FEMINIST FOREIGN POLICY ANALYSIS
A New Subfield

Edited by
Karin Aggestam and Jacqui True

First published in Great Britain in 2025 by

Bristol University Press
University of Bristol
1–9 Old Park Hill
Bristol
BS2 8BB
UK
t: +44 (0)117 374 6645
e: bup-info@bristol.ac.uk

Details of international sales and distribution partners are available at bristoluniversitypress.co.uk

© Bristol University Press 2025

British Library Cataloguing in Publication Data
A catalogue record for this book is available from the British Library

ISBN 978-1-5292-3946-1 hardcover
ISBN 978-1-5292-3947-8 paperback
ISBN 978-1-5292-3948-5 ePub
ISBN 978-1-5292-3949-2 ePdf

The right of Karin Aggestam and Jacqui True to be identified as editors of this work has been asserted by them in accordance with the Copyright, Designs and Patents Act 1988.

All rights reserved: no part of this publication may be reproduced, stored in a retrieval system, or transmitted in any form or by any means, electronic, mechanical, photocopying, recording, or otherwise without the prior permission of Bristol University Press.

Every reasonable effort has been made to obtain permission to reproduce copyrighted material. If, however, anyone knows of an oversight, please contact the publisher.

The statements and opinions contained within this publication are solely those of the editors and contributors and not of the University of Bristol or Bristol University Press. The University of Bristol and Bristol University Press disclaim responsibility for any injury to persons or property resulting from any material published in this publication.

Bristol University Press works to counter discrimination on grounds of gender, race, disability, age and sexuality.

Cover design: Liam Roberts
Front cover image: Liam Roberts
Bristol University Press uses environmentally responsible print partners.
Printed and bound in Great Britain by CPI Group (UK) Ltd, Croydon, CR0 4YY

Contents

Notes on Contributors ... v
Acknowledgements ... xi

1   Introduction: Gender, Feminisms and Foreign Policy ... 1
Karin Aggestam and Jacqui True

2   Ethics ... 16
Fiona Robinson

3   Power ... 32
Columba Achilleos-Sarll

4   Norms ... 49
Jennifer Thomson

5   Networks ... 62
Daniela Philipson García and Victoria Scheyer

6   Diplomatic Infrastructure ... 74
Katarzyna Jezierska and Ann Towns

7   Practice ... 90
Ekatherina Zhukova

8   Leadership ... 106
Klaus Brummer and Karen E. Smith

9   Feminist Decolonial Historiography ... 120
Khushi Singh Rathore

10   Gendered Disinformation ... 137
Elsa Hedling

11   Defence/Military ... 154
Annika Bergman Rosamond and Katharine A.M. Wright

12   Trade ... 167
Roberta Guerrina

13   Aid and Development ... 183
Rebecca Tiessen

14   Peacemaking ... 199
Farkhondeh Akbari

15   Global Environmental Challenges ... 212
Carol Cohn and Claire Duncanson

16	The Advancement of Feminist Foreign Policy Analysis *Karin Aggestam and Jacqui True*	228

References	240
Index	289

Notes on Contributors

Columba Achilleos-Sarll is Assistant Professor in Political Science and International Studies at the University of Birmingham. Her research examines the Women, Peace and Security (WPS) agenda. More broadly, her work focuses on feminist and post/decolonial approaches to international relations, civil society and advocacy, visual global politics, and feminist foreign policy. Her most recent publications include 'Towards an abolitionist feminist peace: state violence, anti-militarism, and the women, peace and security agenda', *Review of International Studies* with H. Wright (2024) and 'Reconceptualising advocacy through the women, peace and security agenda: embodiment, relationality, and power', *International Political Sociology* (2024).

Karin Aggestam is Professor of Political Science and Director of the Centre for Advanced Middle Eastern Studies. She is also Adjunct Professor at Monash University and Honorary Professor at University of Queensland, Australia. Her interdisciplinary research interests include gender, diplomacy, foreign policy, peace and conflict, the Israeli-Palestinian conflict, and Middle East politics. The most recent publications include a special issue on digital disruption in diplomacy with C. Duncombe, *The Hague Journal of Diplomacy* (2024) and *The Politics of Feminist Foreign Policy and Digital Diplomacy* with A. Bergman Rosamond and E. Hedling (2024).

Farkhondeh Akbari is a postdoctoral research fellow at Monash University where she conducts research on inclusive peace, diplomatic actors, feminist foreign policy and the Women, Peace and Security agenda. She received her PhD in diplomatic studies from the Australian National University. Her thesis examined the required characteristics for non-state armed actors to engage meaningfully in diplomacy for the purpose of peace settlements and studied the cases of the Taliban in Afghanistan and the Khmer Rouge in Cambodia. Her publications include 'Geopolitical narratives of withdrawal and the counter-narrative of women's rights activism in Afghanistan', *Global Studies Quarterly* (2024), 'Bargaining with patriarchy in peacemaking', *Global*

Studies Quarterly (2024) and a forthcoming book on women, peace and security in Afghanistan (with J. True).

Annika Bergman Rosamond is Senior Lecturer/Associate Professor of International Relations and Gender at the University of Edinburgh and an affiliate of Lund University where she worked for 10 years prior to taking up her current position. She has been the Chair of the Feminist Theory and Gender Studies section of the International Studies Association of North America and is currently co-convenor of the Gendering International Relations Working Group of BISA. She has published widely on feminist foreign policy, feminist security studies and critical military studies, popular culture/celebrity humanitarianism and world politics, world heritage, indigenous justice and gendered nationalism. Her most recent publications include 'Sweden, NATO and gendered silences on feminist foreign policy', *International Affairs* with K Wright (2024) and *The Politics of Feminist Foreign Policy and Digital Diplomacy* with K. Aggestam and E. Hedling (2024).

Klaus Brummer holds the chair of International Relations at the Catholic University of Eichstätt-Ingolstadt, Germany. He served as co-editor-in-chief of the journal *Foreign Policy Analysis* (2018–2020) and as President of the Foreign Policy Analysis section of the International Studies Association (2015–2016). He has published in peer-reviewed journals such as *British Journal of Politics and International Relations, Government and Opposition, International Affairs, International Studies Review,* and *Journal of European Public Policy*. He is the author of *A Leader-centered Theory of Foreign Policy Change* (Bristol University Press, 2024), co-author of *Foreign Policy Analysis* (Oxford University Press, 2024), and co-editor of *States and Their Nationals Abroad* (Cambridge University Press, 2025).

Carol Cohn is the founding Director of the Consortium on Gender, Security and Human Rights at the University of Massachusetts, Boston. Her research interests have focused on gender integration issues in the US military, feminist approaches to thinking about weapons of mass destruction, the gender dimensions of contemporary armed conflicts, the concept of 'vulnerability' in security and humanitarian discourse, and gender mainstreaming in international peace and security institutions. In addition to her research, she has conducted training and workshops on UNSCR 1325 and provides consultancy on gender mainstreaming for institutions such as the UN Department of Peacekeeping Operations (DPKO).

Claire Duncanson is a senior lecturer in international relations at the University of Edinburgh. She has published widely on issues relating to gender, peace and security, with a particular focus on gender and peacebuilding. Her current work aims to bring a feminist analysis to the political economy of building peace. She is affiliated with the Consortium on Gender, Security and Human Rights on the Feminist Roadmap for Sustainable Peace and Planet Project and has co-authored with Carol Cohn 'Whose recovery? IFI prescriptions for postwar states', *Review of International Political Economy* (2020), 'Women, peace and security in a changing climate', *International Feminist Journal of Politics* (2020) and 'Feminist critical engagements with green new deals', *Feminist Economics* (2023).

Roberta Guerrina is Professor in Politics at the University of Bristol and a visiting professor at the College of Europe in Bruges. She is the co-founder of EQUAL In-Sight, an interdisciplinary project seeking to develop a holistic approach to equality, diversity and inclusion in organizations. She researches the politics of gender, with a particular interest in EU politics, policy-making processes and gender mainstreaming. Her book, *Mothering the Union* (2005), provides a comprehensive overview of maternity rights provisions in the EU. At present, she is working on feminist foreign policy, the evolution of the EU gender regime in the context of crisis; gender and leadership during Covid-19, and equality governance for social justice outcomes. She is co-editor of the *Journal of Common Market Studies* and POST Parliamentary Fellow with the Women and Equalities Committee in the House of Commons.

Elsa Hedling is Associate Senior Lecturer in European Studies in the Centre for Language and Literature at Lund University. She is also an affiliated member of the Europe programme at the Swedish Institute of International Affairs in Stockholm and of the Psychological Defence Research Institute based at Lund University. Her research interests are focused on EU politics, visual international relations, mediatization, digital diplomacy and foreign policy. Her most recent publications include 'Diplomatic representation and online/offline interactions: EU coordination and digital sociability', *International Studies Quarterly* (2024) and *The Politics of Feminist Foreign Policy and Digital Diplomacy* with K. Aggestam and A. Bergman Rosamond (2024).

Katarzyna Jezierska is Associate Professor in Political Science and Senior Lecturer at the International Programme in Politics and Economics, University West, Sweden. She is also Deputy Director of the Gender and Diplomacy Program at the University of Gothenburg, Sweden. Her research interests concern the role of expertise in de-democratization (think tanks), as well as gender in diplomacy and foreign policy with a focus on Scandinavia and Central Europe. Her most recent book is *Resourceful Civil Society? Navigating the Changing Landscapes of Civil Society Organizations* (2022) with Z. Kravchenko and L. Kings.

Daniela Philipson García is a PhD candidate in the School of Social Sciences at Monash University and an ARC Centre of Excellence for the Elimination of Violence against Women (CEVAW) affiliate. Her doctoral thesis focuses on militarization and gender-based violence in Mexico from a feminist political economy lens. Daniela has over ten years of experience conducting policy analysis and mixed methods to advance social justice, collaborating closely with governments and civil society. She holds a Master of Public Policy from Harvard University and is a Fulbright-García Robles Scholar.

Fiona Robinson is Professor of Political Science at Carleton University in Ottawa. Her research and teaching focus on critical, feminist and normative theory in global politics. She is the author of *Globalizing Care: Ethics, Feminist Theory and International Relations* (1999), *The Ethics of Care: A Feminist Approach to Human Security* (2011), and co-editor of *Decentering Epistemology and Challenging Privilege: Critical Care Ethics Perspectives* (2024). In 2014, she was the recipient of the inaugural J. Ann Tickner Book Prize for scholarship on gender and feminist international relations.

Victoria Scheyer is a PhD candidate in the School of Social Sciences at Monash University and an ARC Centre of Excellence for the Elimination of Violence against Women (CEVAW) affiliate. Her research is focused on gender and transnational far-right politics. As a research fellow at the Peace Research Institute Frankfurt, she researches feminist foreign policy and peacebuilding, especially forms of resistance and backlash to gender equality. From 2021–2023, Victoria was co-president of the Women's International League for Peace and Freedom (WILPF) German section.

Khushi Singh Rathore recently received her PhD from the Centre for International Politics, Organization and Disarmament (CIPOD) at Jawaharlal Nehru University and is Associate Editor of *The Hague Journal of Diplomacy*. Her doctoral thesis entitled 'Women in Early Years of India's Foreign Policy: Evaluating the Role of Vijaya Lakshmi Pandit' is a study of the role of Vijaya Lakshmi Pandit as India's first woman diplomat in the history of Indian foreign policy making. Her research interests are gender and diplomacy, feminist IR, diplomatic history Indian foreign policy and Asian foreign relations. Currently, she serves as the incoming programme co-chair for the Feminist Theory and Gender Studies Section and is the at-large representative at the South Asia World Politics Section of the International Studies Association of North America. She is also a co-convener for the Gendering IR Working Group of the British International Studies Association (BISA).

NOTES ON CONTRIBUTORS

Karen E. Smith is Professor of International Relations at the London School of Economics and Political Science. Her main area of research is the international relations of the European Union including EU-UN relations. She has published extensively on common EU foreign policies including the pursuit of 'ethical' foreign policy goals such as promoting human rights and democracy, and policymaking regarding genocide. She is currently investigating the role of women in foreign policy-making, and leading the Women in Diplomacy project at LSE IDEAS. She is co-editor of the Palgrave Macmillan book series on global foreign policy studies, which publishes cutting-edge scholarship on foreign policy with a global focus. Her most recent publications include 'Avoiding an emotions-action gap? The EU and genocide designation', *Journal of European Integration* (2024) and 'The European Union's strategic test in Ukraine', *Current History* (2024).

Jennifer Thomson is Senior Lecturer in Comparative Politics in the Department of Politics, Languages and International Studies at the University of Bath. Her research focuses on gender and foreign policy; gender and security; and reproductive rights in international policy. She is currently PI on the ESRC funded project 'Gender in Foreign Policymaking: the academic and policy implications of feminist foreign policy' and Co-I on the UKRI funded project, Mejara: achieving the right to a good period in low and middle-income countries. She is the author of *Abortion Law and Political Institutions: Explaining Policy Resistance* (2019).

Rebecca Tiessen is a Professor in the School of International Development and Global Studies and Director of the Gender, Peace and Security Collaboratory at the University of Ottawa. Her current research examines feminist foreign aid priorities and the implementation of gender equality programming by civil society actors. Recent publications include, 'Towards a transformative vision for gender and Canadian international policy', *International Journal* (with N. Okoli) and 'Whose feminism (s)? Overseas partner organization's perceptions of Canada's Feminist International Assistance Policy (FIAP)', *International Journal* (with S. Rao).

Ann Towns is Professor of Political Science at the University of Gothenburg and Wallenberg Academy Fellow. She directs the gender and diplomacy programme with funding from the Wallenberg Foundation, the Swedish and Norwegian Research Councils. She received the Bertha Lutz Prize from the International Studies Association in 2018 for her work on women and diplomacy. Towns is the author of *Women and States: Norms and Hierarchies in International Society* (2010) and *Gendering Diplomacy and International Negotiation* co-edited with K. Aggestam (2018).

Jacqui True is Professor of International Relations and Director of the Australian Research Council Centre of Excellence for the Elimination of Violence against Women (CEVAW). She is a Global Fellow, Peace Research Institute, Olso (PRIO) and received an honorary doctorate from Lund University Sweden in 2018. Her research focuses on gendered political violence, feminist political economy and the Women, Peace and Security agenda. Most recently she published, *Hidden Wars: Gendered Violence in Asia's Civil Conflicts* (2024) and *The Oxford Handbook of Women, Peace and Security*, co-editor with S. Davies (2019). In 2021 she was named by Apolitical (UK) as one of the top 100 global experts on gender policy.

Katharine A.M. Wright is Senior Lecturer in International Politics at Newcastle University. Her research focuses on women, peace and security (WPS) and defence. She is interested in gender and security at NATO, including how militarized understanding of WPS influences its transformative potential; and NATO's engagement with WPS. She is the co-author of *NATO, Gender and the Military: Women Organising from Within* (2019), along with numerous other publications. She has extensive experience of engaging with policy-making and civil society communities globally to inform evidence-based decision-making.

Ekatherina Zhukova is Associate Professor in Intercultural Studies at Karlstad University (Sweden). She has a PhD in political science from Aarhus University (Denmark), where she investigated state management of long-term consequences of mass-scale disasters. Her interdisciplinary research interests revolve around feminist foreign policy, humanitarianism and development, disaster and crisis, vulnerability and trauma. She has led postdoctoral projects focused on the role of gender in humanitarian programmes for disaster survivors and the impact of social media on humanitarian photography. As a researcher and senior lecturer at the Department of Political Science at Lund University, she explored external perceptions of feminist foreign policy. She is currently working on a research project on gender equality, renewable energy, and violent conflict.

Acknowledgements

We would like to thank all our contributors for their commitment and constructive engagement in this collaborative book project on feminist foreign policy analysis throughout the development of their chapters, and at the workshop held in September 2023 at the Monash Prato Centre, Italy.

We would like to thank the Australian Research Council for generously supporting the research and workshop conducted for this manuscript through the Discovery Program (DP2110103549). We greatly appreciated the administrative support of Jasmine Mead at Monash University, Melbourne and Sarah Gore at Monash University, Prato in facilitating the workshop organization and travel to the wonderful centre in Tuscany.

Our sincere thanks to Stephen Wenham and Zoe Forbes at Bristol University Press for enthusiastically supporting this timely volume from the outset and ensuring that its production was swift and professional.

We would also like to acknowledge the pivotal role and leadership of former Foreign Minister Margot Wallström in pioneering the world's first feminist foreign policy. We extend our appreciation for her invaluable input with other practitioners to the policy-research dialogue held at the Monash University Prato Centre in September 2023.

Finally, as editors, we would like to thank our respective partners and families – Magnus and Michael, and our young men, Simon, Filip, Seamus and Hugo (who, as it turns out, are the same age!). Collaborating across Australia and Sweden does not make for the best working conditions and often cannot occur in the usual workday. However, collaborating on this project has been a truly rewarding journey, deepening our friendship, and providing us with additional support and intellectual inspiration.

1

Introduction: Gender, Feminisms and Foreign Policy

Karin Aggestam and Jacqui True

Introduction

For over a century, feminists have advocated for women's participation in decision-making on war and peace to achieve a more just global order. There is today a growing recognition among states that promoting gender equality and the Women, Peace, Security (WPS) agenda as part of their foreign policies is not only useful for foreign aid and international development, but that such developments may also contribute to climate change policies to keep global warming below 2°C, to more inclusive trade, the stability of alliances, the prevention of conflict, terrorism and pandemics, and ultimately, the achievement of sustainable peace. At the same time, other powerful governments are contesting these ideas and fiercely resisting such foreign policy change. How can feminist scholarship advance the field of foreign policy analysis to understand contemporary foreign policy actions and challenges? A decade after states first adopted explicit pro-gender equality norms and/or feminist foreign policy strategies, feminist and gender scholarship is now beginning to take off in the field of foreign policy analysis (FPA).

The overarching aim of the book is to provide the latest state-of-the-art in the study of gender, feminisms and foreign policy, and to advance the emerging subfield of feminist foreign policy analysis (FFPA). The volume presents new theories, novel concepts and empirical knowledge for this growing field of scholarship. It builds on innovations in feminist International Relations theory and FPA, both dynamic bodies of scholarship within International Relations (IR). Feminist IR theory is distinguished by its 'plural and interdisciplinary theoretical orientation and multilevel approaches to method and empirical analysis' (Aggestam and True, 2020: 147); while FPA is 'multi-layered and conceptually complex, examining the many agents and institutions, cultures and identities, interests and perceptions that influence foreign policies' in domestic politics and the international realm (Kaarbo and Thies, 2024: 2). In advancing FFPA, the book encompasses both feminist analysis of avowedly 'feminist foreign policies' and new feminist analyses of foreign policies on trade, defence, environment, disinformation, peacemaking and international development assistance. Moreover, it critically explores how diverse and contested gender and feminist approaches and strategies are put into practice across a range of countries' foreign policy.

Gender and feminist strategies in foreign policy are often based on alternative understandings of power. Power politics does not guarantee peace nor can states bring about security and prosperity alone. Thus, gender and feminist approaches promote a logic of empowerment that supports women and men to deliver on development, security, peace and sustainability, inter alia, through fundamental, actionable principles of gender equality and human rights. Furthermore, state and non-state actors in foreign policy have increasingly been drawing upon and expanding gender equality instruments and feminist normative guidance to be applied across security, diplomacy, trade, development aid and humanitarian foreign policy responses.

This book critically examines how and to what extent these norms and practices have been implemented and their likely effects on foreign policy outcomes. Gender and feminist strategies directly engage with people's experiences in finding solutions to problems of cooperation and conflict, security and insecurity. With regard to conflict situations or climate threats affecting national and regional security, foreign policy actors informed by gender or feminist strategies often meet with the groups 'most affected' to listen and comprehend the contexts and identify what actions are necessary and effective to reduce insecurity. As such, these approaches to foreign policy derive their legitimacy from inclusive engagement with many different groups at home and abroad – in other countries and regions.

Gender and feminisms in foreign policy seek not only to respond to crises effectively and inclusively in real time but also to develop a long-term vision and strategy for achieving foreign policy outcomes, including sustainable peace and intersectional gender justice within and across states and societies. Studying foreign policy success and failure of gender and feminist approaches is fascinating and insightful, but it also stands in stark contrast to current revisionist foreign policy trends, which are distinguished by short-term national security concerns, hyper-masculinity and strongman foreign policy postures, which seem to destabilize democracy, human rights, peace and ultimately the liberal world order (Aggestam and True, 2021). With the advent of gender and feminist strategies, this book focuses on foreign policy change. As such, it advances new theoretical and empirical knowledge that provides insight into major shifts in political power and gender relations in contemporary global politics. Moreover, the chapters explore how geopolitical themes as well as states' normative goals and identities are played out by using soft power tools, such as pro and anti-gender equality and feminist branding, as part of their foreign policies. They recognize the political contestation and debate about genders and feminisms with the transnational spread of anti-gender ideology and also actors that co-opt gender equality discourses for discriminatory racist and misogynist agendas.

This introductory chapter introduces the readers to the rise, diffusion and contestation of pro-gender equality norms and feminisms in foreign policy. It presents the core research questions that provide the overarching rationale and the theoretical framework guiding the book and its focus on foreign policy change and continuity. The second part presents the state-of-the-art in the field and identifies new novel avenues for scholarship by drawing upon two strands of research, which seldom engage with one another, namely feminist IR theory and FPA. It notes key synergies across these bodies of research and current foreign policy challenges that are illuminated by their synthesis (Aggestam and True, 2024). This opens the space for the emerging subfield of FFPA to expand. The third and final part introduces the contributing chapters of this book.

Diffusion and contestation on gender and feminism in foreign policy

We have argued that gender is a major fault line of international politics today (Aggestam and True, 2021: 385). The world is currently 'experiencing a reversal of generational gains in women's rights while violent conflicts, military expenditures, military coups, displacements and hunger continue to increase' (UN Secretary-General, 2022). There are internal and external challenges to pro-gender and/or feminist foreign policy as well as heightened threats to women's rights and leaders, and setbacks to gender equality worldwide. As a result of how the COVID-19 pandemic was managed, for instance, there is a further four-decade setback to progress in gender equality, with women on average having to wait 136 years for equality with men, according to the World Economic Forum (2021). This book posits that if we want to understand this visible regression in equality and women's rights and the polarization of global politics, we need to understand how gender plays out in foreign policy by exploring different concepts and types of foreign policy.

Over the past decade, a dual trend in foreign policy has been apparent. On the one hand, gender equality has become a salient foreign policy issue promoted by states and non-state actors, most recently with the diffusion of 'feminist' foreign policies. On the other hand, an opposite foreign policy trend is evident with growing state resistance to gender equality norms with the adoption of anti-gender foreign policies and contestation of multilateral commitments to women's human rights. How do we explain the seemingly contrary developments in foreign policy? In this book, we tackle that research question and ask how gender and FFPA can explain how key foreign policy actors navigate these complex dynamics for the security of all? We are interested in studying how far and in what ways the integration of gender in foreign policy and/or rebranding of foreign policy as 'feminist' is a meaningful agenda generating policy change or a merely symbolic or instrumental agenda legitimizing liberal or authoritarian states vis-à-vis their citizens, or bolstering their status and 'soft power' on the world stage. Scholars have observed how pro-gender equality and feminist foreign policies are being used as a way for countries (and their leaders) to gain or hold on to political capital in different organizations and alliances, and to make military power more palatable to domestic and international constituencies, for example (Chapnick, 2019). It is a complex political context to analyse since some foreign policy leaders and states use progressive gender equality talk to promote regressive neoliberal, neocolonial, anti-gender agendas (Thomson and Whiting, 2022). Feminist principles, however, can be used to evaluate all types of foreign policy, whatever its brand.

These research questions and concerns provide the overarching rationale and theoretical framework for the book's focus on foreign policy change and continuity considering the powerful and increasingly visible gendered dynamics in global politics. We adopt a consistent nomenclature across this volume. We refer to both pro-gender (equality) norms in foreign policy and feminist or feminist-informed foreign policy to identify and investigate where states have adopted a core focus on mainstreaming gender equality and human rights, and the normative values and principles associated with them, that are coined 'feminist'. We also refer to anti-gender norms and foreign policy to examine the antagonistic politics that we argue are part of the dual trend of diffusion and contestation of gender relations.

With these definitions, we gain critical analytical distance from state proclamations and political branding strategies to be able to analyse and evaluate words as well as actions, the saying and the doing of foreign policy. The benefit of such a framing is that we can study states that have committed to gender equality strategies in their foreign policies but who have proclaimed an Indigenous foreign policy rather than a 'feminist' foreign policy (Aotearoa/New Zealand); and states that have announced a feminist foreign policy but have not adopted a WPS National Action Plan (for instance Libya), even though United Nations Security Council Resolution 1325 on WPS is considered a core part of the normative international policy framework adopted by feminist foreign policy states.

The state-of-the-art on gender, feminism and foreign policy analysis

This volume contends that feminist IR theory can advance and bridge some critical lacunae prevalent in FPA. Scholarship on gender in foreign policy remains limited due to the prevailing 'gender blindness' in FPA that does not consider the import of the gender dynamics of foreign policy leadership, institutions and international structure (Hudson and Leidl, 2015; Smith, 2019). Consequently, this chapter identifies several key points of convergence between these two bodies of scholarship, thereby delineating some new avenues of research for the advancement of FFPA. Feminist IR theory can explain the proliferation of pro-gender equality norms and feminism in foreign policy as well as the resistance and contestation engendered by states and other political actors, alongside their ramifications for global politics. These challenges and resistance cannot be explained without understanding and acknowledging the entrenched historical embedding of patriarchal structural and hierarchical principles as part of state identities, diplomatic practices and global order (Enloe, 2017; True, 2017). Thus, feminist IR theory transcends traditional approaches inherent to conventional foreign policy analysis. Furthermore, feminist IR theory offers a dynamic and non-linear framework for understanding policy change and continuity and the role of gender therein. By acknowledging the ongoing construction of norms, it assigns agency to gendered actors in the identification and interpretation of norms and policy dilemmas (Bacchi, 1999). As Zwingel contends, transnational networks 'have their own political agendas and are not automatically supporters of international norms' (2013: 113). These networks engage in iterative processes, both in theory and practice, to discern effective strategies for translating abstract principles into tangible outcomes (Krook and True, 2012: 117).

However, the examination of pro-gender norms and feminist-informed foreign policy has historically been scarce in feminist scholarship. This scarcity is due in part to a prevailing scepticism regarding the effectiveness of state-centred institutional frameworks to further feminist political agendas. States are frequently perceived as entrenched within patriarchal, hierarchical and oppressive power structures (Peterson, 1992; Parashar et al, 2018). Gendered analyses elucidate how states both extend masculine protection to 'women and children' while simultaneously perpetuating social, political and economic inequalities that render women vulnerable in the first place (Parashar et al, 2018). Liberal, post-colonial and religious states alike manifest hierarchies of male entitlement and female subordination; thus, from a feminist perspective, a state cannot be construed as a neutral agent (Stetson and Mazur, 1995). Consequently, for women to advance and thrive as agents of the state, they often find themselves compelled to conform, to some extent, to its norms and discourses, which predominantly reflect a historically male-centred perspective derived from men's experiences in the world. Moreover, reluctance to engage in analysis from within by diplomats and foreign policy leaders may contribute to this disengagement. Token women are also frequently depicted as operating within and adjusting to masculine norms and scripts, thereby becoming co-opted by male power structures that dominate foreign policy. As feminist scholars have long observed, the mere inclusion of women without addressing underlying power dynamics does not lead to transformative policy outcomes (Peterson, 1992). Instead, feminist scholars have directed greater attention to external or structural factors rather than individual-level actor-centric factors, emphasizing the influence of international norms, transnational networks and efforts to restrain patriarchal power.

In light of the scepticism directed towards the state, feminist theory has redirected its focus towards conceiving the state as a complex entity comprising multiple, often conflicting, agencies and actors. This perspective underscores the delineation of spaces and opportunities for feminist interventions (Kantola and Dahl, 2005). Marian Sawer and Sandra Grey (2009) have developed the notion of 'insider-outsider' support structures, which facilitate the connection between women bureaucrats operating within the state and women's movement activists operating outside it, a concept also captured by Eisenstein (1996) as 'femocrats'. Htun and Weldon (2018) have assessed the impact of women's civil society movements on significant state policy outcomes, such as the enactment of new legislation aimed at mitigating and eradicating violence against women. By analysing data from 70 countries spanning three decades (1975–2005), they demonstrate how distinct political logics operate across various policy areas. Notably, on issues concerning violence against women and workplace equality, policy norms are influenced by a logic of (international) status hierarchy among states, whereas in matters concerning family law, abortion and contraception, a logic of domestic doctrinal politics predominates, driven by the influence of religious institutional actors.

Feminist IR theory, contributing to and drawing upon constructivist scholarship, has been at the forefront of analysing non-state actors and transnational forces both below and above the state level, influencing normative changes with implications for state foreign policies (Finnemore, 1996; Zwingel, 2015). Structures such as quotas for equitable gender representation, gender mainstreaming institutions and policies against violence targeting women increasingly shape contemporary foreign policy, fostering specific pro-gender equality norms and strategies. In contrast to constructivism, feminist IR theory emphasizes the role of transnational networks initiated by locally grounded grassroots actors, such as women's groups and organizations, rather than international organizations or expert communities (True, 2019). The research agenda on norm diffusion has been significantly influenced by feminist scholarship, particularly focusing on feminist networks as agents of diffusion (True and Mintrom, 2001; Hughes et al, 2015). These networks are viewed as dynamic entities that actively shape international norms, which are subject to contestation and change. Furthermore, feminist scholars have confronted practical challenges in researching these networks by gathering international data on women's organizations, pro-gender equality laws, quotas and institutions across numerous states, often collaborating with policy, justice institutions and civil society partners (True, 2018). In studying international normative change, feminist theorists have observed the dynamic and non-linear evolution of norms regarding gender and gender equality (Krook and True, 2012). Emphasizing the fluidity and multiple meanings of norms provides a robust analytical framework for understanding why gender equality norms emerge and appear to be widely accepted across states despite often falling short of their intended objectives (True, 2018). This insight has direct relevance to FPA and the assessment of the outcomes of pro-gender equality foreign policies. For example, within the WPS foreign policy, the concept of gender as enshrined in United Nations Security Council Resolution 1325 initially relied on a binary understanding of sex. However, over nearly two decades, the WPS community of practice has increasingly acknowledged greater diversity and intersectionality within the category of 'woman' (including girls, youth, minority ethnicities and those with disabilities), as well as recognizing men and boys (in terms of gender rather than sex) as victims of sexual and gender-based violence and as supporters of women's agency in peacebuilding. Consequently, this increased diversity has altered the prevailing understanding of gender within international discourse and practice concerning peace and security.

Towards feminist foreign policy analysis: new avenues for research

In navigating the complexities of a global world marked by gendered structures and practices, international actors must grapple with how states and individuals present themselves, are perceived, and interact with one another. The emergence of illiberal democracies, right-wing populism and authoritarian leadership, coupled with targeted assaults on women's reproductive rights and bodily autonomy, signal the possibility of significant regression in the outcomes of pro-gender foreign policies. Within this context, our argument posits that analysing these gendered dynamics offers a nuanced understanding of how power and authority manifest in foreign policy. Foreign policy actors continuously navigate the intricate realm of gender symbolism and normative structures on a global scale, influencing the depiction of states, non-state actors and individuals (Aggestam and True, 2021).

Feminist approaches to foreign policy enhance the analysis of situated foreign policy actors by sensitizing them to the material realities where gender intersects with and often reinforces other dimensions of social inequality and identity, such as race, ethnicity, sexuality, class and nationality status. For instance, while contemporary global incentive structures may ostensibly provide a rationale for advancing pro-gender norms in foreign policy, the deep-rooted patriarchal structures entrenched in states and global politics pose formidable obstacles to transformation. Should the existing rule-based liberal order, which upholds international norms including human rights and gender equality, face further erosion, the prospects for advancing pro-gender equality outcomes in foreign policy are likely to diminish. These entrenched patriarchal structures not only constrain feminist and pro-gender equality actions but also engender resistance against them. Therefore, an examination of continuity and change in foreign policy necessitates a focus on the gendered dynamics pervading global politics. In this book, we propose three avenues of research with the potential to advance a novel subfield within IR, namely FFPA.

Political leadership: navigating gendered dynamics in foreign policy

The examination of leadership holds a pivotal position in the analysis of foreign policy, increasingly involving the utilization of global networks and public engagement to address common and often entrenched challenges in inter-state relations (Matthews, 1997: 51–66). However, there remains a notable gap in the literature concerning the analysis of women's and men's foreign policy leadership as gendered beings. Women and men exhibit performances imbued with gendered attributes, deploying gendered imagery, language, tropes and actions. Moreover, gendered structures extend to institutions and their influence on foreign policy processes and decisions. Notably, the emergence of foreign policy changes driven by pro-gender norms typically requires substantial leadership from women or male feminists. As shown in Sylvia Bashevkin's (2018) analysis of US administrations, not all female secretaries of state have endorsed pro-gender norms. Conversely, the agency of political leaders such as Margot Wallström in Sweden, Julie Bishop in Australia, Gro-Harlem Brundtland historically in Norway, Nkozasana Dlamini-Zuma in South Africa and Justin Trudeau in Canada has been instrumental in advocating for pro-gender equality or feminist foreign policies. These leaders have sought to distinguish themselves in the political and international arena through their promotion of pro-gender equality or feminist foreign policies. Nevertheless, their leadership styles can be evaluated in terms of their projection of both masculine and feminine power and their approaches to foreign policy. Some leaders, like Dlamini-Zuma in South Africa, have prioritized gender inclusion in foreign policy by advocating for the involvement of diverse actors, whereas others, such as Julie Bishop in Australia, have focused on making foreign policies more 'gender-sensitive', incorporating gender analysis into foreign aid spending and development programmes. Moreover, certain leaders, like Margot Wallström in Sweden, have aspired to transform the unequal, gendered structures of international politics through Sweden's feminist foreign policy (Aggestam and Bergman Rosamond, 2016).

Thus, various collective leadership styles may manifest concerning the adoption of pro-gender equality and/or feminist strategies, ranging from status quo-oriented (minimalist) to gender-sensitive (inclusive) and transformative (maximalist). One central conundrum pertains to the extent to which individual leaders influence the adoption of pro-gender equality and feminist foreign policies. Undoubtedly, the advancement of pro-gender norms in foreign policy is closely tied to the roles of key foreign policy actors acting as 'norm entrepreneurs' (Nadelmann, 1990). A norm entrepreneur can be conceptualized as a political actor actively and consciously endeavouring to promote foreign policy change by integrating pro-gender equality norms. Unlike non-state actors that set agendas by advocating for new norms, foreign policy decision-makers leverage their positionality and relative power to advance the recognition of certain under-implemented norms by redefining the 'national interest'. Hence, the gender identity and positionality of political leaders are pertinent, potentially facilitating norm diffusion, particularly when juxtaposed with the content of the normative or policy change and when challenging conventional foreign policy actions (Davies and True, 2017).

Gender, feminist branding and foreign policy orientation

The foreign policy orientation of a state serves as a comprehensive framework for elucidating the emergence, persistence, transformation and/or opposition to pro-gender equality norms. States can be analysed comparatively based on the centrality of gender articulation within their foreign policy orientations and practices. Notably, certain countries such as Sweden and Canada have opted to explicitly designate and brand their foreign policies as 'feminist'. The foreign policy orientation also encompasses state identity, which is shaped or reshaped by a diverse array of historical, domestic and international factors, actors and practices. A central concept in this regard is 'state feminism', which focuses on reforming state structures through the institutionalization of women's state machinery, feminist social movements, and women's rights and empowerment (Hernes, 1987). In the cases of Sweden and Norway, the integration of pro-gender norms into foreign policy aligns with their long-standing self-perceptions as 'women-friendly' states. Gender equality has become extensively institutionalized and domestically embedded within the frameworks of state feminism in both Sweden and Norway. Consequently, their conceptions of foreign policy roles reflect the bureaucratic capacity of these states to effectively implement pro-gender norms in their foreign policy endeavours. For instance, Sweden's adoption of a feminist foreign policy stemmed from a long-standing humanistic idea of 'gender cosmopolitanism' (Bergman Rosamond, 2020), while Norway's significant investment in becoming a superpower in peacemaking has facilitated the advancement of gender-inclusive peace processes through enhanced professionalization of diplomats and institutionalization of pro-gender norms (Skjelsbæk and Tryggestad, 2020).

Under Trudeau's leadership, Canada has pursued a strategy of 'rebranding' itself through practices of feminist international development assistance, aligning with broader efforts to project an image of Canada as a compassionate and generous member of the global community (Parisi, 2020). Thus, while states warrant serious consideration, privileging state actors as the primary or sole unit of theoretical and empirical analysis should be avoided. Instead, the traditional domestic–international divide in foreign policy must be challenged by acknowledging the multifaceted nature of the state, encompassing various actors and serving as a site of diverse domestic and international structures, processes and actors.

Nation branding is intricately linked to national role conception, delineating how nations perceive themselves and their roles in the international arena (Holsti, 1970). This conception is influenced by both elite perceptions and societal characteristics, as well as domestic political imperatives that facilitate or impede the advancement of pro-gender norms in foreign policy. The study of gender and democracy underscores the domestic factors that influence the receptiveness of nation-states to the promotion of gender equality norms. Democratically governed states with a significant presence of women in politics and women's movements are more inclined to advocate for pro-gender equality foreign policies, such as with regard to the WPS agenda (True, 2016). Moreover, states identifying with roles such as peacemaker or peaceful democracy are more likely to adopt pro-gender foreign policy norms in alignment with these conceptions. Notably, the adoption of pro-gender norms in peace agreements, as seen in Colombia, or in third-party peace mediation, as exemplified by Norway, can contribute to or reinforce the construction of a peacemaker/peaceful democracy identity.

This book endeavours to examine and delineate how pro-gender norms are anchored and operationalized into specific foreign policy strategies, often through coalition building with both domestic and international actors and other states. For instance, initiatives such as the 'friends of WPS' coalition at the United Nations Security Council and the 'champions of the UK's

Preventing Sexual Violence Initiative' demonstrate such foreign policy coordination efforts. Furthermore, it is imperative to examine the contexts and conditions under which pro-gender equality practices are identified and implemented as significant foreign policy changes. Conversely, exploring the strategies employed by various actors to resist and/or contest such foreign policy changes is also crucial.

Gendered structures in foreign policy and global politics

During periods of crisis and upheaval, which are frequent occurrences in foreign policy and global politics, gendered norms may engender the illusion of fixed and stable structures, which serve to reinforce boundaries – be they of identity, the home, public versus private spheres, or the nation state (Hozic and True, 2016). Gendered norms establish biological differences 'not only as a natural fact but as the ontological basis for political and social differences' (Kinsella, 2005: 271). They not only legitimize differences and inequalities but also produce them, thus generating power and legitimacy. Traditionally, power in the field of IR scholarship, including FPA, has been understood in terms of the material capabilities of states and as a zero-sum quantity within the inter-state realm. However, conceptions of power are manifold and increasingly viewed as ideational rather than positional, shaped by knowledge and symbolic structures as well as military and production capabilities (Strange, 1988). Power is not solely vested in material structures, such as the international gender division of labour or controlled by specific actors; it also resides in 'systems of signification and meaning' that are socially constructed and influence actors' self-understanding and perceived interests (Barnett and Duvall, 2005: 20). In some respects, the term 'soft power' commonly employed in diplomacy encapsulates this ideational, symbolic and performative conception of power (Nye, 1990).

From a feminist perspective, gender relations are deemed intrinsic to the meaning of power itself, with masculinity often synonymous with power and vice versa (Scott, 1986). Power is inherently relational (Tickner, 1988; Sylvester, 1994), conceived less as power-over and more as the power to act collectively, which is integral to the notion of empowerment – both individual and collective. In foreign policy conceptualized as 'gendered multilevel games', such an understanding of power is relational and influenced by gender among other dimensions of identity and structure. For instance, hyper-masculine performances of foreign policy, emphasizing the use of forceful tactics and demonstrations of hard power, may significantly constrain the potential emergence of pro-gender norms in foreign policy. This approach importantly acknowledges the power of identity, ideas and networks, alongside the material capabilities of states. Crucially, it elucidates both theoretically and practically the critical interplay between agency and structure, which can explain both the rise and resistance of pro-gender norms in foreign policy (Aggestam and True, 2021).

It is noteworthy how the global diffusion of pro-gender norms has been perceived as a 'window of opportunity' for foreign policy change by several states in recent decades. Undoubtedly, the global mobilization around the WPS agenda has incentivized states to promote pro-gender norms, underscoring the importance of identifying key representations and discursive structures that legitimize foreign policies. Moreover, certain ideas target specific spheres, and the variation in responsiveness to pro-gender norm diffusion across different areas of foreign policy, such as international aid and humanitarian policy versus national security or international trade policy, warrants analysis.

Transnational networks and coalition building among 'women-friendly' states have been evident in various international forums as a means to advance pro-gender norms. Feminist IR theorists have developed new conceptual approaches to understand transnational structures and networks as non-state actors that directly and indirectly influence foreign policies through advocacy and contributing to international normative change (True and Mintrom, 2001; Zwingel, 2015). These networks, akin to norms, are viewed as evolving entities, crucial in fostering new institutions that promote gender equality, particularly in foreign policy. However, they do not function as a unified social movement, and their effectiveness may vary across different contexts and spheres of foreign policy (Hughes et al, 2015).

Transnational feminist or women's networks engage in global activities, negotiating and localizing international norms to effectuate both social and policy change, even in the absence of favourable foreign policy leadership, norm entrepreneurs or international power structures conducive to such change (Aggestam and True, 2023). Frequently, these networks rely on generations of local and national social movement activism to facilitate such transformative processes by forging new alliances and reframing previous ideas and actions (Zwingel, 2013). The strategy of 'going global' is anticipated to bolster public support and overcome significant obstacles to change, yet the complexities inherent in linking issues across jurisdictions can inadvertently alter both the agents and the norms being advocated (True, 2024). This underscores the critical role played by networks in establishing new institutions that advance gender equality, particularly within the field of foreign policy. However, networks do not operate as a monolithic social movement. As highlighted by Hughes et al (2015), women's organizing across states exhibit significant diversity, often encountering challenges, such as proto-feminist agendas, which undermine efforts to implement electoral gender quotas, despite international support for such measures.

Moreover, networks can be conceptualized as evolving entities, that may be particularly significant in the post-introduction phase of a new norm when the norm in question attains a degree of international acceptance. During this phase, networks often transition from informal and ad hoc structures to more professionalized entities, engaging with governments and intergovernmental institutions in a more formal capacity. Distinct from individual leaders or cohesive groups, networks are loosely connected sets of individuals and groups actively shaping evolving norms, reflecting the changing dynamics within the network itself (True, 2024). For example, networks of women foreign policy leaders existed before the branding of foreign policy as 'feminist', laying the groundwork for such developments by challenging entrenched 'masculine hegemonies' and facilitating new forms of leadership and governance. Feminist foreign policy-informed governance networks (Aggestam and True, 2023) seek to challenge the conventional logic of foreign policy power, promoting an alternative logic of empowerment through diplomacy that advocates for principles of human rights and gender equality, thereby contributing to the realization of peace and prosperity.

Furthermore, when the global environment shifts in ways that challenge the pursuit of soft power arguments, tools and practices, such as in today's situation of rising civil and inter-state conflict, patriarchal structures entrenched in states and global politics may pose formidable obstacles. Consequently, the feminist 'pragmatist' approach adopted by several 'women-friendly' states may face limitations and vulnerabilities when confronted with increasingly hyper-masculine foreign policies, actors and anti-gender norms in global politics. Consequently, if the present rule-based liberal order continues to erode, there is a heightened risk of gender backlash against transformative foreign policies and regression to traditional foreign policy approaches. The contestation through antagonistic discourses and non-implementation as a form of resistance against pro-gender norms may be a barometer of future developments in global politics (True and Wiener, 2019). This book aims to provide new theoretical and empirical insights into the major shifts in political power and gender relations in contemporary global politics in the 21st century, exploring how geopolitical themes intersect with states' normative goals and identities, particularly through the utilization of soft power tools as part of their foreign policies. In the subsequent section, we outline the volume and its chapters.

Outline of the book

The volume consists of 16 chapters. Each contribution critically assesses the state of the art in research and suggests new ways to theoretically and empirically advance the field of study. The chapters in the book variously explore to what extent pro-gender equality norms and feminisms have been adopted and integrated within several countries' foreign policies and across a broad range of foreign policies, such as defence, diplomacy, peacemaking, aid, trade, development and the environment.

Chapter 2 by Fiona Robinson explores ethical foreign policy and considers relational ethics, as articulated by feminist care ethicists, post-humanist and decolonial feminisms as well as many Indigenous ethico-onto-epistemologies. It shows how it can take feminist foreign policy beyond rights-talk towards an understanding of ethics as emerging through complex moral relations and entanglements. Chapter 3 by Columba Achilleos-Sarll focuses on power and revisits the feminist critique of power in foreign policy analyses. It traces how the concept of power has travelled through the language of feminist foreign policy declarations and adoptions as well as civil society framings. It advocates for a more expansive and in many ways radical understanding of feminist foreign policy by theorizing power as intersectional and entangled with macro-structures of colonialism, patriarchy, capitalism and militarism. Chapter 4 by Jennifer Thomson examines gender equality as a norm in foreign policy from a constructivist perspective. It argues that the norm of gender equality allows states to signal an attentiveness to multilateralism and liberal values, while also providing means to distinguish themselves from other states of similar international power.

In Chapter 5 by Daniela Philipson García and Victoria Scheyer the role of transnational feminist and women's rights networks in informing, developing, implementing and disseminating gender-responsive and feminist-informed foreign policies is examined. This chapter argues that feminist-informed foreign policy and governance rely on the knowledge production of (transnational) feminist networks. Chapter 6 by Katarzyna Jezierska and Ann Towns explores the gendered diplomatic infrastructure for the implementation of foreign policies and how it has transformed during the past 300 years. It focuses on the major institutional changes of the 20th century, such as the opening of formal diplomatic positions to women, the global emergence of networks of female diplomats, the spread of ambassadors for women's rights and gender equality as well as Gender Focal Points in Ministries of Foreign Affairs and their embassies. Chapter 7 by Ekatherina Zhukova advances theory on the routinized practices of emerging feminist foreign policy. It shows how practice goes beyond the dichotomy of private and public, personal and professional, and how it includes, but is not limited to, self-awareness, self-care and caring for others. Chapter 8 by Klaus Brummer and Karen E. Smith takes stock of the state of the art on gender and foreign policy leadership. It highlights in what ways leadership is gendered and how various theories in foreign policy analysis, which often are based on case studies of Western democratic leaders, travel to contexts in the Global South across different political systems. Chapter 9 by Khushi Singh Rathore explores decolonial feminist historiography as a method for FFPA and in the case of Indian foreign policy. It explores the feminist strategizing by the early women envoys of independent India, thereby opening accounts of Indian foreign policy to a post-colonial gendered theorization.

In Chapter 10, Elsa Hedling sets the stage for studies of gendered disinformation in FFPA. It examines how this phenomenon both constrains and advances the prominence of feminism and gender considerations in foreign policy agendas. Annika Bergman Rosamond and Katharine A.M. Wright's Chapter 11 on defence analyses the relationship between feminist and pro-gender foreign policy on the one hand, and military and defence on the other, by engaging with feminist ideas on just war, war as experience, pacificism and self-defence. It explores the inconsistencies between states' firm commitment to feminist foreign policy and the lack of feminism in national military thinking and practice. In Chapter 12, Roberta Guerrina examines the gender–trade nexus through the prism of gender mainstreaming, gender regime theory and the European Union as a case study. Trade is a gender issue in so far as it has an impact on employment, consumption and public services as well as foreign relations but the link between these three facets of trade policy remains under-researched even though they may have a greater impact than foreign aid. Chapter 13 by Rebecca Tiessen turns to the consideration of the contributions of feminist foreign policies to aid and development with a focus on Canada's feminist international assistance policy. It elaborates on feminist methodology, monitoring and priorities for feminist aid and development evaluations as a way of deepening feminist commitments to decolonizing aid. Chapter 14 by Farkhondeh Akbari considers the role of peacemaking in foreign policy. Despite major international milestones in 'pro-gender equality' norms, the chapter argues that the foreign policy of peacemaking lacks real politics and strategy to realize and implement them. This is examined in the cases of Afghanistan, Syria and Libya. Finally, Chapter 15 by Carol Cohn and Claire Duncanson considers the potential for feminist approaches to the environment in foreign policy. It surveys the potential and the limitations of each of these feminist approaches and argues that only the inclusion of policies generated by the third feminist strand can offer a realistic response to the environmental, especially climate change, challenges the world faces. The final chapter takes stock of the insights gained from the preceding 15 chapters and advances the case for the emerging subfield of FFPA and its vital new research agenda.

2

Ethics

Fiona Robinson

Introduction

This chapter considers the role and nature of ethics in the theory and practice of feminist approaches to foreign policy. From their earliest articulations, feminist approaches to foreign policy have been framed in explicitly moral terms. In 2015, Margot Wallström – Sweden's Foreign Minister and trailblazer of feminist foreign policy – described it as seeking the same goals as 'any visionary foreign policy: peace, justice, human rights and human development' (Wallström, cited in Rupert, 2015). Similarly, in 2018, Canada's Foreign Affairs Minister Chrystia Freeland delivered a speech emphasizing the connections between a feminist foreign policy, human rights and the democratic values which uphold the rules-based international order (Government of Canada, 2018). In 2021, Foreign Minister Nanaia Mahuta outlined an 'Indigenous foreign policy' for New Zealand, guided by Māori principles. This turn not only centres Indigenous peoples, but Māori values – interconnectedness, responsibility and custodianship. While this is not a 'feminist' foreign policy, striking lines of connection can be drawn between these progressive, value-based turns in foreign policy, as this chapter will discuss. In all these cases, there was a clear effort to position foreign policy as seeking to further not simply the national interest, but the wider moral aims of world peace, global justice and human rights for all. But unlike earlier, post-Cold War efforts to develop ethical foreign policy, these new approaches seek to realize these goals by challenging unequal gender-based and colonial relations of power.

Although it is widely understood that feminist foreign policy is inherently ethical, there has been relatively little critical reflection on precisely what this ethical content is, and how it ought to be reflected in foreign policy that is explicitly labelled feminist. In line with the rhetoric of state officials described earlier, feminist foreign policy has been described as embodying 'broad cosmopolitan norms of global justice and peace' (Aggestam and Bergman Rosamond, 2016: 323). Alternative understandings of ethics – including relational and care ethics – have also been used to theorize feminist foreign policy (Aggestam et al, 2019; Robinson, 2021a). Moreover, it is notable that the ethicality of feminist foreign policy has provided the basis for both praise and disdain; while some commentators argue for the need for a normative reorientation and an ethically informed framework for foreign policy (Aggestam and Bergman Rosamond, 2016), others are critical of the 'saviour narrative' of feminist foreign policy (Novovic, 2023). Unsurprisingly, for foreign policy traditionalists, the ethical nature of feminist foreign policy is taken to be 'idealistic, naïve – and potentially even dangerous – in the *realpolitik* power struggles between nations' (Egnell, quoted in Nordberg, 2015).

The notion of ethical foreign policy began to gain traction after the end of the Cold War, as many Western states began to shift away from the openly declared pursuit of national interests in foreign policy in favour of an approach centred on moral duties to protect the rights and interests of others (Chandler, 2003). Two decades later, feminist foreign policy once again seeks to put values and ethics at the forefront of foreign policy. This chapter argues that, while there are evident similarities between the framing of ethics in contemporary pro-gender equality and/or feminist foreign policy and the ethical foreign policy of the immediate post-Cold War era, the former's commitment to challenging gendered relations of power provides openings for a more sophisticated and critical understanding of the role of the ethical in foreign policy. Specifically, I argue that recent interventions by both governments committed to pro-gender equality and/or feminist foreign policy, and civil society organizations, suggest a move towards an ethical foreign policy. Feminist-informed commitments to resisting intersecting hierarchies of power through relational ethics are a driving force of this foreign policy turn. Using examples from Canada, Mexico and New Zealand, I will point to the moral potential located in recent discursive and policy shifts that are characterized by the following: a foregrounding of quotidian practices of care as a key site of morality; an explicit rejection of individualist, hierarchical and binary logics in favour of reflexivity and contextual ethico-political thinking; and a move beyond the use of intersectionality as a 'buzzword' (Mason, 2019) towards a recognition of the state as a masculinist, colonial institution, and a commitment to listening attentively to and learning from Indigenous values, practices and ways of knowing.

The chapter begins by tracing the development of ethics in feminist-informed approaches to foreign policy, beginning with Sweden – the first country to adopt a feminist foreign policy. It then moves to a more fine-grained consideration of ethics, focusing specifically on key arguments and approaches in feminist ethics. Finally, the chapter presents three examples that embody or point to the potential of relational feminist approaches to ethics in the context of foreign policy. Specifically, it examines the ethical commitments underlying three recent initiatives towards integrating feminist and pro-gender-equality commitments into foreign policy in Mexico, Canada and New Zealand. First, I examine the move by the government of Canada in 2021 to new international assistance funding dedicated to the global care economy, and the extent to which this serves to highlight practices of care and the relational values and ontologies on which they are based. Second, I discuss the rejection of binary and oppositional ethico-epistemologies in Mexico's feminist foreign policy, particularly regarding the domestic–international dichotomy. Here I focus particularly on the interventions of Mexican non-governmental organization Internacional Feminista, one of the only civil society organizations in Mexico to have mobilized and adopted feminist foreign policy language and ethical commitments in their work. Finally, I consider the movement of New Zealand towards a 'First-Nations foreign policy', focusing on the relationship between this and New Zealand's nascent feminist-informed foreign policies. In this case, while there may be tensions between the strategic goals of Indigenous and feminist approaches, the moves beyond colonial understandings of state sovereignty and national interest have the potential to dovetail with feminist values and political commitments, giving rise to a more inclusive feminism. The chapter concludes by reflecting on relational ethics as a normative basis for challenging gender oppression through pro-gender equality and feminist-informed foreign policies.

It should be emphasized that, while all these examples can be linked to particularly feminist ethical commitments, none of them can be understood as illustrations of unproblematically ethical (or feminist) foreign policy. Indeed, as I have argued elsewhere (Robinson, 2021a), there are tensions inherent in bringing feminism to foreign policy, not the least of which are ethical and ontological. Foreign policy centres the sovereign nation state – a colonial and patriarchal institution – that operates according to a logic of absolute exclusion. The very idea of foreign policy thus takes as given a world divided by boundaries, whether as physical borders or limits of jurisdiction and principle (Bigo and Walker, 2007: 730) – an ontology that is antithetical to feminist commitments to relationality. That said, as the idea of feminist foreign policy develops – particularly through the interventions of civil society – space is created to rethink both the ethics and politics of foreign policy in ways that do not reproduce existing binaries and hierarchies in world politics.

Tracing the ethical in (feminist) foreign policy

There is no doubt that Sweden is the singular pioneer of feminist foreign policy; the coalition Social Democratic and Green Party government declared their foreign policy to be feminist shortly after coming to office in 2014. Since that time, many other states have adopted this language, and some have developed specific policies, such as Canada's Feminist International Assistance Policy (FIAP). Of course, feminist foreign policy did not emerge in Sweden out of 'thin air'; indeed, Sweden has been a particularly strong supporter of the Women, Peace and Security agenda since its establishment in 2000, being one of the first states to produce a National Action Plan (Thomson, 2020: 428). The Women, Peace and Security agenda – built upon United Nations (UN) Security Council Resolution 1325 and nine related UN resolutions – is committed to increasing the full, equal and meaningful participation of women in peacemaking, conflict prevention and peacebuilding efforts.

Right from the start, Sweden's feminist foreign policy was recognized as guided by an 'ethically informed framework of cosmopolitanism and human rights that seeks to shape global developments in a gender-sensitive direction' (Aggestam and Bergman Rosamond, 2016: 324). Indeed, the normative direction of Swedish foreign policy at this time was closely associated with then-Foreign Minister Margot Wallström, a strong advocate of gender justice within the work of the UN, having held the position of first-ever UN Special Representative on sexual violence in conflict (Aggestam and Bergman Rosamond, 2016: 325). Wallström's approach was driven by an explicitly human rights-based framework; indeed 'rights' formed the first of the so-called '3Rs' of the policy (rights, representation and resources), and thus the key normative pillar of Sweden's feminist foreign policy. This focus on women's rights as human rights can be seen as instrumental in establishing feminist foreign policy as an explicitly ethical foreign policy. In 2016, Aggestam and Bergman Rosamond (2016: 327) argued that the declaration of a distinct feminist foreign policy signals a departure from traditional, elite-oriented foreign policy practices and discourses towards a policy framework that is guided by normative and ethical principles. Certainly, this is, in many senses, indisputably true; foreign policy is commonly seen as reflecting the national interest, understood in terms of physical national security and economic growth. But 'ethical foreign policy' did not originate with feminist foreign policy. Indeed, the mid to late 1990s saw a marked rise in the use of the language of ethics by Western governments to describe their foreign policy. This move was also dominated by the language of rights, reflecting both the 'end of history' triumphalism of the end of the Cold War, and the space for states like the UK to turn their attention to pressing moral problems, such as global poverty and human (in)security (Frost, 1999).

While the discursive and policy framework of 'human security' spoke to the feminist critique of traditional understandings of national security, the 'human' in human security ultimately reinscribed masculinist universalism and gender-blindness by concealing the gendered underpinnings of security practices (Hudson, 2005: 157). Feminists have emphasized how the human security approach tends to apply 'primarily male norms in valuing and regulating social life', ignoring the everyday significance to people's security of arrangements of care and social reproduction (Truong et al, 2006: xxi). A feminist ethical approach to foreign policy thus differs from human security insofar as it is deeply attentive not only to the moral aspiration of freedom from 'want' and 'fear', but hierarchies, context, relationality and difference, while employing a reflexivity with regard to power relations. In the following section, I turn to a discussion of feminist ethics, drawing on insights from feminist research ethics, feminist epistemology and the ethics of care.

Feminist ethics: foregrounding relationality and power

Ethics is a branch of the academic discipline of philosophy, which engages in the 'systematic philosophical investigation of the ground and nature of ethical principles and values' (Hutchings, 2018: 5). Beyond academia, ethics usually refers to 'codes of behaviour or sets of values that set out what is right or wrong to do within particular contexts' (Hutchings, 2018: 5). Both the academic study and the more everyday understandings of ethics are characterized by vigorous debate surrounding both the content of moral values and their source. While these debates feature numerous, diverse points of contention, they often focus on the problem of universalism – whether there can be moral principles that apply to all, across time and space – and particularism – the notion that moral principles are situated, and become meaningful, in thick historical and sociocultural contexts. As will be discussed in more detail further on in this chapter, feminist ethicists tend to be suspicious of moral universals, arguing that they are, in fact, based on masculinist ontologies and epistemologies, thus reinscribing gendered relations of power.

While cynics and modern-day Machiavellians would claim that politics is a space that is devoid of ethics, this view is both simplistic and reductionist. As Kimberly Hutchings has argued, ethical questions about what is right and wrong to do are difficult to separate from political questions about the kinds of laws, procedures and institutions we should put in place to regulate and mediate human action (Hutchings, 2018: 7). Moreover, while some moral theories – especially those based on rules or principles, may be considered in the abstract or the 'ideal', ethics, in fact, always operates in and through 'the political', which refers to the establishment and constitution of a given social order within which actions, events and other phenomena acquire political status in the first place (Edkins, 1999: 2). Feminists are particularly attuned to the process of delineating the political, as evidenced in the famous feminist slogan 'the personal is political'; and as Enloe has put it, the personal is also international, and vice versa (Enloe, 1989 [2014]).

While not all feminist theory in International Relations (IR) is explicitly concerned with ethics or normative questions, many IR feminists are committed to 'post-positivist' epistemologies and methodologies, thus eschewing the possibility of 'value-free' social science (Robinson, 2009: 79). Feminist methodologies in the study of politics and international relations emphasize reflexivity regarding the positionality of the researcher or 'knower', along with explicit consideration of the ethics of the knowledge–power relation. A feminist research ethic can thus be understood as being committed to self-reflection, and to 'exploring absence, silence, difference, oppression, and the power of epistemology' (Ackerly and True, 2020: 21). Similarly – and importantly for any discussion of feminist foreign policy – Elisabeth Prügl (2016: 25) has emphasized the need for those she calls 'governmental feminists' to reflect on the ethics of their practices. She employs Christine Sylvester's influential notions of 'empathetic co-operation' to understand the agential power of gender experts' ability to engage reflexively with their environment (Prügl, 2016: 26). For feminist policy makers, a reflexive attitude helps to identify power in hegemonic discourses that stifle voices from the margins, and in 'bureaucratic routines that reproduce hegemonies unthinkingly' (Prügl, 2016: 36).

Despite the differences among feminisms – including feminisms in IR – all approaches to feminism are ultimately driven by challenging the exclusions and forms of oppression generated by gendered norms, institutions and structures, and by commitments to alternative futures which are non-hierarchical and inclusive. In this vein, feminist approaches to ethics are thus not oriented in relation to universal reason, but rather in relation to 'cultures, practices, forms of life, care or compassion' (Hutchings, 2013: 27); they eschew universalized accounts of humanness and individualist ontologies, favouring accounts that start with moral subjects in relation and place moral practices in context. Perhaps the best-known approach to feminist ethics that follows this line of thinking is the ethics of care, which foregrounds quotidian practices of care and the 'moral thinking' to which these practices give rise. The different voice of care ethics stands in contrast to dominant, rationalist, masculinist justice-based moral reasoning. It focuses not on the principled grounds for moral judgement, but rather on the relational and contextual (and often messy) process of working though moral-social life in the context of webs of relations and responsibilities of care. Importantly for feminists, care is an embodied ethic. As Maurice Hamington (2020: 25) has put it, 'all care is received and delivered through the body', thus 'our bodies are the epistemological and imaginative basis for care'. To make this claim is not to negate the role of the cognitive and the psychological in the ethics of care; rather, it is to recognize care as a 'holistic and integrated investment of thought, sensation and emotion' (Hamington, 2020: 25). Normativity – moral judgement on what is right, or how we should act – is intimately tied to our relational being that is dynamic and always unfolding in and through our interaction with others.

Recent work on feminist care ethics has sought to decentre it – in other words, to acknowledge the diversity of forms of care, as well as the wide-ranging ways of knowing associated with care ethics (see Bourgault et al, 2024). For example, an ethic of caring has played a crucial role in much Black feminist thought, where 'personal expressiveness, emotions and empathy are central to the knowledge validation process' (Collins, 2003: 62). Collins draws lines of connection between 'women's ways of knowing' and Afrocentric expressions of the ethic of caring, highlighting the shared epistemology of connection, in which truth emerges through care (Collins, 2003: 64). Notably, Collins' relational ethico-epistemology does not erase the individual; indeed, the emphasis is on 'individual uniqueness', where Black people are described as 'profound individualists with a passion for self-expression' (Collins, 2003: 63). This form of individualism, however, differs from the Western conception of the rational (economic) individual (man); Collins uses the metaphor of Black women's quilting, where strong colours and patterns are 'placed next to one another to see the individual differences not as detracting from each piece but as enriching the whole quilt' (Collins, 2003: 62). This is a conception of the 'individual-in-relation', where every individual contributes to the community, and which rests on values of mutual support and empathy.

This rejection of individualistic rationalism in ethics and epistemology is also evident in Black women's political organizing. In 1994, a caucus of Black feminists at a pro-choice conference coined the term 'reproductive justice', a framework that moved a woman's right not to have a child and the rhetoric of 'choice' that accompanies it, but also the right to have children and to raise them with dignity in safe, healthy and supportive environments. Indeed, the language of choice has proved useless – indeed, detrimental – to the argument for public resources that most women need to maintain control over their bodies and their lives (Roberts, 2016: 79–80). As Roberts explains, '(t)he liberal notion of reproductive choice aligns with a neoliberal market logic that relies on individuals' purchase of commodities to manage their own health, instead of the state investing in health care and the other social needs of the larger public' (Roberts, 2016: 81). Not only does the move to reproductive justice reposition reproductive rights in a political context of intersecting race, gender and class oppressions, but it recognized that the complex interpersonal and political dynamics of conceiving, bearing and raising children are profoundly relational experiences, and therefore ones that are laden with multiple and intersecting relations of power.

Care as a radical challenge to oppression can also be seen in Indigenous thought. Relational values are central to Indigenous ways of being and knowing, which focus on deep connections and moral commitments between nonhumans and humans, while taking an historical and anti-colonial perspective (Tuhiwai Smith, 2021). Feminist Indigenous scholars have taken up the potential for women's relationship with the self, the family or the natural world to inspire change in the ways in which we interact with others and our environments (Starblanket and Stark, 2019: 176). Whyte and Cuomo argue that there is a deep synergy among feminist care ethics and Indigenous ways of knowing, especially in the context of ecological wellbeing (Whyte and Cuomo, 2017: 236). And while international relations and foreign policy are arguably centered around territory (and sovereignty over it), the 'flattened ontological frameworks of traditional IR often result in a paradoxical turning away from a focus on place' (Tuck and McKenzie, 2014: 633). By contrast, Indigenous scholars foreground issues of land and place; for example, Tuck and McKenzie's 'critical place inquiry' addresses spatialized and place-based processes of colonization and settler colonization and works against their erasure by furthering generative and critical politics of places via a 'relational ethics of accountability' to people and place (Tuck and McKenzie, 2014: 19).

Although there are several points of intersection between feminist and Indigenous ethico-ontologies and ways of knowing, there are also important differences. Indeed, while feminist ethics and epistemologies still occupy a marginal position in the academic literature, Indigenous ethics and epistemologies have 'more brutal histories of exclusion' (Doucet et al, 2024). Indeed, the violence that Indigenous people in settler colonial contexts endure is under the 'twisted auspices of care for our wellbeing' (Doucet et al, 2024). As Anishinaabe scholar Eva Jewell explains, colonial care is the 'actual clutches' on children that remove them from the care of their original families, working in tandem with settler bureaucracy to enact colonial violence in the lives of Indigenous peoples. And yet, she continues, care is 'at home in Anishinaabe worldviews, and is a vital concept in our onto-epistemologies' (Doucet et al, 2024). It must be recognized that Indigenous understandings of care are as much about absences, rage and 'abandoned and invisible worlds of care' as they are about relationality and interconnection. Feminist ethics must confront these absences and silences in dominant White, Western theorizations of care, and make explicit the onto-epistemological debt owed to Indigenous thought. Thus, while we can recognize points of intersection among Western feminist, Black feminist, Indigenous, and Indigenous feminist ethico-ontologies, particular 'ethics of care', we must also recognize the way that 'caring' discourse and practices have been used as a tool of violence and genocide (Narayan, 1995). As I will discuss, any efforts to bring together feminist and Indigenous ethics (including as a basis for foreign policy) must recognize these exclusions, silences and absences.

In the sections that follow, I will describe initiatives and approaches to feminist foreign policy, by governments and civil society organizations, that demonstrate a move towards relational feminist values. None of the three examples described should be understood as fully formed policies or as representing a wholesale embrace of feminist relational ethics. But all three constitute a recognition that feminist-informed foreign policy must be underpinned by values that do not create moral aporias, but which work with and support intersectional feminist political goals that challenge existing hierarchies of power, working towards more sustainable and equitable feminist futures.

Care ethics and the care economy

In 2017, Canada unveiled its new FIAP. The FIAP coincided with Canada's first integration of feminist language into its foreign policy discourse. To date, development assistance remains the only area of foreign policy in Canada to have an explicitly feminist policy. The language of rights, women's empowerment and poverty reduction through 'smart economics' defined the early narrative of the FIAP; indeed, even though the FIAP expresses a desire to transform gender roles, it does so in ways that are largely instrumental to the overall goal of economic growth and prosperity (Parisi, 2020: 177). And while activists, advocates and academics recognized the importance of the government's discursive and policy shift towards feminism, criticisms of this continued neoliberalization of feminism were evident (Parisi, 2020). In October 2020, Global Affairs Canada solicited views on the subject from stakeholders in Canada and around the world – including civil society – to feed into the development of a White Paper on Canada's feminist foreign policy. Among the many recommendations was an emphasis on the need to recognize the role of unpaid and underpaid care in stifling progress towards racial and gender justice, and the need to advocate for more investments in the care economy to advance women's economic equality. It was noted that this involves investment in public services, social and physical infrastructure, and social protection (Feminist Foreign Policy Working Group, 2021: 21).

Advocates were thus pleased to have their voices recognized when, on 30 June 2022, Prime Minister Justin Trudeau announced CAD$100 million in new international assistance funding dedicated to paid and unpaid care work. It was the first targeted global investment in the care economy by a donor government (Oxfam Canada, 2022). Oxfam Canada was a central player in advocating for this investment. Their *WE-Care* programme works towards a just and inclusive society by recognizing, reducing and redistributing unpaid care and domestic work. Clearly, there is a recognition of the normative implications of 'reframing' the conversation around care: 'In Oxfam's We-Care program we have learnt from feminist economists to avoid using the term "burden" as a default when advocating on care. Why? Because "burden" implies that something needs to be reduced and minimized. Do we want less education, less nourishment, less care?' (Parkes, 2021). Here, Oxfam is seeking to demonstrate the value of care, the skills and labour that unpaid social reproductive labour requires, and the fact that care is not something that needs to be reduced and minimized. While care work is often seen as a burden that prevents women from achieving full empowerment or emancipation – often through paid work outside the home – valuing care means asking why this should be framed as a burden, and continually sloughed off to more and more marginalized women. Valuing care means wanting more of it – for our families, our communities and ourselves. It imagines a form of feminism that is not about the entrepreneurial spirit of individual women, but about the collective recognition of social reproductive labour and the moral value of attentiveness to the needs of others. As I have argued elsewhere, framing care as a burden perpetuates neoliberal logics, reifies the hierarchical, gender binary, and overlooks the value of relational care practices for maintaining wellbeing – at the level of the household and the community (Robinson, 2021b). Oxfam's move to avoid the language of burden, and reframe care as a social good, alters the normative orientation towards valuing caring relations and practices for their contribution to households and communities. That said, while this can be seen as a progressive move, it is important to note the potential dangers of this focus on care work, especially in terms of the narrow focus on the gender binary and heteronormative assumptions about care, which may partly be accomplished through narratives of racialized masculinities. While it is true that care work is feminized and that most of this labour around the world is performed by women, the task of 'ungendering' this work is not a straightforward one. The emphasis by Oxfam and the Government of Canada on the need to 'engage men and boys' could assume what Kate Bedford (2008) calls a heteronormative 'two-partner model of labour and love', thus reinforcing the exclusive gender binary. Moreover, the effort to 'mould' men's behaviour could reinforce assumptions that there are some masculinities – performed by poor, racialized men in the Global South – that are unenlightened and thus in need of transformation. This may not only reinscribe racial stereotypes and strain familial relations but may also bring costs that are borne by the women they are seeking to help, as they may face a backlash from families and communities for colluding with Western norms of feminism.

Although these potential dangers must be recognized, it remains the case that Oxfam's advocacy on care work as a key component of feminist international assistance shifts the ethical register by foregrounding quotidian practices of care and recognizing their value for sustaining households and communities. Feminist philosophers have argued that practices of care give rise to a particular kind of moral thinking that 'takes the concerns and needs of the other as the basis for action' (Tronto, 1993: 195). The recognition of care as a shared aspect of human life may be a descriptive claim, but it is also one that entails important, and often overlooked, normative implications.

Challenging hierarchies in Mexico

Mexico announced its feminist foreign policy in 2019, becoming the 'first country in the Global South to embrace feminism as a guiding principle for its international involvement' (Velasco et al, 2022). Mexico is garnering recognition for its feminist foreign policy; in a 2023 study conducted by the International Center for Research on Women, Mexico was ranked third overall for its feminist foreign policy, behind only Sweden and Norway (Papagioti, 2023). In its discussion of Priority Area I, Peace and Security, the report points to one of the key critiques of feminist foreign policy generally – the lack of coherence between policies and rhetoric at the domestic and international level. It specifically singles out the case of Mexico, where the ongoing militarization of public security since 2006 has led to grave human rights violations. It has been estimated that confrontations between armed forces and alleged criminal groups have contributed to a shocking rise of femicides in Mexico, with ten women murdered per day in 2019. While the Mexican Ministry of Foreign Affairs has acknowledged the issue and pledged to eliminate gender-based violence as part of its feminist foreign policy, the glaring discrepancy between international and domestic remains an important challenge (Papagioti, 2023: 19).

The Mexican research and advocacy organization, Internacional Feminista, has focused on this challenge, defining its mission as 'reappropriating' the international gender equality agenda. They seek to contribute to an alliance of activists and civil society groups to build, monitor and evaluate public policies and initiatives that guarantee an inclusive approach and radical feminist transformation (Internacional Feminista, https://www.internacion alfeminista.com). Their specific interest in foreign policy and security has led them to engage closely with the feminist foreign policy in Mexico; indeed, the organization was born as a response to the need for transparency and accountability regarding Mexico's feminist foreign policy – what it consists of, and what it has achieved (Velasco and Philipson García, 2023). Specifically, they argue that GBV in Mexico is ubiquitous, and that governmental solutions are lacking and negligent (Philipson García, 2022). Despite feminist activists' anti-military demands, the federal government has continued to grow the military's spending and responsibilities in everyday life, including for public safety. This is problematic since it reveals an association between military presence and increased prevalence of violence against women (Philipson García, 2022).

Internacional Feminista co-founders Daniela Philipson García and Ana Velasco have articulated how feminist values must challenge hierarchies and binary logic. They argue that the separation of global and local values is arbitrary and goes against feminist values. For instance, they demonstrate the way that local actors – such as grassroots feminist groups and women farmers – are often instrumental to the fulfilment of foreign policy goals. 'Honing in on gender inequality abroad while disregarding it locally', Philipson García (2022) explains, 'is particularly problematic for countries in the Global North who continue to frame development and human rights shortcomings as unique to the Global South'.

These framings are upheld by a politics of forgetting, which idealizes the Westphalian narrative, and fails to consider the colonial and racialized history of this story (Nisancioglu, 2020). Moreover, when feminists rely on universalizing and idealized moral language in their normative commitments, they reduce ethics to 'one of three modalities: protective, educative or punitive' (Hutchings, 2013: 35). As Kimberly Hutchings explains, this means that they 'identify with the moral position, choices and dilemmas of the *protector, the teacher and the law enforcer*' (Hutchings, 2013: 35; emphasis added). The result is that ethics (or ethical feminist foreign policy) ends up institutionalizing patterns of inclusion and exclusion, thus undermining its normative aspirations to speak truth to power (Hutchings, 2013: 36). Rather than finger-pointing, Western states need to look inward to foreground the intricate webs of relationships – for example, tied to the global arms trade, transnational business interests, systemic transnational racism – that make women's oppression around the world look the way it does (Robinson, 2021a: 30).

Feminist ethics actively resists the hierarchical binaries of Western modernity and, specifically, the forms of patriarchy that value separation (Robinson, 2020: 14). Internacional Feminista's approach recognizes the problem of epistemic injustice in the conceptualization of feminist foreign policy, but argues that embracing such a policy allows countries to blur the arbitrary lines separating the global from the local and to disrupt power asymmetries to address the challenges of an increasingly globalized world (Philipson García and Velasco, 2022).

Internacional Feminista is thus creating a vision of feminist foreign policy for Mexico that is radical and potentially transformative. As a Global South country, Mexico has the potential – through an integrated pro-gender equality domestic and foreign policy – to provide a model for states around the world, particularly those of the Global North. While several states – including Canada and Sweden – have been criticized for not attending to gender-based human rights violations within their borders – for other states, it has been suggested that tacit recognition of their own domestic failings on gender equality has led them to avoid a full embrace of feminist policy (Lee-Koo, 2020). Mexico's feminist foreign policy already challenges the moral high ground of Western states; its next step must be to listen to their own feminist civil society that calls for the state to reject the international–domestic binary and tackle the endemic gender inequality and violence at the local level.

Indigeneity and feminism in New Zealand's foreign policy

In 2021, then Aotearoa New Zealand Foreign Minister Hon Nanaia Mahuta began her inaugural foreign policy speech with a reference to the treaty partnership between the Indigenous Māori inhabitants and the British settlers who arrived on the land, arguing that the principles of partnership and mutual respect embodied in the Treaty of Waitangi provide 'the foundation for how New Zealand can conduct its foreign policy' (Government of New Zealand, 2021). This was a value-based foreign policy, but Mahuta did not use the language of rights or justice. Rather, she stressed Māori values, such as *manaaki* (kindness or the reciprocity of goodwill), *whanaunga* (our connectedness or shared sense of humanity), *mahi tahi* and *kotahitanga* (collective benefits and shared aspiration) and *kaitiaki* (protectors and stewards of our intergenerational wellbeing). Mahuta stressed the importance of relationship and connection, empathy and 'intergenerational solutions for wellbeing' (Government of New Zealand, 2021). This move by New Zealand towards an Indigenous foreign policy can be seen as revolutionary in many respects. James Blackwell (2021) has argued that this approach is 'not merely a progressive take on traditional diplomacy, but a radical departure from traditional thinking. Gone is the state-centric approach in which the states' own self-interest is the only goal. Instead, the focus is on shared goals, shared custodianship, and shared responsibility'. It has been noted, however, that this move is more 'evolutionary' than 'revolutionary', insofar as it reflects significant domestic and foreign policy changes in New Zealand over the last few decades, including regarding its advocacy for Indigenous rights (Smith and Holster, 2023: 1579–1580).

Synergies and complementarity can be seen between Indigenous values and pro-gender or feminist norms in the context of foreign policy. Stephenson and Blackwell argue that both approaches aim to focus on foregrounding previously side-lined, 'unseen' or invisible people and communities, subvert traditional power structures that have oppressed others, and centre individuals' agency, experience, perspectives and worldview (Stephenson and Blackwell, 2022). Moreover, relationality is a defining feature of both Indigenous and feminist onto-epistemologies. Smith and

Holster (2023) describe how the ontological basis of *te ao Māori*[1] as a 'series of entanglements' evokes the concept of relationality, noting how relationality has also been used as an ontological base to theorize feminist foreign policy as representing a shift towards centring moral relations among human beings (Smith and Holster, 2023: 1579, 1589). Yet, despite this affinity, it is evident that relationality can be understood and employed in multiple ways, including strategically or instrumentally. Smith and Holster explain that while *te ao Māori* is strongly relational, the use of this relational ontology to guide Aotearoa New Zealand foreign policy has been inconsistent, especially when comparing the country's interactions in the Pacific with its interactions with allies in the Anglosphere (2023: 1592).

While Smith and Holster address the potential conflicts between values and interests in this context, it is important to consider conflicts *between and among* values and interests as well – including conflicts between feminist and Indigenous values and political aims. For example, there are some fundamental differences between some Indigenous and some Euro-Western cultures regarding to gender relations, and many Indigenous scholars reject Western notions of equality and freedom (St. Denis, 2017). As Verna St. Denis argues, some Indigenous women regard it as unnecessary to appeal for the attainment of the same rights as men; rather they appeal for the restoration and reclaiming of cultural traditions and self-government that would allow them to be restored to their revered position in their communities (St. Denis, 2017). Scholars and communities have identified that structural and system reform is needed that recognizes the enduring effects of colonization on racial and gender hierarchies, also known as 'colonial gender regimes' (McClintock, 2016; Glenn, 2015).

Feminist and pro-gender foreign policies will be faced with a glaring moral aporia if they are not able to recognize the historical and ongoing dispossession of Indigenous peoples, especially Indigenous women, at the hands of the state. It may be that a way to bring together feminism and Indigenous thought with foreign policy is to embrace the radical potential of the former to radically refigure the latter. This requires consideration of how epistemology and ontology inform both ethics and our understanding of the political. Feminist theory has been instrumental in subverting the dominant modernist, masculinist epistemology that presumes a disembodied knower that constitutes abstract, universal truth (Hekman, 1995: 30). As Susan Hekman has argued, the relational self produces knowledge that is connected, a product of discourses that *constitute forms of life*; it is plural rather than singular (Hekman, 1995: 30; emphasis added). The radical implication of this aspect of feminist

---

[1] In English, 'the Māori way', emphasizing the importance of relationships between people, nature and more-than-nature grounded in *tikanga* customary values and knowledge.

thought overlaps with decolonial theory and ethics, in which 'universalizing and monolingual predicates' are foregone to maintain 'openness through multiple imaginaries' (Odysseos, 2017: 451). In this vein, Maggie FitzGerald's work has theorized care ethics in the context of the 'pluriverse'; specifically, she considers the significance of caring for and maintaining multiple distinct yet connected onto-epistemologies or 'worlds' (FitzGerald, 2022; 2023). She suggests that the ethics of care, defined by a relational ontology and situated epistemology, is well positioned to serve as a lens for understanding the pluriverse, which shares these same premises. Furthermore, she argues, the ethics of care normatively values 'repairing and maintaining our relations of care that allow us to produce and reproduce ourselves and our worlds as well as is reasonably possible' (FitzGerald, 2022: 129).

On this view, the colonial sovereign state belongs only to 'one world', and therefore, from the position of both feminist and decolonial ethics, must be decentered and, in some cases, resisted and refused. Ethically, that means recognizing the pluriverse (and the contingency of institutions like the modern state), as well as the gendered and racialized forms of power that serve continuously to recentre the state while marginalizing other worlds. This requires a commitment to thinking and acting relationally, and to practices like what Judy Atkinson calls 'deep listening' (Atkinson, 2002). The emphasis on listening changes the focus – prominent in liberal, masculinist ways of knowing – on speech, voice and discourse. Feminist care ethicists, by contrast, have emphasized the act of listening (Robinson, 2011; Bourgault, 2022), thus interrogating the familiar binary of speech versus silence (Bourgault, 2022). Challenging this binary not only radically refigures the idea of voice in politics, understanding it relationally, but serves to bring the silent into view, so to speak. As Carol Gilligan put it, to have a voice is to be human, but speaking depends on listening and being heard; it is an intensely relational act (Gilligan, 1993).

Of course, the dangers of cultural extractivism are ever-present here; listening to and learning from relational ontologies and values in Indigenous thought is not about wresting this knowledge from its history and place and applying it to the context of Western modernity. On the contrary, it is shifting the self into the position of listener and learner, recognizing the international as a 'zone of mutual constitution' (Barkawi and Laffey, 2006: 114), and that states promoting pro-gender and feminist foreign policies are both deeply implicated in and constituted by the gendered and racialized projects of colonialism.

Conclusion

In this chapter, I have argued that feminist foreign policy has the potential to build a new kind of ethical foreign policy, one that breaks from the liberal rights and rules-based, state-centric models of the post–Cold War era. This will not happen, however, if governments continue to couch their feminist foreign policies in moral discourses of white, Western, liberal feminism – where women are treated as individual rights-holders and potential 'rational economic men' in the making, and justice means that policies are directed only towards 'Third World Women' (Mohanty, 1988) without challenging the binary and hierarchical logics which construct the dichotomy between inside and outside the sovereign state. In order to provide a normative framework that can truly challenge patriarchal, racial and colonial global relations of power, feminist-informed foreign policy should turn to relational feminist ethics. Relationality is central to accounts of morality – as well as epistemology and ontology – in feminist theory, including feminist care ethics, Indigenous feminist thought and Black feminism. These perspectives foreground ethics as practices of responsibility and care – for others, for the self, and the land and water around us. By rejecting separation, individualism and rationalism in favour of connection, context and the relational self, these approaches provide a basis for thinking about feminist foreign policy, which has the potential to move beyond the aporias which it currently faces, towards more sustainable feminist futures.

3

Power

Columba Achilleos-Sarll

Introduction

Power is a critical concept in International Relations (IR) and central to all feminist work, including feminist approaches to foreign policy. Feminists demonstrate that the conduct of foreign policy is a hyper-masculine performance where states pursue national security and economic gains through 'hard' and 'soft' power. This, in turn, constrains pro-gender norms (Aggestam and True, 2020) and alternative approaches to foreign policy that centre, for example, care, welfare and redistribution (Achilleos-Sarll, 2018; Robinson, 2021a). Unpacking the conduct, practice and effects of foreign policy, feminists demonstrate how foreign policy is deeply gendered all the way down. Despite these critical insights, feminist IR and foreign policy analysis (FPA) rarely engage in conversation (for exceptions, see Hudson and Leidl, 2015; Aggestam and True, 2020). While both mainstream and critical strands of FPA conceptualize power differently, the former more concerned with power understood as the material capabilities of states while the latter proposing a more variegated understanding, drawing into the analysis power as relational, ideational and normative, gender remains a blind spot for both (Hudson, 2005; Achilleos-Sarll, 2018; Aggestam and True, 2020). However, for feminist scholars gender is 'intrinsic to the meaning of power itself' (Aggestam and True, 2020: 154), seen as a 'primary way of signifying relationships of power' (Scott, 1988: 1067). This includes drawing attention to 'how power operates in areas where most non-feminists deny there's any power at work' (Enloe, 2013), as well as emphasizing that power is always relationally produced (Tickner, 1995; Sylvester, 1994). Feminism is therefore both a critique and reconceptualization of power.

If feminists understand power qualitatively differently to mainstream approaches, then the question arises whether feminist foreign policies also rest on alternative understandings of, and approaches to, power *and* thereafter foreign policy. This chapter therefore investigates how the concept of 'power' is 'put into discourse' (Shepherd, 2008) in feminist foreign policy. I ask what conceptualizations of power (and by extension what feminisms) are articulated within the discourse of feminist foreign policies and what are the constitutive political effects thereof. While feminists have assiduously unpacked the feminist-informed documents that have been produced by states since Sweden launched its avowedly 'feminist' foreign policy in late 2014 (for example, Thomson, 2020; Parisi, 2020), and often point to frequent mentions to power, and particularly empowerment, within these policies, seldom is the concept of power and its multiple strands the primary focus of analysis. This is reflected in this volume, where power/empowerment are referred to copiously by authors addressing topics from trade to the environment, thereby demonstrating its discursive centrality to understanding what feminist foreign policy is, how it guides the practice of foreign policy, and how it differs from conventional foreign policy. Tracing variants of power is worthy of analytical attention because the way power is understood is central to defining the 'problem' of gender inequality and gender subordination, which is at the heart of feminist foreign policy, with implications for the solutions, or foreign policies, that become possible, plausible and imaginable. This requires deconstructing the assumptions inherent in how power and empowerment are discussed and invoked, rather than presuming that a consensus exists about what they mean and how they travel in pro-gender foreign policies.

The chapter is organized as follows. First, I map different conceptualizations of power in feminist theory and feminist IR, paying particular attention to feminist approaches to foreign policy. Attached to different feminist epistemologies and methodologies, these can be divided between an understanding of power as resource, power as relational, power as intersectional, power as resistance, and power as empowerment. This loose typology serves as a guiding analytical framework rather than an exhaustive account of power. I then trace these variants in the current and former feminist foreign and development policies of Sweden (2014) and Canada (2015), identifying empowerment as the predominate variant. Despite the mutability of the concept of power and empowerment, and while the analysis will demonstrate that there are multiple, overlapping and sometimes conflicting variants of power traceable in these documents, power and especially empowerment are predominantly re-rooted through a neoliberal economic logic that emphasizes efficiency, choice and agency. This, in turn, eclipses other, potentially more transformative variants, therefore offering little hope of bringing into being the secure, prosperous and peaceful world that frame the language – and potential – of feminist foreign policies. The conclusion reflects on the possibilities produced – and foreclosed – by these articulations of power and empowerment in feminist foreign policy.

Feminist foreign policy takes on power

Feminists have always been at the forefront of resisting patriarchy and gender inequality; feminist power has long been wielded through social movements, activism and advocacy. Feminism is therefore emancipatory, moving us beyond ideas of resistance to agency, which is captured by Nancy Hartsock who describes 'the feminist theory of power ... as energy and competence rather than dominance' (Hartsock, 1983: 224; see also Prügl, 2016). According to Hartsock, this explains 'why the masculine community constructed ... power, as domination, repression, and death, and why women's accounts of power differ in specific and systematic ways from those put forward by men ... such a standpoint might allow us to put forward an understanding of power that points in more liberatory directions' (Hartsock, 1983: 226). In what follows, I explore different feminist takes on power, including feminist perspectives on foreign policy, as a challenge to conventional understandings of power that omit gender. Feminist approaches not only identify how gender is central to understanding unequal power relationships but feminism also offers new pathways towards a gender-just world. Feminist power is, crucially, about the possibilities and practicalities of transformation; the capacity to empower or transform oneself and others, at the heart of which lies the transformation of gender relations and, therefore, patriarchal society.

In (feminist) IR and FPA, power is commonly conceptualized as a resource that is unequally distributed within and between individuals and states. According to this view, power is 'a kind of stuff that can be possessed by individuals in greater or lesser amounts' (Young, 1990: 31). For states, this 'stuff' is usually code for either tangible, material assets, often described as 'hard power', which mostly refers to economic and military power, or intangible, ideational and symbolic 'soft power', which includes culture, ideas and identity (Nye, 2011). In this reading, power represents a positive social good, albeit an asset that is unevenly and unjustly distributed. Those who conceptualize power as resource argue that what is significant is less to do with what, and how much 'stuff' a state possesses, but rather how resources convert into the state's capacity to do things and/or influence others' actions to produce preferred outcomes, which describes a version of 'power-over' (Nye, 2011: 13).

Feminist approaches to foreign policy highlight that the unequal distribution of resources, as well as the meanings attached to different resources (for example, Cohn, 1987), is highly gendered and represents a primary marker of gender inequality (see Guerrina et al, 2023a). Feminists attribute the disparity between men and women to socially constructed inequalities which is implicit in the work of liberal feminists who adhere to a male/female, domination/subordination, binary (for example, Okin, 1989: 136). Feminist international political economists go a step further and trace resource disparity to the gender division of labour and globalized economic exploitation of women's labour (for example, True, 2012). They highlight how resource inequality makes women particularly vulnerable, and, among the least able to adapt to, inter alia, climate effects (for example, Cohn, 2023: 14, cited in Achilleos-Sarll et al, 2023), war and conflict (for example, Meger, 2016), financial crises (for example, Hozic and True, 2016) and global health pandemics (for example, Johnson, 2021). As the subject and primary distributor of resources, 'gendered states' (Peterson, 1992) institutionalize these gender relations by 'delineating the sexual division of labor, and structuring state violence along gender lines' (Duriesmith, 2018, quoting Connell, 1987: 125–134). Feminists who conceptualize power as a resource argue that redistributing resources more equitably is a step towards achieving gender equality (for example, Okin, 1989). This distributive model of power (Young, 1990) has, however, drawn several critiques that form the basis of other conceptualizations of power.

Iris Marion Young (1992) explains that power is not simply a 'thing' that can be possessed and therefore re/distributed; rather, it is produced through action and therefore always relational. In other words, power is not only and always repressive but can be productive, producing both subjects and governance structures. While many interpret resources as a vehicle for understanding 'power-over', which follows a pattern of domination/subordination, feminists who derive inspiration from Foucault instead conceptualize power as a 'productive network' existing in all social relations (Foucault, 1977: 119). This follows the idea that 'power circulates and is *exercised* rather than possessed' (Deveaux, 1994: 231). The idea of power as a capillary network in all relationships that 'produce and regulate quotidian practices' (Amigot and Pujal, 2009: 650) is captured by the adjoining statements developed by Cynthia Enloe: 'the international is personal' and 'the personal is international' (Enloe, 2014: 315). In other words, if power is ubiquitous and polymorphous, then limiting and directing our analytical attention to certain foreign policy sites and actors in global politics, typically states, institutions, presidents and prime ministers, is to render partial and incomplete the workings and consequences of power (Enloe, 2014).

While feminists are aligned in demonstrating that the discourse and practice of power is profoundly gendered and relational, there has been a tendency to privilege and prioritize gender as the primary structuring feature of society, so divesting gender of its relationality to race, class and sexuality, for example (see also Collins, 1986; Haraway, 1988; Crenshaw, 1989). Reading gender as an identity marker assumes a static, dyadic and atomistic understanding of power as existing between two unequally positioned, and oppositional, subjects, usually men and women, and thus restricted to binary gender. This approach, in turn, overlooks the wide range of social structures into which all individuals and states are interpolated, which shape individual and state relations of/to power. In other words, it is 'unhelpful for understanding the structural features of domination' (Allen, 2022).

The foregoing variants of power focus predominately on the oppressive and destructive dimensions of power characterized by forms of domination. This focus, however, can obscure how power can and has been mobilized as a mode of *resistance* to certain foreign policies – including those related to the climate emergency or foreign interventions. Power is therefore not simply top-down and dualistic, reproducing a domination/subordination binary that travels only in one direction; rather, as many scholars illuminate, power is never absolutely determining, resistance is always present (Amigot and Pujal, 2009: 651–652). Forms of resistance to structures of power can include a wide range of political action deployed by diverse groups across different scales, from social movements and multiply marginalized people, who often bear the brunt of the most destructive foreign policies (Bouka, 2021), to professionalized policy experts, non-governmental organization actors and policy makers.

Empowerment

Empowerment is a further strand of power, which has been a particular focus for feminist scholars especially in relation to women's empowerment. Indeed, feminist foreign policies and related pro-gender foreign policies are variously framed as a vector for women's empowerment. While power as resistance and empowerment intersect in meaning, empowerment moves beyond the idea of a relationship of/to power to its potential to be harnessed as an emancipatory force or site of possibility, agency and, ultimately, change. Empowerment is therefore a concept, as Claire Duncanson (2019: 113) writes, 'of much interest to feminist scholars both because of its emancipatory origins and potential and because of its salutary lessons about how such terms, and feminist agendas more broadly, can be hijacked and co-opted'. Within the concept of empowerment, it is possible to excavate two overarching strands and genealogies that exist in tension with one another.

Cueva et al (2023: 7) trace the concept of empowerment to 'the theorising and struggles of women from the Global South' (for example, Sen and Grown, 1987; Batliwala, 1993; Kabeer, 1994). Empowerment was originally developed through grassroots struggles to transform unjust and unequal power relations. Kabeer (1994: 129) elaborates on the relationship between power and empowerment by defining power 'as control over material assets, intellectual resources and ideology'. Empowerment is thus understood as 'the process of challenging existing power relations, and of gaining greater control over the sources of power' (Kabeer, 1994: 130). Moreover, empowerment is directly linked to collective action understood as 'power with' in addition to 'power within' (Cornwall and Rivas, 2015: 405). In that sense, it is seen as a process rather than a measurable end point that seeks to challenge and transform not only gender relations operating at an individual level but interlinked structures of patriarchy, militarism, colonialism and capitalism (Batiwala, 1993: 558). Essentially, empowerment is about transforming power relations rather than improving the capacity and fortitude of women in dealing with oppression and injustice (Cornwall and Rivas, 2015: 405).

In the late 1990s, at the tail-end of the United Nations (UN) World Conferences on Women, these transformative ideas were lost to a neoliberal conception of empowerment that emerged as dominant, focused on inclusion in the prevailing neoliberal economic system, as discussed in Rebecca Tiessen's chapter in this volume on development (Chapter 13). It was believed that women's empowerment could be achieved through their integration into global economies so as to produce a liberal, autonomous subject afforded equal rights. While the idea was that women would benefit from economic development initiatives through a focus on labour market participation, they would continue to be marginalized from these same processes – those that it was claimed would ultimately emancipate them (Bandarage, 1984: 500). In addition to an *economic logic* (which highlights women's contribution to economic development often measured in terms of national economic growth), there are other, relational, logics that Cueva et al (2023) explain have also come to structure empowerment discourse across the fields of development, peace and security. These include: a *political logic*, which positions women as agentic actors who can effect political change; a *social logic*, which equates gender equality with the empowerment of women and girls; and a *security logic*, which attributes the ability to achieve a sustainable peace in post-conflict environments to the empowerment of women in these settings (Cueva et al, 2023: 7–8).

How is empowerment put into discourse?

The foregoing discussion demonstrates that power is central to feminist attempts to explain, challenge and transform gender inequality and therefore gender subordination, including how it manifests through the discourse and practice of foreign policy. The meaning and weight attached to such articulations is therefore worthy of analytical attention because how power is conceptualized is part of defining the 'problem' of gender inequality, with implications for the foreign policies that become possible and thinkable and those that are foreclosed (Doty, 1996). As Lene Hansen (2006: 25) theorizes, 'representations and policy are mutually constitutive and discursively linked'. In the sections that follow, I trace these variants of power (resource, relational, intersectional, resistance and empowerment), paying particular attention to empowerment due to its prominence in the (historic and current) feminist foreign and development policies of both Sweden (2014, which they abandoned in 2022) and Canada (2015), and ask why power and empowerment may be understood differently by states. Sweden and Canada are chosen because they were the first two to officially announce and adopt feminist foreign and development policies. Their policies have had a domino effect, resulting in other states adopting explicitly feminist foreign and development policies, as well as influencing the official take-up of language around gender, feminism and foreign policy, and thus they can be described as 'norm entrepreneurs' (Davies and True, 2017). A brief, discourse-theoretical analysis (for elaboration of method, see Shepherd, 2008) of both policies seeks to uncover the variants of power that are dominant so to begin to trace constitutive political effects.

Sweden

Empowerment is the dominant variant of power traceable in Sweden's *Handbook on Feminist Foreign Policy*. It is set within a broadly liberal cosmopolitan framework and social democratic tradition (for example, Bergman Rosamond, 2020). The domestic political context as well as a state's history and identity influences how power is differently understood among states and to some degree also explains why a feminist foreign policy might be adopted in the first place. Sweden's welfare model, gender cosmopolitanism, internationalist tradition, humanitarianism and donor positionality are highlighted as interacting factors in the production of its feminist foreign policy and reason for adoption, as well as in its orientation towards rights discourse, resource allocation, and women's inclusion and participation in decision-making (for example, Bergman Rosamond, 2020). This firmly locates power – who wields it and how – I argue, in a distinctly liberal, and neoliberal, feminist framework.

The two prominent empowerment logics in the policy include an *economic logic* that highlights women's contributions to economic development through labour market participation as a measure of, and necessary for, empowerment, and a *social logic*, which connects women's empowerment to gender equality and equal rights. Both terms are frequently linked together, and thus mostly conflated, despite both concepts reflecting different theories of social and political change (Cornwall and Rivas, 2015: 408). Empowerment and its multiple logics are therefore evident both in the structuring framework of the policy, with its focus around rights, representation and resources – commonly referred to as the '3Rs' – and in the number of mentions of empowerment vis-à-vis other variants of power. Empowerment provides the glue that holds the 3Rs together.

The document states that 'Sweden's feminist government aims to ensure that women and men have the same power to shape society and their own lives' (Government of Sweden, 2018a: 3).[1] Broadly, this reflects an individualistic understanding of inequality as emanating from a power imbalance, usually material, between men and women. As Jennifer Thomson writes, 'Swedish feminist foreign policy is an attempt to address this fundamental problem' (Thomson, 2020: 429). The document posits that gender equality will have an impact not only on women's lives but wider society through economic growth. It follows the idea that gender equality is 'smart economics' and is therefore framed using instrumental arguments, such as: 'It is ... socially smart to invest in women's economic empowerment' (Government of Sweden, 2018a: 27) or, 'getting more women into business and trade is sound economic policy' (Government of Sweden, 2018a; Linde, 2017). Gender equality and women's rights are therefore presented as a necessary precondition to advance other foreign policy goals, predominately economic growth and poverty reduction, while also highlighting that better market access will help overcome other barriers to gender equality.

The '3Rs' are the identified indicators for achieving Sweden's feminist foreign policy goals. First, *rights* – discursively prioritized in the document, are mentioned through attention to Sweden's pre-existing commitments to human rights treaties and declarations, including the UN Declaration of Human Rights, the UN Security Council Resolution 1325 on 'Women, Peace and Security', the Geneva Conventions, and European Union gender equality policies. Under the umbrella of rights, there is specific mention of human rights, economic rights and empowerment, and sexual and reproductive health and rights. *Representation* follows, and refers to how Sweden's feminist foreign policy will promote 'women's participation and influence in decision-making at all levels' (Government for Sweden, 2018: 14), which, alongside market access, is highlighted as a means through which power may be redistributed between men and women.

Resources are listed last in this three-pronged approach, with the document referring 33 times to resources, often linked to economic growth. Resources are discussed in terms of resource disparity between men and women, flagging that gender equality should be an indicator when allocating resources. It states: 'The Swedish Foreign Service shall work to ensure that

---

[1] On 23 August, Minister for Foreign Affairs Margot Wallström launched a handbook on Sweden's feminist foreign policy. www.swedenabroad.se/globalassets/ambassader/zimbabwe-harare/documents/handbook_swedens-feminist-foreign-policy.pdf. Accessed 1 August, 2024.

resources are allocated to promote gender equality and equal opportunities for all women and girls to enjoy human rights' (Government of Sweden, 2018a: 13). Examples of resource disparity between men and women are highlighted in statements such as: 'Globally, 300 million fewer women own a mobile phone compared to men' (Government of Sweden, 2018a: 15), or 'Women own less than 20 per cent of the world's land resources' (Government of Sweden, 2018a: 15). In the case of mobile phones, it goes on to underline that this disparity in turn limits women's access to information and therefore the use of services such as credit, thus preventing women from running companies, businesses and, ultimately, accessing markets (Government of Sweden, 2018a: 15).

Against the broad aims of the policy, it includes 39 mentions of power, out of which 22 are articulated in terms of empowerment, and out of those 22, 17 are referenced in relation to economic rights, mostly described as 'economic rights and empowerment'. As mentioned, this funnels the 3Rs through an economic logic, which highlights women's contribution to economic development, particularly economic growth, combined with a social logic, which associates empowerment with gender equality and equal rights. On balance, however, empowerment is mostly articulated in terms of economic empowerment: 'When women participate in the labour market their economic empowerment increases, and a society's economic growth increases' (Government of Sweden, 2018a: 27). This proffers neoliberal capitalism as the organizing economic rationale through which women's empowerment can be achieved. The remaining 17 mentions of power mostly reinforce a liberal, dyadic and economic version of power as existing between men and women regarding access to 'resources, opportunities and power' (Government of Sweden, 2018a: 78).

The solutions put forward centre around participation in decision-making institutions, better access to the labour market, resource allocation and gender mainstreaming. Regarding participation, the document states: 'Increasing the proportion of women in the world's parliaments and in leading positions is central', concluding 'changes occur when power exists' (Government of Sweden, 2018a: 26). It also states participation will enable women 'to empower themselves, resulting in increased self-confidence and more interest in political engagement and participation' (Government of Sweden, 2018a: 95). This presupposes a binary state of pre-empowerment, where women are positioned as disempowered to post-empowerment where women have control and agency over their lives, and thus more likely to engage politically. In terms of labour market participation, the policy quotes Ann Linde, former Minister for European Union Affairs and Trade: 'When women participate in the labour market as employees or entrepreneurs, their power over their own lives increases and the whole of society is strengthened' (Government of Sweden, 2018a: 85). Gender mainstreaming is the practice that follows and mentioned 21 times, mostly articulated in terms of economic budgeting and resource allocation with gender equality an indicator and measure thereof (for example, Government of Sweden, 2018a: 76).

Canada

Canada's 2017 Feminist International Development Assistance Policy (FIAP) focuses on development, which is the only area of its foreign policy that includes a distinctly feminist approach. The policy was adopted under Justin Trudeau, leader of the liberal party, and self-described feminist, who, once in office, proceeded to place several women in key ministerial positions forming a gender-equal cabinet. Trudeau describes his feminism as equality between men and women (Parisi, 2020). Gender equality is articulated as a central pillar of Trudeau's government, and can be understood as part of a longer tradition in Canadian politics that has focused on women's rights and gender equality in international development which is an established part of its soft power (Parisi, 2020). Parisi explains that Canada's wider approach to development has distinctly liberal feminist leanings dating back to the former Canadian International Development Agency's 1976 adoption of guidelines on Women in Development, which included a 'add "women and stir" type of gender mainstreaming, which positions women as objects of development' (Parisi, 2020: 166, citing Swiss and Barry, 2017: 25). Power and empowerment in Canada's FIAP therefore reflect liberal feminist concerns around increasing women's representation in official bodies as well as emphasizing the role women play in building peace. Central to the FIAP is a belief that 'gender equality and the empowerment of women and girls is the best way to build a more peaceful, more inclusive and more prosperous world' (Global Affairs Canada, 2017: np). The more expansive focus on peace, security and poverty reduction arguably makes Canada's policy more far-reaching than Sweden's in its overarching vision and aims, and a continuation of its approach to development but equally neoliberal in its approach (Parisi, 2020; Thomson, 2020).

Canada's policy makes 79 mentions of power, with the majority of those (64) articulated in terms of empowerment. This skew towards empowerment is unsurprising given its embeddedness within development assistance. Similar to Sweden's feminist foreign policy, Canada articulates empowerment in terms of gender equality following a social logic, with frequent mentions of 'gender equality and the empowerment of women and girls'. Both are cited as 'core action areas' which will be integrated across cross-cutting areas, including 'human dignity', 'growth that works for everyone', 'environment and climate action', 'inclusive governance' and 'peace and security' (Global Affairs Canada, 2017: iii). Like Sweden, the empowerment of women and girls is instrumentalized for development outcomes, particularly, but not limited to, economic growth, which is discursively more prominent than gender equality. Parisi (2020: 164) explains that the document embodies two neoliberal narratives: (1) *feminist neoliberalism*, which argues that gender equality is necessary for economic growth; and (2) *neoliberal feminism*, which posits women's labour market participation as central to achieving gender equality and/or empowerment. What follows is a secondary association that links gender equality and women's empowerment to peace, security and poverty reduction.

Discursively linking gender equality with empowerment is articulated as follows: 'A feminist approach to international assistance recognises that the promotion of gender equality and the empowerment of women and girls require the transformation of social norms and power relations' (Global Affairs Canada, 2017: 9). Here, the use of language around transformation is potentially disruptive to the neoliberal idea of empowerment as it acknowledges that empowerment requires transforming social relations rather than simply rebalancing existing social arrangements in more equitable, and gender-just ways. Interestingly, Sweden's policy makes only one reference to transformation wherein it describes its policy *as* transformative (Government of Sweden, 2018a: 11) whereas Canada's includes several mentions, related to transforming, inter alia, 'households, societies, economies' (Global Affairs Canada, 2017: 2), 'local economies' (Global Affairs Canada, 2017: 8), 'the attitudes of adolescent boys' (Global Affairs Canada, 2017: 10), 'harmful behaviours' (Global Affairs Canada, 2017: 17), 'the attitudes towards women' (Global Affairs Canada, 2017: 51), 'the private sector' (Global Affairs Canada, 2017: 65), as well as making three separate mentions to 'power relations' (Global Affairs Canada, 2017: 9, 11). How, for example, local economies, societies or households are transformed and, indeed, what they might be transformed into is not outlined. This is not to say that this variant of power is more dominant; indeed, it still appears relatively infrequently in comparison with an overriding economic, neoliberal logic of empowerment.

Reflecting its more expansive focus, Canada's policy also includes a variant of empowerment underpinned by a political logic (women's ability to effect political change) and a security logic (the idea that women's empowerment will help achieve peace and security), both of which draw on instrumental arguments. Seven mentions of power (instead of empowerment) posit a political logic which frame woman as 'powerful change agents' (Global Affairs Canada, 2017: vi, 1, 2, 29, 62, 65, 75) compared to one mention in Sweden's feminist foreign policy (Government for Sweden, 2018: 84). For example, the FIAP states, 'women and girls are powerful agents of change for development and peace' (Global Affairs Canada, 2017: 75). Like Sweden, it highlights resources and greater participation as prerequisites to, and a measure of, women's empowerment that in turn enables them to fulfil the role of change agents. This is then directly linked to a security logic; ergo, that the empowerment of women and girls can help 'build a more peaceful, more inclusive and more prosperous world' (Global Affairs Canada, 2017: 74), with improving humanitarian outcomes (Global Affairs Canada, 2017: 29) and poverty reduction (Global Affairs Canada, 2017: vi, 75) given as the overarching examples. Next, I elaborate on what these empirical findings tells us about the significance of how different variants of power, and particularly empowerment, are articulated across both documents.

Empowerment lite, superheroines and structural transformation

There is a discursive circularity in the empowerment logic found in these policies. They converge around an individualized notion of women's self-empowerment through the market and economic neoliberalism. While there are occasional flashes of other variants of power as relational, intersectional and structural as per the typology sketched out earlier, these are buried in, and eclipsed by, pages and pages of neoliberal feminist, 'empowerment lite' (Cornwall, 2018) discourse, which distinguishes it from these other, potentially more transformative, variants. Subordinate to self-empowerment and 'empowerment lite' narratives, these critical variants of power, which are reduced to nothing more than buzzwords, are rarely elaborated upon and therefore remain unable to gain any discursive prominence, without which a feminist alternative to foreign policy based on a radically different idea of power cannot gain traction. But to expect otherwise is naïve; feminists remain sceptical that the state can deliver gender justice. Nevertheless, a key limitation of these policies resides in the understandings of power upon which these documents rest, understandings that have deep roots in domestic political governance structures, histories of state violence and legacies of colonialism.

First, both policies organize the world into two gender categories, 'men' and 'women'. Cornwall and Rivas (2015: 397) discuss the effects of this sex/gender distinction on empowerment narratives as follows: 'Is "empowering women and girls" and "engaging men and boys" – parcelling two genders into categories with one-size-fits-all universalising remedies and ignoring anyone who does not conform – the way to create a fairer world for all?' Despite some vague references to intersectionality, binary gender is positioned as the defining feature of inequality, which must be overcome to transform the purpose and orientation of foreign policy and its institutions. Consequently, both policies underestimate that the purpose and orientation of foreign policy is largely shaped by its relationship to the co-constitution of patriarchy, capitalism, militarism and colonialism, for example (see also

Zhukova, 2023). The earlier, more radical work on empowerment, which emphasized the wider structures that determine power relations, including the effects on women's everyday lives and ability to exercise agency, are practically non-existent in both policies. Shifting a few resources around will do little to alleviate structural violence.

Canada's FIAP makes just three references to intersectionality (Global Affairs Canada, 2017: 8, 49) in relation to identities rather than structures, while Sweden's includes only one reference wherein it describes its policy as intersectional (Government of Sweden, 2018a: 11). First, surface-level interpretations that employ intersectionality merely as a 'heuristic device' (Henry, 2021: 24) hollow-out its transformative potential and render it a buzzword. That said, the intersectional approach of Sweden's feminist foreign policy has been expanded incrementally over time. The policies are then funnelled through recalibrating, rebalancing and reallocating in service of equality understood in measurable terms. This is envisaged through getting more women into political institutions (regardless of how discriminatory or inefficient they may be) or getting more women into jobs (regardless of labour market protections and welfare). As Duncanson (2019: 114) explains, 'the liberal approach does not liberate women but burdens them; burdens them with more work (as they are expected to work in the productive sector whilst having little of the care work lifted from their shoulders)'. This liberal approach is offered as the 'solution' but which leaves little, if any, room for conversations about deep, structural transformations that challenge the foundations of power.

Second, without structural transformation, empowerment easily becomes co-opted and instrumentalized in service of developmental objectives, particularly economic growth, but also security objectives, including interventionist policies. Indeed, the empowerment of women of girls was used by Canada as well as others to justify military engagements abroad, notably in Afghanistan (Swiss, 2012; see also Tiessen, Chapter 13, this volume). Tiessen (Chapter 13, this volume) writes that this includes allocating international assistance for gender equality and women's empowerment programmes in service of defence purposes. There is a distinctly racial, colonial and militaristic logic that undergirds neoliberal empowerment discourse in these feminist foreign policies. It is instrumentalist both in terms of the hierarchies within donor/recipient models of international assistance as well as in those related to national security and defence. Empowerment is invariably, then, about empowering women and girls 'over there' in the 'insecure, Global South' (Haastrup and Hagen, 2020; Achilleos-Sarll, 2023) – with the Middle East and North Africa often profiled and particularly visible within each policy. For example, the section in Canada's policy 'Empowering Afghan Women and Girls' profiles those who are meant to be the beneficiaries of this policy with Canada positioned to 'help Afghan women assert their rights' (Global Affairs Canada, 2017: 20). This is paired with an underlying sentiment across both policies that project Canada and Sweden as having achieved the requisite levels of equality, peace and security, and thus the policy is neither for nor about them, or indeed about finding ways of engaging with states differently. Moreover, while Canada's policy is the product of a settler-colonial state system, it makes no mention of the gendered violence of settler-colonialism related to missing and murdered Indigenous women and girls. The assumption is that the liberal, autonomous, economically empowered, and therefore 'free' subject is White, Western and European. This is different to a feminist approach to foreign policy that centres the ideas and experiences of the most marginalized and, indeed, looks to them for solutions.

Third, the use of empowerment language framed in neoliberal individualized terms raise the same question Cohn asked of the Women, Peace and Security agenda 20 years ago: 'Are we expecting more from women (superheroines) than we expect of men?' (Cohn et al, 2004: 136). Taking up this prompt to unpack the discursive constitution of Security Council Resolutions on 'Women, Peace and Security', Shepherd further argued that women are represented as 'superheroines, agents of their own salvation, capable of representing the needs and priorities of others and with the capacity to effect positive transformation in their given societies' (Shepherd, 2011). The weight of change is firmly placed 'at the feet of women and girls' (Thomson, 2020: 430) but, in particular, at the feet of women and girls predominantly from the Global South. The focus for both policies is therefore less about empowerment understood in terms of cultivating more liveable and just worlds, and more on proffering a version of 'empowerment-as-efficiency' (Thomson, 430, cited in Calkin, 2015: 665).

Finally, this 'efficiency', superheroine, model renders 'women's economic agency complementary to (and usable in) mainstream economic development' (Cueva et al, 2023: 10); that is, an individual resource to be extracted for maximum efficiency. As mentioned, gender equality in Canada's FIAP is instrumentalized in service of the wider aim of its policy, that of economic growth and poverty eradication, and therefore connects empowerment with a market-based logic of development. This presents an 'uncomfortable union with neoliberal economic policy' (Thomson, 2020: 427), placing an enormous burden for sustainable development on women, while expunging power/inequality from the structural root causes of poverty, inequality, war and underdevelopment. It does this in part by erasing the 'serious, (infra-)structural inhibitors that may well impede the (superheroic) activities of the women' (Shepherd, 2011: 511).

Consequently, both policies offer very little, if any, reworking of the broader macroeconomic framework that acknowledges, for example, the gendered division of labour, the globalized economic exploitation of women's labour, particularly of those who are poor and marginalized, as well as the feminization of poverty. While disparities in resources between men and women are mentioned ad infinitum in both reports, with occasional, fleeting references to global resource inequality, there is no great reimagining of redistribution in majority-minority world terms that radically rejects the notion that the free market will allocate resources either efficiently or fairly. This skew towards economic empowerment conceptualized in broadly feminist neoliberal, neoliberal feminist and liberal feminist terms, means that insights from feminist political economy that both challenge this economic model and present viable alternatives, such as around degrowth (for example, Dengler and Strunk, 2018) or community economies (for example, Dombroski et al, 2018), remain invisible. Rather, it is about both making women work for the global economy, for development, for security, to make the global economy more efficient, rather than transforming the global economy, development and security in ways that would emancipate all genders. Therefore, it not the focus on economic empowerment per se that is the problem, but rather how narrowly conceptualized economic empowerment is in relation to binary gender and resource imbalance conceptualized on an individual basis, and how that, in turn, eclipses other, potentially more transformative variants of power as intersectional, structural and relational that would require a fundamentally different approach to foreign policy, including to the global political economy.

These initial observations appear to be supported in other feminist foreign policies. For example, a cursory glance at France and Spain's feminist policies suggests similar empowerment narratives. For example, France's International Strategy for Gender Equality (2018–2022) states that women's economic empowerment constitutes 'a main vector for progress and development' (French Ministry for Europe and Foreign Affairs, 2018: 18). Empowerment is also a principal objective of Spain's Feminist Foreign Policy (2021–2026), with most mentions focusing on 'women's economic and political empowerment'. It would be pertinent, therefore, to expand these initial observations beyond a focus on Sweden and Canada, which have been particularly visible in feminist foreign policy scholarship to date. To that end, more recently, Mexico, Libya, Chile and Colombia, among others, have adopted, pledged to adopt, or have shown an interest in adopting, a feminist foreign policy in the future. A worthwhile investigation could focus on whether and how empowerment, or other variants of power, figure in these pronouncements/policies and, if so, through what discursive articulations, attachments and logics, and with what political implications, observing points of convergence, fracture and tension. Moreover, it would also be useful to examine whether civil society uses of power/empowerment differ (or not) from state policies and pronouncements, and how central they are in advocacy materials, as they have the potential to challenge these logics and inject feminist foreign policies with much-needed criticality.

Conclusion

This chapter sought to provide a critical overview of power in feminist IR and feminist theory, with a particular focus on feminist approaches to foreign policy. In doing so, it emphasized several, intersecting, strands, including power as a resource, as relational and intersectional, as resistance and empowerment. This theoretical and conceptual overview provided the groundwork to trace these variants across the feminist foreign policies of both Sweden and Canada, revealing a dominant focus on empowerment. Different logics of empowerment are found to be frequently re-rooted through an economic logic based on self-empowerment, self-improvement, liberal and neoliberal market-based feminist narratives. This follows from the premise of writing women in, predominately from the Global South, as change agents (a political logic) and contributors to peace and security (a social logic), thus affixing gender equality to empowerment. Surrendering empowerment, understood as the transformation of power relations, into empowerment 'lite' through economic liberalism, over-simplifies the role of women in society, politics and economics, the efficacy of the (gendered) subject, and the structural barriers to subject agency, choice and opportunity. Resultingly, these feminist foreign policies expunge the transformative potential of empowerment, despite the concept serving as conceptual glue in these policies.

Challenging this individualized notion of self-empowerment is not to downplay the significance and necessity for material relief and the redistribution of resources. Rather, the chapter suggests that by taking a neoliberal approach to power as empowerment, feminist foreign policies remain unable to challenge the very structures of domination that necessitate emancipatory, transformative foreign policies in the first place. This might include using feminist foreign policies as a vehicle to commit to reparations to formally colonized and enslaved populations, for example. Indeed, with the partial exception of Germany's feminist foreign policy, there are minimal to no references to colonial histories and legacies of violence. At stake in the analysis are the possibilities produced – and foreclosed – by particular articulations of power, as well as by representations of women's empowerment. As a travelling concept, observable is how empowerment gets stripped of its emancipatory potential to produce 'governance feminism', a feminist agenda conflated with the dominant security agenda.

To deliver gender-justice through foreign policy and to move feminist foreign policies beyond these cul-de-sacs, 'we need new words and new frames. Or, at least, we need to take our old language out of circulation for "cleaning"' (Cornwall and Rivas, 2015: 408). When informed by women's resistance, collective action and grassroots mobilizations, empowerment can be transformative of women's lives.

4

Norms

Jennifer Thomson

Introduction

Gender equality is increasingly accepted as a norm within states' foreign policy and international actions. From the role of international mechanisms, such as United Nations Security Council Resolution 1325, to adherence to international legal frameworks, such as the Convention on the Elimination of All Forms of Discrimination Against Women, and involvement in multilateral agencies, gender equality is increasingly taken seriously by states in relation to their external role. Yet, at the same time, a growing backlash to these pro-gender norms has been developing. In both individual states (Korolczuk and Graff, 2018; Korolczuk, 2020a) and in transnational coalitions (Goetz, 2020; McEwen, 2023), liberal gendered rights are under attack. In response to the well-developed literature on gender norms in foreign policy (Aggestam and True, 2020; Haastrup, 2020), which tends to focus on liberal uptake, some scholars have explored the contemporary resistance to pro-gender norms (Sanders, 2018; Sanders and Jenkins, 2022) and how conservative actors are acting to fundamentally challenge or replace them (Bloomfield, 2016; Goetz, 2020; Schneiker, 2021).

The status of gender equality as a norm in foreign policy is therefore far from fixed. Gender as a normative power is at work in many diverse and often contradictory ways in foreign policy. On the one hand, gender is institutionalized in many states' foreign policy work, and a central component of how they act and present themselves on the international stage; yet, on the other, gender equality measures are increasingly under attack and states are consciously adopting regressive positions on gender in their international work. Even when viewed within liberal states alone, the meaning of gender equality is not static, but rather changing and evolving – better understood as 'content-in-motion' and a norm in 'flux' (Krook and True, 2012; Zwingel,

2017), rather than a fixed thing. Furthermore, when referenced by states and key actors, gender equality is often a signifier that speaks to the 'bundled norms' of gender, democracy and liberal modernity (Towns, 2009; Donno et al, 2022) in global politics, not just an idea unto itself.

To capture the fluctuating state of gender equality in foreign policy, and the competing presentations of it in international politics, this chapter adopts the concept of 'normative configuration' from Pratt (2020). I consider this concept in relation to a range of key empirical examples from the national state level, across both progressive and illiberal policies around gender. These two sets of examples highlight some of the most important trends in gender and foreign policy in the last 30 years, which have been dominant in both the literature in this area and in setting trends in the international arena. Taken together, these progressive and illiberal issues help to show that gender in foreign policy is a set of diffuse, evolving and often contradictory ideas. As I illustrate here, understanding gender in foreign policy as a normative configuration better helps us to capture the changing nature of gender in international relations, and to allow for a clearer analysis of it as a phenomenon within global politics.

Norms, gender and foreign policy

Norms are 'one of the major conceptual innovations' (Peez, 2022: 3) in International Relations in recent decades. Gender, understood not just as material sex difference but as a culturally and socially constructed set of ideas shaping society, has been a key topic in this subfield and much of the major contributions have helped to elucidate states' foreign policy work in relation to it. For example, Finnemore and Sikkink define a norm as 'a standard of appropriate behaviour for actors with a given identity' (Finnemore and Sikkink, 1998: 891). Their influential model (Finnemore and Sikkink, 2001: 405–407) argues that norms go through a life cycle, in which they emerge (often promoted by norm entrepreneurs), then 'cascade' to other organizations and situations, and are finally internalized by states, bodies and individuals, to no longer require specific elucidation. Examples of this model in relation to gender-related norms in international politics abound. Female suffrage, for example, first emerged in a small number of relatively minor states on the international stage (New Zealand, or most of the Nordic countries) but rapidly cascaded until it was largely unquestioned as a key right across the majority of the world by the mid-20th century (Towns, 2019). More recently, and albeit in a much more limited fashion, same-sex marriage was adopted by several 'entrepreneurial' states in the early 2000s, but is now widespread across the Western world to the extent that '"gay-friendliness" ... [is] a key factor in assessing a country's modernity' (Slootmaeckers et al, 2016: 1). Although very different examples, both highlight the utility of the norm life cycle model for explaining how gendered norms become entrenched in international politics and are clearly established and often reinforced through international treaties and law (True, 2016).

Further work on norms complicated this model. A 'second wave' (Acharya, 2004) of norms scholarship has developed an understanding of how norms might be seen in a more complicated fashion that better captures the complexity of their adoption. This second wave of norms scholarship, and particularly its idea of a more dynamic model for norms, has been especially helpful in understanding the evolution and contestation of gender equality, as argued by Krook and True (2012). First, scholars have highlighted the way in which the locales in which norms emerge (within international institutions, but also among transnational advocacy networks or domestic civil society) need to be seen as diverse agents in their own right who have the power to shape, change and contest norms (Acharya, 2004; Krook and True, 2012; de Almagro, 2018; Bodur Ün, 2019). The ideas of *norm localization* (Acharya, 2004), *norm translation* (Zwingel, 2005; 2016) and *contested compliance* (Wiener, 2004) all suggest that norms need local translation to be politically acceptable. Second (and as the idea of contested compliance also infers), norm adoption and diffusion are understood as a continually evolving process as opposed to an event with definitive start and end points – particularly those norms which relate to gender (Krook and True, 2012: 117).

In relation to this work, developing attention is increasingly paid to the ways in which gender equality is under attack in many states' international work. Attention has been paid to how certain states attack pro-gender norms as foreign imports which are perceived to be enforced on them by international bodies such as the European Union and as being unrelated to their country's traditional values (the idea of 'gender bashing' – Bjarnegård and Zetterberg, nd; also Gaweda, 2021; Korolzcuk and Graff, 2018; Fodor, 2022) Relatedly, a developing literature considers how autocratic states selectively adopt pro-gender norms to encourage a favourable international standing (Tripp, 2019; Bush and Zetterberg, 2021; Drumond and Rebelo, 2023). As Donno et al note, movement on gender equality may be perceived by the international or donor community as making up for democratic failings, such that 'advances in one area may serve to compensate for a lack of progress in another' (2022: 452). Such states may adopt quotas or key policies around women and security in a selective or pointedly narrow fashion to be associated with the 'bundled norms' of gender equality, democracy and liberal modernity. These actions have been referred to as 'gender washing' (Bjarnegård and Zetterberg, nd). The more dynamic understanding of norms that the second wave of literature presents has thus been taken up by scholars to show that ideas around gender equality are also moving in a regressive direction.

Yet further theorization is required to capture the contradictory ways in which ideas about gender play out in foreign policy. As the following empirical examples show, ideas around gender are often moving in multiple directions at once, and even when they do reach a level of international acceptance, they are still open to not only regression but also manipulation and strategic employment by states. Existing concepts go far in explaining this, but do not fully help us to capture this fluctuating nature.

In this vein, I adopt Pratt's (2020) concept of the normative configuration as 'an arrangement of ongoing, interacting practices establishing action-specific regulation, value orientation, and avenues of contestation'. This understanding extends and amplifies that second wave of norms scholarship to show in greater depth the dynamic nature of norms. Such an understanding is also helpful methodologically because it acts to dereify the idea of norms. Normative configurations are the result of 'institutions, actors, means, formal and informal regulations, and practices generating stability in normativity over time' and 'points of tension, where problems of implementation or disagreement may spark innovation and transformation' (Pratt, 2020: 75). The examples of gender equality in foreign policy in the work of both liberal and illiberal actors illustrate how normative configurations about gender circulate and have an impact in international politics. Gender equality is a fluctuating idea in international relations, which the previous definition's understanding of formal and informal processes, points of tension, and a variety of different actors, helps to capture. The following sections and their empirical examples of gender equality illustrate the utility of this concept to a consideration of gender equality in foreign policy.

Pro-gender equality norms in foreign policy

Understanding gender equality within foreign policy as a normative configuration may therefore help to capture more accurately its fluctuating nature. Here, I set out three examples of feminist norms in foreign policy that have gained significant attention in the International Relations literature but which have also been key trend-setters. All have been influential in setting the tone for gender equality measures at the international level and have encouraged the development of their ideas by other states and international bodies alike. First, the 'Hillary Doctrine', with its idea that the status of a nation's women is related to its security; second, the UK's Preventing Sexual Violence in Conflict Initiative (PSVI), which was pivotal in setting an international standard for commitments and discourse around this issue; and third, Sweden's feminist foreign policy, which, although no longer utilized by the country, started a trend which saw over a dozen countries to date adopt this framework. Taken together, these examples of feminist norms in states' foreign policy show the slipperiness and fluctuating nature of the concept. Although these examples share many common elements and understandings, I show here that even across a liberal understanding of gender equality within foreign policy, the concept remains fluid and difficult to pin down as one specific idea. I suggest that the diffuse nature of gender equality as a norm can be seen in two ways here – the evolving nature of ideas around gender equality and international politics; and a lack of political commitment and resourcing to match normative discourse.

The 'Hillary Doctrine'

In recent decades, feminist international norms around gender equality have widened further to include ideas of state security and economic growth. Whereas gender equality was for a long time coded as a development issue in international politics, in the new millennium it is now increasingly discussed in relation to broader ideas around national (and, relatedly, international) stability and economic development. This is in large part due to the growth of the United Nations' Women, Peace and Security agenda, and the explicit connections that this encourages states and the international community to make between women and state security. It is however, also connected to the actions and discourse created by the so-called 'Hillary Doctrine' and the work of Hillary Clinton as US Secretary of State under the Obama administration. Clinton argued that 'the subjugation of women is ... a threat to the common security of our world and to the national security of our country'.[1] As Hudson and Leidl summarize, the Hillary Doctrine proposed that 'the situation of women and the destination of nations are integrally linked' (Hudson and Leidl, 2015: xiii–xiv).

In previous decades, this elevation of gender equality as an integral part of national stability would have been not perhaps unthinkable but difficult to foresee as part of a mainstream conversation around security. The connection of gender (often coded as a 'soft' political issue and, as previously mentioned, far more likely to be related to the 'softer' area of international development and aid funding) with security was a fundamental change in how national and international security was perceived, and what policies might be pursued in relation to it. The central premise of the Hillary Doctrine was incredibly influential and is increasingly seen in the work of other states' foreign policies (including in many so-called feminist foreign policies, a further evolution of this norm, discussed later on in this chapter) and international organizations. Gender equality has developed as an international norm from being an oft-segregated side issue of lesser import, to now being increasingly viewed as

---

[1] 'Remarks at the TEDWomen Conference', Secretary Clinton's Remarks at the TEDWomen Conference (state.gov).

a fundamental part of national security policy. It has therefore evolved and changed as a normative framework, morphing from a development to a security issue. Gender equality in the foreign policy realm has been dynamic and changeable, moving across issue areas. Furthermore, it might be seen not in isolation but as part of a 'bundle' of norms (Winston, 2018), closely related to wider norms around modernity, democracy and human rights (Thomson, 2022a) which are understood as central to security.

Preventing sexual violence in conflict initiative

The UK's PSVI was launched in 2012 by then-Foreign Secretary Lord William Hague. Still ongoing more than a decade later, the proto-feminist policy aims to challenge attitudes towards survivors and victims of sexual violence in conflict; deliver better access to healthcare and support; and improve security forces' response to addressing perpetrators. Hague, along with the actress and humanitarian Angelina Jolie, Special Envoy for the United Nations (UN) High Commissioner on Refugees, hosted a high-profile Global Summit to End Sexual Violence in Conflict in London in 2014, which was attended by over 1,700 international delegates from politics and civil society, and concluded with 113 states endorsing the UN Declaration of Commitment to End Sexual Violence in Conflict (Independent Commission for Aid Impact, 2020: i). Although tackling violence against women and girls (VAWG) has been an accepted global norm since 1993, such a summit was ground-breaking. It brought global attention to an area of VAWG which has hitherto been seen as more taboo; raised the profile of a more neglected area of VAWG; and ultimately resulted in a cascading commitment to work to end conflict-related sexual violence from a large number of states (Lawrinson, 2023).

Yet following this initial high profile, and the related spending and political attention given to PSVI, it has since dramatically withered. Although the policy continues to this day, it is in a much-reduced form. Promises made during the initial summit were seen as largely rhetorical or merely repeating existing commitments (Kirby, 2015). Following the 2015 general election and with Hague moving away from a formal association with PSVI the same year, the issue was not given as high a profile (Lawrinson, 2023). It is now no longer represented by the Foreign Secretary, but responsibility has passed to the lower level of a Special Representative. An independent evaluation of the PSVI initiative conducted by the Independent Commission for Aid Impact (ICAI) published in 2020 was damning of its legacy. In addition to critiquing the loss of central leadership around the issue, the ICAI report said that there 'has never [been] a strategic vision or plan driving [PSVI's] work' (independent Commission for Aid Impact, 2020: 14) and that although it has been continually linked to the UK's wider work on the Women, Peace and Security agenda, this does not fully provide 'an adequate framework from which to develop a coherent approach to programming' (Independent Commission for Aid Impact, 2020: ii).

PSVI continues in a hollowed-out fashion compared to original commitments, the policy prevails, and the UK continues to progress it. A smaller international summit on sexual violence in conflict was held in London in 2022. Yet while it continues, the policy lacks the level of enthusiasm and institutional commitment seen following its initial launch. Funding and political energy for PSVI may have largely disappeared but it discursively continues within UK foreign policy. There is still an eagerness to present as a 'good' state and actor, even if these promises appear largely empty (Independent Commission for Aid Impact, 2020). While PSVI continues, therefore, it acts as a reminder of the messiness of gender equality in action in foreign policy. There is a hollowness to this policy in terms of an absence of commitment via funding and institutional support. While states may speak the language of gender equality in terms of their international work, there may be less concrete action. As such, it can be understood in some contexts less as what it signifies in and of itself, and more as what it works to represent for the states that adopt it (Towns, 2009; Jezierska and Towns, 2018). Adopting gender equality measures helps to present a positive self-image on the world stage, and to signal a commitment to liberal values and actions.

Feminist foreign policy in Sweden

Relatedly, several states are now choosing to refer to their entire foreign policy as 'feminist'. Sweden was the first country to do so in 2014, and feminist foreign policy was a flagship policy of its government's foreign policy until 2022. Following the 2022 Swedish elections, a new right-wing minority government was formed with support from the far-right Swedish Democrats who gained over a fifth of the popular vote. The new Foreign Minister, Tobias Billström of the conservative party 'Moderaterna', announced on his first day in office that Sweden would no longer use the term feminist foreign policy, but stated that gender equality is a core value in its foreign policy.

Throughout its adoption and promotion of feminist foreign policy between 2014 and 2022, Sweden stressed the ways in which its policy and actions were novel and ground-breaking. Sweden's *Handbook on Feminist Foreign Policy* opens proudly with the pronouncement that '[i]n October 2014, Sweden became the first country in the world to launch a feminist foreign policy'. In her Statement to Parliament on Sweden's Foreign Policy position in 2019, Wallström stated that '[t]he Government will continue to pursue a feminist foreign policy – wholeheartedly, throughout the world. We see that a growing number of countries are being inspired and are following our lead'. In the plan of action for the feminist foreign policy from 2019 to 2022, the country describes itself as a 'frontrunner' (Swedish Ministry for Foreign Affairs, 2016) in relation to its work on gender equality in the international arena. Sweden was also pivotal in bringing about the Feminist Foreign Policy + Group at the UN, an informal network of states who have adopted feminist foreign policy or are sympathetic to its aims. It is therefore keen to see itself as a leader in this area and to project an image of itself as a steward of the norm of gender equality in international politics. This is reflected in developing literature which shows that other states consider Sweden to be a leader in relation to gender equality in response to its feminist foreign policy (Sundström and Elgström, 2020; Zhukova et al, 2021).

Yet, despite the emphasis Sweden has placed on its leadership in this area, specific outputs remain more difficult to see. Doubtless, there have been clear achievements, not least of all the cascading of feminist foreign policy to so many other states, but much literature has argued that it is difficult to see concrete results and actions emanating from the policy in the ways that it has been formulated (Cadesky, 2020; Parisi, 2020; Concord, 2017). Furthermore, more fundamental critiques and accusations of hypocrisy abound about the state's feminist aims. During the period that Sweden first adopted and promoted its feminist foreign policy, it met with and sold arms to Saudi Arabia including throughout the period of conflict in Yemen (although the resulting national debate saw this arms deal cancelled). It also signed an arms deal with Colombia, which a Swedish non-governmental organization described as 'in complete contradiction to a feminist foreign policy' (Concord, 2017: np). There was also a further restriction of Sweden's migration policy, including making the potential for family reunification more difficult (Concord, 2017). This failure to link domestic and international action (Concord, 2017; Ansorg et al, 2021), as well as a continued militarization (including its 2022 application to join the North Atlantic Treaty Organization), suggest that the policy has not been particularly transformative. Although a recent evaluation is more positive, suggesting there is a 'stickiness' to Sweden's FFP (particularly in relation to civil service practices – Towns et al, 2024) that may survive its overturn, Sweden's eagerness to project its leadership and novelty in this area, coupled with significant policy challenges, again illustrates the adoption of a norm to create a brand and place for the state on the world stage (Zhukova et al, 2021).

As with the foregoing discussion of PSVI, consideration of Sweden's near-decade-long association with feminist foreign policy shows the 'messiness' of gender equality as a norm in action. States may be strongly supportive of gender equality in their words and may back this up in action (through the creation of new policy agendas, positions and funding), but still ultimately fall short in these aims. The case of Sweden's feminist foreign policy shows that gender equality may also work in contrast to other areas of state policy (for example, migration). The concept of a specific norm does not therefore fully capture what is happening in these examples. Instead, the coalition of actors involved and the changing political landscape in each are better captured by the idea of a normative configuration. This allows for an understanding of them as both anchored around specific normative ideas, but also underpinned by 'points of tension' and 'problems of implementation' which have messier, less coherent results (Pratt, 2020: 75).

Backlash against feminist and pro-gender norms in foreign policy

The idea that gender equality in foreign policy is a fluctuating norm can be seen, not only in the work of pro-gender equality states such as those described earlier, but also in its adoption in illiberal states, and contestation by anti-gender actors. This section turns to consider developing trends in the ways that feminist and gender equality norms are being contested and co-opted by states in their foreign policy work, arguing again that this adoption reiterates a sense of gender as a diffuse, contradictory and constantly shifting idea in global politics.

The very fact that gender equality is adopted by anti-liberal actors shows its fluctuating nature, but also, as with the previous discussion of liberal actors, how it is used differently by different illiberal actors. The International Relations literature on norm adoption has been slower to theorize how illiberal norms develop and spread, or how backlash to liberal norms emerges (Bloomfield, 2016; Peez, 2022). Nonetheless, there has been some developing conceptualization in these areas, and some study of particularly entrenched resistance to dominant norms (Blok, 2008). These attempts to address the relative blind spots in the literature on illiberal norms or resistance to norms are particularly important in any contemporary consideration of gender given the well documented backlash around gendered (and human) rights in both domestic and international contexts in recent years (Goetz, 2020).

Norm spoiling refers to the ways in which actors attack existing norms to limit their 'development and diffusion' and create 'space for competing norms' (Sanders, 2018; Sanders and Jenkins, 2022). Antipreneurs 'defend the entrenched normative status quo against challengers' (Bloomfield, 2016: 321) and resist the introduction of new norms. Relatedly, norm saboteurs 'oppose an already accepted norm and seek to obstruct other actors' collective efforts to adhere to this norm' in an attempt to 'undo the normative status quo' (Schneiker, 2021). Here, three empirical examples show the diverse, fluctuating and sometimes contradictory way that feminist norms regarding gender equality are used by illiberal states. First, I address the contestation of reproductive rights by states at the international level. Then I turn to consider the concepts of 'gender bashing' (particularly in relation to Poland and Hungary) and 'gender washing' (particularly in relation to Rwanda), illustrating again how these show the very different ways in which gender is adopted and manipulated by states to their own ends in foreign policy.

Reproductive rights

The developing literature on norm spoiling (Sanders, 2018) builds from an understanding of the role that conservative state and non-state actors have in stymieing the development of women's rights norms, but also in laying the ground for alternative norms to emerge (True, 2016; Sanders, 2018; Bodur Ün, 2023). Reproductive rights have been one key area in which these actors have worked to contest norms, and to create alternative ideas and coalitions. The Vatican, alongside a constellation of conservative states and international non-governmental organizations, has worked to erode international gains around reproductive rights. Such work has largely focused on the UN and its bodies, given the belief by conservative actors that the UN has been 'hijacked' (Sanders, 2018: 280) by feminist interests, and is thus hostile to religious actors and more conservative positions on abortion. Relatedly, in 2020 the anti-abortion Geneva Consensus Declaration was signed by over 30 countries, showing that conservative forces can also use tools that were long considered to be intrinsic to only the development of liberal international norms (such as transnational alliances; human rights discourse; utilizing membership of international bodies and working within them to control the agenda). Furthermore, new international alliances are forming among states with illiberal positions on gender issues such as reproductive rights, but also LGBTQIA+ rights, fomented not only by well-known US-based actors but also across the 'post-Western international order' (Mcewen, 2023: 112). These are having demonstrable impact on the language and framing of international policy making around sexual and reproductive health and rights (Gilby et al, 2021). Such changes are a reminder that international bodies and alliances can be key sites of contention and debate around women's rights, and that pro-gender norms are not necessarily guaranteed a position of safety in international institutions.

Furthermore, individual states have helped to set this tone, most notably the United States and, under the Trump and Bush presidencies, its adoption of the Global Gag rule which strongly prohibits American aid money from being taken up by any organization which provides abortions. The difficulties that this poses for development funding and women's health organizations at the global level has in turn encouraged other states to take strong positions against it. The Netherlands' lead campaign, 'She Decides', aims to refocus global conversation and campaigning on bodily autonomy and reproductive rights. The first area of focus for the campaign is an explicit acknowledgement that '[a]ccess to safe legal abortion is a human right' (She Decides, nd). This swing between pro- and anti-choice politics reiterates the fluctuating nature of gender in states' foreign policy and how gendered issues can exist as areas for broader contestation between conservative and liberal states.

Gender bashing

While norm spoiling suggests how conservative actors work to challenge established liberal gender norms, more recent work has been interested in considering how autocracies attack or incorporate dominant international ideas about gender equality. The concepts of gender bashing and gender washing have emerged to explain how states adopt or resist gender norms to further non-gender-related goals (Bjarnegård and Zetterberg, nd).

Gender bashing refers to how states resist gendered norms, consciously arguing against gender equality by relating it to ideas of 'gender ideology' or the notion that it is a foreign, Western or European Union-imported notion (Korolczuk and Graff, 2018; Korolczuk, 2020a; Gaweda, 2021). If gender equality is part of the 'bundled norms' of democracy, human rights and liberalism then, by association, it is related with the institutions that promote those norms – the European Union, the UN and Western states more broadly (Bjarnegård and Zetterberg, nd). In Poland, for example, gender is presented and understood by the right-wing through a 'colonial' framework, in which it is one facet of outside intervention into the Polish state and national values (Korolczuk and Graff, 2018). In 2019, the leader of the ruling right-wing PiS (Law and Justice) political party, Jaroslaw Kaczynski, said about LGBTQIA+ rights that 'We are dealing with a direct attack on the family and children [in Poland] – the sexualization of children, that entire LBGT movement, gender. This is imported, but they today actually threaten our identity, our nation, its continuation and therefore the Polish state'(Kacznyski, 2019). In Hungary, the teaching of gender studies has been banned in universities and discriminatory laws against LGBTQIA+ individuals have received sharp criticism from the European Union. In response, Prime Minister Viktor Orbán declared that:

> We central Europeans know what it is like when the state party or the dictatorial system and the power monopoly it operates, want to raise children instead of their parents. ... We did not allow it to the communists, so we will not allow these self-appointed apostles of liberal democracy to educate the children instead of Hungarian parents either. (Rankin, 2021)

Gender bashing is now an established autocratic tool whereby gender equality measures are clearly coded as foreign, invasive and antithetical to national values and interests.

Gender washing

Relatedly, gender washing refers to how autocratic states or those experiencing democratic backsliding selectively adopt gendered norms as a diversionary tactic to prove their commitment to democracy to the international or donor community (Reyntjens, 2011; Tripp, 2019; Bjarnegård and Zetterberg, nd). This adoption may do little to further women's and gendered rights within these societies. The adoption of such norms allows states to project an image of themselves as liberalizing and progressive by the association that gender equality has with the bundled norms of democracy and human rights. As such, the movement on gender distracts from these states' democratic failings and furthers their international image as 'good' states (Lawler, 2013). Rwanda, for example, has done much to promote itself as a country which champions women's rights and empowerment. It has the highest rate of female parliamentary representation anywhere in the world (continuously over 50 per cent since 2008), high female labour participation, and in 2023 became the first African nation to host the prestigious International Women Deliver conference (World Bank, nd). President Paul Kagame has been particularly personally associated with such endeavours, winning the 'Gender Champion Award' from the African Women's Movement in 2016 (World Bank, nd). Yet Rwanda's democracy has severe failings (Bjarnegård and Zetterberg, 2022). Kagame has ruled since 2000 and has stated that he aims to run again in 2024. The country is designated as 'Not Free' by Freedom House. The government has suppressed opposition candidates and stopped them from running in elections, engaged in the torture, intimidation and potential murder of political opponents, and the media is strongly skewed in favour of Kagame and the ruling party. Intimidation of political opponents continues outside of the country's borders as well, with Rwandans living abroad fearful that any vocal opposition might cause harm to their family or friends in the country (Harding, 2020). By adopting strong measures around gender equality domestically and championing women's rights on the global stage, the association that gender norms have with democracy and human rights protections help to obscure the country's democratic failings.

The ideas of norm spoiling, gender bashing and gender washing and their examples illustrate the diffuse nature of gender equality within states' foreign policy. Gender equality is vilified and attacked in some states' foreign policy, and often codified as 'colonial' and external to the nation. Yet autocracies are also eager to use the language of gender equality to put forward an understanding of themselves on the global stage as progressive, modern and democratic. Although the content – gender equality – remains largely the same, it is employed to very different ends and does very different things for different actors. Gender equality is being adopted strategically by some autocratic states, but also critically attacked by other anti-gender actors. Seeing the discourse(s) of gender equality in foreign policy as a normative configuration helps to capture both the diversity around it, and its flexible nature.

Conclusion

The literature on gender and norms in states' foreign policy is now well established. It has moved on from the first and second wave in which interest was largely in explaining how liberal norms develop, spread and take root. A new body of scholarship is currently interested in explaining pushback and regression around gendered norms in addition to the way that gendered norms are used to give legitimacy to autocracies or to obscure democratic backsliding. Within this, literature on gender and norms is now firmly established, including in relation to foreign policy Yet, this literature also acknowledges that gender equality is a particular example within our broader understanding of norms. Gender equality as a global norm is understood as 'content-in-motion' and in a state of 'flux' compared to other established norms (Krook and True, 2012; Zwingel, 2017). Indeed, as the examples given in this chapter show, gender equality can mean very different things when adopted by liberal states with regards to their foreign policy. The 'Hillary Doctrine' and the evolution of feminist foreign policy show the changing nature of gender equality in international relations, and the implications that gender is now understood to have for national security and economic growth. The UK-led PSVI policy and Sweden's now-defunct feminist foreign policy illustrate the challenges of implementing norm configurations. Similarly, across illiberal states and anti-gender actors, the meaning of gender equality as a norm shifts according to context, in relation to political climates, the involvement of key actors and often the presentation that states wish to create for themselves on the world stage.

Gender equality has become at once strongly embedded in states' foreign policy and is being pushed further by some through the increasing use of feminist language; yet at the same time, it is contested or used instrumentally by illiberal actors. It is pulled in different directions by different actors according to their own aims. Normative configuration (Pratt, 2020) helps to capture the dynamic picture of gender within foreign policy as illustrated in this chapter. Gender equality in foreign policy is the result of different informal and informal practices, institutions, and actors, which creates both tensions and alignments. This more dynamic understanding helps to better explain the contrasting and often contentious ways that gender equality works as a normative force in foreign policy.

5

Networks

Daniela Philipson García and Victoria Scheyer

Introduction

Transnational feminist networks (TFNs) have been crucial to formulating and diffusing gender equality norms (True and Mintrom, 2001). They have advanced legislation and policies to uphold women's rights (Weldon and Htun, 2012), reinforced shared ideals of gender equality (Moghadam, 2005) and affirmed identity-solidarity among women globally (Alvarez, 2000). Feminist networks organize locally, nationally and transnationally and coalesce around various issues, from economic policy to environmental justice. More generally, feminist networks engage in collective action to contest patriarchal social, economic and political power structures and norms (Tarrow, 2011; True, 2024).

Feminist networks are manifestations of social networks that describe social and political problems using a gender and power-critical perspective (Tarrow, 2011; Krinsky and Crossley, 2014). Social networks 'coordinate their efforts, pool their resources and act collectively' (Krinsky and Crossley, 2014: 2). These networks use different strategies, such as framing, to create shared meanings and make sense of their reality (Benford and Snow, 2000). By framing collective understandings of injustices and inequalities, feminist networks lay the groundwork for initiatives (see Tarrow, 2011; Caiani, 2023). Hence, feminist networks extend their engagement beyond the descriptive realm to one that encompasses actionable demands and solutions.

Transnational networks connect organizations and ties across borders 'through common ways of seeing the world ... and contentious relationships with their targets' (Tarrow, 2011: 241). Moghadam (2005: 4) defines TFNs as structures that 'unite women from three or more different countries around a common agenda'. TFNs played a particularly relevant role in international politics during the 1980s and 1990s, when they lobbied states to guarantee and expand women's human rights and achieved concrete policy outcomes (Moghadam, 2005). The recent proliferation of feminist foreign policies has put feminist-informed foreign policy and governance at the forefront of international politics once again. With the diffusion of feminist foreign policy, what is the role of TFNs in advancing feminist-informed foreign policy and governance? This chapter seeks to answer this question.

One of the main criticisms of TFNs is that the shift in focus from the local to the transnational oversimplifies local complexities. For instance, Markland (2020: 20) argues that 'combining global, regional, national and sub-national spaces can undermine and/or mask existing social forms whose function cannot be reduced to a greater whole'. Transnational activism is critiqued for diminishing sense of place and flattening differences based on national origins and identities (Conway, 2017). Moreover, networks have been denounced for reproducing asymmetric power structures. According to Conway (2017: 219; De Almagro, 2023), TFNs constitute a form of 'placeless cosmopolitanism that reinscribes race and class privilege on a global scale'. Lastly, the failure of TFNs to scrutinize existing political and economic structures is also a common critique. Instead, they are pointed out for becoming unintentionally complicit in the policy structures they sought to undo in the first place (for example, Schild, 2014: 253). Similar criticisms emerge from research on the implementation of the Women, Peace and Security (WPS) agenda in Burundi and Liberia (Martin de Almargo, 2018).

Putting these assessments aside, it is important to acknowledge that networks have undoubtedly influenced the course of transnational politics and translated them into domestic contexts (Weldon and Htun, 2012). The consequent changes arising from feminist expertise, norms and practices in international politics have further reshaped the nature of international relations (True and Mintrom, 2001). Thus, TFNs and the long-term ripple effects they've triggered require scholarly attention. Overall, this chapter argues that feminist foreign policy would not have been possible without the knowledge produced within and by TFNs. Thus, feminist foreign policy is informed by and relies on TFN knowledge production.

This chapter proceeds in the following way. First, it describes how networks, particularly those in the Global South, have built the groundwork and avenues for gender-inclusive and feminist-informed foreign policy and governance to ripen and mature. Second, it argues that feminist-informed foreign policy and governance rely on the knowledge production of TFNs. It highlights how TFNs have developed and provided a backbone to feminist foreign policy through: thematic and technical expertise; gender-inclusive language and policies; and everyday feminist practices and values. Third, it describes feminist foreign policy networks, consisting of state and non-state actors. This chapter argues that states rely on TFNs and civil society not only because of their knowledge but also for legitimacy. Although states are the main drivers of feminist foreign policy, TFNs are the gatekeepers of feminist knowledge, values and practices that produce feminist-informed foreign policy and governance. Lastly, we discuss the challenges for TFNs in the context of growing feminist foreign policies.

Over a century of transnational feminist network activism

Transnational feminist demands, activism and knowledge have historically played a critical role in the formation of gender-inclusive and feminist-informed foreign policy and governance. Their efforts span a broad range of policy areas, such as security, peace, disarmament, trade and development. Feminist networks are grounded in diverse positionalities and have proactively crafted demands and policy propositions directed not only at the foreign policy agendas of national governments, but also towards the broader landscape of global politics. Aggestam and True (2023) argue that non-state actors, including transnational feminist and women's rights networks, have prepared the ground for governments to advance gender equality, enabling and supporting transformative policy making. Moreover, they have been critical in holding governments accountable (Aggestam and True, 2023). Hence, we argue that the adoption of feminist foreign policy and their policy content rests on a diverse set of transnational feminists and women's rights networks formulating policy and carving out spaces for more than a century.

The first international women's organization, the International Council of Women, founded in 1888, exhibited a focus on justice, human rights and peace (International Council of Women, nd). Similarly, the early women's suffrage movements in Britain in the 1890s connected 'militarisation as the enemy of both civilization and women' and campaigned against the imperial British forces' violence against women and children in the Boer War (Etchart, 2015). The genesis of distinctly oriented women's peace and anti-war networks in the Global North can be traced back to the First World War (see Tickner and True, 2018). It was in 1915 when the first international women's congress convened in The Hague. During this congress, the transnational women's anti-war organization, Women's International League for Peace and Freedom (WILPF), was founded. At the congress, WILPF adopted its first resolution, demanding that 'foreign politics shall be subject to democratic control and declares that it can only recognize as democratic a system which includes the equal representation of men and women' (WILPF, 1915).

The history of feminist networks relevant to foreign policy not only takes place in the Global North. Women in the Global South and Indigenous networks, especially in formerly colonized countries, have a strong history of resisting and contesting global power structures and international politics. Nonetheless, they are seldom considered relevant to foreign policy making in the Global North and are considered local instead of international expertise. Jayawardena (2016) shows that women's movements in the 'Third World' – India, Sri Lanka, Vietnam and the Philippines, among others – not only fought for women's liberation nationally but strongly linked their national struggles with anti-imperialism. Moreover, Indigenous women's networks have historically led the resistance against the extractivism of resources, such as mining minerals or fossil fuels by transnational corporations (Lindio-McGovern, 2019).

TFNs in former colonies and Black women's abolitionist activists, such as the 'Third World Women's Alliance' (TWWA), formed in the 1960s. They strongly advocated against colonialism and imperialism at the international level (Mendez, 2021). TWWA expanded as a network of solidarity with several African anti-colonial movements and advocated against the US intervention in Vietnam (Kannan, 2018). Among other Global South women's rights networks, TWWA also played an important role in the anti-war movement (Spector, 2019). Transnational feminist and women's rights networks with different positionalities have always linked gender-based inequalities with international systems of power. Furthermore, they have a long history of addressing structural forms of oppression and hegemony in global politics.

Since the Commission on the Status of Women in 1946 many women's rights policies and laws have been achieved. These achievements relied on the continuous efforts of TFNs, such as the International Council of Women, WILPF and TWWA. The United Nations has played an important role in institutionalization processes, including in the facilitation of the International Women's Conferences in 1975, 1980, 1985 and 1995; the promotion of the Beijing Platform for Action and Goal 5 of the Sustainable Development Goals; and the adoption of the WPS agenda.

Together, these policy frameworks and tools form the foundations for gender equality commitments in the international political arena. States that adopt feminist foreign policy today not only draw on these international women's rights conventions for their state policies but use them to legitimize and recognize their feminist-informed foreign policy and governance. While we acknowledge that not all networks in the women's rights, gender equality and LGBTQIA+ rights spaces use a feminist terminology to describe their work, in the following paragraphs we refer to these as TFNs.

Knowledge production and transnational feminist networks

Where do feminist foreign policy guidelines come from and what sources do policy makers use to draft gender-inclusive policies? In this section, we argue that feminist networks produce the knowledge that policy makers and states use when designing feminist foreign policy. Knowledge production from a feminist perspective goes beyond academic research; it includes constructing various narratives and forms of resistance that aim to challenge unequal power structures and advance social justice. This section identifies three types of knowledge that have informed feminist-informed foreign policy and governance: thematic and technical expertise; gender-inclusive language and policies; and everyday feminist practices and values. These three categories are informed by the literature on social network theory and TFN theorists (Keck and Sikkink, 1998; Benford and Snow, 2000; Krinsky and Crossley, 2014).

Thematic and technical expertise

TFNs in the foreign policy realm vary in their thematic and technical expertise. Moreover, they vary in how they produce knowledge according to their respective themes and positionalities (Achilleos-Sarll et al, 2023). Some networks combine themes or form a larger network, such as the NGO Working Group on Women, Peace and Security. There are also thematic networks focusing on the interlinkages between gender inequality and specific global challenges, such as human rights, conflict, climate justice or sexual rights and reproductive health. While all these networks aim to promote gender equality in foreign policy as their main goal, they differ in their specific areas of focus, their strategies and target audiences (Caiani, 2023).

Moghadam (2005) identified five thematic types of TFNs that are relevant to the field of foreign policy: human rights; peace, anti-militarism and conflict resolution; reproductive health and rights; ending violence against women; and economic and environmental policy. However, networks continuously adjust themselves in response to new challenges. In the past years, queer feminists have increasingly pushed for LGBTQIA+ rights. Similarly, feminist advocacy against imperialism and colonialism and in defence of Indigenous rights are gaining prominence. Thus, building on Moghadam (2005), this chapter identifies two more types of TFNs of relevance to feminist and pro-gender equality foreign policy: those focusing on LGBTQIA+ and Indigenous rights.

Overall, TFNs are crucial for formulating feminist demands and consequently communicating them to the wider public, including policy makers, agencies and government departments. Depending on their thematic focus, these networks target different actors, such as ministries and United Nations (UN) agencies. For example, WILPF built a strong advocacy strategy around members of the UN Security Council when advocating for the implementation of the WPS agenda. At the same time, WILPF's disarmament programme, 'Reaching Critical Will', works with disarmament agencies and ministerial departments of defence. Women Environment Development Organisation (WEDO), among others, addresses international financial institutions and trade organizations, whereas the Women's Global Network for Reproductive Rights (WGNRR) does advocacy with the World Health Organization. Hence, thematic networks develop different linkages depending on their theme and target groups to become a cross-cutting issue among all themes of foreign policy.

Thematic feminist networks also use different tools to produce knowledge. They publish resources, participate in conferences and promote advocacy campaigns. For example, during the Pacific Feminist Forum in Fiji in 2023 conference, participants developed a call to act on decolonization and the re-indigenization of the Pacific. Furthermore, networks create international campaigns, such as the Women's Global Network for Reproductive Rights campaign's 'Global Day of Action for Access to Safe and Legal Abortion', which was initiated by TFNs in Latin America and the Caribbean, focused on demanding access to safe abortion.

Lastly, TFNs engage in thematic knowledge production for government-specific policies, for example, by giving speeches, conducting workshops and delivering policy briefings. Governments often invite feminist networks to participate in the making of feminist foreign policy. In 2022, Germany invited several feminist networks and transnational non-governmental organizations to submit their recommendations and to participate in panels and workshops at an international conference in Berlin titled 'Shaping Feminist Foreign Policy' (Federal Foreign Office, 2023b). In 2023, Australia invited several feminist networks to contribute to their International Gender Equality Strategy.

Feminist language and policies

TFNs have developed gender-inclusive language and policies that are pivotal to the formulation of feminist-informed foreign policy and governance. Moreover, they have been central for the innovation of international norms and politics. Transnational activists and gender experts have coined terms like 'gender mainstreaming' and 'meaningful participation', forever transforming international politics (Krook and True, 2012). However, the meanings behind these norms continue to be contested, re-negotiated and diffused.

This section traces the genealogy of feminist foreign policy language and policies back to the feminist networks' formulation and diffusion of gendered norms. Drawing on the pillars of the WPS agenda and the institutionalization of gender mainstreaming, we argue that the language formulated and diffused by these networks are the bedrock for feminist-informed policy and governance, including the first-ever feminist foreign policy by Sweden in 2014. Feminist foreign policy has since revolutionized the fields of foreign policy and development programming by (re)formulating and (re)developing gender-inclusive language.

The language of Sweden's feminist foreign policy can be traced back to the WPS agenda, which was supported by transnational networks, such as WILPF and the NGO Working Group on Women, Peace and Security (Tryggestad, 2009; Pratt, 2013). Fourteen years after UN Security Council Resolution 1325, the Swedish Ministry reframed language from the WPS agenda to develop the core of the first-ever feminist foreign policy, also known as the 3Rs (Rights, Representation and Resources). According to the Swedish *Handbook on Feminist Foreign Policy* (Government Office of Sweden, 2018), 'the Swedish Foreign Service, in all its parts, shall strive to strengthen all women's and girls' Rights, Representation and Resources, based on the reality in which they live'. Thus, the first WPS pillar, participation, can be likened to Sweden's notion of representation. Both the WPS agenda and Sweden's feminist foreign policy call for the participation of women in decision-making processes at all levels (UNSCR, 1325; Government of Sweden, 2018a).

The WPS protection and prevention pillars are similar to Sweden's feminist foreign policy mission to 'promote all women's and girls' full enjoyment of human rights, including by combating all forms of violence and discrimination that restrict their freedom of action'. Likewise, the WPS agenda calls for the protection of women and girls from sexual and gender-based violence and the prevention of violence against women. The WPS relief and recovery pillar calls for more and better funding for women and girls. However, while the WPS agenda focuses specifically on 'measures to address international crises through a gendered lens', Sweden's feminist foreign policy sought to 'ensure that resources are allocated to promote gender equality and equal opportunities for all women and girls to enjoy human rights' (Government of Sweden, 2018a).

Given that the WPS agenda can be considered the heart of feminist foreign policy, we argue that without TFNs, the progressive language needed for the innovation of feminist foreign policy would not exist. One example is queer-feminist criticism of the WPS agenda. While LGBTQIA+ language might not pass in the UN Security Council, feminist networks have pushed for the inclusion of LGBTQIA+ language in feminist foreign policy at the national level. Germany, for instance, has integrated this criticism into its feminist foreign policy. Going beyond binary language on women and girls only, the German feminist policy mentions marginalized communities and LGBTQIA+ people.

Lastly, gender mainstreaming, a concept developed by feminist networks, is a crucial component of feminist foreign policy. Out of the 16 countries that had adopted or announced a feminist foreign policy in September 2023, 11 included languages on gender mainstreaming (Achilleos-Sarll et al, 2023). In an analysis of the spread of gender mainstreaming institutions across states, True and Mintrom (2001) found that TFNs were responsible for enabling domestic institutional change in line with the international mainstreaming policy norm. Feminist foreign policies are reliant on prior gender-mainstreaming institutions and would not have been possible without the knowledge produced by TFNs.

Everyday feminist values and practices

Beyond influencing policy change, feminist networks nurture everyday values and practices that are foundational to feminist-informed foreign policy and governance. TFNs have further shaped feminist-informed foreign policy and governance by fostering values and practices that embody a feminist worldview. These networks underscore that feminist values, such as a commitment to peace and accountability, among others, are key to feminist foreign policy (Cheung et al, 2021). Other similar values include intersectionality and the 'respect for and reciprocity with nature' (Achilleos-Sarll, 2023). Moreover, these networks have been crucial to 'transforming politically marginalized identities' and to promoting feminist values and practices of solidarity and care (Alvarez, 2000: 31).

Feminist values and practices insist on developing bonds of solidarity across time and space, particularly among those who share marginalized identities. Mohanty (2003) writes that 'engaging in ethical and caring dialogues (and revolutionary struggles) across divisions, conflicts and individualistic identity formations' is crucial to overcome the challenges of multicultural feminism. Solidarity-building in feminist spaces has facilitated the creation of epistemic communities and helped dismantle the construction of 'Third World Women' as a homogeneous, powerless group (Mohanty, 1984). For feminist-informed foreign policy and governance to succeed in any context, it is indispensable for it to be grounded in feminist solidarity. Feminist solidarity is the basis for recognizing 'common differences' and 'unequal power relations among feminists' to advance a cross-national, non-colonizing feminist project (Mohanty, 2003). Such a basis is relevant for feminist-informed policy and governance because it is an inherently cross-national endeavour that spans differences and contexts to address global issues and provide feminist alternatives as solutions.

Another value and practice shaped and applied by networks of feminist movements, activists and scholars is care. A care perspective adds to human rights and justice commitments in conflict and peacemaking settings (Pettersen, 2021). An ethics of care as discussed in Chapter 2 by Fiona Robinson shifts attention to the so-called 'private', to households, making space for care and those in need of care, such as children, the elderly, people with disabilities and caretakers. It emphasizes the importance of considering the perspectives of carers in how we see the world. As a value and practice, feminist scholars and advocates use care ethics to inform their research and knowledge production as well as in the formulation of policy (Robinson, 2021a).

Feminist foreign policy networks: non-state and state actors

Unlike policy changes driven by TFNs, feminist foreign policies were instigated by state actors (Aggestam and True, 2023). With feminist foreign policy, states define the agenda and consequently identify allies from civil society and academia to transform foreign policy (Aggestam and True, 2023). In this section, we show how state actors drive feminist foreign policy and argue that non-state actors, including national and TFNs, have often taken a back seat in the efforts to advance feminist foreign policy. As a result, we conclude that feminist foreign policy is predominantly state-centric in its approach to embedding feminist policy and principles within foreign policy.

Several feminist foreign policy networks that vary in form and purpose have emerged in recent years. Social network theory distinguishes between advocacy networks, connective structures and interpersonal networks (Tarrow, 2011). In this chapter, we highlight four networks that vary in form and structure but share efforts to advocate for feminist foreign policy: the Global Partners Network for Feminist Foreign Policy; the Feminist Foreign Policy Plus Group; the Coalition for Feminist Foreign Policy in the United States; and the Australian Feminist Foreign Policy Coalition. These networks can be divided into two categories. First, those that operate at the transnational level, which include the Global Partners Network for Feminist Foreign Policy and the Feminist Foreign Policy Plus Group. Second, those that operate at the national level – the United States and Australian Feminist Foreign Policy coalitions.

At the transnational level, the Global Partners Network (GPN) is composed of several local, regional and international non-state actors from several countries. However, unlike traditional TFNs, the GPN includes state actors (that is, the governments of Chile, Canada, France, Mexico, Spain, Luxembourg, the Netherlands and Germany, among others), all of which hold significant power within the network. Within the GPN, there are three types of membership: core partners, members and friends. All state actors involved in the GPN are core partners or members, which grants them additional access to decision-making processes and spaces. The Feminist Foreign Policy Plus (FFP+) group represents an important outlier relative to other TFNs; the FFP+ group cannot be defined as a traditional TFN because it is composed exclusively of states. The FFP+ group consists of 19 countries, some of which have formally adopted a feminist foreign policy. The FFP+ group is unique in that statehood is a membership condition and does not include any civil society members. Nonetheless, the FFP+ group has been instrumental in advancing and promoting feminist foreign policy in multilateral fora. During the 78th UN General Assembly, the group issued the first political declaration on feminist approaches to foreign policy (Feminist Foreign Policy Plus Group, 2023). At the national level, the Coalition for Feminist Foreign Policy in the United States includes both national and international non-governmental organizations, such as the African Women's Development and Communication Network (FEMNET), Amnesty International, Women Environmental Development Organization (WEDO) and CARE. Similarly, the Australian Coalition is exclusively geared towards feminist foreign policy at the national level and includes national and international non-governmental organizations.

Both types of coalitions – transnational and national – are state-centric in the sense that they seek to operate within and influence state action. They differ in that the former category – transnational feminist foreign policy networks – includes states as members (and, in one instance, includes states exclusively). The implications of the composition of these networks suggest that decision-making power and resources primarily reside with states. On the other hand, non-state actors continue to play an advocacy and consulting role that seeks to hold states accountable for their feminist foreign policy commitments.

Challenges to transnational feminist networks

Feminist networks face several challenges in the context of advocating for feminist-informed foreign policy and governance. The challenges are both external and internal. External challenges include the unequal distribution of resources and power stemming from the North/South divide, the increased connection between non-state and state actors and the rise of increased authoritarian, far-right and illiberal governments. Internal challenges include the lack of transnational solidarity and increasing divisions in the understanding of feminism(s), including trans-rights and pacifism.

Feminist networks continue to be challenged by structural North–South divides that not only impact the distribution of and access to resources but also 'the building and sustaining of solidarities across colonial, racial, sexual, class and national borders' (Carty and Mohanty, 2015: 85). TFNs function within political systems that are driven by neoliberalization, meaning that 'all areas of life and the resources for human well-being fall under the control of the market' (Carty and Mohanty, 2015: 85). The scarcity of resources and the need to professionalize to manage these resources puts increased pressure on solidarity between and within feminist networks. Growing dependency on governmental funding can compromise the ability to resist the co-option of feminism by state structures – including policies like feminist foreign policies.

TFNs have to grapple with different meanings of feminism and inequalities along the lines of race, class, nationality and sexuality. Feminist scholars of colour and from the Global South stress the importance of anti-colonial and anti-imperial knowledge production, especially regarding the 'diagnostic language' of 'the West as liberator' (Carty and Mohanty, 2015: 87). These views shape the discussions on feminist foreign policy, especially the tendency for these policies to focus exclusively on women's rights.

Practising solidarity has always been a significant challenge within the feminist movements. Feminist networks struggle with practising solidarity, listening to each other and overcoming power differences between them. This is not only a North–South divide but has many more layers. For example, feminist networks in the post-Soviet region and Ukraine have criticized the lack of transnational feminist solidarity of Western feminists after the full-scale invasion of Russia in supporting their right to self-defence. The question of pacifism versus self-defence as a feminist principle caused controversy between feminist networks, which continues today (The Feminist Initiative Group, 2022). Feminist networks also struggle with the questions of sexuality, especially supporting the rights and protection of transgender people and sex workers. These divisions cause a major disruption of transnational solidarity between feminist networks. As we stated earlier, a common understanding of the problems and root causes causing gender inequality is crucial for strong collective action.

Lastly, the lines between state and non-state actors continue to be blurred with the professionalization of feminist non-governmental organizations and proliferation of feminist foreign policy bureaucrats. The motives of some feminist foreign policy-centred organizations are unclear and their dependency on donor governments is high. The question remains open whether networks seek to promote feminist foreign policy as a genuine means to advance gender justice at the multilateral level or if feminist foreign policy is instead being used as a vehicle to promote personal brands and maximize profits as state subcontractors and consultants. In the case of the latter, the professionalization of feminist foreign policy-focused organizations and their state-centrism poses an even bigger challenge. It may result in the marginalization of smaller groups and collectives that challenge state actors and espouse more radical ideas. This criticism is not new. Increasing institutionalization of feminist knowledge has often served to enhance the careers of individuals and selected organizations while promoting incremental change only.

Conclusion

This chapter focuses on the pivotal role that TFNs assume in shaping feminist-informed foreign policy and governance. We emphasized the historical importance of these feminist networks and their instrumental role in making visible the 'personal' not only as 'political' but as 'international'. TFNs contribute significantly to knowledge production and connecting gender equality policies with other thematic policies, such as climate change or peace and war. It is imperative to acknowledge the diverse forms of knowledge generated by these networks, extending beyond conventional policy briefs to various forms of resistance. We traced how this knowledge has been adopted and institutionalized in forms of international norms and how they continuously develop with the help of these feminist networks. Finally, networks also play a more indirect role in fostering feminist values and practices, such as solidarity and ethics of care, resulting in role models of feminist actions.

Following Sweden's introduction of a feminist foreign policy, we have seen the emergence of new types of feminist networks. Exploring these recent network developments, it becomes evident that there is a trend for these networks to focus centrally on the state. Our chapter concludes with a concern about this shift. The adoption of feminist principles by states as cornerstones of their foreign policy is commendable. Yet for over three decades feminist international scholars and activists have noted the limitation of state-centric approaches to foreign policy and international security, calling instead for a stronger focus on the human dimensions of international relations (Tickner, 1992; Enloe, 2000; True, 2018).

As relatively new actors within feminist spaces, states rely on TFNs and civil society not only because of their knowledge but also for legitimacy. Although states are the main drivers of feminist foreign policy, feminist networks and civil society produce the feminist knowledge, values and practices that informs feminist-informed foreign policy and governance. Hence, states that act unilaterally in implementing feminist or pro-gender equality foreign policies are doomed to achieve little more than co-optation or 'pink-washing'. Feminist networks and civil society are needed to hold governments accountable regarding their feminist commitments. Without such accountability 'feminism' is reduced to a meaningless and 'hollow term', thereby stripping feminist foreign policy of its transformative potential (WILPF, 2023).

6

Diplomatic Infrastructure

Katarzyna Jezierska and Ann Towns

Introduction[1]

Until recently, official diplomatic positions, such as those of ambassador, envoy and diplomat, were exceptionally male-dominated. Particularly through the professionalization of diplomacy in the 19th century, institutions, such as foreign ministries, embassies and permanent missions were made to be masculinized institutions, attributed putatively 'masculine' traits, and made to accommodate men and male roles. Starting in the 20th century, often due to mobilizations by women, the diplomatic office was not only opened to women, but several institutional features developed that challenged the male dominance of foreign policy. This chapter aims to identify, map and theorize some of these changes over time. Our key argument is that such institutional features may be related to the implementation of foreign policy and that both diplomacy and foreign policy scholars should pay more attention to the links between diplomatic institutional infrastructure and foreign policy contents.

With this aim, our chapter brings novel knowledge to the study of gender, diplomacy and foreign policy analysis (FPA). In the large academic literature on diplomacy, there has been a remarkable growth of studies on gender and diplomacy in the past decade (for overviews, see Aggestam and Towns, 2018; 2019; Niklasson and Towns, 2022). The aim of these studies has primarily been to document and analyse the gendered institutional features that advantage men to the detriment of women. Our chapter turns this question around, centring on institutional changes that help challenge the androcentrism and male dominance of diplomacy. We also suggest that these institutional features may shape the concrete form foreign policy comes to

---

[1] Funding for this chapter was provided by the Knut and Alice Wallenberg Foundation, KAW 2020.0186 and the Swedish Research Council grant 2017-01426.

take when it is implemented. In other words, with new institutional forms that enable or promote the participation of women in diplomacy, we may also see new foreign policy content.

We also speak to scholarship on continuity and change in diplomacy (Leguey-Feilleux, 2009; Hamilton and Langhorne, 2011; Neumann, 2020). Diplomatic change and continuity have been debated for over a century – the impact of democracy and technological changes have been of particular interest – but this voluminous body of work has not yet looked at transformations in the gendered features of diplomacy over time. In turn, FPA has recently seen a vibrant research agenda on gender emerge, with a slew of innovative agenda-setting pieces (Achilleos-Sarll, 2018; Aggestam and True, 2020; 2021; Smith, 2020) and careful empirical analyses (Dean, 2001; Haastrup, 2020; Lee-Koo, 2020; Thomson, 2020). Our chapter contributes to FPA scholarship by shedding light on some of the institutional infrastructure through which foreign policy is concretized and implemented. Ministries of foreign affairs (MFAs) and their foreign missions are crucial as the operative divisions of foreign policy. We thus seek to draw foreign policy scholars' attention to how institutional features may shape policy implementation.

In doing so, we rely theoretically on feminist institutionalism, with its focus on gendered formal and informal institutional features and 'rules of the game' (Krook and Mackay, 2011: 1). We focus on institutional changes that help break the male domination of diplomacy, opening the way for women to enter diplomacy and for new institutional forms, changes which may shape concrete foreign policy contents. Diplomacy here designates the formal representation of a state abroad, institutionalized in the form of the MFA including its agencies and embassies. As noted earlier, diplomacy is the operative division of foreign policy, the apparatus that implements foreign policy objectives. In this view, 'foreign policy is the architect; diplomacy is the engineer and builder' of foreign relations of any given state (Weisbrode, 2017: 2; see also Hocking, 2016). As the engineer, diplomacy concretizes foreign policy through its implementation. The two should thus be considered in tandem, we suggest. Rather than examine one or two MFAs, we focus on diplomatic institutional features and initiatives that have developed and spread to become common among all or some subset of MFAs.

In sum, the chapter will identify and map changes over the past 50 years that have served to break the male monopoly on diplomatic positions and bring an increasing number of women into diplomacy. The chapter focuses primarily on more formal institutional features, such as recruitment rules, formal networks and new types of diplomatic positions. We point to considerable changes in the gendered institutional infrastructure of diplomacy, ranging from the emergence of recruitment efforts targeting women and networks of female diplomats to the creation of Ambassadors for

Women, MFA Gender Focal Points and the institutional demands embedded in feminist foreign policy. There are now a range of institutional features in play to advocate for and increase the number of women in diplomacy, we contend. If these features do their work, the share of women in diplomacy should continue to rise in the coming years. While diplomacy may be late in including women when compared to state institutions such as legislatures or domestically oriented ministries, the emergence of multiple institutional features to advance women shows that diplomacy is not impervious to change. Crucially, these institutional changes may also shape foreign policy contents, as institutional features enable and disable various courses of action. Throughout the chapter, we will point to ways in which institutional change may shape gender in foreign policy, underscoring the need for more scholarship investigating these links.

The chapter provides an overview of gendered diplomatic infrastructure and how it affects foreign policy by tracking large historical institutional trends globally. Our analysis is based on many years of studying diplomacy as a gendered practice, including both site-specific case studies and global mappings and statistical analyses. We also draw on our research on the implementation of feminist foreign policy (Towns et al, 2023; 2024). We thus have an extensive cache of primary documents, interviews with diplomats and quantitative data as well as a comprehensive command of secondary sources on gender, diplomacy and feminist foreign policies. Drawing insights from this material, the chapter shows how thoroughly male-dominated (and masculinized) diplomacy has been, to then feature some central changes in the institutional infrastructure of diplomacy that have helped challenge that male domination. We also discuss how gendered institutional features may be linked to foreign policy implementation.

The remainder of the chapter is organized into four main sections. The first discusses the feminist institutional framework that informs the analysis. The subsequent section then provides a brief historical background discussion of the gendered institutional infrastructure of diplomacy before the 20th century. The main section identifies and maps institutional changes to break the male dominance in diplomacy in the 20th and 21st centuries, including what these might mean for the gender contents of concrete foreign policy. The chapter ends with a concluding discussion suggesting future avenues for studies of gender in diplomacy, including the relation between formal and informal institutions, as well as between descriptive and substantive representation.

Feminist institutionalism

Scholarship on gender and diplomacy often relies on some form of feminist institutionalist framework to identify the institutional features that have disadvantaged women and advantaged men. We build on this framework. Institutional perspectives approach institutions as coherent and semi-autonomous sets of 'roles, routines, rights, obligations, standard operating procedures and practices' (March and Olsen, 1996: 249). Diplomacy thus conceived would be understood as consisting of diplomatic roles and formal positions (for example, diplomat, consul, envoy or ambassador), diplomatic routines, standard operating procedures and practices (for example, sending of diplomatic cables, agreement rituals, seating arrangements at diplomatic dinners, networking) and the rules and norms governing such roles, routines and practices.

Institutional analyses place primacy on how institutional features shape and condition not just the options of actors but also their very identities, thoughts and emotions. As March and Olsen (1996: 249) argue, 'in the institutional story, people act, think, feel and organize themselves based on exemplary or authoritative (and sometimes competing or conflicting) rules derived from socially constructed identities, belongings and roles. Institutions organize hopes, dreams, and fears as well as purposeful actions'. Feminist institutionalists have developed and enriched institutional analyses by insisting that scholars need to interrogate how institutions are gendered, consisting of masculinizing and feminizing rules, roles and norms that order actors, relations and actions in differentiated ways (Kenny and Mackay, 2009; Mackay et al, 2010; Krook and Mackay, 2011; Waylen, 2014). Diplomacy scholars have shown that MFAs are characterized by gendered divisions of labour (Niklasson and Towns, 2022), that the formal hierarchy of MFAs is gendered, with more men at the top of the organization than at lower levels (Niklasson and Robertson, 2018), that diplomatic networking is gendered (Niklasson, 2020; Towns, 2022) and that the professional role of diplomat is masculinized (Neumann, 2012) but also feminized (Towns, 2020) in multiple ways. Some scholarship has also tried to explain how the gendered character of diplomacy has changed, focusing on campaigns and intentional efforts to alter diplomatic rules and procedures (McCarthy, 2014) and on more incremental and less intentional changes (Chappell, 2016).

Our chapter identifies institutional changes over time, leaving questions about how and why those changes came about to future scholarship. Hence, we align with feminist institutionalism in prioritizing structural elements (Mackay et al, 2010: 573), while acknowledging the role of critical actors and other factors in establishing these institutions and making them count (Bergman Rosamond, 2020; Aggestam and True, 2021). Obviously, no institutional change appears without agents. The role of policy entrepreneurs and leaders in the introduction and upholding of these institutions is not the focus of our chapter, however.

What is more, we focus primarily on formal diplomatic institutional features, recognizing that there are also a range of informal practices at work. By formal, we refer to professional roles and practices that are formalized into explicit rules, policies and statements by and for diplomatic agents. Formal marriage bans for female diplomats, affirmative action regulations to attract more women to the diplomatic profession and the creation of 'Ambassadors for Women' are some examples of such formal institutional features. We seek to identify formal institutional changes, by which we mean institutional features that are new to diplomacy, such as affirmative action recruitment rules. Features such as affirmative action may of course already be in play elsewhere, so we are not claiming that the features we identify were first to appear in diplomacy.

Finally, in an exploratory discussion, we seek to tie these changing institutional features of diplomacy to the content of foreign policy. The way the implementation of foreign policy is organized in diplomatic institutions may shape the concrete contents foreign policy takes when executed around the world, we suggest. We thus connect institutional infrastructure with foreign policy content, focusing on gender, and suggest fruitful avenues for future research.

A brief history of institutionalized masculinized diplomacy

Diplomacy in the late 19th century and the first decades of the 20th century was not just an elite institution but also remarkably male-dominated. Interestingly, diplomatic practice before this period made more room for women, in both formal and informal roles. For instance, diplomatic interactions between Native American polities and among Native polities in their interactions with the male envoys of European colonial powers also included women in formal diplomatic roles (Barr, 2007). In contrast, the European diplomatic systems centred around royal courts and almost exclusively relied on male diplomatic envoys and ambassadors. Some European empires, kingdoms and principalities were headed by women, and these female rulers were at the centre of formal diplomatic interactions with the (male) envoys. Thus, although the formal diplomatic representatives of these rulers were almost exclusively male, diplomatic interactions took place between these envoys and rulers that were at times female. If we look beyond formal diplomatic positions, women within and around the courts performed crucial but informal diplomatic functions. As queen mothers, daughters, concubines and ladies-in-waiting, they had some influence over male rulers and envoys and came to facilitate diplomatic interactions in a range of ways (Fry, 2013; Iyigun, 2014; James and Sluga, 2016). For instance, in the Ottoman Empire, harem women were at times entrusted with managing correspondence and gift exchanges with less prominent foreign polities (Peirce, 1993).

One early institutionalized feature that formalized a role for women in diplomacy was that of 'ambassadress', the wife of the (male) ambassador. In the 16th century, wives of European ambassadors sometimes accompanied their husbands (Allen, 2019; Kühnel, 2022). They assisted their husbands at diplomatic meetings, helped with the reception of envoys at the embassy, served as translators and gathered information through establishing female networks and friendships (Allen, 2019; Kühnel, 2022). In the 19th and early 20th centuries, ambassadresses instead became referred to as 'diplomatic wives'. National MFAs and the institution of diplomacy relied heavily on these women and their unpaid labour. Indeed, heterosexual marriage was indispensable to the functioning of foreign missions, as female spouses supported and enabled the diplomatic duties of their husbands in many ways (Enloe, 1989 [2014]; Hickman, 2002; Mori, 2015).

By the early to mid-20th century, the male monopoly on diplomatic office was challenged by women seeking a formal place in international affairs. The bans on women from pursuing a diplomatic career were lifted between the 1920s and 1960s (Aggestam and Towns, 2018; Demel, 2020). However, the bans on women in diplomacy were quickly replaced by marriage bars – women were not allowed to combine marriage with a diplomatic career whereas male diplomats were expected to marry a woman – limiting both women's entry to diplomacy and their career advancements (Rajagopalan, 2009; McCarthy, 2014). Heterosexual marriage was thus institutionalized into diplomacy in a way that advanced the careers of men (who had a 'diplomatic wife' as support) and hindered those of women (who had to take on the function both of the male diplomat and his wife). The marriage bars remained in place for decades, being lifted in the late 1960s and early 1970s (McCarthy, 2014; Aggestam and Towns, 2018; 2019).

During the period when official diplomatic positions were dominated by men, foreign policy was simultaneously masculinized in particular ways. This was an era both of *realpolitik* and of masculinized status signalling and status competition between states. In a context of clear and stark gender segregation, exceptionally little foreign policy was devoted to issues considered feminine or expressly related to women.

Once women began entering MFAs, institutional gender patterns developed. Studies of contemporary MFAs have shown that persisting divisions of labour have developed between men and women in diplomacy (Aggestam and Towns, 2018; Niklasson and Towns, 2022). On the one hand, gender divisions of labour have developed in foreign policy domains: women cluster in 'soft' foreign policy issues such as foreign aid and human rights whereas men are dominant in positions dealing with 'hard' issues such as security and finance. On the other hand, women have become overrepresented at lower ranks and in administrative positions and men in positions of higher rank and leadership. For instance, the UK 'Foreign & Commonwealth Office Diversity and Equality Report' from 2021 (Foreign & Commonwealth Office, 2021) highlighted that while women comprised

47 per cent of the overall personnel, they mostly occupied lower foreign office grades (making up 71 per cent at the lowest A1 level, and 37 per cent at the highest senior management structure). Similarly, LGBTQIA+ workers in the Foreign & Commonwealth Office were mostly found in the lower ranks (15 per cent at the A1 level, and 5 per cent at the highest SMS level).[2] What is more, representation in bilateral and multilateral tracks of diplomacy also seem to be gendered. While more research is needed to establish overall trends, case studies suggest that women may be excluded from the multilateral missions of states that prioritize the multilateral arena, such as Japan (Flowers, 2022). When states downgrade multilateral venues, we may instead see more women in these missions. For instance, Nash (2020) suggests that the United Nations – of secondary status to US foreign policy – has become a 'dumping ground' for US female diplomats.

In sum, historically, diplomacy has been constructed as a masculinized institution dominated by men, and foreign policy was masculinized accordingly. Official diplomatic positions have overwhelmingly been occupied by men, with women performing key but often unofficial and undervalued support services. The advancement of women in formal diplomacy and the recognition of non-heterosexual diplomats are relatively new phenomena. However, there are now a range of efforts underway to increase the number of women in formal diplomatic positions. In the remaining parts of this chapter, we map institutional innovations that have developed to recruit women and support their diplomatic careers, thus seeking to challenge the gendering of diplomacy as male. We also highlight some ways in which the new institutional features may relate to foreign policy contents.

New institutional features that advance women in diplomacy

Following internal and external pressures, MFAs around the globe, however unevenly, have undergone several institutional changes that help to bring more women into diplomacy and to support their diplomatic careers. In the following, we discuss some of these institutional features. Our selection of new institutional features is not exhaustive – there may well be other important features that our discussion overlooks and that merit attention

---

[2] Highlighting the issue of division of labour, after the 2020 merger between the Foreign & Commonwealth Office and the Department for International Development, the ratio of women in higher grades significantly improved (in 2022, women made up 42.5 per cent of all senior civil servant roles) but were still overrepresented at lower civil service grades (Foreign, Commonwealth & Development Office, 2022).

in future scholarship. We have chosen to discuss some new recruitment rules, diplomatic positions and foreign policy in order to illustrate our argument that the gendered institutional features of diplomacy have changed significantly over time, and that such institutional features may be related to the implementation of foreign policy. This, in turn, informs our overall contention that both diplomacy and foreign policy scholars should pay more attention to the links between diplomatic institutional infrastructure and foreign policy contents. The feminist institutionalist perspective helps us direct focus to the analysis and recognition of institutions that seek to address the underlying structures which underpin institutionalized advantages and disadvantages according to gender (Krook and Mackay, 2011: 3). Crucially, some of the institutional features discussed also serve the purpose of promoting gender equality as a thematic policy priority in a given state's foreign policy.

Affirmative action and active recruitment efforts by ministries of foreign affairs

Affirmative action, including gender quotas, has been used for decades by various states to level the playing field among aspiring diplomats and compensate for past and contemporary discrimination (Clayton and Crosby, 1992). Depending on what is possible in a given national legal framework, as well as on current political tendencies and particular histories of inequality, some MFAs around the globe have introduced direct or indirect forms of affirmative action in the recruitment of diplomats to speed up the process of diversification of their staff. Within diplomacy, such equalizing measures are admittedly more common with respect to ethnic diversity than gender, which might explain why scholars of diplomacy have paid attention to ethnic diversity in MFAs before noticing gender diversity (Cassidy, 2017; Lequesne et al, 2022). For instance, since the 1950s and with several expansions, the Indian foreign service has had quotas, known as 'reservations', in place to amend unequal opportunities of candidates coming from low-caste backgrounds (Levaillant, 2017). In 1993, the US Department of State launched a programme to increase the numbers of African Americans in diplomacy and development by recruiting undergraduate students into summer internships with USAID missions, assuming that early exposure would create a career pathway (Wellons, 2019). Another example of affirmative action policies focusing on ethnicity in the MFAs is the Brazilian Itamaraty. Since 2003, Afro-Brazilians have been offered scholarships in preparation for the entrance exams. In 2011, a quota policy was also implemented for the recruitment process (Lima and de Oliveira, 2018; Lequesne et al, 2022).

While widespread in other institutions (Franceschet and Piscopo, 2013), mandatory gender quotas are not common in diplomacy (Cassidy, 2017).

Quotas might be seen as the most explicit institutional mechanism to increase the nominal representation of women in diplomacy, overcoming such barriers as societal and cultural biases and stereotypes, lack of role models, and lack of support networks for female diplomats (Uličná, 2023). While quotas are rare, we assess that softer institutional measures of supporting the recruitment and career advancement of women in MFAs are more common. Such measures may include informal attention to the gender composition of incoming diplomatic academy cohorts. They may also include policies enhancing work–family balance in diplomacy. As women are still largely responsible for caretaking tasks at home, they are disproportionately affected by a lack of work–family balance. As Zuzana Fellegi and colleagues show with their study of the Czech MFA, there are concrete measures that can be taken to support women in diplomacy in this regard (Fellegi et al, 2023).

Affirmative action and active recruitment and retainment efforts by MFAs show how diplomacy is changing as an institution in the direction of lessening gender inequality and increasing the number of women (Waylen, 2014: 212). A larger share of women may, in turn, shape the contents of foreign policy. There is a massive body of research on the policy consequences of increasing shares of women in legislatures and executives demonstrating that while women (obviously) are a heterogeneous group without a coherent policy stance, women are nonetheless more likely to place policy issues on the agenda that tend to be ignored in male-dominated institutions: reproductive health, childcare, child development and women's rights. Sylvia Bashevkin's important work on male and female foreign policy leaders corroborates such findings (Bashevkin, 2014; 2018). She shows that female foreign ministers and ambassadors are more likely than men to pursue gender equality in foreign policy. This is not to suggest a simple and clear relationship between institutional rules that increase the number of women and heightened attention to these issues. Indeed, feminist institutionalism cautions that 'no institution is a blank slate' (Mackay, 2014: 552) and that entrenched patriarchal norms will likely affect new diplomats' chances to change the state of affairs. But we should not assume that the policy focus of diplomats will necessarily remain the same when large(r) numbers of women enter diplomacy, as Bashevkin's work and prior scholarship on women in legislatures and executives have shown. Indeed, much more research is needed to examine what has happened to the implementation of foreign policy in practice with the rising share of female diplomats. For instance, scholars might ask questions about whether female diplomats involve different constituencies in the implementation process, whether they advocate for different kinds of policy change abroad (such as lending support to efforts to pass parental leave legislation, maternal health initiatives or struggles to curb violence against women) and other differences.

Networks of female diplomats

Another example of an institutional innovation is the self-organization of female diplomats into formalized women's diplomatic networks (True and Davies, 2020). Such networks have developed around the world, both within MFAs and among diplomats from different countries posted to the same capital. They often take a semi-formalized form, with a name (for example, WAW, Women Ambassadors in Warsaw), membership and a regular schedule for getting together. These networks are often a response to the informal, unrecognized and homosocial male networks that permeate diplomacy (Towns, 2022).

First, women's networks have developed within the MFAs of several states (Niklasson and Robertson, 2018; Bashevkin, 2018; Martins Yassine, 2022; Niklasson and Towns, 2022), to support female diplomats in their careers and to identify MFA structures that are discriminatory and inhibitive for women. These networks are an expression of female diplomats collectively mobilizing to push for reform in their respective MFAs. The Women's Action Organization in the US Department of State, established in the early 1970s (Bashevkin, 2018), and the Network formed in the Swedish MFA in the 1980s (Niklasson and Robertson, 2018) were pioneering. Such institutional networks might be unique to the military and diplomacy – we are not aware of similar, formalized networks in other state ministries. Given that MFAs, alongside ministries of defence, are slower than other state institutions to pick up on gender equality measures, it is perhaps not surprising that female networks cropped up there. Interestingly, since the early 2000s, this type of organization has multiplied across European, Latin American, Middle Eastern and African MFAs. There are currently more than a dozen such networks, with varying degrees of formalization. As Amena Martins Yassine's research shows, these more recent mobilizations emerge for the same reasons as their US and Swedish predecessors, pointing to the female diplomats' continuing sense of disadvantage and discrimination in their respective MFAs (Martins Yassine, 2022).

Women are not only forming networks within their home MFAs, but they are also forming networks with foreign counterparts in the capitals where they are posted. Indeed, in the past decade or so, formalized women ambassadors and women diplomats' networks have popped up in capitals around the world. To make sense of this institutional feature of diplomacy, one must understand that networks are central to both bilateral and multilateral diplomacy, including pro-gender and feminist foreign policy (Neumann, 2012; Aggestam and True, 2023; Chapter 5, this volume). Diplomats network to access individuals in key positions, to influence them, learn important information from them, coordinate policy positions and more. Networks also manifest the status and resources of the state the ambassador represents (Towns, 2022). Depending on their international position, and to some extent on the individual skills of diplomats, networks connect various actors in the hosting state, from formal state representatives to civil society and business actors. There are also diplomats-only networks, among diplomats from different states posted in the same capital. These networks often reflect established state relations, such as networks among diplomats representing European Union or Association of Southeast Asian Nations states, or the Nordic or Caribbean states (Towns, 2022).

Given that the overwhelming majority of diplomats in most capitals are men, diplomatic networks are largely male-dominated. With more women in diplomatic positions, women have now joined some of these networks. However, the enduring male homosociality of some of the more informal networks has become a barrier for women. When diplomats meet in bars, on the golf course or in other masculinized contexts, female diplomats may not have the same easy access (Aggestam, 2018). What is more, as women, female diplomats still stand out, becoming visible tokens in an overwhelmingly male environment (Niklasson, 2020). As Iver Neumann (2012) and Birgitta Niklasson (2020) have discussed with regard to Norway and Sweden, female diplomats play up or play down their femininity in various ways, trying to adapt to the male standards of interaction in diplomatic networks.

In the last decade, in the context of the male-dominated and masculinized nature of diplomacy, female diplomats have also started organizing separate networks for women, following similar initiatives among women ministers of foreign affairs (for example, Madeleine Albright's network from the late 1990s, Aggestam and True, 2023). 'Women ambassador networks' seems to be the most common form. These networks connect female ambassadors accredited to international organizations such as the United Nations, the European Union and the Organization for Security and Co-operation in Europe, as well as those posted to various capitals around the globe. While many of the networks can be found in Europe, women ambassadors placed in Asian, African and American capitals also utilize this form. There is even a Women Ambassadors' Network in the Vatican (Sailer, 2021). Women ambassadors' networks vary in terms of how frequently they meet, how formal the structure of the network is, and what the meetings are used for.

In a study of Women Ambassadors of Warsaw (WAW), Ann Towns poses the pertinent question: 'what is it about diplomacy that creates impetus for "women" ambassadors to organize separately?' (Towns, 2022: 357). The fact that women organize in women-only networks is quite remarkable, as these networks cut across the usual alignments along geopolitical, regional and international status lines. While such networks are a response to exclusionary androcentric practices in diplomacy, the members of WAW did not univocally embrace the notion of diplomacy as androcentric in ways that inhibit women's professional efficiency (Towns, 2022: 358). This, in turn, highlights the double bind of women in diplomacy – as a male-dominated institution, diplomacy is harder for women to navigate, but highlighting this disadvantage might reproduce women's purported inability to manage the diplomatic profession.

Feminist institutionalist studies show that alternative institutional spaces might prove effective in circumventing male dominance of given institutions (Wagle et al, 2020). Alternative institutional spaces may also serve as policy incubators, where members discuss and develop new policy goals or ways of interpreting and implementing policy. Female ambassador networks may serve to support women diplomats in their careers. These networks, apart from providing mutual support for women in a masculinized institution, potentially also allow to form alternative policy agendas, transforming the content of foreign policy (Aggestam and True, 2023). Again, more research is needed to examine the relation between the institutional form and substance of foreign policy.

Gender focal points

For a growing number of states, a gender equality agenda is becoming an integral part of their foreign policy (Aggestam and True, 2020). To institutionally manifest this policy priority and to practically coordinate gender equality work, many MFAs and international organizations around the globe have instituted Gender Focal Points which are positions dedicated to coordinating work with gender equality in foreign policy. These focal points oversee the implementation of gender action plans and gender mainstreaming initiatives (Norwegian Agency for Development Cooperation, 2015), and they are thus central to the practical realization of the lofty gender equality goals expressed in policy declarations. Often, they also serve as internal nodes coordinating the increased inclusion of women in diplomacy. Their specific tasks vary among MFAs and their embassies. In most cases, Gender Focal Points are expected to bring expertise in gender issues and disseminate it among colleagues across the whole organization or department. This often concerns both attention to gender equality in foreign policy *and* to representation of women and non-binary staff within the MFA, its embassies and agencies. Gender Focal Points are thus an additional institutional innovation that in practice shapes policy content.

As scholars of feminist institutionalism have highlighted, resources are crucial for new institutions to have any real chance of enhancing gender equality (Haastrup, 2023). The resources of Gender Focal Points vary enormously (Towns et al, 2023). Some are assisted by a team and gender equality work is their only responsibility, whereas others are appointed on top of many other tasks and do not even have a specified instruction detailing their roles and responsibilities. What is more, while undoubtedly an important infrastructure for promoting gender equality in foreign policy, Gender Focal Points are often selected from junior staff, leading to marginalization in their respective organization (OSAGI, 2001; European Commission, 2020).

Ambassadors for gender equality

Another institutional feature that has emerged to coordinate and concretize pro-gender foreign policy is issue-specific ambassadorships with a focus on women's rights and/or gender equality. In 2009, the United States was the first country in the world to appoint an Ambassador-at-Large for Global Women's Issues (Bro and Turkington, 2020). Since then, many more countries around the globe, including Seychelles, Australia, the Nordic countries (except Denmark), the UK, Spain, the Netherlands, and Canada have followed suit, appointing their own ambassadors or envoys for gender equality, global women's issues, women and girls, or Women Peace and Security. The fact that these posts are given the rank of ambassador or special envoy is significant, signalling the importance of gender equality efforts abroad and at home.

While Gender Focal Points may be created in embassies as well as in MFA divisions, Ambassadors for Gender Equality typically work from the home MFA. Similar to Gender Focal Points, their resources vary. For instance, the Finnish Ambassador for Gender Equality has no team at all (Vastapuu and Lyytikäinen, 2022) and the Swedish equivalent is supported by a minimal team of two collaborators. In contrast, the Ambassador-at-Large for Global Women's Issues in the US Department of State heads an office of four employees. The specific mandates of these envoys vary as well. Some ambassadors have primarily external focus, promoting the rights and empowerment of women and girls abroad; others work more to mainstream gender equality within their departments. For instance, in the UK the Special Envoy for Gender Equality is tasked with promoting gender mainstreaming throughout the Foreign, Commonwealth and Development Office, sensitizing its staff to the overt and covert operation of gender-based discrimination. Since the first appointment in 2017, the envoy has organized gender equality courses, introduction talks to new members of staff, and briefings of outgoing ambassadors (Bro and Turkington, 2020). Apart from states, some international organizations have also instituted special representatives or ambassadors for gender equality, for instance, the North Atlantic Treaty Organization's Special Representative on Women Peace and Security or the European Union's Ambassador for Gender and Diversity.

Ambassadors for Gender Equality are highly visible single-person posts. Undisputably, the leadership of individuals (predominantly women) occupying these positions matters. In line with basic tenets of feminist institutionalism (Mackay et al, 2010: 573), however, while critical actors might play an important role, the formal institutionalization of these positions allows for an infrastructure that outlives a particular individual's term of office. The impact of Ambassadors for Gender Equality on policy contents is a research area in need of much more attention. For instance, what difference does having such an ambassador make for how widely and deeply pro-gender goals are integrated into foreign policy? What resources and institutional placement are needed for Ambassadors for Gender Equality to be effective?

Feminist foreign policies

The emergence of expressly feminist foreign policies has also contributed to the focus on bringing more women into diplomacy. What is more, having an expressly feminist foreign policy puts pressure on MFAs to become more operative, systematic and integrative in how they work with gender equality. Since 2014, more than a dozen states, mostly from Europe and the Americas, have adopted or declared an intention to adopt a feminist foreign policy. In addition to pledging to make gender equality a foreign policy priority, most feminist foreign policies have included personnel parity measures for their own MFAs (Green et al, 2023). For instance, the Swedish feminist foreign policy, in place between the years 2014 and 2022, was concretized into six external and one internal objective. 'Objective 7: Swedish Foreign Service internal activities support and advance the policy' included a number of measures to increase gender equality within the MFA such as a 'human resources policy, management and operational support' (Government of Sweden, 2017: 17). This last objective recognizes the need to transform the MFA from within. Similarly, Chile's guidelines and feminist foreign policy strategy published in 2023 'recognize the persistence of gender gaps that hinder the full participation of women in all decision-making areas of the Ministry of Foreign Affairs' (Government of Chile, 2023: 50).

For many states with feminist foreign policies, international credibility as global gender equality promoters hinges upon a simultaneous domestic observance of gender equality goals, including within their own MFAs (Green et al, 2023). As France made clear after its declaration of feminist diplomacy in 2018: 'Gender equality has been declared the great cause of President Macron's term. It is now at the centre of France's work around the world. The credibility of this commitment depends on setting an example through France's diplomatic network by working towards gender equality in the workplace' (Ministère de l'Europe et des Affaires Étrangères, 2019).

Apart from the declared ambition to increase gender equality in the MFAs, increases in the share of female ambassadors is one easily observable check of whether these states 'set an example'. It is not clear that feminist foreign policies have led to larger increases in female ambassador shares when compared to world averages (Niklasson and Towns, 2023). If we look at states three years after the launch of their feminist foreign policy, Sweden increased the share of its female ambassadors from 41 per cent in 2014 to 47 per cent in 2019, Canada from 41 per cent in 2017 to 45 per cent in 2021, and France from 26 per cent in 2018 to 27 per cent in 2021. These changes follow the world average increase in female ambassador postings, which has gone up at a similar pace (Niklasson and Towns, 2023).

Feminist foreign policies are primarily designed to reorient the content of foreign policy, giving priority to gender equality issues in various foreign policy domains such as trade, aid and security (Towns et al, 2023). The increase of women in diplomacy is a related goal, enhancing international credibility of those states. This is illustrated by the fact that internal matters are usually discussed at the end of feminist foreign policy declarations or set as the last objectives. Nevertheless, feminist foreign policies are the most explicit institutional attempt to pair substantive and descriptive representation of women in foreign policy – aiming to even out the distribution of rights, resources and representation of women and girls around the world, feminist foreign policies also facilitate women's presence in diplomacy. Setting expectations about what is to be achieved in external relations, they establish new standards within the MFAs, explicitly targeting its current gendering (Mackay et al, 2010).

Conclusion

This chapter traces shifts in the gendered infrastructure of diplomacy to capture broad changes to the gendering of diplomacy and suggest how this may relate to the contents of foreign policy. We observe a shift from the active marginalization of women in diplomacy, expressed for instance by bans on women and marriage bars, to active inclusion efforts concerted by many MFAs around the globe. We map several institutional innovations that all aim to compensate for the persisting underrepresentation of women in diplomacy. However, this is by no means a story of smooth progression towards a more gender-equal diplomacy. Both historically and contemporarily, there are examples of pushback. For instance, when bans on women were lifted in the MFAs, marriage bars were introduced; the establishment of Gender Focal Points or 'Ambassadors for Gender Equality' does not always entail the allocation of sufficient resources; and there is reluctance, mostly among male diplomats, to accept new recruitment strategies. As Elise Stephenson (2024) concludes in her study of the gendering of the Australian case, a feminist institutionalist lens reveals 'pockets of progress and undercurrents of resistance'. Our mapping of the institutional innovations that aim to further gender inequality at the MFAs is by no means exhaustive. What is more, the features we selected are observable in several MFAs around the globe but are certainly not universal. Future studies could try to map the patterns and effects of these various constellations of institutional innovations more systematically.

The chapter demonstrated that diplomacy, while still predominantly masculinized, has undergone significant changes over time and can be challenged and reformed. Feminist institutionalism cautions that formal institutions, which we have focused on in this chapter, are only part of the story. While the formal rules have gradually changed towards broader inclusion of women in diplomacy (but still lagging when it comes to inclusion of non-binary people), informal institutions, or rules-in-use, might complement but also counteract these changes. Existing research on informal norms and perceptions about how diplomacy should be practised has pointed to gendered ideas about who constitutes a skilful diplomat (Standfield, 2022). Informal norms might still block women's full inclusion and appreciation in the diplomatic profession even when formal rules appear to be gender-neutral. Future research could expand on these findings, especially the connections between formal and informal institutions in the gendering and transformation of diplomacy. Another interesting direction for future studies is to explore the relationship between descriptive and substantive representation in diplomacy. While we acknowledge that 'numbers do not translate to authority and agency' (Cassidy, 2017: 215), there is sufficient evidence from other institutions that the connection between descriptive and substantive representation is significant. However, it remains to be shown by future studies whether and how changes to diplomatic institutional features and gender patterns accompany changes in the manner and content of diplomatic relations and foreign policy.

7

Practice

Ekatherina Zhukova

Introduction

How is feminism conducted in everyday foreign policy and what feminist routines do foreign policy actors practice? We know that men have long been doing foreign policy in homosocial environments ranging from golf courses, saunas and billiard rooms to hotel lobbies, smoking corners, banquets and bars (Nair, 2020). Since women (less so non-binary people) entered foreign policy institutions in the 20th century, it becomes important to understand how their contribution to diplomacy has changed the everyday practice of foreign policy (Aggestam and Towns, 2018). Practice is defined as the routine and innovative everyday behaviours that enable both continuity and change.

In recent work on International Practice Theory (IPT), we learn, for example, that because of the changes in women's status in foreign policy institutions, the understanding of a diplomatic spouse has started to transform (Standfield, 2022). For instance, the male-homosocial practice of playing golf has lost momentum in certain parts of the world because women as foreign policy actors are not interested in reproducing the traditional practices of their male counterparts (Nair, 2020). Given these changes, it is worth asking whether feminist practices of foreign policy are emerging and, if so, what they entail?

Drawing on International Relations (IR) feminist scholarship, this chapter shows how feminist practices of foreign policy involve an inclusive dialogue based on partner-oriented listening and respect for difference (Park-Kang, 2011; Robinson, 2011), self-reflective listening and attentiveness to positionality (Ackerly and True, 2008; Harcourt et al, 2015), and collaborative engagement in 'third spaces' (Nnaemeka, 2004; Kamaara et al, 2012).[1] I argue that traditional practices of foreign policy can enable and constrain feminist practices of inclusive dialogue aimed at achieving empathetic cooperation in global politics (Sylvester, 1994). I thus look at how traditional foreign policy and new feminist practices coexist in everyday encounters of foreign policy actors and how these practices influence each other.

The chapter aims to contribute to IPT scholarship that has not comprehensively considered the role of gender and feminisms in foreign policy practice (Pouliot, 2008; Bueger and Gadinger, 2015; Bremberg, 2016). This neglect has led IPT to focus more on conflict than cooperation ignoring the role of social structures, such as gender, sex, class, race and others in shaping international interactions (Nair, 2020). Focusing on feminist foreign policy allows for investigating the possibilities of non-rival relations among foreign policy actors as well as difficulties in achieving cooperation due to inequalities stemming from intersections of different social structures. In addition, examining feminist practices of foreign policy reveals the importance of broader and general practices of foreign policy actors rather than only the narrow practices of elite specialists, as IPT would suggest (Wilcox, 2017).

The chapter is structured as follows: In this first part, I review the literature on both foreign policy and feminist practices leading to a discussion of the use of certain feminist practices in foreign policy. In the second part, I use illustrations from interviews with foreign policy actors in states advocating feminist foreign policies (Sweden, Canada, France, Luxembourg, Mexico, Spain) and key actors in states that are the aid recipients or targets of feminist foreign policies (such as from Latin America, Europe/Eurasia, Africa, the Middle East and Asia). In the final part of the chapter, I consider the challenges and opportunities of practising feminism in foreign policy and how they can be addressed as well as suggesting directions for further research on foreign policy.

Practice and feminist theory

Scholars, advancing practice theory into the IR field, suggest looking at practice as a process of a simultaneous reproduction of continuity and facilitation of change (Bueger, 2014; Bueger and Gadinger, 2015). Pouliot argues that practices 'are the result of inarticulate, practical knowledge that makes what is to be done appear "self-evident" or commonsensical'

---

[1] A 'third space' implies a meeting place collaboratively chosen, arranged and financed by all negotiation partners, which emerges outside of traditional spaces of engagement and protocols of foreign policy.

(2008: 258), while Bremberg argues that practice represents 'the tension between routine and innovation' (2016: 425). Routine means that what is known from the past is mobilized to act in the present with continuity. Innovation implies that the present opens a 'window of opportunity' to introduce new practices of change. This tension does not allow a transformative change to take place but rather, it leaves room for 'more subtle instances of change' (Bremberg, 2016: 425). Foreign policy actors can select from the available repertoire of actions because 'change often takes the form of broadening a given repertoire, rather than clean cuts between the past and present' (Bremberg, 2016: 427). The task of this chapter is to examine how engaging with gender and feminisms in foreign policy can bring innovation to the conduct of foreign policy in the context of a traditional *modus operandi* in foreign policy, which works to co-opt gender and feminisms to the already existing order.

Practice theory distinguishes between routines and innovation as well as between reflective conscious knowledge (what foreign policy actors think about) and unreflective background knowledge (what foreign policy actors think from) (Pouliot, 2008). This distinction has often set practice theory against normative approaches in IR. While normative approaches may focus on what rules create consensus and guide collective action, practice theory is interested in what creates these normative rules in the first place (Bueger and Gadinger, 2015). However, this chapter focuses on gender and feminisms in foreign policy and demonstrates that practice theory has a limited understanding of norms. As feminist theories of norms in IR have shown, gender norms can refer to tacit, bodily norms (True and Wiener, 2019; Wiener, 2023). While for Bueger and Gadinger 'norms, then, exist primarily in practice' (2015: 453), for feminist scholar Wilcox 'practices never fully embody norms' since 'acts that may seem to comply with norms can have unintended consequences' (2017: 800). This is because practices do not stand alone, independently of each other; they are always embedded or related to other practices, the latter influencing the realization of the former.

But how do foreign policy practices relate to feminist practices? Do they facilitate or hinder feminist practices? To address this question, we need to understand what feminist practices are. Inspired by feminist theory, I define feminist practices as ways of engagement in inclusive dialogue based on partner-oriented, self-reflective, and embodied listening and collaborative participation in 'third spaces'. I elaborate on each of these constitutive elements of feminist practices in what follows.

Drawing on Joan Tronto's understanding of care ethics, Fiona Robinson (2011: 851) argues that feminist practices constitute morality. These practices include 'attentiveness, responsibility, nurturance, compassion and meeting others' needs'. Such practices are crucial for minimizing the negative effects of unequal power relations between international partners so that a more inclusive dialogue can take place. These practices do not aim to eradicate inequality, but to raise awareness about inequality to smooth its negative effects. Feminist practices stem from the assumption that we can never be equal. Instead of imagining how we can eradicate inequality, we should learn how to deal with this inequality in an ethical manner. This learning does not take place in the form of a one-off event but requires patience and continuous discussion over a long time (Robinson, 2011).

A continuous discussion over a long time contributes to an inclusive dialogue. An inclusive dialogue means not just bringing people to the table ('adding women and stirring'), but listening to what these people have to say, understanding their needs, the conditions of their dependency and vulnerability, and discussing the possibilities of addressing these needs and conditions (Robinson, 2011). To listen, in other words, is to be sensitive to and receptive of difference. To listen is to be open to challenging one's assumptions, beliefs, convictions and values. As Robinson argues, 'effective listening requires learning how to be truly attentive to others, as well as nurturing the virtues of patience and trust' (2011: 856).

Inclusive listening is also embodied listening (Wilcox, 2017) since dialogue partners are always constituted by their social location, gender, sexuality, class, race, religion, and other identity structures that they embody and perform (Nair, 2020; Standfield, 2022). Wilcox argues that '[n]orms of heterosexuality stabilize the apparent naturalness of sex, gender, and sexuality through a "grid of intelligibility" that creates the limits within which "practitioners" can appear as proper "practitioners", that is, subjects' (2017: 796). Similarly, Nair contends that 'there are barriers to what kinds of sociability one can access owing to differences in race, gender, and social class' (2020: 200).

An inclusive dialogue also means being attentive to the context and conditions of how the negotiation table is set up; who pays to set up the table, who chooses its location, who sets the agenda, who chooses the participants, what language(s) is spoken, who speaks, and who moderates the conversation (Kamaara et al, 2012: 55). In an inclusive dialogue, setting up the table can allow a new 'third space' to emerge (Nnaemeka, 2004), 'a space that is collaboratively chosen' (Kamaara et al, 2012: 56). This space 'involve[s] the voices, resources, and perspectives of all conversation partners from start to finish' (Kamaara et al, 2012: 56).

To minimize power and hierarchies between the participants in international collaboration, an inclusive dialogue would consist of partner-oriented and self-reflective listening in spaces of collaborative engagement. According to Park-Kang, partner-oriented listening means 'to listen rather than to give advice' (2011: 862). Here, 'the emphasis is on the person I am in dialogue with rather than on myself or my rationale for listening' (Park-Kang, 2011: 875). Similarly, Ackerly and True (2008: 695) suggest that it is important to 'always listen for new voices, always (respectfully) hearing cacophony, always suspicious of certain harmonies or recurring themes'.

Partner-oriented listening is a constitutive part of 'nego-feminism', which is feminism based on non-egoistic negotiation, and which moves beyond the homogeneous status quo 'anesthetized by the comfort of the familiar/"home" towards the "foreignness" that challenges and promotes self-examination' (Nnaemeka, 2004: 378). By contrast with practice theory, nego-feminism invites us to familiarize ourselves with and appreciate the unknown everydayness of the Other rather than reproduce the taken-for-granted routines of the Self. Nnaemeka argues that such a practice 'needs the different, the out of the ordinary, that defamiliarizes as it promotes the multiple perspectives and challenges rooted in heterogeneity' (2004: 278). Hence, nego-feminism is about compromising with the Self and accommodating the Other. While the Self familiarizes with the Other, it simultaneously defamiliarizes and refamiliarizes with the Self. As Park-Kang argues, 'a good and constructive dialogue begins within oneself' (2011: 863). This contributes to self-reflective listening, being 'attentive to the constraints on his or her imagination coming from all global social processes' (Ackerly and True, 2008: 696). Self-reflective listening implies an ability to rethink, change and adapt the policy based on what one has learned with others.

Both self-reflective listening and partner-oriented listening can become possible in spaces of collaborative engagement. These spaces emerge based on learning with each other, rather than learning about or from each other. As Nnaemeka argues, 'learning about often produces arrogant interrogators; learning from requires humble listeners' (2004: 374); learning with makes the interconnection of positionalities of dialogue partners possible.

Based on these considerations, the following sections address how traditional foreign policy practices such as official policy documents and concepts, bilateral and multilateral spaces of engagement, and stages of policy design and implementation can facilitate, or hinder, feminist practices of inclusive dialogue based on partner-oriented, self-reflective, and embodied listening and collaborative engagement in 'third spaces'.

Practising inclusive dialogue through foreign policy

Creating and using new documents is a traditional way to practice foreign policy. Policy documents 'belong to the very basic material out of which the field of political practice is made. They are basic glue by which people relate to each other and organize their activities' (Bueger, 2014: 398). They 'are sometimes read, sometimes processed, sometimes admired, sometimes shelved, and sometimes immediately discarded' (Bueger, 2014: 398). Documents as a part of foreign policy practice can influence and be influenced by feminist practices (Wilcox, 2017: 800); they can facilitate or hinder inclusive dialogue. One example of facilitation of the inclusive dialogue can be found in the use of Sweden's *Handbook of Feminist Foreign Policy* (Government of Sweden, 2018a). While the Swedish government was an initiator of the dialogue, it was up to its partners to decide how to relate to this document. As one key informant stated: "I read the policy paper of Sweden and I liked it ... Sweden is very close to our heart, so that's why we are willing to follow them, to be inspired by them, with this policy paper. And we are developing our own policy paper."[2] Here, a specific foreign policy document becomes a part of broader 'empathetic cooperation' (Sylvester, 1994) that has already been established earlier between Sweden and an aid recipient country.

An example of a hindrance to an inclusive dialogue can be found in the translation of the United Nations (UN) Security Council Resolution 1325 on Women, Peace and Security into the National Action Plans (NAPs). NAPs can reproduce old routines in foreign policy practice due to the difficulty of applying universal principles of gender equality into particular cultural and religious contexts where the conflicts take place. Instead of using NAPs as a meeting point for an inclusive dialogue, they can be used to sustain power and reproduce hierarchies between states in the Global North and South. For instance, one research participant from an aid recipient country stated:

> We want other things being added when it comes to the implementation of the Resolution 1325 because we can't implement it the same way Western people implement it. Because of the religion and culture, everything is totally different when it comes to the MENA region, we can't implement it the same way. So they need to understand, we have other problems facing us, other obstacles.

Here we see a lack of partner-oriented listening to the needs of the representatives from the Middle East (Park-Kang, 2011). This lack of partner-oriented listening contributes to a lack of understanding between the partners from the Global North and the Global South. It reproduces the traditional *modus operandi* of foreign policy since the representatives of the Global North assume in advance that they know best what the needs of their partners in the Global South are (Nnaemeka, 2004).

In addition to using documents as a traditional way of practising foreign policy, Bueger argues that concepts 'are part of practices and using them allows for different forms of action' (2014: 398). Let us go back to the

---

[2] This and future quotations of research participants are from digital interviews conducted at various geographical locations between July 2021 and October 2022.

concept of feminist foreign policy. It can enable new practices in foreign policy 'through which actors relate, transform their behaviour and compete over authority' (Bueger, 2014: 398). Not all states that have adopted a feminist-informed foreign policy engage with the concept of feminism, but may instead focus on gender equality as their goal is to improve women's conditions. For example, the large-scale events that countries with feminist foreign policies organized have gender equality in their titles: Stockholm's Forum for Gender Equality 2018 (rather than the Stockholm Feminist Forum) or the Generation Equality Forum 2021 (rather than the Generation Feminism Forum). Staying with the widely accepted concept of gender equality rather than incorporating the more political concept of feminism into the foreign policy practice may facilitate an inclusive dialogue or hinder it depending on the context.

The facilitation of an inclusive dialogue using gender equality instead of feminism can be seen as a practice of nego-feminism through which foreign policy actors rely on compromise to engage with as many dialogue partners as possible. The conversation partners do not have to agree with each other; what matters is that they sit down at the negotiation table and start listening to each other in a partner-oriented and self-reflective manner (Park-Kang, 2011). In the words of Nnaemeka, nego-feminism 'knows when, where, and how to detonate patriarchal land mines; it also knows when, where, and how to go around patriarchal land mines. In other words, it knows when, where, and how to negotiate with or negotiate around patriarchy in different contexts' (2004: 378).

Nego-feminism becomes crucial in navigating the persisting anti-feminist stands within the foreign policy institutions. As one interviewee explained:

'How do you bring these conversations with the policy makers who oppose the advancement of women's rights? How do you get these different parties, who have gender biases, interested in even speaking about feminism? In some spaces, the word is not even allowed to be used! How do you navigate yourself around those spaces?'

This prevalence of gender biases does not only apply to national policy making and bilateral relations, but also stretches to the international organizations and multilateral collaboration:

'Everyone feels comfortable to use "gender equality" rather than "feminism". We had a session once and the consultant was intentional to include the word "feminist" into a number of documents. But some of the government officials did not feel comfortable, even the UN did not feel comfortable, to use the term "feminist" in the policy document!'

While using the concept of gender equality instead of feminism can facilitate inclusive dialogue with less like-minded partners, it can simultaneously risk reproducing the old routines in foreign policy practice. At the same time, choosing the concept of feminism over gender equality can facilitate inclusive dialogue with more like-minded partners, and through that challenge the old routines in the practice of foreign policy. Challenging the old routines in foreign policy practice can take place when countries with feminist foreign policies mobilize the word feminism strategically to distinguish their left-leaning policies from the rivals to the right: 'When [diplomats in] biateral [states] name themselves and push a feminist agenda, it is significant in terms of the sort of message that is communicated out there.' Having feminism endorsed at the highest political level can help feminist non-governmental organizations to have their work recognized and legitimized by the government. At the same time, the research participants point out the possible gap between the feminist words and actions in feminist foreign policy: 'But also there is a bigger question about what does that mean? Does it mean that they are ready to invest in actions that are feminist?' Similarly, for those not directly involved in the drafting or implementing the policy, the idea of feminist foreign policy remains unclear: 'Why do we assume such a policy? It is still not clear for the general public.'

Hence, creating and using new documents and concepts as an integral part of foreign policy practice can simultaneously facilitate and hinder feminist practices of inclusive dialogue. Facilitating inclusive dialogue can work through nego-feminism where foreign policy actors navigate the language use in negotiations in order not to antagonize their conversation counterparts (Nnaemeka, 2004). The hindrance to the inclusive dialogue can occur when partner-oriented and self-reflective listening is not practised by at least one or both sides of the negotiation table (Park-Kang, 2011). This means that feminist practices do not necessarily depend on introducing a feminist foreign policy, while states with a feminist-informed foreign policy may not automatically engage in inclusive dialogue. Hence, states without a feminist foreign policy may also incorporate feminist practices into their foreign policy routines.

Collaborative engagement through different spaces

The COVID-19 pandemic has opened new technological possibilities to normalize digital meetings of foreign policy actors. Interviewees report having regular informal digital meetings once or several times a month among Gender Equality Ambassadors and foreign ministers, to which representatives from like-minded countries and international organizations working on gender issues (for example, Gender Equality Ambassadors, envoys, special envoys, and so on) can be invited. In these informal meetings, foreign policy actors exchange ideas and discuss possible responses to crises. They also use this space to work on strengthening their position on gender equality issues in the UN organizations. The informality of these networks plays a crucial role in ensuring flexibility and vitality of cooperation and exchange.

This digital meeting space can be thought of as a 'third space' (Nnaemeka, 2004; Kamaara et al, 2012), compared to traditional physical formal diplomatic spaces. The only requirement to participate is having time to join and a device with Internet access. The dialogue partners can be physically based at any geographical location, be it private or public, and use any available device, mobile phone or computer. This space provides conditions for practising partner-oriented and self-reflective listening since it is a safe space, and the performance stakes are low (Park-Kang, 2011).

An example of the effort to create an alternative space for 'other-oriented' listening and reflection is the Global Partner Network for Feminist Foreign Policy launched in 2021 at the Generation Equality Forum co-organized by Mexico and France. It 'is an informal, global and multi-stakeholder network and dedicated space for the advancement of feminist foreign policies. Its main purpose is to promote the articulation and implementation of feminist foreign policies worldwide, deepening analysis, understanding and impact' (Paris Peace Forum, 2022). At the same time, as one interviewee put it, 'this collaboration is in an embryonic state'. Although as Aggestam and True (2023) point out, the international community working on gender and feminist issues is not limited to states with feminist foreign policies but includes transnational networks involving non-state groups and an incipient of feminist foreign policy movements. Thus, even if certain countries abolish their feminist foreign policy, for instance, Sweden, there exists a community of practice to continue carrying this work further.

In addition, foreign policy actors utilize well-established practices of organizing small- and large-scale events as a part of their public diplomacy toolkit. These events can be considered collaborative spaces where inclusive dialogue can take place (Park-Kang, 2011; Robinson, 2011). For example, France and Mexico co-organized the Generation Equality Forum in 2021; Canada and France held the G7 presidency in 2018 and 2019, where gender equality was a key topic; Sweden organized the Stockholm Forum for Gender Equality in 2018. These events allow for discursive visibility of gender equality and for establishing anew and strengthening the old community of practice. Large-scale events are also supplemented by smaller events such as organization and participation in webinars, starting a course or giving a lecture at universities.

While potentially being spaces for partner-oriented and self-reflective listening (Nnaemeka, 2004; Kamaara et al, 2012), organizing small- and large-scale events as a part of states' public diplomacy also raises questions about the obstacles to inclusive dialogue. These obstacles include who can support these events financially and under what conditions, who can participate in them and who cannot, and whose voices can be heard at them and whose cannot. For example, when France held the G7 presidency in 2017, feminist organizations were not invited to raise their concerns at the G7 leaders' summit. An Open Letter to President Macron from civil society organizations stated on 13 June 2019: 'Civil society's expertise must be acknowledged, recognized and heard at the highest level so that the decisions taken by G7 leaders are not disconnected from the reality and needs of the people who will be directly affected by the G7 outcomes' (Action contre la Faim, 2019). This example shows that large-scale events might not always foster partner-oriented listening and be attentive to the needs of the people on the ground.

This example also indicates that there are conflicts within the epistemic community of practice where disagreements arise on who sets the terms of what is to be done and how, whose feminism is prioritized, and whose interests are addressed. According to one research participant:

'A lot of it is about control. Are they willing to genuinely let go of the process and give it to the local or national movements? The other element is mistrust. Some activists would not want money from the INGOs or donors because it is more damaging to them than anything else. And vice versa, some donors and INGOs might think they [activists] are too radical, they are too political.'

Furthermore, due to global structural inequalities, it is the educated middle- and upper-class elite that constitutes the gender and feminist epistemic community, since the subaltern remains silent:

'You have women at the very-very bottom who can't afford to join. You need to be able to afford to fight for your rights. And if you are working every day, and if you miss one day of work, that means that you don't get food that day. So, of course, you can't join. So they are the ones that everybody else can join has to work for.'

Hence, even though feminist epistemic communities can bring foreign policy innovations, they can also reproduce old routines because they remain embedded in global class inequality (Nair, 2020). The question then remains how to listen to the subaltern who cannot join the struggle and speak for themselves, how to create and sustain an inclusive conversation despite global class inequality (Wilcox, 2017).

Finally, collaborative engagement does not only take place among like-minded actors across countries but also among actors within the same country across different foreign policy domains. It can be done by setting gender equality at the centre of policy making across all domains – development, trade, security, climate change, and so on. This means that every embassy and consulate can be tasked with mainstreaming gender equality in their diplomatic, trade, defence and development collaboration in a partner country. However, mainstreaming gender equality in each foreign policy domain does not always translate into making this policy cross-sectoral, where each foreign policy domain can benefit from the activities done in other domains. This applies particularly to countries that prioritize only one domain of foreign policy for gender equality promotion over others (for example, international development). But even in countries that try to have gender equality as a foreign policy priority in every domain, there is still work to be done to make their foreign policy cross-sectoral: "More integration between multiple [foreign policy] arms of Sweden could help to push the change initiatives through, even if it's just the ones that are in alignment with other SIDA's [Swedish International Development Agency] objectives. I don't think it's quite holistic in its perspective, it's a little siloed still." Hence, while making gender equality a foreign policy priority can contribute to the creation of new routines in foreign policy practice, having siloed projects in each foreign policy domain that do not 'talk' to each other risks reproducing old routines.

The challenge with siloed projects can be addressed by setting up a community of feminist practice across foreign policy domains within the same country, which can later be expanded to other countries. The obstacles of setting up such a community of practice domestically can come from actors representing one domain of foreign policy who consider gender equality less relevant than actors in other domains do, or from actors representing different political parties with conflicting policy priorities. For example, actors representing the security domain can resist learning from the actors in the development domain who have more experience with working on gender equality. Such resistance can hinder partner-oriented and self-reflective listening between foreign policy actors of the same country (Park-Kang, 2011).

Hence, organizing small- and large-scale events as an integral part of foreign policy practice and creating new collaborative 'third spaces' such as informal digital meetings and networks can simultaneously contribute to and challenge inclusive dialogue. Inclusive dialogue can flourish through the setup and maintenance of the community of practice which different groups can join (Aggestam and True, 2023), including across foreign policy domains within the same country. The challenges in sustaining inclusive dialogue lie in the global class inequality between those who are supposed to participate in it (Nnaemeka, 2004) and in the competition between actors from different foreign policy domains (Nair, 2020). Once again, these examples show that the adoption of feminist foreign policy by a state does not always mean conducting feminist practices; foreign policy actors can engage in feminist practices with or without a feminist foreign policy.

Embodied listening through all stages of foreign policy

Wilcox criticizes IPT for its focus 'on limited groups or communities with specialized knowledge' (2017: 298), which risks excluding those who do not belong. Feminist practices are not just practices of and for the elite; non-elite knowledge is central to all stages of foreign policy from a feminist perspective (Kamaara et al, 2012). Feminist practitioners promote participatory approaches to policy making, which support minorities and marginalized people to share their stories without mediation, interference or framing by institutions or those in power. These stories then serve as a basis for drafting and implementing policies, from problem formulation to its solution.

Drafting and implementing policies based on the voices of minorities and marginalized people from bilateral partner countries, which most of the time represent the Global South, facilitates an inclusive dialogue in international collaboration. As one practitioner remarked with respect to Germany's adoption of a feminist foreign policy:

'There's some difference there with how they cooperate, they were very much involved in the development of the programme. They were more consultative, there was clarity of frames, they didn't object to some of the things ... and it felt more empowering to do so, rather than to be tools instructed to do this, do that.'

This example demonstrates certain elements of the participatory approach in foreign policy practice where partners in the Global South are involved in co-designing the programme with their funders from the Global North. This feminist practice challenges the historically dominant practice of the Global North being the agent who teaches the Global South what to do.

One of the challenges that remains is how to get the policy to the destination, to an ordinary person, even if it is possible to develop it in collaboration between foreign policy actors from the Global North and South:

'To the extent where you can see the real actions of these instruments, they are still not very clear. Of course, they are then placed into national frameworks, action plans, and so on. But how this translates to the ordinary woman, to the ordinary girl, is still very difficult to achieve.'

Another challenge is that foreign policy actors rotate from country to country and do not always have time to get to know the context of a particular country well enough, which hinders their capacity to tailor the policy to this context:

> 'Empowerment comes from knowledge. When it comes to policies, we often have to go outside to bring a consultant into design policy, who's not going to know the context, who's not going to have an appreciation, and be able to really design a policy that's relevant. And so a lot of the policies don't yield fruit.'

This is in line with Robinson's argument about 'the need for patience and commitment in the recognition that responsibilities to others are fulfilled over the long, rather than the short, term' (2011: 847).

A lack of time for learning about the local context can hinder partner-oriented and self-reflective listening. As one participant expressed:

> 'Sometimes, it comes with a backlash, when the Western perspective of feminism comes. It just erases everything else that happened before. ... There is no clear understanding of how things work in different cultures. I mean, there were feminist activists since the 1920s in our country, fighting for women rights!'

This backlash also has to do with the deeply seated superiority that Western perspectives can bring and a sense of inferiority they can create in the local population:

> 'It was just White activism. We were expected to do exactly what they do and do exactly what they think. And even though they never said that, they also allowed us to do things our way. But I always felt that our version of things was not as legitimate as their version of things.'

One of the examples this interviewee shares is about the organization of a gay pride parade in a Middle Eastern capital city:

> 'I remember we had a discussion once, it was "Wouldn't it be important to have a pride in the country?". I was like "I don't think this is a priority to have a pride parade in the capital city". Because the priority is safety, the priority is for people to feel safe. ... Sometimes we did have pride parades, but they were not official ones. We had areas in the city where you go to an area in downtown with stained coffee shops, and basically 90 per cent of people sitting there are gay people. They didn't need a parade. They created a community themselves. And just not to see them as liberated just because they don't have a pride parade is insane. They actually liberated themselves within that

margin of freedom they had. And we can't just dismiss that just because we don't have a gay parade!'

This example shows how foreign policy actors working with bilateral partner countries may lack awareness of how their structural privileges can affect the wellbeing of people they collaborate with. The partiality of foreign policy actors can lead to a self-centred rather than partner-oriented dialogue. Wilcox argues, for instance, that when we do not listen, 'we erase and in fact make unintelligible a multitude of practices defined as incompetent, practices that may turn out to be quite subversive' (2017: 805). In order to make multiple perspectives and practices intelligible in international cooperation, intersectionality becomes paramount. Intersectionality can contribute to an inclusive dialogue when foreign policy actors become attentive to the situatedness of all negotiation partners in cultural, social, economic and political power structures. According to one key informant, an intersectional analysis enables an understanding that the gender issues

> 'faced by women in a rural setting will be quite different from issues that women face in an urban setting, but also even there, what are the issues that Muslim women face, what are the issues in terms of religion. Or, for instance, the scholarship programme to young women, how does that affect young women with special needs?'

In other words, an intersectional analysis would mean that foreign aid actors would tailor the policy content to different groups of women even within a bilateral partner country.

However, the challenge is that intersectional feminism requires a significant amount of contextual knowledge to make sense of the gendered situation. As one interviewee reflected:

> 'To understand things, intersectionality is actually hard work. And this is where the problem is. I don't think a lot of people are willing to do the hard work to understand everything intersectionally. ... It is hard work to be able to understand where the person standing in front of you is coming from. And when we talk about policies, when we talk about politics, when we talk about regimes, they are more leaning toward standardizing things. We cannot just accommodate everything to every single person and their own experiences, and this is where the problem comes.'

One way to address the complexity of intersectional understanding is to start by recognizing intersectional power differentials within own foreign policy institutions. As one informant stated:

'A lot of the institutions that are doing development work are patriarchal, in their understanding of the work and within their own organizations. So they implement policies from a patriarchal stance, and there's rarely any time for self-reflection. So, I've actually been curious to know if the feminist foreign policy comes from some level of introspection.'

This means that in addition to achieving gender parity between men and women in own foreign policy institutions, it is important to look at what kind of men, women and non-binary persons get access to these institutions in the first place (for example, are they all children of former diplomats or have other privileged backgrounds or are there individuals representing the working class? Are they all of the same racial or ethnic background or is this background mixed?) (Aggestam and Towns, 2018). Introducing intersectionality into own foreign policy institutions would contribute to an inclusive dialogue with bilateral partners. That is because foreign policy actors with different life experiences are more likely to be more attentive to diverse life experiences of others. That would also contribute to changing the *modus operandi* of foreign policy where not only patriarchy (Standfield, 2022) but other structures of global inequality (for example, capitalism, colonialism, racism, and Eurocentrism) are considered in policy design and making.

Hence, drafting and implementing foreign policies with bilateral partner countries can simultaneously contribute to and challenge inclusive dialogue. Foregrounding the voices of the minorities and marginalized people from bilateral partner countries and recognizing intersectional power differentials within own foreign policy institutions can facilitate an inclusive dialogue in international collaboration (Kamaara et al, 2012; Aggestam and Towns, 2018). A lack of time for learning about the local context and challenges to reaching non-elites through the foreign policy can hinder embodied listening (Robinson, 2011; Wilcox, 2017). This implies that a feminist foreign policy and practices do not always go hand-in-hand; some countries can adopt feminist foreign policy without the simultaneous introduction of feminist practices, while other countries can engage in feminist practices without the need for adopting a feminist foreign policy.

Conclusion

This chapter has asked how foreign policy actors do feminism on a daily basis. It has attempted to provide an answer to this inquiry by exploring whether there are specific feminist practices that are emerging in foreign policy, and if so, how they manifest in everyday life of foreign policy actors. Drawing on IR feminist scholarship, the chapter looked at how attentive listening to others and self-reflective listening to one's own assumptions within and outside the traditional spaces of engagement in foreign policy can contribute to inclusive dialogue in international encounters. It argued that feminist practices do not stand in isolation, but shape and are shaped by the already existing foreign policy practices. Acknowledging the coexistence of different practices in foreign policy brings us to several conclusions. First, in order for feminist practices to shape foreign policy in an effective way, foreign policy institutions need to engage more in self-reflective work on what structures of power and inequality they unintentionally reproduce. This can be achieved through the inclusive dialogue within each foreign policy area and among different foreign policy domains in the same country (for example, cross-sectoral policy through the recognition of intersectional power differentials within own foreign policy institutions). This mutual learning could then improve the performance of foreign policy machinery overall.

Second, in order for feminist practices to bring positive change to the lives of the most marginalized people around the world, foreign policy actors need to engage more in inclusive dialogue with non-elites at each area of foreign policy whose knowledge can serve as a basis for transforming the design and implementation of foreign policy. Dialogue with non-elites requires the expansion of spaces for foreign policy encounters and including non-traditional 'third spaces'. This stands in stark contrast to the traditional practices of foreign policy, which do not usually consider internal or external consultations as a necessary part of policy making. As this chapter has shown, even feminist foreign policies do not necessarily include feminist practices in policy design and implementation, while states without a feminist foreign policy can conduct actual feminist practices in their everyday routines.

This chapter has prioritized feminist practices in relation to the most marginalized groups, however, future research could also look at feminist practices among foreign policy elites as well as among non-elites. Feminist practices between elites occur within and across domains of foreign policy and actors representing different countries in global politics. Feminist practices among non-elites also exist on the ground, in those spaces where foreign policy actors engage. Understanding how feminist practices are conducted by diverse people who hold different positions of power will contribute to more ethical practice of foreign policy. Above all, feminist practices are practices for everybody, not just for specialists. They can be performed by men, women and non-binary people, feminists or not, elites or not, and by foreign policy actors across geographical and ideological division.

8

Leadership

Klaus Brummer and Karen E. Smith

Introduction

Gender is now a foreign policy issue on which some states are trying to lead, to promote either pro- or anti-gender norms (see Aggestam and True, 2021: 318). Over the past decade, a growing number of countries have pledged to adopt a feminist foreign policy while, at the same time, in other countries, authoritarian governments have rolled back gender equality norms (Chenoweth and Marks, 2022). In this chapter, we ask what drives some states to espouse a feminist foreign policy and others to lead an anti-gender movement? To answer this question, we focus on state leadership on gender and foreign policy, that is, states leading on pro- and anti-gender foreign policies in the international realm. As part of the explanation for state leadership, the chapter considers the role of political leaders advocating for these policies within states.

Leadership matters in foreign policy. We define leadership as being in the vanguard (Zhukova et al, 2022: 198). Through leadership, states seek prestige to bolster the country's image and status in international affairs (see Towns, 2010), but also their domestic legitimacy. Displaying leadership is a way for states to try to shape the international normative and institutional context, thus establishing their international status for years to come, and 'locking in' corresponding domestic policies. Furthermore, political leadership entails defining and clarifying goals for a group, and then bringing the group together to pursue those goals (Keohane, 2020: 236). Thus, state leadership with respect to feminist foreign policy means not only clarifying it as a goal and mustering the resources to pursue it but also setting an example for other states and leaders to follow.

Pro-gender equality state leadership may include the explicit adoption of the label feminist foreign policy, which adds a new quality to the pursuit of foreign policy goals. Many states have pro-gender equality foreign policies, but only a few have declared they are pursuing a feminist foreign policy. Aggestam and Bergman Rosamond (2016: 323) suggest more generally that 'adopting the "f-word" … elevates politics from a broadly consensual orientation of gender mainstreaming toward more controversial politics, and specifically toward those that explicitly seek to renegotiate and challenge power hierarchies and gendered institutions that hitherto defined global institutions and foreign and security policies'. As Vastapuu and Lyytikäinen (2022: 4) argue, 'adopting an explicit feminist foreign policy has transformative potential' and 'provides a window of opportunity for governments to redefine and sharpen their gender equality policies in foreign affairs, as well as reinforce coordination efforts with other governmental actors and with civil society'.

While some states seek to advance pro-gender norms on the international level, other states act as 'norm antipreneurs' in their efforts to push back against such norms (Scott and Bloomfield, 2017). Actions to that effect include normative contestations of pro-gender rights internationally (and possibly the outright eradication of such rights domestically), for example by sponsoring corresponding resolutions at the United Nations (UN) and organizing groups of like-minded states to that end. Often, such actions are embedded in a broader struggle against Western values, and the West in general. This chapter sets out a framework for explaining why some states have put themselves in the feminist vanguard group and others have tried to lead a reactionary group.

To build that framework, we draw on the literature on feminist foreign policy, role theory and policy entrepreneurship. While there is a burgeoning literature on feminist foreign policy (for overviews see Thomson, 2022a; Achilleos-Sarll et al, 2023), most scholarship has focused on the key actors and factors that have led to its adoption by states – or its implementation (IWDA, 2021; Thomson, 2022a: 174). Aggestam and True (2020) have put forward several factors that can be used to help explain the rise of pro-gender equality foreign policies, based on a systematic comparison of cross-national trends and diverse contexts. Building on this and other literatures, such as role theory and policy entrepreneurship (Holsti, 1970; Davies and True, 2017; Mintrom and Luetjens, 2018), we develop an analytical framework that seeks to explain why some states have forged ahead in terms of adopting a feminist foreign policy and the obstacles for implementation and continuity of such policy; and why other states have pushed back forcefully against gender equality.

The chapter first distinguishes the key concepts of 'feminist vanguards' and 'reactionaries' in terms of gender and foreign policy leadership. Next, the chapter sets out the analytical framework that considers three main explanations for why feminist vanguards declare feminist foreign policies and why reactionaries push back in international fora. The following sections explore these explanations related to the international strategic environment, national role conception and state policy entrepreneurship in depth. The final part of the chapter analyses contemporary examples and identifies further potential areas for research on leadership and foreign policy.

Feminist vanguards and reactionaries

Several scholars suggest that the launching of a feminist foreign policy is a way for small states or middle powers to 'gain relevancy' in international affairs (Thomson, 2022a: 183). As Zhukova et al (2022: 198) argue, 'being a pioneer by initiating a feminist policy attracts attention and can consolidate a country's image as a vanguard and frontrunner'. But if adopting a feminist foreign policy is about demonstrating leadership, then why have many pro-gender equality countries chosen not to adopt this label? Haastrup (2020) and Lee-Koo (2020) point to the importance of the domestic context in limiting the 'uploading' of pro-gender equality norms and policies. Aggestam and True (2020: 153) have also argued that we can expect to see pro-gender foreign policies in democratic states where women's political presence is manifest and with a national role conception as a peacemaker. Yet there is a puzzle here in that states with favourable domestic contexts and conducive national role conceptions may still not adopt feminist foreign policies (for example, Finland, Norway, Sweden post-2022) whereas other states with relatively unfavourable domestic contexts may do so (Libya, Mexico).

In contrast, few states explicitly declare themselves to be anti-gender equality, but there are certainly several states that have staked out positions as leaders in favour of 'the traditional family' or traditional values and against 'gender ideology'. Such anti-gender governments are for the most part authoritarian, but some democracies and hybrid regimes have also proved hostile to pro-gender equality policies (Thomson and Whiting, 2022). Chenoweth and Marks (2022) note the growing number of explicitly misogynistic authoritarian leaders that suppress or eradicate women's and LGBTQIA+ rights domestically also contest the pro-gender equality agenda at the international level. The leaders include those in the 'Western camp', such as former US President Donald Trump, Recep Tayyip Erdogan in Turkey and Viktor Orbán in Hungary. At the UN, a 'Group of Friends of the Family', which includes Belarus, Egypt, Iran, Pakistan, Russia and Saudi Arabia, among others, stresses that the 'traditional family is the foundation of human civilization' (Ministry of Foreign Affairs of the Republic of Belarus, 2015). Those states, plus others including China, have pushed back against sexual and reproductive rights and opposed initiatives regarding sexual orientation and gender identity (Smith, 2017; Dukalskis, 2023).

Vladimir Putin's Russia has linked gender and traditional values to forge a 'counterpoint' to the West (McInnis et al, 2022).

On the continuum defined by feminist vanguards at one end and reactionaries at the other, there are many possible in-between categories, such as states that are generally in favour of integrating gender equality into foreign policy without, however, placing particular emphasis on it, or states who are essentially agnostic to the pursuit of such policy goals. However, since those in-between categories are not about exercising leadership, we do not explore them further in this chapter.

Explaining gender and foreign policy leadership

In this section, we first set out an analytical framework for explaining 'vanguard state leadership' on gender issues, and then show how it could also be used to explain 'anti-gender state leadership'. Our framework subscribes to analytic eclecticism. Thus, 'rather than privilege any specific conception of causal mechanism, analytic eclecticism seeks to trace the problem-specific interactions among a wide range of mechanisms operating within or across different domains and levels of social reality' (Sil and Katzenstein, 2010: 419). Against this background, we suggest that a certain combination of structural and agent-related factors render states' leadership in the promotion of feminist foreign policy goals most likely.

More specifically, spanning different levels of analysis, our framework emphasizes the role of the strategic international environment, national role conceptions and the presence of policy entrepreneurs in the executive. Systemic factors provide crucial background conditions for state action. However, echoing a core claim of foreign policy analysis scholarship, we suggest that systemic factors do not determine foreign policy outcomes. Rather, their concrete meaning for foreign policy strategies and actions is ultimately determined by domestic factors. In this regard, national role conceptions provide indications concerning the overall compatibility, or lack thereof, of feminist foreign policy goals with a country's general foreign policy orientation. Finally, policy leadership by key decision-makers is required to actively push for, or against, the pursuit of feminist foreign policy goals. We draw on examples from several 'vanguard' and 'reactionary' states, such as Sweden, Germany, Mexico and Hungary, to illustrate the utility of the framework.

Opportunities for international leadership

Realists would point to the inherent unsustainability of normative foreign policies like feminist foreign policy, which will have to make way for more 'hard-headed' policies if the state's security is threatened (Fukuyama, 1998).

Hence, if at all, the pursuit of normative foreign policies should occur in a permissive international security environment, which is characterized by remote and weak 'threats and opportunities that states face' (Ripsman et al, 2016: 52). However, the strategic environment in the past few years – and especially since the 2022 Russian invasion of Ukraine – is hardly permissive: indeed, it has been described as one of immense danger, what with US–China tensions, the clear threat to European security posed by Russia, the rise of authoritarianism and anti-democratic parties, and the existential threat posed by climate change (see, for example, NATO, 2022; von der Leyen, 2023). The rise of countries adopting a feminist foreign policy, including relatively powerful states such as France and Germany, is thus a puzzle from this perspective.

Pointing to the indeterminacy of structural factors, we suggest that the very restrictiveness of the international system has opened a window of opportunity for the pursuit of normative agendas. Indeed, with gender equality 'one of the major fault-lines in contemporary global politics' (Aggestam and True, 2021: 385), competition among states is as much about material factors as it is about normative ones. Thus, the increasing polarization between authoritarian powers and more liberal states has prompted mobilization around key values and identities and is not just about economic and military power. In this context, then, the restrictive international environment provides governments with opportunities to clarify their values and take clear stances that distinguish themselves from 'the other' – whether that other is explicitly pro-gender equality or anti-gender (Thomson, 2022a: 179–180).

Global developments, for example, provided a key impetus for the launch of a feminist foreign policy by Sweden. Sweden's then Foreign Minister Margot Wallström referred to 'unsettled times' in which '[g]ender equality and a feminist foreign policy' as well as 'standing against the systematic and global subordination of women' more broadly were presented as key 'building blocks' for Sweden to 'take global responsibility' (Government of Sweden, 2015; Nordberg, 2015). In a similar vein, Wallström's successor as Foreign Minister, Ann Linde, emphasized that '[t]he rights of women and girls are under attack. Conservative forces are trying to restrict the right of women and girls to decide over their own bodies and lives. ... To reverse this trend, courageous action is needed at all levels. This is why we are pursuing a feminist foreign policy' (Government of Sweden, 2020). Likewise, in Germany, the pursuit of, as well as the general necessity for, feminist foreign policy has been explicitly connected to the increasing polarization between liberal and authoritarian states. Russia's invasion in Ukraine has served as the key reference point in this regard. Feminist foreign policy is presented as a viable strategy to counter the 'attack against the ... rules-based international order' (Federal Foreign Office, 2022b), and to increase the stability of societies around the world more broadly (Federal Foreign Office, 2023a).

International polarization is also referenced by the Hungarian government, as it seizes leadership that is explicitly anti-gender and pro-family. Hungarian Prime Minister Viktor Orbán has claimed to be a leader in the fight against the international liberal order: 'Hungary is an old, proud but David-sized nation standing alone against the Woke Globalist Goliath' (Orbán, 2022). Orbán's speeches attack 'the Left', 'Brussels', 'gender ideology', 'illegal migration' and George Soros, and put forward a nationalist vision of 'Hungary Before All Else' (Orbán, 2022; 2023). In Orbán's speech to the US Conservative Political Action Conference in Dallas, Texas in August 2022, he told his audience that the secrets of his electoral victories lay in the values of 'the nation, Christian roots and the family'. He warned that: 'If traditional families are gone, there is nothing that can save the West from going under' and that they must protect children against gender ideology (Orbán, 2022).

However, international polarization is not the only window of opportunity for leadership on gender issues. Countries may seize the opportunity simply to differentiate themselves from others. When Mexico launched its feminist foreign policy in January 2020, it vaunted the fact that it was 'the first Latin American country to adopt a feminist foreign policy' (Gobierno de México, 2020). The global pushback against gender equality does not explicitly feature in the government's rhetoric. Instead, it positions itself as a leader in Latin America and the Global South and only implicitly differentiates itself from the United States, which at the time of Mexico's announcement was governed by Trump pursuing an anti-gender foreign policy (Zhukova et al, 2022: 212; Thomson, 2022a: 182).

Compatibility with national role conceptions

The strategic environment does not automatically translate into the pursuit of feminist foreign policy. Rather, two additional factors need to be in place for this to happen, in terms of compatibility of such goals with a country's national role conception and domestic political entrepreneurs. National role conception relates to the compatibility of feminist foreign policy goals or anti-gender leadership with a state's foreign policy vision and ambition. Here, the argument draws on role theory, which zooms in not only on states' conceptions of themselves and their role in the world (the 'ego' part) but, importantly, also on other states' perceptions and acceptance of those conceptions (the 'alter' part). This is important for our argument in that states must not only want to take on a leadership role, but such role must also be socially accepted.

More specifically, for a state to aspire to taking on a leadership role in the promotion of either feminist foreign policy or anti-gender goals, we suggest that such goals must be compatible with the state's national role conception. Following Holsti, national role conceptions are defined as:

> [P]olicymakers' own definitions of the general kinds of decisions, commitments, rules and actions suitable to their state, and of the functions, if any, their state should perform on a continuing basis in the international system or in subordinate regional systems. It is their 'image' of the appropriate orientations or functions of their state toward, or in, the external environment. (Holsti, 1970: 245–246)

Thus, the pursuit of leadership on gender issues must fit squarely with a country's image of itself, suggesting the need for fit between states' domestic and external self-conceptions.

As a liberal inside-out perspective suggests, feminist foreign policy goals should typically rank high on the domestic political agenda and are translated from there into external affairs (Müller and Risse-Kappen, 1993). In other words, the political prominence as well as the actual pursuit and implementation of feminist foreign policy goals in the domestic realm should provide clear indications as to whether a state ascribes relevance to, and identifies itself with, such goals. It is those states where feminist concerns align with the national role conception that are most likely to seek to promote those norms beyond their borders. Arguably, leadership requires alignment between the domestic context for gender equality and other feminist goals, and the external pursuit of a feminist foreign policy.

Moving to the alter-dimension, the pursuit of a feminist foreign policy leadership role by a state must also be perceived as credible and sincere by other states. In role-theoretical terminology, if role expectations by ego and alter diverge, role conflict emerges and role enactment is significantly inhibited, if not rendered outright impossible, so that role adaptations are required (Harnisch, 2011). In our context, role conflict and ensuing role adaptions might eventually entail the shedding of feminist foreign policy goals altogether. In short, then, it is those states that are most likely to seek a leadership role in the promotion of feminist foreign policy goals whose national role conception aligns with such goals and whose efforts are perceived as credible and sincere by other states.

For example, feminist foreign policy goals align closely with 'Swedish internationalism'. In pursuit of that role, governments of different colours have sought to promote 'human rights and "gender cosmopolitanism," including promoting women's security and protection beyond borders' (Bergman Rosamond, 2015: 462). The pursuit of such policy seems like a natural extension of Sweden's domestic gender policy and welfare regimes and of its state feminism more broadly (Bergman, 2007), with the country being 'often pictured as a paradise for gender equality' (Bergqvist,

2015: 56). Germany's 'civilian power' role conception also seems to be highly compatible with feminist foreign policy goals (Maull, 1990; Brummer and Kießling, 2019). Among other things, this role conception considers human rights and democracy as core values, emphasizes the promotion of social balance and justice at the global level and supports multilateral cooperation along with norms- and rules-based international order more broadly (Kirste and Maull, 1996: 300–303). What is more, those feminist policy goals have also increasingly been embedded, pursued and implemented in the country's domestic political context. Feminist foreign policy has been expressly presented as the extension of gender mainstreaming from domestic politics to external affairs (Federal Foreign Office, 2023b: 9).

However, the case of Mexico illustrates the importance of external credibility. Its feminist leadership matches its multilateral diplomatic efforts to promote human rights and gender equality, such as its co-hosting of 'Generation Equality', to celebrate 25 years since the Beijing Platform for Action on women's rights, or its push for the consideration of gender in climate policy (Delgado, 2020; Deslandes, 2020). However, many observers have also pointed out that there is a serious clash between Mexico's feminist ambitions internationally and the appalling level of femicide within the country, as well as a highly militarized and masculinist law enforcement culture (see Deslandes, 2020; Zhukova et al, 2022: 212; García, 2022; Thompson et al, 2021: 15; Internacional Feminista, 2023). As Deslandes (2020) argues, '[u]nless the metrics on gendered violence within Mexico improve, it will be difficult for the country to continue to convincingly prosecute the case for equity on the international stage'.

National role conceptions also help explain anti-gender leadership. We argue that states likely to push back against feminist foreign goals are those who consider the latter as incompatible with their national role conceptions. It is such lack of alignment of feminist goals with a state's conception of itself which opens the way for active pushback against such norms. The lack of domestic pursuit of feminist concerns should be a viable indicator for such incompatibility. For example, in Hungary, a fundamental element of its foreign policy approach is the appeal to Christian, 'pro-family' values. This external role matches domestic legislation and policy as enacted by the Orbán-led government since his first electoral victory in 2010, for example, banning sex change, reforming the constitution to define marriage as between one man and one woman, banning material that 'promotes homosexuality' in schools, and banning gender studies programmes in universities (see, for example, Fodor, 2022). These changes have sparked sustained criticism in the European Union and beyond, but they give Hungary's gender 'antipreneurship' credibility: internal policies match the foreign policy rhetoric (see Scott and Bloomfield, 2017).

Policy entrepreneurs

While the existence of a permissive international strategic environment as well as a general compatibility of feminist foreign policy goals with a state's national role conception might be conceived as necessary conditions for a state to pursue feminist leadership, they are not sufficient for the outright and explicit adoption of a feminist foreign policy. Nor do such factors alone explain anti-gender leadership. We suggest that policy entrepreneurs located within governments are required to better explain such foreign policy choices.

Acting out of formal positions of power, one or more members of the executive must take the lead in ushering in feminist foreign policy. As a first step, this means placing feminist foreign policy concerns high on the foreign policy agenda. The literature points to several different instruments and strategies at the disposal of policy entrepreneurs, who are generally outside of the state. They include leading by example, team-building and networking, and the transformation of institutions (for example, Davies and True, 2017; Mintrom and Luetjens, 2018; Mintrom and Luetjens, 2019). Hence, these policy entrepreneurs within the state can translate feminist concerns into the formal adoption of feminist foreign policy.

Policy entrepreneurs pushing for the adoption of a feminist foreign policy are clearly motivated by a strong attachment to gender equality. This does not necessarily mean that they are only women. Although Sylvia Bashevkin (2014) has found that in several developed democracies, female decision-makers voiced more gender equality claims than male decision-makers, gender-sensitive policy makers could be promoted by men or women (True, 2003). A supportive domestic context, which enables such entrepreneurs to lead, however, is linked to the overall gender balance, gendered practices and power structures within the ministry, as well as to gender equality within the state, and the presence of an active pro-gender civil society (True, 2003; David and Guerrina, 2013; Brysk and Mehta, 2014).

The domestic political context in which policy entrepreneurs operate varies significantly from state to state and should impact the likelihood of feminist foreign policy adoption. All else being equal, single-party governments should put policy entrepreneurs in a better position to realize their goals compared to coalition governments since inter-party coordination and contestation over policies (and voters) is absent (Oppermann et al, 2017). Also, the more feminist policy concerns are mainstreamed across policy areas (foreign policy, development, trade, military, and so on), thus seeing buy-in by other members of the executive and their respective ministries, the lesser the likelihood of inter-ministerial conflict, or bureaucratic politics (Allison and Zelikow, 1999), and the greater the chances of the adoption of a feminist foreign policy. Further, a policy entrepreneur is more likely to succeed in seeing through the adoption of feminist foreign policy the more powerful his or her formal position within the executive and, more specifically, within the foreign policy executive (Hill, 2016: 62) is, suggesting that leadership by the foreign minister and even more so by the head of government are most likely to succeed. Lastly, a policy entrepreneur should be more likely to succeed the less pushback feminist foreign policy experiences from the state's key partners and allies, which connects to the previous discussion on role enactment and role conflict.

In Sweden, the key policy entrepreneur was Margot Wallström, who took over the post of foreign minister in 2014 in the centre-left government led by Stefan Löfven and who 'championed the [feminist foreign policy] agenda' until 2019 (Achilleos-Sarll et al, 2023: 3). Wallström carried high personal authority on the issue, which resulted from her previous role as first-ever Special Representative of the UN Secretary-General on Sexual Violence in Conflict (2010–2012). To broaden the acceptance of feminist foreign policy, Wallström tied its pursuit to Sweden's broader foreign policy goals: 'Striving toward gender equality is therefore not only a goal in itself, but also a precondition for achieving our wider foreign, development and security policy objectives' (Rupert, 2015). Wallström and her ministry, where for example the post of 'ambassador-at-large for global women's issues and coordinator of Sweden's feminist foreign policy' was created, undertook various measures to put the policy into practice. For starters, conceptual work was done to spell out what feminist foreign policy stands for, evolving around the '3Rs' in terms of rights, representation and resources (Government of Sweden, 2018a: 13–15). Further, Wallström engaged in advocacy activities, giving numerous interviews and speeches in which she made the case for feminist foreign policy (for example, International Peace Institute, 2018). In turn, her ministry unfolded a range of project-based activities aimed at fostering women's education, economic empowerment and political participation (Government of Sweden, 2018b) and co-organized workshops and conferences, including the 'Stockholm Forum on Gender Equality' in 2018 which brought together actors from both governments and grassroots organizations (Government of Sweden, 2018b).

The crucial role of policy entrepreneurs is evident in the case of Germany, which has only recently taken on a leadership role in the latter's promotion. While sympathetic to feminist foreign policy goals as such, the Merkel governments (2005–2021) pursued those goals essentially 'by stealth' (compare the case of Australia in Lee-Koo, 2020). As Aran and Brummer (2024) argue, the two key, and interrelated, reasons for this were that the feminist foreign policy label found little sympathy within Merkel's conservative party and that Merkel herself (or any other member of the executive for that matter) refrained from championing feminist foreign policy goals. Only under the new government led by Olaf Scholz did Germany adopt a feminist foreign policy, and crucial for this was the entrepreneurial role played by Annalena Baerbock, first in her role as co-chair of the Green party and then as foreign minister. Indeed, it was upon the insistence of the Greens that feminist foreign policy was enshrined in the coalition agreement (FAZ, 2022). Subsequently, after taking over the post of Foreign Minister, Baerbock has used her key position in the foreign policy executive to further promote and implement feminist foreign policy (Narlikar, 2022). For example, Baerbock gave numerous policy statements (speeches, interviews, and so on) in which she presented her understanding of feminist foreign policy – which explicitly follows Sweden's '3Rs' to which diversity has been added as an additional dimension (Federal Foreign Office, 2022a) – as well as the need for its pursuit in the first place.

The conceptual work culminated in the publication of Germany's first-ever feminist foreign policy guidelines in March 2023 (Federal Foreign Office, 2023b). Crucially in terms of broadening the political support for the pursuit of feminist foreign policy goals, there has been a buy-in from at least one minister hailing from one of the other parties of the governing coalition. The Federal Minister for Economic Cooperation and Development, Svenja Schulze from the Social Democrats, pursues a feminist development policy, details of which were outlined in a strategy that was also published in March 2023 (BMZ, 2023). By extension, a future change in government could mean that Germany gives up its leadership role and returns to the pursuit of feminist foreign policy goals 'by stealth' – and in so doing possibly once again following in the footsteps of Sweden.

In Mexico, the key policy entrepreneurs pushing for a feminist foreign policy were serving in the foreign ministry: Foreign Minister Marcelo Ebrard, and, in particular, Undersecretary Martha Delgado (Deslandes, 2020). In contrast, López Obrador, Mexico's president, has either ignored gender equality (García, 2022: 20) or undermined it by dismissing reports of violence against women as 'fake' (Thompson et al, 2021: 15). Delgado's resignation from the foreign ministry in May 2023 (Gobierno de México, 2023a) and Ebrard's resignation in June 2023 (to run for president) could have signalled a substantial weakening of the commitment to a feminist foreign policy, but the new Foreign Minister, Alicia Bárcena, reaffirmed the commitment to a 'responsible, more humane and feminist foreign policy' (Gobierno de México, 2023b).

In anti-gender states, for active pushback to occur, actors must emerge who take the lead in actively advocating against the promotion of feminist foreign policy goals in the international arena. Such anti-gender actors could be male or female, with the case of Italian Prime Minister Giorgia Meloni being an example of the latter. Those actors turn themselves and their states more broadly into antipreneurs who act as 'defender[s] of the normative status quo' (Scott and Bloomfield, 2017: 231) or try to roll back certain normative changes to a status quo ante, depending on how deeply entrenched the norms that they are advocating against already are. In pursuit of their goals, norm antipreneurs can draw on a range of discursive and institutional instruments, such as counter-framing, feet-dragging, coalition building and scaremongering (Scott and Bloomfield, 2017: 240–242).

In Hungary, Orbán is clearly the key policy entrepreneur, backed by loyalists that now dominate the foreign ministry. The structural and doctrinal changes in Hungarian foreign policy were not immediately undertaken by the post-2010 government; instead, they were implemented after another landslide election win in 2014. A self-proclaimed Orbán-loyalist, Péter Szijjártó, became the new Foreign Minister (Müller and Gazsi, 2023: 405), and set about replacing the 'old guard' in the foreign ministry with loyalists and reforming training programmes to reflect the 'historical endeavour of defending Christian values' (Müller and Gazsi, 2023: 409). At the same time, foreign policy making was increasingly centralized in the Prime Minister's Office (Müller and Gazsi, 2023: 407).

Analysis

In the global political arena, women's rights and gender equality have been increasingly contested. While some states have become fervent advocates of women's rights, others seek to cement traditional gender roles and the male-dominated political order more broadly. We refer to such states as 'vanguards' and 'reactionaries' respectively. Vanguards are states who not only pursue feminist foreign policy goals but do so under the explicit label of feminist foreign policy. Conversely, reactionaries are states that actively oppose many of the goals of feminist foreign policy.

To answer the question of why some states pursue a feminist foreign policy while others agitate for pro-family and anti-gender norms, we have suggested an analytical framework that highlights opportunities for international leadership, national role conceptions and policy entrepreneurship as the key explanatory factors. International leadership opportunities emanating from a perceived struggle between progressive and conservative forces concerning the role of women have provided a key impetus for states' actions in either direction (that is, vanguard or reactionary). Similarly, compatibility, or lack thereof, of feminist foreign policy goals with states' key national role conceptions helps explain why there is a general openness to feminist foreign policy goals on the part of some states but not others. Lastly, policy entrepreneurship, or for that matter antipreneurship, by members of the state executive branch has been key for translating a general openness to feminist foreign policy goals into the explicit proclamation and pursuit of feminist foreign policy or, conversely, for actively working against the promotion of those goals. We illustrate the utility of our framework by drawing on the cases of Sweden, Germany, Mexico and Hungary.

At the same time, our analysis points to additional factors that seem to warrant greater attention and might help fine-tune the framework and its underlying assumptions. First, party ideology seems to serve as a key transmission belt between the general alignment of feminist foreign policy goals with a country's national role conception on the one hand and the emergence of policy entrepreneurship required to get to a formal proclamation of feminist foreign policy on the other. So, a 'dual alignment' of feminist foreign goals might be required, with respect to both a country's national role conception and a ruling party's ideology, to trigger the emergence of policy entrepreneurs. In terms of ideologies, the empirical discussions suggest that, all else being equal, leftist ideology aligns more closely with feminist foreign goals so that policy entrepreneurs are more likely to come from left or centre-left parties, as evidenced by Wallström (Sweden), Baerbock (Germany) and Delgado (Mexico). Conversely, rightist/conservative ideology, hence parties, are less open towards feminist foreign policy goals, as 'tradition, family, religion, country' tend to be their defining elements. However, the case studies suggest that this does not necessarily have to translate into outright rejection of feminist foreign policy goals, as has been the case in Hungary, but could also mean a rejection of the terms feminism and feminist foreign policy while still being generally sympathetic to feminist foreign policy goals such as the Merkel governments in Germany or the current Swedish government. Finally, in countries with coalition governments party ideology could also be a key reason for enabling or limiting the spread of feminist foreign policy goals, in the sense of it being pursued by just a single ministry, thus rendering it merely a departmental policy, as opposed to turning it into an essentially whole-of-government policy based on buy-in by other ministries. The Mexico case, though, shows that restricting feminist foreign policy to a single department can occur even in countries governed by a single party.

Second, while our definition of leadership argues that vanguards are only those states who explicitly proclaim a feminist foreign policy, the latter as such does not automatically qualify a state for a vanguard role. The proclamation of feminist foreign policy should not be considered as inevitably mirroring or extending domestic gender regimes. For example, Mexico has a much weaker track record concerning the domestic status and empowerment of women not only compared to Germany and Sweden but, noticeably, also compared to Hungary (GIWPS and PRIO, 2021: ii). Thus, the mere proclamation of feminist foreign policy without a meaningful reflection of such goals in a country's national role conception or anchoring in its domestic gender regime might amount more to an example of 'rhetorical action' referring to 'the strategic use of norm-based arguments' (Schimmelfennig, 2001: 48) than to actual policy leadership, and likely also limits the extent to which other states accept a state's vanguard role.

Third, from a temporal perspective, the example of Sweden illustrates that policy entrepreneurs are critical not only for the adoption of feminist foreign policies but also for their continuation. When the 'driving forces' of feminist foreign policy move on or are removed from office, then commitment to feminist foreign policies is revealed to be quite fragile. The German example may show how to build a broader internal coalition in favour of feminist foreign policy so that it survives a change of personnel, or even government, though it is obviously too early to tell. Conversely, should the Orbán government ever be replaced by a government committed to liberal democracy, Hungary will presumably no longer be in the reactionary category of anti-gender leadership – but it may not switch to the feminist vanguard category if the national role conception – and corresponding domestic context – does not also shift.

Conclusion

To conclude with a few suggestions for future research, there is an obvious need for ascertaining the extent to which countries' proclamations of feminist foreign policy are accepted by third countries, thus extending the work by Rosén Sundström and Elgström (2020), who asked this question for the case of Sweden vis-à-vis fellow European Union members. Is there a systematic relationship between the quality of domestic gender regimes of feminist foreign policy proclaiming states and the latter's acceptance by third parties? Second, we used democracies (however flawed) to illustrate the utility of our framework. There is therefore scope to use it to explain why some authoritarian governments seek to demonstrate antipreneurial leadership and others do not. Finally, to what extent is there a competition for global gender leadership? Are pro-gender equality states influenced by feminist foreign policy proclaiming states: do they note the possibilities of global gender leadership by proclaiming a feminist foreign policy, and do they fear losing credibility as pro-gender actors if they do not follow suit? Likewise, do pro-family norm antipreneurs compare themselves with other states, and does this influence the policies they pursue?

9

Feminist Decolonial Historiography

Khushi Singh Rathore

Introduction

This chapter situates itself on the crossroads of non-Western International Relations (IR), feminist theory and foreign policy analysis (FPA), introducing feminist decolonial historiography as a methodological disruptor for the androcentric narratives of foreign policy and IR.[1] In this pursuit, the chapter uses the case of Indian foreign policy and Indian IR to illustrate how feminist decolonial historiography can be employed to highlight the gendered nature of IR and its resultant post-colonial IR and FPA iterations.

The study of India's foreign policy has often been referred to as under-theorized in the IR discipline. As scholars studying Indian foreign policy have contended, its study is mostly distanced from the larger frameworks of IR theorization as well as frameworks of FPA (Ganguly and Pardesi, 2015; Hansel et al, 2017). In recent times, scholars of Indian foreign policy have made commendable attempts at bridging this gap. However, these explorations have been largely silent on the question of gendered foundations, even when looking at non-Western IR theoretical frameworks, thus giving the impression that the Indian foreign policy terrain/ecosystem is gender-neutral. This chapter attempts to fill this lacuna in the literature by employing the tool of feminist decolonial historiography to understand the theoretical exploration of India's foreign policy by centring gender therein. In this pursuit, this chapter proposes feminist decolonial historiography as an important method to counter the androcentric narratives in IR theorizations and FPA.

---

[1] Parts of this chapter are drawn from my doctoral thesis titled 'Women in Early Years of India's Foreign Policy: Evaluating the Role of Vijaya Lakshmi Pandit'.

Looking at the early years of independent India's foreign policy making, this study provides a preliminary exploration of the foreign policy visions of two of the pioneer women in the Indian foreign office at the time, Vijaya Laksmi Pandit and Lakshmi Menon. In doing so, the chapter argues that when we employ a feminist decolonial historiography in the study of foreign policy, it brings forth new actors, who had earlier been marginalized. Thus, it contributes to the larger pool of evidence for FPA and adds to the under-explored terrains of international history and IR at large. Hence, this chapter argues for engaging and (re)formulating these fields from a non-Western standpoint, thus making the case for post-colonial knowledge production in the emerging field of gender and foreign policy. The chapter provides evidence of foreign policy contemplations of two of the earliest women leaders in the Indian foreign policy establishment. Thus, it also establishes a contemporary point that women have long belonged to the terrain of post-colonial foreign policy narratives, even if erased or side-lined from its theorizations.

This chapter pushes to narrow the visions of these women practitioners of international politics to questions of active foreign policy making and to explore the possibilities of feminist strategizing by the early women envoys of independent India, therefore opening up the accounts of India's foreign policy to a gendered theorization. This chapter borrows the idea of 'useable history', which is explained in the following sections, to look at the formative years of Indian foreign policy and women's narratives therein to explore the possibilities of a feminist future.

Indian International Relations and foreign policy analysis: where are the women?

The discipline of IR is built on erasures. Indian IR is no different. In recent years, there have been deliberations on the under-theorization in the field of Indian foreign policy. While there have been promising developments to locate the theoretical footholds, including a decolonial approach to the discipline, the larger terrains of inquiry remain ambivalent to the question of gender. Alongside this, there is the concern about the underdeveloped state of FPA in the study of India's foreign policy. As Ganguly and Pardesi (2015) argue, FPA, as a subfield of IR, has largely been missing in the Indian context. This is not to say that the study of foreign policy has been absent in India. Instead, they argue that 'FPA as an approach' did not entirely take off in India due to several factors varying from the state of the field, available resources and most importantly access to foreign policy archives. Thus, constraining the study of Indian foreign policy to frameworks that remained in want of robust theorization. However, the increased declassification of Indian archives in recent years has, for the first time, opened space to engage with the history of Indian foreign policy in ways not done before. Thus, opening space for new alternative analyses of the same. This also allows for re-examining the gendered omission in the formative conceptualization of Indian IR and FPA. Hence, this chapter aims to take on this opportunity to situate women actors within Indian foreign policy discourse.

Situated in the Indian context, this chapter recognizes that FPA, as a field of study, has long been centred on Western geographies and has continued to employ 'Western-born concepts and methods that continue to be inadequate in addressing non-western foreign policy imaginations' (Hansel et al, 2017). L.H.M. Ling (2017) characterizes disciplinary IR as 'the domain of Hypermasculine-Eurocentric Whiteness' that premises itself on a Protestant-based, 'realist/liberal mode of interacting with the world', thus taking North America and Western Europe as the point of origin for world politics. Therefore, creating what Vitalis calls a 'white world order' (Vitalis, cited in Bilgin and Ling, 2017). When extrapolated to the non-Western academy, the discipline of IR continues to emanate trappings of this West-centric world order, particularly while engaging with questions of foreign policy.

The chapter outlines the state of Indian foreign policy theorization and the intervention made in this study operates at two distinct levels. First, it raises the question of incorporating gender through the international thought of women in the study of foreign policy and IR. Second, it highlights the gendered marginalization of women's voices from the history of Indian foreign policy. This chapter looks at women's history as an entry point into a gendered study of the subfield by employing the idea of 'useable history' (Delap, 2021).

The central question here is: How does centring gender in the study of Indian foreign policy alter our understanding of the discipline as well as of the processes underlying the subfield? This inquiry is driven by the feminist assertions that, first, question the state of IR as a gendered discipline and, second, how the subfield of FPA fails to account for the place and influence of women in foreign policy decision-making processes (Smith, 2019). The chapter approaches this line of inquiry through the route of history. Thus, locating women actors in the early years of India's foreign policy making as figures who cannot be left out in the quest for theorization in the study of Indian foreign policy (IFP). Looking at the ideas of two of the early women envoys of India, this chapter employs feminist historiography as an initiation into a gendered study of Indian foreign policy through the concept of 'useable history'.

'Useable history', as interpreted by Lucy Delap (2021), is a history that is in conversation with the present. Such an approach to history highlights the questions of 'feminist strategy, priority and focuses on the contemporary moment' by telling us how feminist questions were addressed in the past.

Thus, rendering such a history 'useable' to attain the feminist aspirations of the present moment. In short, Delap writes, 'a useable history is not one that judges the past by today's standards. Instead, useability reminds us of the use of the variable ways in which feminisms have been used, rhetorically, intellectually and materially, in the lives of historical actors' (Delap, 2021: 23).

In the Indian context, two of the important women envoys of independent India are central to this study. Getachew et al (2022) remind us that women were serious international thinkers throughout the 20th century. Though they remain missing from the IR canons, they wrote 'some of the earliest and most powerful theoretical statements of what would later become core approaches to contemporary international theory' (Getchaw et al, 2022: 1). This chapter thus excavates these statements of these women leaders of independent India in the mid-20th century and encourages asking questions, such as what current visions of foreign policy can this history be foundational to? How does anti-imperial Indian women's thought inform the contemporary discourse on feminist foreign policy? And, how does centring of women's voices in the birth of independence in India's foreign policy help us better theorize the latter?

In 1947, India started a new chapter in world history as a modern nation state. As Mallavarapu writes (2015), in these formative years, there existed a 'critical mass of thinking and theorizing on various facets of India's foreign policy' (2015: 36). Literature so far has primarily located this theorization in the accounts of diplomats and academicians (all men), thus overlooking the role of women in this 'latent theorization'. Gender, as a category of analysis, remains absent from the dominant attempts at theorizing, even when the need for considering 'diverse strands of theorization' is advocated for in the discipline. The latter pushes for advancing theorization, prioritizing an Indian vantage point that is peculiar to the post-colonial identity and trepidations of the country in the sphere of foreign policy. The international as well as the universe of foreign policy is predominantly imagined as masculine in Indian IR, even when not iterated as such. Gender as a category of critical analysis does not play a role in this theoretical endeavour, much like it did in the earliest iterations of larger IR theory. This chapter is a nascent attempt towards problematizing this lacuna.

How does bringing women's international thought to the forefront transform the study of Indian foreign policy and IR at large? What does gender as a category teach us about the origins, evolution and execution of IFP? As this chapter concerns itself with the historical beginnings, it elucidates upon what such an approach teaches about the origins. To begin with, it exposes the hegemonic masculinities in the varied imaginations of these disciplines where women as actors and gender as a category of analysis are absent. The study of women here not only adds new subject matter to the discipline but also gives thrust to a critical re-examination of the premises of the existing body of knowledge(s) (Scott, 1986). The use of gender brings to attention the aspect of relationality in our analytical vocabulary, thus making ground for examining the skewed gender power relations in the study of Indian foreign policy. The historiography as we know it predominantly evades questions of gender, while the burden to prove why it matters continues to be borne by feminist scholars in the field. A labour of love for most, but also a necessity for existence and labour which is nonetheless cumbersome and exhausting.

The study of Indian foreign policy began with inadvertently emulating the gendered hierarchies of Western IR. Even while it interrogated India's post-colonial positionality, questions of femininities and masculinities embodied in India's foreign policy iterations remained underwhelming, barring important works by Indian feminists. Thus, resulting in a discipline devoid of gendered theorization, as has been stated earlier. This, however, does not mean that gender is not at play in accounts of Indian foreign policy. Looking back at history enables us to identify the point of disjuncture where women were dropped off from discourses on India's engagement with the world. Women were key architects in the national struggle for independence and the founding of the post-colonial state. They were also critical to the transnational alliance building, which predated independent India's foreign office-centred official diplomacy. However, as the post-colonial Indian state was consolidated, women's internationalism underwent a gradual erasure from Indian foreign policy history. The choice of 'history' and not 'discourse' is deliberate while making this argument here because women were present in India's international history but were left out from the very foundation of Indian foreign policy discourse.

Feminist decolonial historiography: recollecting, rewriting, reconceptualizing history

How does history inform FPA? Tracing the historiography, scholars draw our attention to the established standards for what has so far constituted history that informs FPA. Fahrmeir (2017), explaining the European and North American historical traditions, outlines how these, going as far back as Thucydides's *History of the Peloponnesian War*, included 'empirical histories of war and peace, international interaction and treaties in this tradition for centuries to come'. Thus, constituting texts composed by (near) contemporaries of events who had either been involved personally or could claim authentic knowledge based on participant recollection or surviving documents. Essentially, as Fahrmeir sums it up, this drew from a close look at long prehistories to the events unfolding in the present.

A feminist inquiry into the historiographical character of FPA mandates asking about the gendered nature of these texts. Where are the women therein? Who were the actors in these histories that came and continue to inform FPA? The quest for finding women in these histories looks at them as both actors as well as subjects of foreign policy making and implementation. This intervention becomes particularly critical when we study contemporary debates in FPA in post-colonial states such as India. This chapter does so as it broadly articulates the gendered nature of FPA by locating it as being reflective of the characteristics of the larger discipline of IR. The rationale for doing so is also driven by the lack of conceptualization of Indian IR in the frameworks of FPA (Ganguly and Pardesi, 2015). Thus, it makes sound reason to locate the gendered erasure in the study of Indian foreign policy by employing the analytical framework of IR as a discipline, instead of FPA as a subfield. Such demarcation also bursts the myth that FPA literature, even if desired, in its current state is not located in or necessarily reflective of non-Western foreign policy discourses while writing from within the region. Therefore, making non-Western histories of IR and diplomacy better suited to unseat the Western-centrism that has long dominated the discipline. However, such a disruption does not necessarily dislodge the inherent gender bias in the non-Western discourses themselves, the case in point here being that of IFP.

The historical turn in Indian IR is nascent and it has only begun to expand in recent years at an impressive pace. This has allowed for attempts towards generating a more comprehensive analysis of contemporary IFP, considering the various tilts and shifts in history. For example, it would not be possible to analyse India's relationship with China solely based on contemporary diplomatic accounts that circulate primarily with well-guarded elite governmental networks. History provided much-needed context and informed the consistencies and disruptions in foreign policy making and execution, especially when both countries are aggressively propelling the model of a civilizational state. History in this context educates and informs the understanding of foreign policy decision-making and diplomatic manoeuvring. History here is 'useable', as this chapter argues.

Gendering the history of foreign policy opens an avenue to locate women within the historiography of FPA from where they largely remain missing. Gendering here is employed as beginning with the excavation of women's histories as actors in the foreign policy archives and inquiring whether/how their policy visions influenced post-colonial India's foreign policy; it also makes us ask whether questions of gender even percolated into vocabularies of the post-colonial foreign office or were they subsided in the larger anti-imperial discourse? As evidence shows, it was more of the latter. Women were not recognized as foreign policy actors, nor did gender become a category of analysis in Indian FPA. Thus, rendering Indian foreign policy discourse with what this chapter calls a 'men only' problem, where the so far utilized diplomatic archive predominantly accounts for the ideas and experiences of male members of the foreign policy establishment, as if it was 'gender-neutral'. Feminist decolonial historiography challenges these claims of gender neutrality by asserting that 'every aspect of reality is gendered' (Sangari and Vaid, 1989, cited in Nair, 1994), and this is a political struggle to reclaim the 'personal as international'. While feminist decolonial historiography is employed largely in understanding feminist forces and women's agency within the domestic political landscape in the Indian context, diplomacy and foreign policy continue to remain alien territories for such an intervention. Something that is also reflective of the nature of the latter fields of study and raises the question of whether foreign policy as we know it even permits feminism to cohabit in the same space.

Feminist scholars in recent years have asked for the reconceptualization of foreign policy as 'gendered, sexualized and racialized', thus making 'gender, sexuality and race' central to the study of foreign policy, as well as practice (Achilleos-Sarll, 2018). This post-colonial feminist intervention in the study of foreign policy, as well as FPA, speaks generatively to the aims of feminist decolonial historiography as employed in this chapter, central among them being the disruption of foreign policy knowledge(s) as we know them.

Nair (1994) argues that the burden of feminist historiography is not just restricted to correcting historical biases by bringing forth women's narratives. While that is important, mere questioning of categories of historical analysis does not translate into challenging the so-called 'gender-neutral' categories. While it is imperative to bring women's histories into the discussion, it is essential to address the transformative potential of such rewriting of history on the understanding of contemporary issues and solutions addressing them. Thus, making history 'useable'. Gender-neutral categories, writes Nair, are sustained by 'structures of conventional archive' that privilege the public sphere of production instead of reproduction, which then renders women invisible from public history (Nair gives examples of disruptions made by feminist historiography within the field of economics to substantiate this point). However, the history of foreign policy applies here as women were very much part of the public sphere that is the international, just not counted when histories of diplomacy and foreign policy making were written. This study counters this gap and asks how employing feminist historiography reconceptualizes the study of Indian foreign policy; this is studied to understand the insights, policy visions and prescriptions of Indian post-colonial women foreign policy actors.

Feminist historiography, Bashevkin (2018) argues, opens a promising door for studying international politics and leadership and exploring circumstances that can potentially make a difference. It poses questions such as 'What structural patterns permit, or conversely restrict women's influence?' And how have others received the presence of women in foreign policy decision-making and analysis (Bashevkin, 2018: 1)? Similarly, outlining gender as a useful category of historical analysis, Joan Scott (1986) reminds us that in history, 'it was a term that was offered by scholars who believed that women's scholarships had the potential to transform the disciplinary paradigms'. This concurs with the feminist assertion that the study of women does not merely add new subject matter to the field; instead, it also performs the crucial function of forcing us to critically re-examine the premise and standards of prevailing scholarship (Scott, 1986). Extrapolating this argument to this study, women not only become a new subject of research, but such a scholarly endeavour educates the field about its own omissions and provides alternative research agendas within FPA that have yet to be fully explored or integrated.

Feminist decolonial historiography as used here works towards the recovery of women and their life experiences and to establish their centrality in the historical foreign policy narratives that can be employed to inform contemporary FPA. Thus, the larger proposition is to build a comprehensive narrative of the early history of Indian foreign policy making.

Gendering Indian foreign policy narratives: (re)locating women

Feminism, as has been elaborated in this chapter, does not make it to the lexicon of Indian foreign policy theorization, even if feminism and internationalism are closely interlinked in the period. Partly this can be attributed to the tense relationship of the anti-imperial Global South women of the early to mid 20th century with 'feminism' as a label. While their politics would very well fall within the modern-day understanding of feminism, these female actors rejected being labelled as the same. Thus, feminism and feminists as a category were engulfed in the larger anti-imperial vocabularies with the struggle for women's rights largely a part of the nationalist struggle rather than being a distinct category of feminist contestation therein. This was challenged by feminist historians a few years into independence who carved out and emphasized the distinctiveness of Indian feminist histories and that of feminist iterations of post-colonial India. It is no surprise then that feminism as an approach did not percolate the imagination of Indian foreign policy discourse, especially when compounded with the androcentric nature of foreign policy and diplomacy.

This study builds upon Tickner and True's (2018) assertion stated earlier that women and feminism did not come late to the study of IR. Rather it is the latter which has remained reluctant to engage with the former. Thus, importing the hierarchies of IR to the study of Indian foreign policy and IR at large. Chadha Behera (2007) unpacks the possibilities of re-imagining Indian IR by highlighting how the poor conceptualization of Indian IR is owed primarily to the hegemony of Western IR over the epistemological foundations of the disciplinary core of Indian IR theory, that is, traditional

IR. She also problematizes the intellectual dependency of Indian IR, which fails to take ownership over 'scholarly endeavours inspired by feminism, critical theory, development studies and postcolonialism – termed as new IR' (Chadha Behera, 2007). Thus, arguing for the creation of an alternative site of knowledge construction, which is free of the intellectual dependency on Western IR theory.

Following along these lines, feminist decolonial historiography can be a powerful tool to disrupt this intellectual dependency by moving gender from the periphery to the core of the study of Indian foreign policy. This point aligns with Chadha Behera's (2007) argument for creating 'alternative sites of knowledge by devising different sets of tools' that allow for exploration of new repertoire of resources that have thus far been delegitimized or rendered irrelevant from knowledge production in IR'.

The women pioneers in foreign policy: Vijaya Lakshmi Pandit and Lakshmi Menon

The history of women envoys of an independent India brings to the forefront new knowledge(s) of their visions of the world and what they were actively working to achieve within the foreign policy and diplomatic terrain. While women leaders from the Indian struggle for independence continued working in arenas of domestic politics post-1947, there were two who became officials of the Indian foreign office, that is, the Ministry of External Affairs. They were Vijaya Lakshmi Pandit and Lakshmi Menon. Pandit was the first woman diplomat of India and served in key postings during her tenure as an Indian ambassador. Her first posting was to Moscow (1947–1948). She was subsequently posted as the Indian Ambassador to the United States and Mexico (1949–1951), the UK (1954–1961) and Spain (1958–1961). Intermittently, she served as the leader of the Indian delegation to the United Nations (UN) on several occasions, headed the Indian Goodwill Mission to China (1952) and was elected as the first woman President of the United Nations General Assembly (UNGA) in 1953. Lakshmi Menon, on the other hand, was a teacher, lawyer, activist, politician and an Indian envoy to the UN. In 1948, she was appointed as a member of the alternative Indian delegation to the UN. Thereafter, she headed the UN Section on the Status of Women and Children (1949–1950) and, in 1952, was appointed as a Minister of State in the Ministry of External Affairs of India. Both women were an integral part of the Indian Ministry of External Affairs (MEA). Therefore, making them important figures in the formative years of independent India's foreign policy making.

It is thus unfortunate that as one picks the definitive texts of Indian IR, there is marginal mention of these two important actors therein. Even when references to Pandit are made, she is mostly written about as the Prime Minister's sister, who was also an ambassador, thus, reducing her to her relationship with Nehru. There are, though, a few recent (and important) works that centre Pandit's role as an Indian international figure and diplomat (Bhagavan, 2012; Thakur, 2013; Ankit, 2016). On the other hand, Menon does not even make it to these accounts as a key actor, arguably because she did not enjoy the same familial association with Nehru. The hegemonic narratives of Indian foreign policy, thus far, do not account for women as agents in foreign policy making and implementation, and neither do they acknowledge the role of gender. Thus, creating and perpetuating its characteristic gender-blindness. This chapter looks specifically at the foreign policy iterations of these women and brings to light their ideas of international politics. The purpose here is not necessarily to claim distinctiveness in their ideas from the larger post-colonial thought dominant in the early years of Indian foreign policy. Rather, it is to establish their centrality as pioneering practitioners in the field.

A close look at the Indian archives provides an entry into the international thought of both Menon and Pandit. Both made appearances at the UN and at home, actively participating in the All-India Women's Conference discourse. The primary focus here is on women's rights, human rights and racial equality, among others. While these are iterations are made in a multilateral forum such as the UN or in local women's organizations, this chapter primarily looks at Pandit and Menon's key ideas on matters of foreign policy aims for India. For the former, the chapter looks at Pandit's practical roadmap for achieving Asian solidarity in the aftermath of the Asian Relations Conference (ARC) in pre-independence India in early 1947. For Menon, it closely outlines what she envisioned as the primary aims of Indian foreign policy and what was her idea of India's role in world affairs.

Pandit's roadmap for Asian unity

The idea of a united Asia was important to Pandit. When she spoke on international platforms, since her first appearance at the UN, she stressed that she was speaking for all people of colour and especially for the people of Asia. In 1947, when she had her first win on the floor of the UNGA against South Africa's General Smuts, she called it an 'Asian victory' (Bhagavan, 2012). New nations had emerged, resulting from two generations of nationalism that were the motivating force in Asia (Pandit, 1955). Countries such as India, Burma, Ceylon and Indonesia, to Pandit, were examples of nations where the spirit of nationalism was directed into constructive channels reflected in the adoption of the democratic way of life. However, there were also places where nationalism met with continued resistance, for various reasons, and it was in these societies that people turned to 'the ideology which gave them the promise of fulfilling their basic needs' (Pandit, 1955). The ideology referred to here is Communism.

Asia, pleaded Pandit, who did not need war. The people of these countries did not need war. The only war she said they could appreciate was the one waged against hunger and poverty and desperation. The finer points of differing political philosophies lost all meaning in a world plagued with deprivation. It was unfair that what were considered fundamental human rights in Europe and America were interpreted as privileges in the case of the people of Asia, who had to earn them to prove their worth to be treated with dignity. To Pandit, the rationale for why, in such a case, the people of Asia would turn to Communism lay in the realization that the only nation that supported these demands of freedom and dignity was the one 'politically opposed to the free world'. Thus, making the contestation on the continent about the 'prestige' and 'loss of face' of the opposing political forces and not so much about seeking the most earnest attempts at finding solutions that serve the wider interests of democracy and peace.

Pandit was a serious thinker and practitioner of diplomacy who looked through the grand ideological declarations of the two camps. For her, it was democracy and freedom that was paramount. At the same time, it was the criticality of sharing means to grow and develop that occupied her mind. Her personal belief in these values was also reflective of the trepidations young India was going through. Pandit understood the value of resources and how mere political declarations won't solve real problems. However, an anti-imperialist, she also understood why it was important to draw a line and not get drawn into a great power bargain. The post-colonial world, India and beyond, had to develop its own identity. India was the leader of this world, and one could not lead by merely falling in line.

Asian relations conference

On the path of Asian unity, the ARC of 1947 was the first tangible step. The ARC (23 March to 2 April 1947, New Delhi) was a precursor to the Bandung Conference. However, it is unclear what transpired at the conference and how the discussion there affected the ideas of 'third world' internationalism. As is well documented, many women delegates from across Asia attended the event (almost 38 women's organizations and eminent women leaders in Asia were invited), which was presided over by Sarojini Naidu, an Indian nationalist leader.

The writings that do throw light on the proceedings of the ARC fall short of fleshing out the role of women delegates at the conference. Beyond occasional mentions, much needs to be understood from the interactions of these women at this 'opening act of decolonial solidarity' (Thakur, 2019), thus asking, where were the women in the international imagination of this landmark event of post-colonial world-making? Though nominally a cultural conference, the ARC was the fruition of similar ideas brewing in many minds in Asia at the time. Broadly, it was a deliberate continental attempt to interrogate and understand the post-war political future of Asia. This idea of the future was not a narrow focus on foreign policy, instead, it was the holistic account of the political-economic needs of Asian nations and their peoples; and the world they could collectively envision (Mansregh, 1947). It was a moment of liminality in modern Asian history where attempts were made to carve a collective aim for all Asian peoples. The success and impact of this endeavour, though, requires a closer historical analysis, which this study would do from the point of women's diplomatic participation.

The conference covered five principal topics of discussion, namely: national movements for freedom; migration and racial problems; economic development and social services; cultural problems; and women's problems. It had an attendance of around 400 people including delegates and observers from across Asia and some foreign observers (Mansregh, 1947). A cursory glance at the nature of conversations at the ARC gives the impression of how from it emerged the first possibilities of practical political and economic solidarities across Asia. Broadly the attendees shared the feeling echoed in the words of Nehru, how the colonial exploitation had kept the people of Asia away from each other and now it was the time to come together. This does not mean that there weren't disagreements, for example, while there was shared distrust of Western imperialist intentions, similar concerns about the Indian and Chinese influence in the region were raised by the delegates of Ceylon, Burma, Indonesia and Malaya. The tensions between smaller and bigger Asian nations were evident in the various articulations at the conference.

Pandit reflects on the opportunities laid out by the ARC in one of her undated entries (Pandit, nd). Why this piece of writing is important for understanding her diplomatic thought is because she moves beyond the broader proclamations of Asian solidarity therein, which are critical, and lays out a roadmap for how that could be achieved by the inhabitants of the continent. She writes that the experience of the first ARC in the context of the developing world situation indicated a desirability for fostering closer contacts among governments within the region. The ARC was primarily a non-governmental gathering, and Pandit appreciated the work undertaken by such exchanges. However, to her, if Asia was to 'exert its rightful influence in the counsels of the world', it was important for the governments therein to encourage opportunities for a 'collective exchange at an official level of views periodically on matters of common interest' (Pandit, nd).

Pandit argues that since the first meeting of the ARC in India itself, Pakistan, Burma and Ceylon had become independent. Together with China, Egypt and other independent Asian countries, these comprised a population almost equal to that of the rest of the world. Yet, laments Pandit, world issues continued to be viewed and decided through the 'occidental point of view' (Pandit, nd). To disrupt such a situation, free countries in Asia needed to act in unison on matters of international importance. She was realistic about the timeline for the fruition of such a unison, owing mostly to the disparities in the national development of various states and the lack of mutual knowledge among them. This made cooperation difficult to achieve in the immediate years after 1947. But that was precisely the challenge the Asian statesmen had to overcome. It made no sense to Pandit that if the Western countries could achieve agreement on vital issues of economic policy, defence and larger matters of common interest, then why could not the countries of Asia? Why could not countries work towards peace in the aftermath of decolonization and for the upliftment of vast masses of their population agree on working together in the interest of common aims? Thus, she writes about measures to be considered for what she describes as closer cooperation among the 'free peoples of Asia'. In this, Pandit is careful about not breaching the sovereign right of each country to make its own decisions on matters of national as well as international importance, according to the will of its people (Pandit, nd). The latter is important to take note of here as people continue to remain central to Pandit's international imagination. They are not to be side-lined for the will of the state; rather, they are indispensable to the idea of a reformed world order. Thus, continuing reflections on the anti-imperialist roots of her diplomatic and international thought.

The measures for closer cooperation in Asia were focused on deep people-to-people connections while operationalizing greater governmental cooperation. At the same time, Pandit recognized the need to consider how some of the countries were still struggling to gain formal recognition as free states, such as Indonesia. For these, she suggested that until they were recognized as sovereign states and therefore able to participate in formal governmental activities, they be allowed to send observers to government conferences as well as pursue internal activities of cooperation as means available to them allowed.

Considering transcontinental non-Western anti-imperial solidarity, Pandit writes how countries such as Turkey and Egypt had 'historical and intimate interest in more than one continent', both representing the intersections of Europe–Asia and Africa–Asia, respectively. Similarly, the Arab countries had 'interests in their kinsmen and co-religionists in North Africa' (Pandit, nd). To Pandit, the proposed vision of Asian cooperation had to take into account these special interests and not limit them by focusing only on continental understanding of cooperation. Thus, indicating a vision for broader diplomatic cooperation, reflections of which can be seen in the early 20th-century transnational anti-imperial internationalism.

As mentioned earlier, Pandit made concrete suggestions for closer Asian cooperation. These were:

- Greater collection and dissemination of information among Asian countries – the central driving force here was to build better acquaintance between the peoples of Asia as the intelligentsia in the continent at the time knew more about Europe than countries in Asia.
- Regular diplomatic exchange of information and views concerning regional as well as international issues of importance to Asian countries, individually as well as collectively.
- Maintenance of closer contact among country representatives at UN Headquarters as well as between the Permanent Delegates. This cooperation in the multilateral landscape was to extend to 'free and frank consultations' among Asian country representatives during UNGA sessions as well as sessions of specialized agencies of the UN.
- Periodical meetings of government representatives in rotation in their respective capitals, preferably. While making this suggestion, Pandit also provided an opening for deeper engagement with the civil society groups as 'democratic governments depend for the support of their policies from the will of their people'. Thus, she recommended that every effort was required to associate 'representatives of popular groups or institutions' that could influence public opinion with the governmental delegations to such conferences as proposed here (Pandit, nd).
- Increased cultural exchange by facilitating exchange of teachers, technicians and students.
- Formation of a national committee in each state, that would instruct and facilitate active support of their people in the promotion of closer cooperation and better understanding among the Asian peoples (Pandit, nd).

This rather clear roadmap for Asian solidarity is one of the pieces of evidence of the clarity in Pandit's diplomatic thought as well as her brand of diplomacy that intended to be rooted in a holistic communication aligned with the democratic principles she envisaged for India and the world. These suggestions were to lay a roadmap for where Asia would ensure peace for itself as well as play a significant role in world peace and development while remaining outside the influence of the simmering Cold War. One gets a glimpse of Pandit's strategizing for bringing Asian countries together. The influence of the ARC is apparent in this document as that set the ball rolling for this conversation, and so is the leadership role for India in the continent as the suggestions were being made by an Indian diplomat, namely Pandit. However, one does not see either inclinations for regional hegemony or conceptualization of collective security like in Europe, of which Pandit was critical. She also did not envisage this proposal to build what she calls a 'super-Asian state' or an Asian bloc designed with hostility towards any other group or to rival the UN. Rather, this was an avenue of close cooperation where Asia was central to IR and not a peripheral actor in the workings of the Western power. The aim of this proposal was more effective cooperation among the peoples of Asia to work towards broadening freedom, raising standards of living, and establishing peace and justice the world over. These, wrote Pandit, epitomized the purposes and principles of the UN Charter, which the 'free Asian countries' had pledged support to. Peace in the world, she contends, was threatened by the Western conflict of ideologies and ambitions. Asia did not need to be dragged into this contest, which is what is implied in her proposal. Rather it was to devise its own path to safeguard a peaceful world, and Pandit here had proposed a step in that direction.

Interdependence and coexistence: Menon's vision for India's foreign policy

A close look at the Indian foreign policy archives makes clear the importance of Menon in the early years of the MEA. Menon's visions for Indian foreign policy can be traced to her speeches and writings, which tell us about how she envisaged India's place in the world as well as the new world order. In her writings, the recurrent themes are those of peaceful negotiation, avoidance of war at all costs and coexistence and interdependence rooted in the principle of non-alignment. The idea of international morality was central to this conceptualization.

In Menon's analysis of internationalism and foreign policy, one sees a convergence with the Nehruvian ideas of the time. The latter was a post-colonial worldview that was critical as well as wary of the hierarchical nature of the emerging post-imperial world order. This 'internationalist nationalism' of Nehru, as Chacko (2011: 180) argues, was reflected in his rejection of the 'assumption of the equivalence of the "nation" and the "state" and his "consistent advocacy of the post-sovereign-state world order"'. The aim of this vision was the achievement of a world order in which nationalism would be subordinated to an international ethic embedded in 'ethical, non-exploitative relations with others' (Chacko, 2011: 180–181). India's policies on non-alignment, co-existence, active involvement in the UN and rejection of collective defence were all means of working towards this end (Chacko, 2011: 190). Though much has been written about the idea of non-alignment, the existing foreign policy literature barely ever touches upon the women proponents of this idea. Menon, along with Pandit, was one fierce advocate of it. A close look at both their writings also opens the door for a feminist historiographical inquiry into the non-aligned movement as approached through the corridors of the foreign office.

For Menon, non-alignment was one of the core tenets of IFP. It was 'an expression of opinion as well as a statement of clear intention ... an article of faith of countries which have emerged out of colonialism of one kind or the other'. It was a policy that fostered international cooperation for sustaining the national freedom of the decolonized independent states, helping them build national economies, stabilizing political organization and conserving the values distinctive of their cultures (Menon, 1955). The pursuit of security through military pacts, to Menon's mind, was a pursuit of an illusion (Menon, 1962). The use of force, she wrote, could only be resorted to when the national sovereignty of a state is violated. At the same time, she held the belief that the solution to international problems cannot be found in hate campaigns but in promoting mutual understanding and respect for international obligations (Menon, 1962). In an undated article on Indian foreign policy, she expresses how it is imperative to understand that a country's foreign policy is 'determined by its ideals, traditions and most of all by the compulsions of its domestic or internal world' (Menon, nd). Thus, invoking, for us studying IFP, what can be called questions about the roots of India's foreign policy by encouraging a closer look at the background of the international thought of the Indian state.

Conclusion

Feminist decolonial historiography exposes the gendered power relations in the landscape of foreign policy history. It thus brings to the forefront actors and ideas that have thus far been side-lined in mainstream IR and FPA. When applied as a methodology in the context of Indian foreign policy, feminist historiography reveals the gendered nature of the IR discipline and the gendered politics of what constitutes the legitimate sources of FPA. Feminist analysis, moreover, reveals the erasure of women actors and their theory and practice of internationalism from the analysis of post-colonial foreign policy making.

By centring Pandit and Menon's ideas of Asian unity and the core tenets of Indian foreign policy, respectively, this chapter also brings to attention the post-colonial 'utopian' world vision that held the promise of transforming the scales of power and redefining the international system. These ideas also draw our attention to ethics of redistribution, justice and equality that in today's parlance would converse with principles of feminist foreign policy. With the burgeoning conversations on feminist foreign policy in recent years, it is critical to examine the foundations of feminist thinking applied to foreign policy. State pronouncements, beginning with Sweden as the first country to outline and adopt a feminist foreign policy, require more complex deliberation and closer engagement with world history. This chapter also disrupts the notion that feminist foreign policy is a 'Western' idea. Recovering the histories of post-colonial feminist actors holds a mirror to the world prior to the decolonization era of radical world-making (Raza, 2020). This 'post-colonial utopia' was not allowed to survive in the push and pulls of Great Power politics. Feminist decolonial historiography as a method to study contemporary foreign policy discourse and its core concepts, however, opens a novel route for a more equal field of study. It is also a humbling exercise to not forget an era of non-Western world history when utopias were revolutionary visions that were achievable.

10

Gendered Disinformation

Elsa Hedling

Introduction

The rise of digital disinformation as a threat to liberal democracies confronts the role of gender relations in foreign policy in new ways. The acceptance of 'gendered disinformation' as a foreign policy issue signals a gender-informed understanding of digital disinformation as a security concern. Digital disinformation campaigns that emanate from hostile actors around the world deliberately fuel misogyny, stereotypes and biases to manipulate public opinion and voting behaviours. These campaigns thereby intersect with and overlap public debate. Gendered disinformation is often successful because it resonates with the domestic contestation of gender norms. The construction of gendered disinformation as a security concern thereby implicates the sensitive relationship between disinformation and public opinion. The rise of gendered disinformation in the realm of foreign policy therefore challenges the status of gender norms in the liberal order by exposing the vulnerabilities of domestic polarization over gender equality. This chapter aims to introduce gendered disinformation as a foreign policy issue, and to discuss how studying this phenomenon may draw from previous scholarship on gender and feminism in foreign policy.

Digital disinformation, the diffusion of false information on digital platforms with the intent to deceive, strategically targets the foundations of democratic discourse and public deliberation by exploiting societal division around contested norms. It is a valued foreign policy instrument because it allows actors to exploit socio-political cleavages to spread confusion, amplify conflicts and further divide societies. Gender identities and norms have proven particularly susceptible to this form of manipulation (Bradshaw and Henle, 2021). Disinformation narratives gain traction in online networks when they resonate among audiences by connecting with local narratives, myths or identities (Schmitt, 2018). Digital disinformation thereby insects with and amplifies the known effects of online gender-based violence, such as the silencing and censoring of voices (Suzor et al, 2019). Disinformation campaigns, often favoured by autocratic regimes or groups and their allies, thus further weaponize sexist narratives within domestic debates as part of a foreign policy strategy (Di Meco and Brechenmacher, 2020). Analyses of foreign interference in democratic elections have demonstrated how prominent female candidates like nominee Hillary Clinton in the US presidential election of 2016, are disproportionately targeted through disinformation campaigns that exploit stereotypical and biased attitudes in voters (Jensen, 2018; Nee and De Maio, 2019). An increasingly common objective in efforts to distort the democratic process is, therefore, to dissuade women or gender non-conforming persons from pursuing political office, leadership positions or other public roles. These individuals, who are often already vulnerable to discriminatory conditions, are targeted through attacks that instrumentalize gender identity to reinforce a culture of hate (Bradshaw and Henle, 2021). Other targeted communities include perceived representatives of so-called 'gender ideology' contributing to the construction of LGBTQIA+ rights as a critical site for the domestic and geopolitical struggle over values (Edenborg, 2022b; European External Action Service, 2023).

Gendered disinformation is not marginal; it is increasingly recognized as a widespread deliberate and transversal strategy favoured by actors seeking to weaken the foundations of representative democracies (Wilfore, 2022; United Nations, 2023b). It is a transversal strategy because this is a global phenomenon happening across contexts of deliberative politics. As a tactic for foreign interference, it is foremost associated with actors known to invest heavily in information warfare, such as states like Russia and the People's Republic of China and terrorist and far-right and extremist groups (La Cour, 2020: 710; Hameleers, 2023: 2). In times marked by populism and a regressive approach to gender equality in many states (Agius et al, 2020), gendered disinformation is a 'divide and conquer' strategy. It is by fuelling division over gender norms that this form of disinformation serves adversary interests by distorting public debate or even democratic processes such as elections. States and groups that engage in malign influence operations are increasingly seizing upon this opportunity (Tomz and Weeks, 2020). Importantly, digital infrastructures and social media platforms serve as conduits to expand these disinformation campaigns' reach, volume and impact, often cleverly evading automated detection and regulation systems (Martens et al, 2018). Over the past decade, heightened concern surrounding this issue has prompted states such as the United States and the United Kingdom and organizations like the United Nations (UN) and the European Union (EU) to make statements and issue reports recognizing gendered disinformation as a critical foreign policy concern and global threat to democracy (Di Meco and Wilfore, 2021; EU DisinfoLab and #ShePersisted, 2022; United Nations, 2023b; U.S. Department of State, 2023b). During this time, efforts have materialized to assess and counter the harmful effects of digital disinformation through new foreign policy practices (Hedling, 2021), but more gender-informed analyses are needed to address this form of influence and the vulnerabilities that condition it.

This chapter sets the stage for studies of gendered disinformation in foreign policy analysis (FPA). It examines how this phenomenon both constrains and advances the prominence of feminism and gender considerations in foreign policy agendas. The chapter first traces the emergence of gendered disinformation as a security threat. This involves understanding the role of digital technologies and infrastructures, such as social media platforms, in transforming the reach and logic of disinformation as a strategy in foreign policy. Subsequently, it analyses how gendered vulnerabilities become involved in foreign policy and how authoritarian regimes, groups and actors exploit and amplify polarization around gender norms. To discuss how domestic conditions for gender equality become vulnerable in this context, the role of gender norms, representation and state responses are discussed. Finally, the chapter argues for introspection to prompt a gender-informed understanding of societal resilience to disinformation threats in foreign policy. Societal resilience in this context refers to democratic states' ability to withstand foreign interference through disinformation campaigns. Seen in this light, the rise of gendered disinformation may paradoxically serve to bolster the prominence of feminism and gender considerations within foreign policy discourse. Attention to gendered disinformation contributes to codifying gender and women's vulnerability in terms of security in ways that may contribute to challenging mainstream security concerns. Still, these efforts of countering gendered disinformation rest on contested grounds not just because of the polarization around gender norms but also because of the stakes of introspection and the promise of regulation to cope with the challenges of an increasingly digital society.

The rise of digital disinformation

Disinformation has resurfaced as a pressing foreign policy concern in parallel with the rapid advancement of digitalization. Disinformation is 'the distribution, assertion, or dissemination of false, mistaken, or misleading information in an intentional, deliberate, or purposeful effort to mislead, deceive, or confuse' (Fetzer, 2004: 223). Furthermore, disinformation advances political goals such as 'discrediting opponents, disrupting policy debates, influencing voters, inflaming existing social conflicts, or creating a general backdrop of confusion and informational paralysis' (Bennett and

Livingston, 2020: 3). In foreign policy, disinformation is used in malign influence operations, intending to spread false information to pursue a goal, sometimes alongside military operations. Disinformation is not a new phenomenon (Martin, 1982). Propaganda and influence operations are ancient practices in states' attempts to reach foreign policy goals. However, the modern incarnation of disinformation is noteworthy due to its reliance on and patterns of digital dissemination, setting it apart from traditional propaganda efforts. While the academic study of disinformation in its traditional propaganda form has flourished since the Second World War, the current dominant conceptualization of the study of digital disinformation or 'networked propaganda' is relatively new, emerging around 2017 (Benkler et al, 2018; Freelon and Wells, 2020). It was in conjunction with Russia's illegal annexation of regions of Ukraine in 2014 that many governments became aware that Russia had weaponized its digital capacities for disinformation campaigns (Mejias and Vokuev, 2017). The reinvigorated research agenda resulted from the aftermath of the 2016 US presidential election when social media companies acknowledged that both foreign and domestic actors had manipulated their platforms.

Unlike propaganda, digital disinformation often serves political goals through a more fluid approach to ideology. Political goals can range from influencing candidate selection, gaining momentum for a party or issue position or causing general harm (that is, fuelling cynicism and distrust towards the government) (Hameleers, 2023: 3). This is notable in its intersecting with political polarization in a 'post-truth' era where digital media is the main space for contentious propagation (Bennett and Livingston, 2018). Disinformation campaigns exploit existing divisions and vulnerabilities within societies, adapting their messaging to resonate with different audiences or exploit specific issues or events (Reddi et al, 2023). This adaptability allows disinformation to transcend traditional political boundaries and makes it a potent tool for those seeking to manipulate public opinion and shape political discourse. The proliferation of disinformation in the digital age can be attributed to several factors, including the ease of sharing information on social media platforms, the speed at which false narratives can spread, and the anonymity digital channels provide to those who propagate it. Disinformation campaigns leverage the interconnected nature of social media, operating under a 'networked logic' (Friedland et al, 2006). This approach amalgamates diverse behaviours of various actors who collectively create, spread and consume disinformation across various online platforms (Hameleers, 2023). These campaigns can manifest in different forms, including authentic social media users, influential figures, domestic and foreign political entities, alternative and mainstream news outlets, and trolls or automated bots. Those who initiate disinformation campaigns adeptly exploit this networked logic, often enlisting the involvement of other actors who may not necessarily share the explicit goal of deceiving their audience. These actors could include opinionated social media users or news media outlets. By doing so, they exploit the genuine, often passionate expressions of opinions and beliefs in social media spaces, as well as the competitive and fast-paced nature of news media, all of which further blur the lines between truth and falsehood in the digital space (Lanoszka, 2019; Ördén, 2022). This strategic orchestration of various participants within the networked public sphere amplifies the reach and impact of disinformation campaigns, making them increasingly challenging to detect and attribute. The complexity of the digital diffusion of disinformation presents unique challenges for foreign policy makers and governments worldwide (Bennett and Livingston, 2020).

Gendered disinformation as a security concern

Despite a steep increase in attention to the disinformation problem in foreign policy scholarship in the last decade, relatively few studies have focused on its gendered characteristics, although there are a few exceptions (Edenborg, 2022b; Wilfore, 2022; Esposito, 2023). In exploiting existing divisions and vulnerabilities within societies, gender norms and other identity-based differences, such as class or race, are favoured targets to mobilize polarization and suspicion for political gain (Farkas and Neumayer, 2020). This manipulation is performed in tandem with overarching matrices of power, for example, White supremacy, heteronormativity and patriarchy (Reddi et al, 2023: 2203). While attacks on gender thus belong to a broader set of issues prone to polarization in Western societies, gendered disinformation alone has been lifted to a security concern of its own standing (U.S. Department of State, 2023b). Gendered disinformation or 'gender-based disinformation' are terms interchangeably used by governments, organizations and activists to refer to the convergence of disinformation and gender, leading to a situation where women, gender non-conforming individuals and marginalized groups, including LGBTQIA+ individuals, are disproportionately subjected to targeted harassment through the dissemination of deceitful or erroneous content about them, often on social media platforms. The tactics employed in spreading gendered disinformation vary widely. They may include misogynistic remarks that perpetuate gender stereotypes, the dissemination of explicit content with sexual connotations, and online harassment involving threats of violence, often in tandem with cyberattacks (EU DisinfoLab and #ShePersisted, 2022).

In a widely cited report describing the problem of gendered disinformation, Lucina Di Meco and Brechenmacher (2020) defined it as 'the spread of deceptive or inaccurate information and images used against women political leaders, journalists, and female public figures, following storylines that draw on misogyny and stereotypical gender roles'. Gendered disinformation not only diffuses misogynistic narratives but also seeks to reinforce that bias (Sessa, 2020). This strategy is crafted to leverage pre-existing gender narratives, linguistic constructs and, in essence, discrimination itself to accomplish specific social and political objectives. These objectives encompass the preservation of a current state of gender inequality and the cultivation of a more divided and polarized electorate. In a report to the UN Secretary-General, the Special Rapporteur on the promotion and protection of the right to freedom of opinion and expression, Irene Khan, explained that 'gendered disinformation is gendered because it targets women and gender non-conforming individuals because of the gendered nature of the attacks and their gendered impact, and, very importantly because it reinforces prejudices, bias and structural and systemic barriers that stand in the way of gender equality and gender justice' (United Nations, 2023b: 25).

As a foreign policy tactic, disseminating gendered disinformation harnesses deeply ingrained societal beliefs, stereotypes and linguistic conventions surrounding gender to nudge individuals to adopt increasingly extreme positions, deepening political divisions, and making productive dialogue and compromise more challenging. Moreover, this strategy often uses divisive gender narratives to divert attention from other pressing social and political issues. Highlighting gender-related controversies framed as 'gender ideology' can distract the public from addressing critical matters such as economic inequality, healthcare and environmental concerns. This diversionary tactic effectively serves the interests of those who wish to maintain the status quo by preventing meaningful discussions and actions on these pressing issues. In practice, this strategy can manifest in various forms, including exploiting gender-based fears, stereotypes and biases in political campaigns, media narratives and policy debates. It manipulates language and imagery to reinforce these biases, further entrenching discriminatory practices and fuelling division within society.

A growing awareness of the weaponized potential of gendered disinformation has led to calls for seeing the gravity of the problem beyond a narrative tactic alongside others. Recent reports agree that gendered disinformation is a global trend; it comes in different shapes and forms but serves the same purpose and it is often successful (Sessa, 2020). Since 2020, states like the US and the UK have recognized gendered disinformation as a national security concern (Di Meco and Wilfore, 2021). The construction of gendered disinformation as a security concern has broader implications for the nexus of gender and disinformation. Addressing the exploitation of gendered narratives in political debates in foreign interference disrupts the normalization of online gender-based violence by which accepting it as the new and tougher rules of the political game effectively disqualifies those not capable of coping. On the other hand, the effects of the threat construction itself can be used for political gain. For instance, populist and far-right parties using pro-gender norms as a benchmark against multiculturalism have claimed nationalist ideas of gender equality (Towns et al, 2014; Scrinzi and Blee, 2023) and their externalization as a frontier of Western boundary-making (Agius and Edenborg, 2019; Edenborg, 2022b). In the context of foreign policy, a gender perspective on disinformation challenges the militarization of hybrid threats by further problematizing the protection of public opinion. To this end, it is essential to recognize that the polarization around gender norms is more complex than the conservative/progressive scale. The construction of gendered disinformation as a security concern, therefore, serves multiple interests of domestic groups, states and non-state actors with stakes in the politicization of gender norms.

Foreign policy and gendered vulnerabilities

To grasp the aggressive nature of gendered disinformation, we must consider how polarization around gender equality and gender norms present domestic vulnerabilities in foreign policy. This volume demonstrates that gender and foreign policy intersect across various areas and practices, warranting the intersection of international feminist theory and FPA (Aggestam and True, 2020). Recent research on feminist foreign policy has demonstrated how gender norms and feminism can be leveraged as foreign policy assets (Thomson, 2022a). Gendered disinformation adds to the list of how gender norms and their policy outcomes become situated in the interests of and interactions between states in the international system. Disinformation as a communicative practice contributes to reinforcing or manipulating public deliberations of facts and values that are productive of state identity (Wells and Friedland, 2023). Gendered disinformation thereby contributes to externalizing the role of gender equality through the deliberate contestation of its role in state identity. The status of gender foremost in terms of gender equality thereby becomes a source of weakness in need of recognition and protection in the foreign policies of the targeted states. In foreign policy, vulnerability refers to a state's susceptibility to various external threats, challenges or risks that can compromise its security, stability, status or wellbeing (Foster, 2008). Gendered disinformation, therefore, operates as a catalyst that prompts states to identify their 'gendered vulnerabilities'. The construction of gendered disinformation as a distinct security concern forces nations to confront and acknowledge their susceptibilities in terms of the status of gender equality and the societal anchoring of gender norms. By emphasizing these vulnerabilities, the discourse surrounding gendered disinformation compels states to re-evaluate and fortify their stance on gender-related issues within the broader context of their foreign policies. In essence, the intentional distortion and manipulation of gender-related narratives serve as a mechanism through which states grapple with and respond to the perceived threats posed by geopolitical struggles over gender norms.

International Relations feminist research has explored how gender is constitutive in constructing and reproducing state identities (Sjoberg, 2011) and in the political ordering of international hierarchies (Tickner, 2001). Militarization reinforces gender roles (Agostino, 1998) and security practices construct gendered bodies as ontologically vulnerable (Wilcox, 2015). Gendered vulnerability is further invoked in status-seeking and boundary-making processes where gender and sexual politics are recast along 'national(ist) and civilisational lines' (Edenborg, 2022b: 511). In the context of foreign policy, states advancing pro-gender norms in the global arena, gender is complicit in the constitution of agent and structure in 'gendered multileveled games' (Aggestam and True, 2021: 151). In the construction of gendered disinformation as a security concern, gender is invoked in terms of vulnerability, where 'gender' represents both valued assets and perceived liabilities that hostile states can target. Therefore, studying gendered disinformation in FPA involves attention to the various ways states expose gendered vulnerability. In the remainder of this section, I present a framework for considering gendered vulnerabilities as domestic factors within FPA with focus on clashing norms, the stakes of representation and state responses.

Clashing norms

The role of gender as a focal point in adversarial geopolitics underscores the persistent theme of clashing norms within the global landscape (Razack, 2005). As more states have committed to standards of gender-balanced decision-making and gender mainstreaming since the mid-1990s, strategies to increase the gender balance in political and public life have spread worldwide (Krook and True, 2012). But these norms have also been resisted within domestic politics (Thomson, 2022a) and on international stages for norm contestation, such as in the UN (Ün, 2019). This construction of gender norms as a geopolitical boundary has been reproduced both by states positioning themselves as conservative gender regimes and their progressive 'others'. Gender norms have therefore become central to processes of constructing and safeguarding political and cultural communities, not least as a way of distinguishing Western commitment to progressive values, secularism and gender equality from their reactionary alternatives (Edenborg, 2022b: 499). Most notably, the trend in proclaiming feminist foreign policies instrumentalizes confrontation over gender norms through global positionings and externalization of feminist state identities. At the same time, the threat against these norms in the domestic arena is foremost vocalized through anti-immigration discourse (Towns et al, 2014). Russia has further instrumentalized these narrative complexities through the advancement of its traditional values doctrine that serves both domestic and global interests of political homophobia and 'moral or sexual sovereignty' as foreign policy (Moss, 2017). Hence, the role of clashing gender norms in foreign policy results from the value-driven and strategic interests of states positioning themselves on the global stage (Aggestam and True, 2021: 401).

Disinformation, as a malign foreign policy tactic, serves to weaponize contestation over gender norms by reinforcing state positions along these lines while at the same time exploiting democratic deliberation and freedom of expression by fuelling division and polarization. The salience of clashing gender norms may thus serve the construction of foreign policy roles, such as in the example of Russia. However, producing domestic fragmentation over 'gender ideology' in targeted democracies is a further tactic to distort, distract and divide (Morgan, 2018). Through disinformation campaigns strategically aimed at shaping public opinion by amplifying polarization, gendered narratives gain traction and become visible in political struggles across societal levels. The narrative unfolds as disinformation campaigns strategically exploit societal fault lines, emphasizing perceived clashes between divergent cultural norms. This narrative, rooted in multiculturalism posing a risk to liberal European values, resonates within democratic public spheres where concerns about preserving cultural identity and core values are particularly salient (Edenborg, 2022b).

While there are undoubtedly multiple political interests involved in the antagonistic portrayal of clashing gender norms, the active participation of women and sexual minorities in politics often presents a significant and formidable challenge to entrenched illiberal and autocratic political regimes (Aggestam and True, 2021). Increased participation of women has disrupted the predominantly male-dominated political networks that have traditionally played a central role in fostering corruption and the abuse of power throughout history (Swamy et al, 2001). While the relationship between gender and corruption is more complex (Stensöta et al, 2015), the gradual involvement of women in the political arena exposes a fear of the perceived dismantling of the long-standing societal structures. Furthermore, the active participation of women and sexual minorities in politics can lead to a transformative shift in policy priorities. Issues that have been side-lined, such as gender equality, LGBTQIA+ rights, and social justice, come to the forefront of the political agenda. This shift challenges the prevailing illiberal and autocratic policies that have neglected these vital concerns.

Understanding how gendered disinformation activates these clashing gender norms, therefore, requires understanding how state positions along gendered lines become vulnerabilities to the targeted states. This includes accounting for variations in how disinformation intersects with clashing gender norms across political contexts. In South Asia, for instance, disinformation is most often encountered along lines of division on gender, religion and caste (Nguyễn et al, 2022). In sub-Saharan Africa, it is common for women politicians, journalists and human rights defenders to be portrayed as attacking family values, often through the lenses of neo-colonialism, where women's rights activists and gender rights defenders are seen to be succumbing to 'Western values' (Tripp, 2015; Cloward, 2016; United Nations, 2023b: 25). In Latin America, women and gender non-conforming persons are often attacked for spreading 'gender ideology', further positioning gender norms as proxies for all forms of social dissatisfaction (Beltrán and Creely, 2018). In countries where women have emerged as some of the most vocal critics of what is often referred to as 'hypermasculine populism', broadly understood as radical right-wing movements mobilized by sexism and misogyny, gendered disinformation is a strategy for perpetuating the belief that politics is inherently tainted, cynical and prone to violence (Marwick et al, 2022).

Rising stakes of gender representation

As efforts of gender mainstreaming have gradually increased the representation of women in public and political life, the stakes of safeguarding such representation and its underlying democratic principles become higher. This is true beyond the context of democracies; research has found that electoral autocracies are perceived as more democratic when women's descriptive representation is greater (Bush and Zetterberg, 2021; Bjarnegård and Zetterberg, 2022). When gender representation is recognized as a democratic status signal and as a symbol of societal advancements, malign influence to distort or decrease the gender balance becomes a threat to the state. This threat is potentially even graver in contexts where states have actively externalized gender equality as an identity marker in their international politics, for instance, through the incorporation of the UN's Women, Peace and Security agenda as a core pillar in their foreign policies (Aggestam and True, 2020). For example, gender-balanced governments have been found to receive a disproportionate amount of gendered online harassment (Van Sant et al, 2021). As the stakes of gender representation have increased, so has the vulnerability to campaigns seeking to erode its status from within.

Among the tactics recognized as gendered disinformation are attempts to target women (and other minority groups) in positions of power and visibility, such as politicians, journalists or activists. These campaigns often pass below the radar of detection and attribution because gendered slurs and hate speech are normalized and less regulated than other forms of discrimination (Weston-Scheuber, 2012). These campaigns vary from using gendered stereotypes to dehumanize the 'out-group' comprising women or individuals within the LGBTQIA+ community to very specifically targeted campaigns against individuals by spreading lies, mobilizing hate speech, threats, cyberbullying, and so on (European External Action Service, 2023: 20). By reinforcing existing preconceptions and biases, it fosters an environment conducive to discrimination and hostility, worsening the marginalization and isolation experienced by the already vulnerable 'out-group' members.

Among the long list of politicians and foreign policy leaders that have been targeted by gendered disinformation are US Vice President Kamala Harris, Elisa Loncon, the former President of the Constitutional Convention in Chile, and the Federal Minister for Foreign Affairs of Germany, Annalena Baerbock. Harris and Loncon were both targeted on social media platforms through campaigns aimed at discrediting them as representatives of historically marginalized communities by sowing doubts about their racial identities and feminine respectability (Ibarra, 2023; Orchard et al, 2023). Baerbock (co-leader of Alliance 90/The Greens party) was a lead candidate (and the only woman in the race to succeed Angela Merkel) in Germany's federal election 2021. Her popularity, however, plummeted after she pledged to block a gas pipeline project between Russia and Europe and became the target of a Russian state-backed disinformation campaign on social media. Baerbock was disproportionately targeted by disinformation compared to the other candidates, and the drive was misogynic in nature, including fake and photoshopped nude images depicting her as a former sex worker. She was also targeted by sexist attacks questioning her ability to balance the responsibilities of chancellorship with motherhood. Baerbock's high approval rate decreased radically, resulting in a lost election. The isolated influence of foreign interference on election results is challenging to assess; there were fact-based revelations of Baerbock's flawed CV, voiced criticism as well as domestic actors that engaged in the gender-based attacks on Baerbock (Faas and Klingelhöfer, 2022). In addition, sexism in media coverage during political elections is an established phenomenon within democracies regardless of external involvement (Haraldsson and Wängnerud, 2019). The ability of foreign actors to exploit and amplify this vulnerability, however, makes this a key concern in foreign policy.

The goal of deterring women from political and civic participation is often aimed at individual women leaders and activists. Still, the scale of the problem has led it to become a threat to the preservation of gender representation in democratic systems. Leaving aside the human toll of these campaigns on those targeted, or even the potential ability to manipulate elections, this phenomenon is also constructed as a security concern because of its relative success rate. Whereas some other areas of democratic deliberation have proven resilient to disinformation (Humprecht et al, 2023), gender-based campaigns often result in silencing the targeted individuals who cannot cope (without sufficient support) and, therefore, are effectively pushed out of public sight. When political candidates are forced out of election races or journalists are discouraged from covering specific stories, democratic principles and processes are weakened.

State responses

Recognizing gendered disinformation as a concern has set policy responses that are expanding the foreign policy toolbox in motion. In March 2023, Canada, the European External Action Service, Germany, Slovakia, the UK and the US commissioned a joint report to assess the tactics used to 'sow gendered and other identity-based disinformation across the world' (U.S. Department of State, 2023a). Accepting this problem as a joint problem and a global threat facing 'countries invested in preserving democracy' signals an increased understanding of gendered vulnerabilities in foreign policy. Other times, it is instead the choice or absence of responses that exposes vulnerabilities. For instance, despite pioneering feminist foreign policy (2014–2022), Sweden never included freedom of speech as a crucial priority in its outward-facing promotion of gender norms (Government of Sweden, 2018a).

Among state responses to gendered disinformation and the broader set of weaponized information capacities it represents, more and better regulation of digital platforms is often the prioritized strategy. Policies towards digitalization and the digital economy have been rapidly added to foreign policy strategies (Riordan, 2019). Most states recognize that managing security and foreign policy interests involves understanding and acting on Internet governance and platform regulation (Srivastava, 2021). Within the broader frames of the expanding digital portfolios, governments and their Ministries of Foreign Affairs have become increasingly involved in international or regional attempts to establish better regulatory frameworks for the tech industry and their social media platforms. A key motivating factor for these regulation efforts is the problem of disinformation and the external threat of election manipulation (Datzer and Lonardo, 2022). The EU and its member states have gone furthest in their attempts to counter disinformation, first through voluntary adherence to non-binding regulations, such as the Code of Practice on Disinformation (European Commission, 2018) launched in 2018 that was further strengthened in 2022 (European Parliament and the Council of the European Union, 2022). Since August 2023, the Digital Services Act has significantly increased the EU's mandate to control and manage social media platforms to prevent harmful online activities and the spread of disinformation (European Parliament and the Council of the European Union, 2022). Similar enhanced regulation processes exist elsewhere, such as in Australia, Brazil and South Korea.

The construction of disinformation as a critical threat to democracies and regulation as the path towards greater societal resilience is characterized by techno-solutionism (Wijermars and Makhortykh, 2022), institutional turf battles and geopolitical interests (Datzer and Lonardo, 2022). Framing disinformation and gendered disinformation as an issue that can be solved through greater control of the online sphere and its actors avoids confronting the role of the patriarchy in reproducing gendered vulnerabilities. Instead, it serves opportunities for further global positioning. The EU's mandate to regulate makes it the most suitable course of action on disinformation (Bouza García and Oleart, 2023). It also presents opportunities to exercise regulatory leadership in the digital economy (Council of the European Union, 2023). Moreover, the focus on regulation as the primary strategy for state responses to disinformation largely ignores the fact that it is challenging to distinguish disinformation from other forms of political communication, such as contentious politics, tendentious interpretations or satire. As a solution, it therefore also undermines the complexities in which disinformation campaigns exacerbate societal divisions. Therefore, the problem of gendered disinformation demonstrates the many shortcomings of the regulatory approach.

In addition to regulation, other public state responses focus on strategic communication, censorship, media literacy and media pluralism. Since digital disinformation emerged as a key concern in 2017, many governments have encouraged various strategies to counter disinformation by strengthening societal resilience. These include countermeasures such as fact-checking, myth-busting and censorship in situations of threat, as was the case in the EU following Russia's invasion of Ukraine in 2022 (Golovchenko, 2022). In addition to designated agencies and groups involved in these strategies, efforts have been directed at educating and training state officials in digital literacy and disinformation awareness, especially those engaged in international domains (Hedling, 2023). While these efforts increasingly include attention to gendered disinformation, this is not a policy area in which gender perspectives are salient. This is partly explained by the fact that hybrid threats and influence operations are dominated by traditional and masculine conceptions of security (Tickner, 2004). In addition to the risk of side-lining gendered disinformation as identity-based narratives among all others, this dominance results in the continuous focus on the aggressor (foreign interference) and the defence of the state (societal resilience) rather than on the (gendered) vulnerabilities.

Introspection and gendered resilience in foreign policy

Gendered disinformation emerges as part of a broader political strategy. As this chapter demonstrates, these tactics exploit gendered vulnerabilities within societies in the pursuit of foreign policy goals. Gendered disinformation flourishes in environments characterized by limitations on gender equality, legislative backlash and constraints on women's freedom of expression. This phenomenon is not confined to authoritarian states but is increasingly manifesting in emerging and well-established democracies (Yildirim et al, 2021; Off, 2023). This trend represents a pattern marked by the erosion of human rights and a pushback against women and sexual minorities' rights within the democratic framework (Cupać and Ebetürk, 2021). Geopolitics, identity politics and turf battles in both the construction of the problem and the mobilization for solutions shape these patterns. While efforts to counter these forms of foreign interference are symptomatic, addressing gendered vulnerability also calls for preventive strategies. Since the launch of the UN's Women, Peace and Security agenda, gender-responsive approaches have gained momentum in foreign policy and materialized across domains such as diplomacy, peace, security, aid, and so on. Gendered disinformation as a set of problems recognized as a broader societal challenge intersects with these domains in various ways. There is thus ample opportunity to include gendered disinformation in the study and practice of feminism and gender in FPA. The digital nature of how gender disinformation operates, however, brings domestic factors to the forefront of FPA in new ways. Therefore, theorizing, studying and fostering 'gendered resilience' in foreign policy requires attention to both the internal sources of vulnerability and the opportunity to advance feminism and gender considerations in foreign policy agendas in new ways. To address the vulnerability, we must first identify, analyse and accept gender inequality as a subsisting and homegrown problem. To strengthen the ability to withstand the external attempts to exploit this vulnerability, we must engage in both introspection and recognition of the causes and effects of gendered disinformation.

First, fostering resilience in this context requires a better awareness of how and why gendered vulnerabilities within societies become suspectable to foreign interference. This includes introspection and reflexivity in understanding the structures productive of gender inequality as well as the absence of adequate protection against gender-based hate speech and online violence in the domestic context. For instance, when female politicians are disproportionately framed in sexist terms by the news media, media pluralism and free speech contribute to producing gendered vulnerability (Lazarus and Steigerwalt, 2018). Research confirms this enduring bias against women across media contexts (Haraldsson and Wängnerud, 2019). This phenomenon does not result from social media; instead, the known difficulty in regulating gendered hate speech on social media platforms results from normalization in everyday public discourse (Weston-Scheuber, 2012). This is not to say that restrictions on media pluralism or free speech are solutions; instead, it is about identifying the root causes. Gendered slurs are reoccurring because they resonate with sexist attitudes and stereotypes: they activate entrenched beliefs and fears about who is and is not worthy of trust, power and visibility in the political arena. To build resilience against manipulation of this societal problem in foreign policy, it might be better to deal with the legal protection of equal rights at home. This is a highly sensitive endeavour in the context of digital disinformation because of the tensions with the values and principles of freedom of expression. However, drawing a line in the water between foreign interference and domestic debate is neither accurate nor particularly useful. Digital disinformation, and perhaps especially so in its gendered form, thrives from the intersection of the manipulated and the homegrown polarization around gender norms. Therefore, engaging in introspection promotes gender-informed analysis of why this form of disinformation is effective and pairs foreign policy initiatives with measures to address these vulnerabilities.

Second, to foster gendered resilience also involves the recognition of misogynistic disinformation campaigns as an articulate and consistent global phenomenon rather than a series of isolated events of online hate speech targeting individuals left with the burden to report occurrences and cope with harassment (Sessa, 2020). Better regulation can indeed assist these processes in the accountability of risks. Still, it must be met with judicial measures and control that involves a whole-of-society approach to gendered disinformation. To grasp the transnational dynamics of how disinformation stories travel and are recirculated across national border, will require more multilateral cooperation. The methods for reporting these instances to digital platforms and ultimately to the domestic law-enforcing institutions are currently based on singular reports of hate speech rather than the ability to launch investigations into orchestrated and transnational campaigns. Moreover, the public needs to be informed about the global scope of this problem through aggregated publicly available data rather than through the media reports that victimize individuals who have been targeted and pushed out of elections or from public roles. These stories of victimhood reinforce the campaign's effect by reproducing narratives of these groups as weak, fragile or incapable of the demands of public scrutiny (Orchard et al, 2023). Governments and Ministries of Foreign Affairs should instead invest more effort in educating the public about the shapes and forms of disinformation campaigns and their relationship to domestic challenges, including but not limited to contestation around gender norms on a global scale. To recognize this as a transversal strategy includes fostering gender analyses in the study and the politics surrounding digital disinformation. Policy experts have conducted most attempts at gender analyses in the field and these need to be strengthened by more systematic academic scholarship. Ultimately, gender disinformation is successful because it resonates with domestic debates and because the individuals targeted by these campaigns do not receive adequate support and backing because of (often gendered) ideas of the high price of public office. Acknowledging the disproportionate targeting as a global pattern should also produce more protective measures for state servants in this community, not least at local and regional levels, where representatives of the targeted communities often start their political careers. The steps taken towards international cooperation are essential in recognizing gendered disinformation as a shared societal challenge. More research with global gender perspectives can further this goal.

Conclusion

Advances in digital technology and the widespread use of social media platforms have extended opportunities for expression, deliberation and the rapid dissemination of information on an unprecedented scale. The same surge in digital media is productive of the rise of online risks and threats. Gendered disinformation is not a new phenomenon, but its expressions and harmful impact have been significantly magnified, making it an effective weapon used to weaken and undermine states committed to inclusive democracy. This form of digital disinformation is, however, more than just one example of the weaponization of identity politics; gendered disinformation exploits deeply engrained patriarchal structures to further challenge the status of gender equality in democracies.

This chapter has examined how the threat of gendered disinformation has entered the domain of foreign policy. Attention to gendered disinformation complements a growing literature on the intersection of gender and foreign policy by illuminating how progressive values and commitment to gender equality are productive of both foreign policy goals and threats to them. The intentional framing of gender equality as a battleground in the clash of norms underscores the nuanced ways geopolitical actors may manipulate public discourse. However, identity-based disinformation does not create these biases against specific social groups. Instead, they find resonance within audiences where pre-existing biases are firmly established (Schmitt, 2018) and where the backlash against gender norms finds domestic engagement and support (Kuhar and Paternotte, 2017). Gendered disinformation intersects with domestic debate and public discourse in deeply troubling ways.

As a field of research, gendered disinformation is uncharted territory in FPA. There is a need to systematically explore how and why gendered disinformation becomes recognized as a security concern, with what consequences for foreign policy, and, not least, the diverse political interests this construction can serve. This chapter has only scratched the surface of how this problem, its consequences and solutions have entered the levels of FPA. More scholarship is needed to theorize and study this phenomenon. The insights discussed in the chapter also prompt a re-evaluation of counter-disinformation strategies. Instead of exclusively concentrating on the malicious content or the legal complexity of attribution, more significant efforts are needed to comprehend and address the foundational and gendered biases that make individuals susceptible to manipulation. Foreign policies are therefore required to support multilateral frameworks to address gendered disinformation. This includes global recognition of the disproportionate amount of gendered disinformation facing women and gender non-conforming individuals in the digital age and acknowledging that these campaigns are often orchestrated. Shifting focus in this way could result in more precise and impactful interventions, tackling the root causes of vulnerability to disinformation and cultivating a more resilient and discerning public.

11

Defence/Military

Annika Bergman Rosamond and Katharine A.M. Wright

Introduction

In the past decade, feminist and pro-gender foreign policies have emerged across a range of countries as an ethical alternative to traditional foreign policy practices driven mainly by security and national interests. Rather than reproducing narrow definitions of these security interests, which tend to sediment prevalent global inequalities, feminist-informed foreign policies seek to further equality, justice and collective security through a transformation of the global gender order (Aggestam and True, 2020). Despite the growth of war and conflict in global politics, scholarship on gender and feminist approaches to foreign policy has rarely addressed the increasing militarism and militarization of state foreign policies. To address this gap, we ask where and how defence is addressed in feminist-informed foreign policies. The chapter calls for greater attentiveness to feminist scholarship on war as experience, just war theory, pacifism and self-defence to develop a more robust ethical content of pro-gender and feminist foreign policies. We argue that the lack of examination of military and defence policy in existing pro-gender and feminist foreign policies is a silence echoed in feminist scholarship.

We posit that defence is a core part of most states' foreign policies,[1] including those states which have adopted pro-gender and feminist approaches to foreign policy. Defence refers to activities focused on the protection of the state from external attack, whereby a range of institutional

---

[1] A notable exception is Costa Rica, for example, which reinvested its whole defence budget in health services.

and material capabilities (the armed forces and the military) are employed to defend the nation against war. Importantly, defence

> is distinct from security, which can be defined more broadly and holistically to focus beyond (just) the state, to include the individual and thus can include a range of issues, such as the environment. It is therefore possible to see why defence with its support for realpolitik can come into tension with feminism, which seeks to challenge such state-centred approaches. (Wright, 2024)

This chapter analyses the relationship between feminist and pro-gender foreign policy on the one hand, and military and defence on the other by engaging with feminist ideas on just war, war as experience, pacifism and self-defence (Ruddick, 1995; Hutchings, 2019). We argue that for foreign policy to be transformative, it must also encompass the broad compass of a state's foreign policy concerns, including defence. We propose that a feminist approach to just war can help to address some of the ethical tensions of applying feminist principles to defence. To illustrate this argument, the chapter draws on a range of examples, including the recent war in Ukraine. This enables us to explore the right to self-defence versus (some Western) feminist defence of pacifism. Both concepts come to a head when a feminist-informed foreign policy is applied to defence and the military. Furthermore, the 2021 withdrawal of North Atlantic Treaty Organization (NATO) forces from Afghanistan showed the limits of practising pro-gender and feminist foreign policies in the face of pressing geopolitical developments.

The chapter consists of three main parts. First, we identify a lack of attentiveness to matters of defence in scholarship on pro-gender and feminist foreign policies. Second, we explore the absence of defence and notions of just war in existing feminist-informed foreign policies. Third, we reflect on feminist interventions in debates on just war, pacifism and the right to self-defence (Ruddick, 1995; Sjoberg, 2006; Hutchings, 2019) to understand what such an approach might add to normative considerations of how feminist and/or pro-gender foreign policies apply to defence.

The absence of defence in pro-gender and feminist foreign policy

Traditionally, foreign policy analysis has been critiqued for being 'gender blind' (Smith, 2019). Yet, since the 1960s, feminist peace studies scholars have highlighted the importance of taking account of gender-based insights to understand foreign and security policy (Lyytikainen et al, 2021). This is mirrored in the work by scholars located within feminist International Relations who began to analyse foreign policy through a feminist lens from the 1980s onwards (Enloe, 1989 [2014]; Tickner, 1992). The adoption of pro-gender foreign policy by an increasing number of states (Aggestam and True, 2020), and most notably, the adoption of fully fledged feminist foreign policies, tell us that sensitivity to gender and intersectional variation is central to foreign policy analysis. This involves recognizing that people's lives are affected by interlocking structures of oppression, domination and inequality based on gender, class and race/ethnicity (hooks, 2015).

The adoption of pro-gender and feminist foreign policies among several states has triggered the emergence of prolific research, adding feminist insights to the analysis of foreign and security policy. Key here is research that explores the close relationship between the Women, Peace and Security (WPS) agenda, gender-just peacebuilding, and feminist and pro-gender foreign policies (Aggestam and Bergman Rosamond, 2019). For example, Aggestam and Bergman Rosamond (2021) propose that peace diplomacy undertaken within the frames of feminist foreign policy needs to be inclusive, dialogical and intersectional, and, as such, challenge the structural inequalities that produce gendered harms and armed conflict worldwide. Worth mentioning here is also research on the peacebuilding ambitions of Sweden's former feminist foreign policy, not least in relation to women's roles in multilateral peacebuilding and peace negotiations (Bergman Rosamond and Wibben, 2021).

However, to date there has been little effort to study defence within scholarship on feminist and pro-gender foreign policies (Wright and Bergman Rosamond, 2024; Bergman Rosamond, 2024; Wright, 2024). We propose here that scholarship on pro-gender and feminist foreign policy would benefit from a stronger focus on defence, not least in times of militarism, war and armament around the world. Feminist International Relations and security studies scholars have long explored the gendered effects of war, conflict and militarism on women's lives and political communities more broadly (Stern and Stavrianakis, 2018; Enloe, 2023). Others have studied war as embodied and emotional lived experience (Enloe, 2010; Sylvester, 2013; Bergman Rosamond and Kronsell, 2022). As Sylvester (2013: 65) has noted, '(t)o study war as experience requires that the human body come into focus as a unit that has agency in war and is also the target of war's violence'. As such, there is feminist scholarship on the ethical and gendered underpinnings of national militaries, which identifies a strong link between militarized masculinities and national military policy (Kronsell, 2012; Duncanson, 2013).

Nonetheless, feminist understandings of just war, pacifism and self-defence have been insufficiently considered in the literature on pro-gender foreign policy, but also by states that have through their foreign policies sought to transform the global gender order. Specifically, we explore the absence of meaningful consideration of defence and militarism in feminist-informed foreign policy in relation to the Gaza war in 2023, the full-scale Russian invasion of Ukraine in 2022, and the withdrawal of NATO from Afghanistan in 2021.

Feminist-informed foreign policy engagements with defence

Defence is a core part of the foreign policy apparatus, though not necessarily recognized as such. Indeed, many states have not articulated how a feminist or pro-gender foreign policy framework could inform their strategic thinking on defence, or the actual use of armed force in the event of an armed attack on them or their allies. This is not to say that states have not sought to apply pro-gender norms, notably by the application of the WPS agenda, to their approach of defence, and in some cases have begun to consider what a feminist or pro-gender approach to defence might look like. Even so, such an approach usually has not required a wholescale reprioritization of defence from a feminist ethical perspective.

Nonetheless, some efforts have been made to operationalize and integrate the WPS agenda in the military. For example, in 2019 the UK published Joint Service Publication 1325 to provide guidance on the military application of WPS (subsequently updated to Joint Service Publication 985 in 2021) (Ministry of Defence, 2019; 2021). Militarily neutral Ireland, which branded itself as a pro-gender state in its successful bid for a seat on the United Nations (UN) Security Council (Bergman Rosamond and Wright, 2023) has not shied away from engaging the WPS agenda in defence policy by adopting the third iteration of its Defence Action Plan in 2020 (Irish Defence Forces, 2020). Australia, which is another state pursuing a feminist-informed foreign policy by stealth (Lee-Koo, 2020), has engaged extensively with WPS in defence, with the Australian Defence Force's work on WPS being recognized as an example of best practice by UN Women (UN Women, 2015).

Sweden is an interesting case here given that the WPS agenda has been a consistent pillar of its defence policy, informing the armed forces' operational work and military training (Bergman Rosamond and Wibben, 2021). Nonetheless, defence and military policies were omitted from the country's overarching feminist foreign policy framework throughout its life cycle (2014–2022). This omission arguably contributed to the gendered silencing of feminist foreign policy as Sweden sought to join NATO in response to Russia's full-scale invasion of Ukraine with the newly elected Conservative-led government formally dropping the feminist framing of its foreign policy in October 2022 (Wright and Bergman Rosamond, 2024). While such silencing could (wrongly) be interpreted as an effort to demilitarize Swedish foreign policy, Bergman Rosamond and Wibben (2021) have argued that it is better understood as a pronounced reluctance to locate defence inside the feminist foreign policy framework. The introduction of feminist foreign policy coincided instead with Sweden's gradual increase in the national defence budget and with the securitization of its national borders.

Other states have begun to consider what incorporating defence into their approach to feminist-informed foreign policy might entail. Luxembourg has stated that its feminist foreign policy will include defence as part of its 'three D's' of 'diplomacy, development and defence', though the country has yet to fully articulate what this will look like (The Gender Security Project, 2023). While the German Ministry of Defence is not formally in charge of the implementation of the country's feminist foreign policy, the Federal Office views it as a key partner helping to ensure 'coherent joint efforts' to implement feminist foreign policy across all external facing policy portfolios (Federal Foreign Office, 2023b). In practice, what German defence policy's engagement with feminist foreign policy should mean has yet to be fully articulated beyond advocacy at the European level for the inclusion of the WPS agenda in the Common Security and Defence Policy (Federal Foreign Office, 2023b). Indeed, the German Greens have been active in promoting feminist foreign policy in the European Parliament (Guerrina et al, 2023a). Spain, another state adopting a feminist foreign policy, has incorporated gender training into its military operations and supported the increased representation of women in the EU Common Security and Defence Policy (Government of Spain, 2021). What is more, through their support for the WPS agenda, a key aspect of most feminist and pro-gender foreign policies, Western states have sought to make multilateral peacekeeping operations more gender-just. For example, Germany's 2021–2024 WPS national action plan seeks to add more women to international peace operations, actively reduce conflict-related sexual violence, sexual exploitation and abuse in missions as well as supporting women in local peacebuilding processes (Federal Foreign Office, 2021). Yet, increasingly states in the Global South are the ones that contribute to international peacekeeping operations, rather than Western states that have adopted feminist foreign policies. This is indicative of the hollowness of Western' states feminist commitments to multilateral peacekeeping commitments.

In sum, states with a feminist-informed foreign policy have not fully applied feminist approaches to military matters. Evidence of this can be seen in their responses to the withdrawal of all NATO forces from Afghanistan and Russia's full-scale invasion of Ukraine.

Western withdrawal from Afghanistan

The way in which the US and its allies withdrew their troops from Afghanistan lacked a strategy for sustaining the rights and livelihoods of Afghan women. They left Afghan women more vulnerable to gendered harms, violence and discrimination given the new regime and the rapid and generally ill-thought-through withdrawal by Western forces. Notably, the US and the 'coalition of the willing' continuously justified their prolonged military presence in Afghanistan on the basis of women's human rights and bodily integrity (Akbari and True, 2024).[2] However, the consideration of the status of women in Afghanistan was not part of the decision to withdraw the NATO Resolute Support Mission with little warning. This decision came from the US, with allies having little choice but to toe the line given the weight of US geopolitical power. The result was the resurgence of the Taliban and a devastating setback for women's rights and freedoms in Afghanistan (Akbari and True, 2022). There was seemingly no room for pro-gender or feminist approaches to foreign policy in defence. The gendered logics of the invasion could also be seen in the use of Female Engagement Teams in Afghanistan, a strategy that was employed by some states with a feminist-informed and pro-gender foreign policies, notably Sweden, to both extract intelligence from local populations, not least Afghan women, but also as a way of lending credence to their long presence in Afghanistan (Bergman Rosamond and Kronsell, 2018; Greenberg, 2023).

Germany's policy towards Ukraine

In the current geopolitical climate, Germany is also an interesting case to consider: The country has developed its feminist foreign policy in the context of Russia's full-scale invasion of Ukraine. The German government has rejected the notion that feminist foreign policy requires pacifism, rather opting for policy pragmatism in the face of war. This is a clear message put across in its guiding feminist foreign policy document, which states that 'feminist foreign policy does not provide a magic formula that can be used to eliminate immediate threats Russia's war against Ukraine in the face of brutal violence' and that 'human lives must be protected by military means ... Thus feminist foreign policy is not synonymous with pacifism' (Federal Foreign Office, 2023b: 13). This is seemingly the position in a range of European states with France, Luxembourg, the Netherlands, Slovenia and Spain also having decided that their feminist foreign policies are reconcilable with both NATO membership and support for Ukraine' war efforts.

Despite such pronounced support for Ukraine's self-defence by states committed to pro-gender or feminist foreign policies, there is gendered

---

[2] Some Afghan feminists, however, such as, Malalai Joya, a former Afghan parliamentarian, had long called for the withdrawal of troops from Afghanistan, being of the firm view that the presence of American and allied troops could never lead to sustainable and gender just peace in their country (see *The Independent*, 2021).

silence on what the broader feminist and WPS implications of this move might be (Wright, 2022a; 2022b). Thus, the invasion of Ukraine, though large in European discourse, lacks a more meaningful feminist ethical analysis (Bergman Rosamond, 2022). It is important to unpack such silences by asking questions regarding the lack of distinct feminist principles in states' approaches to defence and deterrence. Some might attribute this silence or side-lining of feminist concerns to policy pragmatism, for example, as a way of countering Russian claims that feminism and gender equality are western imports, which is something feminists in Russia strongly object to (Bias, 2023). However, we see little evidence that the return to *realpolitik* without feminist insight supports this position, given how it has been applied, for example without consultation with Ukrainian women on the ground. More broadly, we should consider here whether the side-lining of feminist concerns at this critical juncture is a result of the silence around the relationship between pro-gender and feminist approaches to foreign policy and defence more broadly. It should also be noted that such pragmatism and silencing of feminist principles and gender equality have not generally been favoured by Ukraine, rather the latter updated its National Action Plan on WPS in 2023, becoming the first state to do so during an active conflict (United Nations, 2023a). Thus, feminist scholarship needs to consider the consequences of such silences.

Responses to the war in Gaza

The Gaza war in 2023 is another case in point where feminist ethical considerations have not been applied to the responses of some states with pro-gender and feminist foreign policies. For example, both the Netherlands and Germany have expressed their unequivocal support for Israel's right to self-defence in the face of the Hamas attacks on Israeli civilians without thoroughly reflecting on the humanitarian effects this would have on the Palestinian civilians in Gaza. Moreover, there have been clampdowns on pro-Palestinian protests in France. Interestingly, Mexico, another state committed to feminism in foreign policy, took a more neutral position (Jayakumar, 2023). While we might have expected states such as Germany, the Netherlands and France to engage in a more thorough feminist analysis of the gendered harms of the war, given their commitment to feminism in foreign policy, there has been little such reflection, despite many of the victims of the war being women and girls. For example, a good number of the Israeli hostages captured by Hamas were elderly women (Thompson, 2023) and sexual violence was widespread during Hamas' initial attack in early October 2023. Meanwhile, the siege of Gaza has had a devastating impact on Palestinian women and girls, with the lack of antenatal and reproductive care being a key example here (Barr, 2023).

The silencing of feminism across the two examples accounted for earlier, at least in part, are attributable to the lack of consideration of what a feminist lens on defence might look like. In terms of the wider WPS agenda, as we have demonstrated here, tensions remain between the purpose of defence and the normative and anti-militarist foundations of the WPS agenda (Wright, 2022c). It is therefore unsurprising that the inclusion of defence in feminist foreign policy – envisioned as a transformative approach to the practice of foreign policy, which can operate within current geopolitical realities – in particular has struggled to move beyond declaration and an engagement with the WPS agenda. We therefore propose that feminist engagements with just war theory could help to address these tensions.

Feminism, just war and pacifism

As we have argued, defence is largely missing from feminist and pro-gender scholarship on foreign policy, along with the practice of feminist-informed foreign policies. By implication, there has been little or no effort to locate the analysis of pro-gender foreign policies within a just war framework, in particular feminist attempts to rethink that tradition. Just war theory emerged as a way of addressing the question whether it is ever ethically permissible to resort to war (Rengger, 2002) or military intervention (Bellamy and McLoughlin, 2018) to save human lives from brutal leaders, oppression and violence. Thus, just war theory provides a platform for the analysis of *jus in bello* (justice in war) and *jus ad bellum* (justice of war), and more recently *jus post bellum* (Sjoberg, 2008). This enables reflecting on what the conditions must be for a war to be deemed just, including questions of rightful authority, just cause, rightful intention reasonable hope of success, last resort and proportional use of force.

Of relevance for our argument is the dominance of a male ethical agenda within the just war tradition, whereby large ethical schemes are employed rather than a situated relational ontology (Robinson, 2011; Aggestam et al, 2019). This male dominance, however, has been challenged by feminist scholars who take issue with the gendered and masculinist logic prevalent within just war theory (Sjoberg, 2013; 2016). This also involves exploring feminist ethical reasoning on pacifism and non-violence (Ruddick, 1995; Hutchings, 2019). Of relevance here is also scholarship that unpacks the gendered and militarized underpinnings of Western interventionism (McBride and Wibben, 2012; Bergman Rosamond and Kronsell, 2018).

What then can a feminist approach to just war add to scholarship on pro-gender and feminist foreign policies? Can war ever be justified in feminist terms, and, if so, does this mean that it is compatible with pro-gender and feminist foreign policies? Key to most feminisms is a commitment to non-violence, pacifism and disarmament, and, as such, notions of what constitutes just war are redundant because violence should never be a response to violence. Yet, not all feminists adhere to such pacifism or non-violence no matter what the situation might be, as the case of Ukraine highlights. Many Ukrainian feminists have been clear since the outset of the war that their country requires military means to defend itself, vocally stating this position (Tsymbalyuk and Zamuruieva, 2022; Tsymbalyuk et al, 2022). Far from being passive victims in need of protection, an attribute often assigned to women in war, Ukrainian women have demonstrated considerable agency in their resistance to Russia's invasion (Phillips and Martsenyuk, 2023). Women have joined the military campaign, serving on the frontline, exercising impact on prevalent attitudes towards women within Ukraine (Mathers and Kvit, 2023). On the civilian side, women have a significant role in government and politics, with the female deputy Minister for Defence and women members of parliament proving crucial mobilizing support for Ukraine, while Ukrainian women have mobilized both inside and outside the country to support the war effort and respond to humanitarian emergencies in the conflict areas. As such they have supported survivors of sexual and gender-based violence perpetrated by Russian soldiers while Ukrainian women abroad have organized fundraising initiatives (Phillips and Martsenyuk, 2023: 5). Such efforts have taken place against the backdrop of the wartime economy with women experiencing the gendered impact of the war. This in turn exacerbates gender inequality by placing the burden of care work on women, reinforcing existing economic insecurities, which have been intensified through the imposition of austerity and militarism post-2014 (Mathers, 2020). The Ukraine case has brought to the fore the relevance of distinctively feminist perspectives on ethical questions pertaining to self-defence, pacifism and what constitutes rightful responses to war, all of which have been insufficiently addressed in both feminist foreign policy scholarship and practice. More specifically, the gendered burdens of the war efforts rarely figure in feminist foreign policy discourses. Along with the domestic impact of the war in Ukraine, which is challenging but also entrenching, it is salient to remember that this is a war being waged in deeply gendered ways by Russia. Conflict-related sexual violence is an integral part of Russia's war tactics, which has produced gendered harms affecting the security of women, in particular. Also, key here is Russia's ideological attack on 'Western' values including gender equality, having long favoured traditional family values and anti-gay rights (Edenborg, 2022a).

Sjoberg (2008) has through various interventions on just war theory challenged its location within gendered and heteronormative binaries (Sjoberg, 2016). She argues that 'the just war tradition is built on, reliant on and inseparable from gendered narratives of innocence and guilt in war', a connection that is reproduced in international relations. Feminist just war theory enables us to disrupt the links between the just war tradition and 'gendered notions of warfare' (Sjoberg, 2006). This, in turn, enables the reconceptualization of the 'gendered nature not only of war ethics, but also of war justificatory narratives, war practices and war experiences'. War is more than military power and dominance – it involves dealing with economic destruction, gendered oppression as well as environmental concerns (Sjoberg, 2008).

The analysis of justice in and of war then needs to go beyond the violence that might play out in a battlefield or in trenches by paying close attention to the lived experience of those subjected to war, whether during the war or in its aftermath. This involves deliberating on what care needs the victims of war might have in conflictual and post-conflictual contexts, and, involving those whose lives have been affected by war rather than engaging in 'paternalistic caring' (Narayan, 1995: 135). As Sjoberg posits, 'an ethics of care recognizes war as an emotional experience, and the victims of war (soldiers and civilians) as human beings with dignity' (Sjoberg, 2008: 8). Beyond states, some Western feminists have struggled to reconcile their pacifist principles with Ukrainian feminist calls for the West to provide arms, with such responses often running counter to Ukraine's right to self-defence. It should be noted here that this is also a position held by Ukrainian feminists who are fundamentally anti-militarist in their convictions. For example, Lutyi-Moroz, active within the Ukrainian feminist collective FemSolution, whose ethos rests on anti-militarism, notes that: 'A large-scale invasion forced Ukrainians to fight for their survival. As feminists we strongly support the right to self-defence ... we are critical of possible negative consequences of militarisation. At the same time, we defend the right to resistance, and we will support those who protect us' (quoted in openDemocracy, 2023: 8). This further points to the challenges of states engaging in a feminist response. For example, Nela Porobić of the Women's International League for Peace and Freedom has argued that:

> The doubling down on the militarisation that is piggybacking on the Russian invasion of Ukraine has led us to a point where war has become sanitised, perhaps even glorified; a point where our empathy and desire to stop criminal and aggressive acts of Putin has become co-opted into the militarised and binary ways of the political and economic elite, where the only option presented is more escalation, never de-escalation, never dialogue and negotiations. (Porobić, 2022)

Again, this tells us that it is central for any state committed to the principles of feminist foreign policy to address the current war through a feminist just war theory lens, with Sjoberg and others advocating an empathetic and care-based approach to war that does not reproduce gendered binaries. In the context of Russia's war in Ukraine and Ukraine's existential struggle, the silence on feminist foreign policy and the WPS agenda at a state level is perhaps more explicable. As a result, feminists struggle to articulate what solidarity and empathy with Ukraine should look like, which might explain why they have not lobbied their governments to apply feminist and WPS principles in policies directly targeting the war. Another reason, as we have shown in this chapter, is that most states that have adopted a feminist platform for their foreign policy conduct have not paired that endeavour with a feminist approach to defence.

By highlighting empathy, care and dialogue as well as individual experience, a feminist perspective on just war and post-conflict can inspire peaceful transformations of war-torn regions by disrupting gendered practices of militarism and violence. A feminist approach to just war, and war more broadly, involves recognizing people's relational and subjective embodied experiences of war and interventionism (Enloe, 2010; Sylvester, 2013; Bergman Rosamond and Kronsell, 2022). This, moreover, requires an intersectional mindset that recognizes a variety of gendered bodies rather than solely those whose gender roles are steeped in heteronormativity (Sjoberg, 2016).

However, states that adhere to a pro-gender equality agenda in foreign policy while engaging in armament and militarism rarely engage in these ethical questions. For instance, while most of these states, notably within NATO, recognize that Ukraine is entitled to self-defence, that recognition is not paired with a meaningful discussion of pacifism and non-violence. An obvious question here then is whether feminist notions of war should always be grounded in pacifism? Elshtain (1987: 241) addresses this broad difficult question by noting that: 'even as some women have turned Beautiful Soul assumptions into dramatic forms of anti-war protest, others have joined the camp of the warriors', pointing to women joining armed forces in larger numbers. Yet, some influential feminisms are intellectually and ethically rooted in pacifism (Ruddick, 1995; Hutchings, 2019). Sara Ruddick's work on maternal thinking and the fostering of a politics of peace is insightful here, with the author noting that maternal care, as a feminist ethical framework, can produce a politics of peace since it 'illuminates both the destructiveness of war and the requirement of peace'. Yet she concedes that maternal care can be militaristic and that at times 'an antimilitarist maternal perspective is an engaged vision that must be achieved through struggle and change' (Ruddick, 1995: 136). Most notably, she argues that 'a sturdy suspicion of violence does not betoken absolute renunciation' and that though 'pacifists perform an essential service among peace activists by requiring every act of violence to be critically appraised, it is unnecessary and divisive to require of all peacemakers an absolute commitment not to kill' (Ruddick, 1995: 156).

It is also useful to consider Kimberly Hutchings' (2019) differentiation between absolute and contingent pacifism. The former refers to an absolute denouncement of any kind of violence at any time, whereas contingent pacifism recognizes that 'pacifism is contingent on facts about the contemporary world ... we should reject war in current circumstances but this position, in principle, is revisable' (Hutchings, 2019: 177). This ethical framework enables reflection on the sticky nexus between feminist-informed foreign policy, pacifism and the right to self-defence. There are instances when we need to ask whether a feminist approach to peace and war requires an absolute commitment to non-violence, thus, absolute pacifism? Ukrainian feminist activist Sganoabsja notes in this light that 'I have an anti-war stance on life because I love unicorns more than blood. But we live on the strong side of the fence to have an anti-war stance' (openDemocracy, 2023: 8). Few scholars of feminism and foreign policy have ethically reflected on the nexus between pacifism and anti-militarism and the right to defend the nation from an imperial aggressor. What is more state proponents of existing feminist and pro-gender equality foreign policies are strikingly silent on this dilemma. To address such silences pro-gender and feminist-informed state actors should engage in more self-critical diplomatic dialogue on the reconcilability between self-defence and the principles of feminist foreign policy. While constellations such as the Feminist Foreign Policy Plus (FFP+) group within the UN is an important diplomatic initiative, bringing together 18 self-defined pro-gender and feminist states, its political declaration on 'Feminist Approaches to Foreign policy' issued in September 2023 did not specifically address defence and military matters, let alone questions pertaining to self-defence (Government of the Netherlands, 2023). Yet, UN Women has encouraged states with feminist-informd foreign policies to engage with the question whether such policies are compatible with militarism, asking specifically if 'increases in military spending can be justified under these policies'. For fruitful diplomatic dialogue on the nexus between pro-gender and feminist foreign policy and self-defence to emerge civil society actors need to be part of the conversation, not least women and other vulnerable groups, whose lives have been directly affected by war and conflict.

Conclusion

This chapter has made a case for applying pro-gender and feminist approaches to all areas of foreign policy including defence. At the same time, we have identified the absence of feminist scholarship on what pro-gender and feminist foreign policy practice could look like if they engaged more profoundly with issues of defence. While there is a place for distinct WPS principles in pro-gender approaches to defence policy, we propose here that feminist and pro-gender foreign policies need to move beyond that agenda to reckon with the ethical aspects of defence. Through the illustrations of the US-led withdrawal from Afghanistan, the Gaza war as well as Russia's full-scale invasion of Ukraine, the chapter argues that geopolitical considerations need to be accounted for in applying feminist considerations to the practice of defence. This does not let states off the hook but rather demands space for broader normative engagement with what transformative feminist defence could look like. Feminist approaches to just war theory are one avenue for realizing such an aspiration by grappling with the challenges of applying feminist foreign policy approaches to defence. Such approaches involve moving beyond a focus just on 'adding WPS and stirring', to consider broader ethical considerations from a feminist perspective.

12

Trade

Roberta Guerrina

Introduction

Like other external policy domains, mainstreaming gender in the context of trade requires political leadership, that is, the willingness to include gender equality as an objective of trade policy. It demands an understanding of the link between domestic consumption and global production chains. This process is dependent on both expertise in gender mainstreaming *and* an institutional architecture prepared to accept the challenge posed by feminist critiques of foreign policy objectives and practice (Eveline and Bacchi, 2010; EIGE, 2019). Whereas feminist political economists have long demonstrated the gendered impact of trade policy (Garcia, 2021; Hannah et al, 2020), policy makers and practitioners have lagged in applying these insights to policy-making practice and strategy (True, 2009).

Trade is an interesting area of foreign policy in so far as it establishes a direct link between the personal, in which social reproduction largely occurs, domestic economic and social policies and global politics. As a policy domain, trade has also been traditionally defined by competition and advantage without much consideration for the social and historical context within which many trade agreements have been signed and international trade policy has been defined (Watson, 2016). The challenge for gender scholars has been to centre these connections, or interactions, to expose the hierarchies of power that support global economic structures. International trade policy is just one of the policy domains through which these hierarchies become normalized and reified. For instance, one of these hierarchies is the assumed neutrality of trade as a field of practice that is implicitly outward-facing, underpinned by the pursuit of state interests, and driven by the logic of competitive advantage. In the face of these global hierarchies, centering social reproduction to understand the impact of trade on socioeconomic relations thus becomes particularly challenging.

This chapter explores the contributions of feminist approaches to foreign policy analysis that centre the continuum between social reproduction and global trade. It argues that the insights stemming from this policy domain help us to understand the nexus between domestic and international politics in shaping foreign policy. Specifically, the chapter, like the rest of the chapters in this book, starts from the assumption that trade, as all other areas of foreign policy and external action, is gendered even though it has been frequently portrayed as gender-neutral or gender-free. These omissions are not what sets trade apart from other domains of foreign policy. Rather, trade warrants detailed examination for the way it exposes how gender structures patterns of consumption, employment and investment. This analysis is rooted in feminist International Relations' claim that the personal is international, however, it also opens the space to an investigation of the links between state institutional processes such as diplomacy and political leadership and the construction of the national interest. It is therefore an entry point for the development of feminist-informed foreign policy analysis a field of study that centres the politics of the everyday to understand global politics.

One of the purposes of this edited collection is to draw out not only the contributions of feminist-informed foreign policy analysis to the field as it is currently defined but also to identify the missing pieces and the biases that have become normalized by the canon that have defined the boundaries of the field itself. In so doing, it provides more detailed and comprehensive insights into the social, political and economic forces that define foreign policy action and practice, thus helping the field itself to understand the impact of policy choices on a wider range of social and economic groups (Guerrina and Slootmaeckers, 2023). This is a normative project rooted in feminist theory's commitment to social change and inclusion. It is a project that requires feminist scholars, activists and practitioners to navigate complex institutional structures and interests. Feminist-informed foreign policy analysis thus must embrace complexity and find pathways to engage with contradictory claims and ambitions. Trade, as a policy domain, provides a useful illustration of these tensions, including possibilities for engagement, transformation, as well as co-optation.

The chapter is divided into three sections. The first section introduces the key debates and scholarship on feminist research on trade. Drawing on international feminist political economy, it provides the analytical framework for a detailed discussion of the trade policy domain in the context of foreign policy. The second section examines some of the latest developments in mainstreaming gender in the field of trade. Specifically, it investigates the way trade has been included, or not, in the context of the Sustainable Development Goals (SDGs) and the way they feed into the development of feminist approaches to foreign policy. Finally, the third section considers the European Union (EU) as a case study of gender mainstreaming in trade. As a multilateral organization, the EU proclaims to be a gender equality trailblazer. This normative identity raises important questions about the impact of gender mainstreaming as a transformative tool of foreign policy on global economic structures.

Gendering trade and the global political economy

There is increasing recognition among scholars and policy makers that trade policy, and specifically trade liberalization, does not happen in a vacuum, but rather it has clear and defined gender implications (European Parliament, 2018; Dommen, 2021). As a policy domain, it feeds into wider economic policies with a clear link to employment, consumption as well as access to public services. In so far as all those facets of economic life are gendered, then trade is defined by global gender hierarchies and is one of the best examples of the interconnected nature of domestic and external policies. It is this link that opens a space for the application of a sociological theory of gender regime to foreign policy analysis as it highlights the relationship between economics, civil society, violence and the polity. This section begins with a discussion of the contributions of feminist international political economy to our understanding of the link between social reproduction and global trade to highlight the interconnected nature of the domestic and the international. It then turns to Walby's (2015) gender regime theory to draw out the impact of domestic gender regimes on states' approaches to trade and, conversely, the impact of global trade on these gender regimes.

Feminist critiques of global trade structures

Enloe's (2004) examination of the 'globetrotting sneaker' provides one of the most evocative illustrations of the way international trade policies interact with gender structures and support global economic hierarchies. As she explains, the end of the Cold War opened a space for multinational companies to grow their market share of new 'high value' commodities, sneakers. Targeted marketing campaigns accompanied this shift in focus with the overarching aim to increase traction among specific consumer groups. In the case of the globetrotting sneaker examined by Enloe, the target demographic was children. Trade liberalization affects socioeconomic structures and relations in multiple and multifaceted ways. First, there are the women who, as consumers, need to access funds to pay for these new 'high value commodities'. Second, we have the women who manufacture the goods intended for the global market. These women often work in low-paid and highly insecure positions, which increases their vulnerability.

And finally, there are the women who support those working in the factories, often engaged in care work. The globetrotting sneaker thus raises issues around care, consumption, employment and human rights. The key point that Enloe wants to make through this illustration is that global production chains are designed to exploit women at every stage of the process. Enloe's (2004) work draws attention to the impact of buying into gender-blind economic drivers to determine the priorities of trade policy, which all too often result in trade liberalization and prioritization of competitive advantage above social and gender justice. Perhaps more pointedly, given the accepted wisdom that trade liberalization can facilitate women's empowerment, it helps to uncover a mixed picture in terms of the impact of trade on gender equality.

A feminist analysis of trade policy presents complex and often contradictory trends. Whereas some studies find that trade liberalization can lead to increased opportunities for women's participation in the official labour market, others warn that socioeconomic inequalities underpin global value chains as women are primarily involved in cheap and atypical work (Hannah et al, 2020). Enloe's 'globetrotting sneaker' illustrates this pattern of productive and export specialization, which leads to the segregation of the labour market and the concentration of women in key sectors such as textiles and footwear manufacturing (Berik, 2011). Trade liberalization thus becomes a vehicle to reproduce socioeconomic hierarchies at a domestic, local, national and global scale. In this context, the interests of women in the Global North are pitted against those of women in the Global South. At a local level, it reproduces women's position as atypical workers, thus maintaining their precarious relationship with the labour market and embedding everyday insecurities within economic policy (Hannah et al, 2020; Garcia, 2021).

Much of the feminist international political economy literature builds on this premise, thus drawing attention to the impact of globalization and trade liberalization on the social, political and economic rights of women across both the Global North and the Global South (Hannah et al, 2020). Going back to the globetrotting sneaker discussed earlier, labour market concentration in specific sectors is a cross-national trend. Trade liberalization facilitates the relocation of manufacturing across national boundaries, creating a zero-sum game for women's employment, particularly as they are often seen as a low-wage labour reserve that creates a competitive advantage (Berik, 2011; Garcia and Masselot, 2015). This position contrasts with the argument advanced by a range of economic actors that trade can bring about women's economic empowerment (Garcia, 2021; Korinek et al, 2021). The latter part of the chapter returns to this in the discussion of the EU as a gendered economic actor. The picture is a very complex one that includes both opportunities for economic empowerment and progress as well as contradictions in the way key principles, for example, gender equality, are mainstreamed in foreign policy domains.

Recognition that international trade policy is gendered in terms of its impact also has to acknowledge that race, class, ethnicity, age, and so on will intersect with gender hierarchies to add an extra layer of complexity to the analysis. A feminist-informed foreign policy analysis of trade thus needs to be intersectional and decolonial to account for multiple patterns and sites of exploitation that arise from this policy domain. This means that it needs to be conscious of the impact of gender, race and class on the beneficiaries of trade policy, as well as actively decentring the interests of the Global North in establishing the parameters and ambitions of global trade policy. This is a long way to say that 'gendered and other power relations shape and are shaped by trade relations at multiple site and scales' (Hannah et al, 2020). Understanding the entanglement between the political economy of the everyday practices, for instance, gender divisions of labour, international trade policy is key to addressing the 'unintended' gender consequences of this policy domain.

Gendered entanglements between domestic gender regimes and foreign trade policy

The addition of gender regime theory highlights the role of gender structures, hierarchies and ideologies in the way policy is defined. It not only brings the politics of the 'everyday' to the centre of the analysis (Elias and Rai, 2019) it also establishes how common (gendered) practices are part of governance and decision-making processes. Elias and Rai theorize the 'everyday' in social reproduction as a site for the performance of agency and structure. The inclusion of space, time and violence in their tripartite understanding of everyday politics helps to elevate Walby's gender regimes to the international. In this context, Walby's (2015; 2020; 2023) analysis of the interaction between gender practices within key institutional domains (civil society, economy, polity and violence) in determining gendered social relations that underpin social and economic policy. Varieties of gender regimes are located on a continuum between domestic and public, which is then subdivided into authoritarian, neoliberal, conservative and social democratic. For Walby, the movement on the continuum is not unidirectional, but rather it allows for contestation, multidirectionality and the emergence of different trajectories. Whereas she once considered a movement towards a public gender regime as a move towards empowerment and emancipation, the emergence of an authoritarian gender regime that intersects with the neoliberal gender regime opens a space for a more complex understanding of the evolution of gender regimes that does not necessarily assume inevitable progress. Originally designed to help us understand patterns of gender relations and patriarchy at the national level, the growth in transnational governance allows for its application to the work of international organizations, for example, the EU (Walby, 2004).

For Walby, gender regimes theory is a macro-level approach that examines structures, hierarchies and practices that underpin all state action. Although this framework does not directly look at foreign policy and external action, it looks at the interaction of gendered practices across key areas of state action. As such, the analysis of the socioeconomic impact of gendered regimes on inequality opens a space for its application to the external domain. The assumptions about gender practices that underpin different gender regimes permeate all areas of policy. The inclusion of violence as a domain is a clear opening to include a discussion of security and securitization as resulting from state action. What is important for the analysis presented here is the way gender regimes approach the issue of social reproduction. Whereas a domestic gender regime locates social reproduction within the familial sphere, public gender regimes recognize it as a form of economic production. Social reproduction thus sits at the nexus between the four domains, and the state's approach to governing social reproduction will reflect the position of equality within the wider political agenda.

This analysis offers important insights into a feminist approach to foreign policy analysis, both in terms of actors as well as levels of analysis. Taking each domain identified by Walby, it is possible to draw a link between domestic and international policy. Starting with the *economy*, it looks at which interests are prioritized in economic policy, including the position of women's waged labour. The *polity* considers the quality and level of engagement with democratic processes and accountability. *Civil society* speaks to the depth of participation, ownership and engagement by focusing on legitimacy. Finally, *violence* draws attention to state regulation and sanction of violence. When applied to the field of foreign policy, and especially trade, this allows feminist scholars to ask questions about whose interests are included in the formulation of national (*economic*) interests, whose voices are included in the development and implementation of key policy objectives (*civil society*), the effectiveness of scrutiny and accountability processes (*polity*), and finally, the (gendered) trade-offs that are factored into the pursuit of the national interest (*violence*). In terms of the distinction between public gender regimes between neoliberal and social democratic, Walby (2020) focuses on the depth of democracy and the level of integration of feminist voices within formal governance structures.

Moving beyond the impact of trade on global socioeconomic and gender inequalities, already well established by existing research (Larking, 2019; Garcia, 2021; Hannah et al, 2023), the application of gender regimes theory to the analysis of trade allows us to interrogate the kind of gender regime that is being promoted through the governance of international trade. For Shire and Walby (2020: 409), gender regimes theory helps us to 'think about the gender of "scale" and [is] part of the return to analysing structural inequality'. In order words, this framework allows us to understand the connection between different levels of governance, from the national to the transnational. In this context, trade policy can exacerbate existing social, political and economic hierarchies, however, it can also be a generative space for constructive resistance through women's organizing (Enloe, 2004). By shifting our assessment to trade governance as a site of research, a feminist-informed foreign policy analysis starts to map the limitations of a global political economy predicated on growth and a narrowly defined set of economic interests (Hannah et al, 2020; 2023). As Larking (2019: 311) outlines, 'trade and investment liberalisation has benefited large companies at the expense of smaller enterprises, producing a high degree of corporate concentration'. Gender inequalities, Larking (2019) further explains, are manifest both in terms of the impact of trade policy on producers and consumers, as well as the governance structures that regulate international trade, for example, women's under-representation in key decision-making bodies.

Gender regimes theory thus allows us to examine the way national and transnational institutions have adopted the language of gender mainstreaming to advance global trade without embedding feminist critiques of those same institutions and the global patterns of inequalities (Hannah et al, 2023). Gender regimes theory enables us to unpack how gender hierarchies underpin social, political and economic institutions and shapes both internal and external policies. The next section of this chapter focuses specifically on trade governance as a site of gender relations. It will specifically focus on the minimal engagement of feminist foreign policy as a new state-led policy paradigm on the issue of trade, highlighting the missed opportunities for integrating development and security policies. It is in the context of governance that feminist-informed foreign policy analysis exposes the opportunities and limitations of gender mainstreaming in external affairs. It is also through this discussion that we can start to unpack the role of and relationships between different actors in the global political economy.

Trading places? Technocratic governance and foreign policy omissions

The inclusion of gender equality in the SDGs (SDG 5) has helped to raise awareness of the multiple ways in which gender intersects with mainstream policies, including foreign and security policy, development and trade. SDG 5 has also institutionalized a particular framing of gender equality that revolves around participation and empowerment rather than social and gender justice (Cornwall and Rivas, 2015). In a way this represents a success for gender mainstreaming, in so far as discussions about gender equality and women's empowerment have become ubiquitous, however, it fails to acknowledge the way gender structures policies, practices and processes. Perhaps most importantly, it represents a call to increase women's representation across a range of sectors, including employment and decision-making, but fails to acknowledge the way such structures are both hierarchical and gendered (Hannah et al, 2022a). Within this context, empowerment, and by extension equality, are achieved through economic production and participation in the public sphere, which signals a move towards Walby's public gender regimes.

Feminist scholars engaged in mapping the gendered impact of trade have noted a shift in recent years for states and international organizations to include a 'gender dimension' in trade agreements. This is in response to both civil society's call for mainstreaming gender across all policy domains, but also economic arguments about the cost of non-equality. The emergence of feminist triangles and successful transnational organizing by civil society have resulted in increased institutionalization of gender equality norms at the national and international levels (True, 2003; Guerrina et al, 2018). The challenge that has been set by scholars and activists is how to engage with formal processes and hierarchies without becoming co-opted (True, 2010). In other words, can mainstreaming be true to its transformative potential when gender equality norms become institutionalized and therefore are part of the socioeconomic order (Squires, 2005)? This is also the same socioeconomic order that supports gender regimes, and in this context, it denotes that this approach to trade contributes to the emergence of public gender regimes. In Walby's framework, this means a shift from a focus on domestic relations to state regulation of gender/equality (Walby, 2004). This is arguably one of the main by-products of gender mainstreaming. The question that ensues is whether this denotes a neoliberal or social democratic gender regime. Feminist critiques of trade point to the reification of neoliberal regimes, as will be illustrated by the discussion in this section.

The main tools for including gender in the context of trade are straight out of the mainstreaming playbook and include the following: gender impact assessments; women's economic empowerment; and initiatives aimed at women's entrepreneurs (Hannah et al, 2020). These are subsequently institutionalized through the inclusion of 'gender chapters' in trade agreements. These are a particular type of innovation in the context of trade governance in so far as they are supposed to integrate the ambition of gender mainstreaming for ensuring gender is treated as a cross-cutting issue. They are also a step change in the piecemeal approach of including gender provisions in trade agreements. As Hannah et al (2020: 7) explain, 'like the WTO Declaration, gender chapters aim at advancing gender and increasing women's participation in trade'. The focus of this more extensive approach is to tackle socioeconomic inequalities generated by global trade structures through participation in formal institutional structures and processes (Hannah et al, 2020). In terms of the domains of the gender regime, we can see that this approach links directly to civil society (women entrepreneurs), the policy (women's participation) and the economy (women's economic empowerment).

The International Trade Centre 'SheTrades Initiative' is an example of gender regimes at work in the context of economic policy through the process of mainstreaming gender. This initiative deploys the mainstreaming toolkit through the launch of an action plan (2022–2025), increased data collection, partnership and programmatic funding for flagship initiatives. Seeking to contribute to the SDGs agenda – specifically SGD 5 (gender equality), SDG 8 (decent work and economic growth) and SDG 17 (partnership for goals) – it sets out to provide a framework for women's (economic) empowerment through increased participation in economic activities and decision-making. This approach is captured in most of the documents produced by the initiative: 'All women everywhere have the right to a decent income, employment, working conditions and a choice and voice in shaping their economic context' (International Trade Centre, nd)

The initiative is designed as a multi-level intervention working with transnational, regional and national bodies to affect change in terms of policy and support for women entrepreneurs. The initiative seeks to bring together key stakeholders to create a more inclusive environment for women's participation in economic production. It does so by funding national hubs and individual projects. The theory of change underpinning this initiative is predicated on the assumption that higher levels of participation will lead to women's empowerment and therefore redistribution of economic resources within the domestic sphere, that is, emancipation.

The real question is whether the inclusion of gender equality norms and programmes in established institutional structures can open a space for transformative feminist action and policy either at the national or international level (True and Prügl, 2014). In other words, can such programmes displace accepted economic wisdom and imperatives that reproduce gendered and racialized hierarchies, in favour of a model that 'centres the experiences and voices of people, particularly women and marginalized groups' (Hannah et al, 2020: 6) and in so doing engenders a shift in gender regimes. Initiatives such as 'SheTrades' are welcomed in so far as they address some of the concerns around the material impact of everyday inequalities, however, they also help to reproduce socioeconomic hierarchies in so far as they only focus on one aspect of trade (participation) rather than engage with the wider impact of trade on reproducing global gender hierarchies (Hannah, 2020). From the perspective of a feminist global political economy what is required is a shift from growth-based, individualized models of economic development to a new model that revolves around sustainability and care ethics (Hannah et al, 2022a). It is a call for a more nuanced and radical understanding of progress that acknowledges the importance of improving individual material circumstances but also calls for a new imagination (Stirling, 2015; David et al, 2023). Such a change requires a substantial transformation of gender regimes that far exceed the opportunities for emancipatory politics included in Walby's social democratic regime.

Hannah et al (2022a) capture the complexity of the task at hand. For them, the key question is 'whether the new gender and trade agenda marks a transformative movement in global trade governance, or whether it serves to cement what we refer to as the trade orthodoxy' (Hannah et al, 2022a: 1368). From this perspective, the inclusion of gender mainstreaming in trade governance adds to the technocratic nature of the policy domain and helps to detach it further to the political economy of everyday life (Elias and Roberts, 2016; Elias and Rai, 2019; Hannah et al, 2022a). Tensions start to emerge between the ambition that gender mainstreaming might open the door for transformative approaches to policy making (Squires, 2005) and the potential for institutionalization and co-optation. As Hannah et al (2022a: 1372) explain, '[w]hile biding and enforceable commitments to gender equality, human rights, and social and environmental protection can disturb the trade orthodoxy, they have also been seen as a "Trojan horse" that is being used to extend the legal remit of the WTA and FTAs'. Given the impact of trade on a vast array of policy domains that affect women's ability to participate in economic life – including care and health – it is worth turning our attention to the idea that a feminist foreign policy approach can and/or should be transformative in nature, as outlined by the list of 'key ingredients' included in the International Center for Research on Women's Feminist Foreign Policy's (2022) framework: '1. Purpose, 2. Definition; 3. Reach; 4. Outcome; 5. Plan.'

The launch of a feminist foreign policy by the Swedish government in 2014 is seen as a critical juncture in the way this policy domain is conceptualized. The inclusion of an explicitly 'feminist' approach to foreign policy is intended to signal the methodical inclusion of a gender dimension to all areas of foreign policy, including trade. Most countries purporting to have adopted feminist-informed foreign policies nominally include trade within the policy portfolio. However, only Sweden and Canada have fleshed out what this means in practice. The Swedish government's *Handbook on Feminist Foreign Policy* (Government of Sweden, 2018a) includes a chapter on trade, making it a key tool for the implementation of feminist foreign policy. It is worth noting that thus far Sweden is the only country to have included a focus on trade as part of its feminist foreign policy commitments. And yet, this is a limited and contained approach. Unsurprisingly, there are echoes of the 'SheTrades' initiative in this chapter with a focus on empowerment, access and voice. Perhaps most pointed is the acknowledgement that the pursuit of the national interest remains central in the context of feminist foreign policy: 'One aspect of foreign policy involves promoting Swedish values and spreading the image of Sweden around the world. Gender equality is an important part of this image' (Government of Sweden, 2018a).

What this chapter does not include is a detailed examination or commitment to review Sweden's approach to international trade, including its continued export of arms to countries with a record of supporting and advancing human rights and gender equality (Thompson and Clement, 2019). Perhaps it is worth taking a step back to consider what is feminist foreign policy and what are the ambitions encapsulated in this discursive pivot in the field of foreign affairs. Thompson et al define feminist foreign policy as follows:

> [A] complete, consistent and coherent approach to a body of work encompassing all auspices of foreign policy and international relations. If done right, the approach will include (but not be limited to) aid, trade, defence and immigration, in addition to diplomacy, using all the tools in the foreign policy toolbox to advance a more equitable world. And most importantly, it will be informed by and amplifying the voices of the rights-holders it seeks to celebrate and support. (Thompson et al, 2021: 26)

What is key here is the focus on the transformation of a policy field that has traditionally been dominated by the pursuit of the national (economic) interest, understood as driven by growth and inherently gender-neutral or gender-free. As discussed previously, global feminist political economy challenges these assumptions drawing attention to the links between the global and personal. A feminist approach to trade thus starts by asking questions about whose interests are being advanced through trade agreements and who is left behind. The point about Sweden's arms trade discussed earlier is particularly important in so far as it is irreconcilable with the ambition of a feminist foreign policy.

A feminist approach to foreign policy analysis thus opens a space to discuss the way social hierarchies are entrenched in decision-making processes around trade. It does so by exposing bridges between policy domains, specifically between internally facing economic policies and external affairs. The question that has remained unresolved in the context of the gender and/or feminist turn in foreign policy is which institutional strategies and mechanisms can be deployed to institutionalize long-term feminist principles and objectives within state institutions? Gender regime theory urges us to consider the way these feminist principles interact with and are shaped by gender hierarchies and practices within domestic states and civil societies, in so far as different gender regimes allow for the integration, or not, of feminist principles within foreign policy, and specifically trade. For instance, changes in how trade, development and aid policies are addressed at the national and transnational level indicate a strong move towards a neoliberal public gender regime, with clear implications for the way human rights (violence domain), participation (polity and civil society domains) and exchange (economy) feed into the production of national gender regimes.

The next section will thus turn to our case study, the EU. This analysis will allow us to evaluate the contribution of this approach to foreign policy analysis both in terms of the role of the EU as a gender equality actor, as well as its approach to mainstreaming gender in trade.

Mainstreaming gender in European Union trade policy

The EU is an interesting and important illustration of gender regimes in action within the field of trade. Not only is the EU the largest trading bloc in the global political economy, but it also purports to be a gender equality actor that has adopted gender mainstreaming as its main strategic tool for advancing equality between men and women within all policy domains (Damro, 2012; Chappell and Guerrina, 2020). Walby (2004) first posed the question about the EU's gender regime in the context of the impact of enlargement in the early 2000s, claiming that it is a public gender regime moving towards a social democratic model. Chappell and Guerrina (2020) have developed this idea by looking at the project of the EU's gender regime in external affairs through the EU's Action Plan on Women, Peace and Security, and Guerrina et al (2023a) analysed the impact of the crisis on the EU's gender regime, pointing to fluidity in the model projected by the EU internally and externally.

Despite gender mainstreaming being included in the Treaty of Amsterdam (1998) and the Treaty of Lisbon (2009) explicitly extending the mandate to external policies, gender has been largely missing from EU trade policy until 2015 with the adoption of the Trade for All strategy (True, 2009; Garcia and Masselot, 2015; Gammage, 2019; 2022; Garcia, 2021). A welcomed shift to include values as part of this policy domain also sets out the EU's limited approach to integrating gender in trade (Garcia, 2021). To unpack the multiple ways that gender hierarchies have come to be integrated into the EU's trade policy, we need to examine two key concepts and how they manifest in this policy domain: market power Europe; and feminist power Europe. Looking at these two analytical frameworks alongside each other we can expose some of the biases that have been institutionalized through an approach that favours the integration of narrowly defined gender equality norms, as opposed to mainstreaming gender-sensitive lenses across all stages of the policy-making cycle to develop more inclusive and potentially more radical approaches to trade.

The idea of 'market power Europe' was introduced to describe the EU's identity above all as an economic power. It looks at the way the EU has sought to exercise power and influence through economic integration. In this context, market power Europe has three core pillars: market integration; expansion of regulatory capacity; and externalization capacity. The third pillar is particularly important here as it directly relates to international trade. Key to our analysis is the way the EU claims to link the social and economic agenda in the pursuit of its external strategies (Damro, 2012). The social agenda is the focus of our analysis here and links to a new concept in feminist theorizing about the EU, 'feminist power'. The idea of 'feminist power' was first coined by Prügl (2016) to describe the complex relationship between feminist activism and the institutionalization of feminist norms that have resulted in legislative and programmatic change. Focusing on the role and impact of knowledge transfer from advocacy to institutions, Prügl's analysis centres on the experience and impact of gender experts working within institutional hierarchies. Applied to the analysis of the EU, feminist power manifests in the idea of feminist or velvet triangles (Woodward, 2015). What is interesting to note here is the dearth of literature on the link between a feminist political economy of European integration (that is, internal-facing policies) and feminist critiques of trade (that is, external-facing policies). This is a missing link that can be captured by deploying feminist power Europe as a conceptual and theoretical tool.

It is important to note at this point that drawing on the idea of feminist power Europe does not equate with accepting that the EU is or has ever been a feminist power (Guerrina et al, 2023a). Rather it is to acknowledge the role of different feminist actors operating within the institutional architecture of the organization. It also provides a space to ask important questions about silences and omissions in trade, given that gender equality norms were originally included in the founding treaties to avoid social dumping and unfair trading practices within the newly established Common Market (Garcia, 2021).

Looking back at the way gender equality norms were included in the founding treaties is useful in establishing a degree of path dependence in the way the principle of gender equality has been subordinated to economic interests and rationalities. Article 119 was only included in the Treaties of Rome (1957) to ensure fair competition in the newly established Common Market. The principle of equality at the European level is thus inextricably linked to trade governance, something that is often forgotten in the way international and foreign trade is often executed. Most importantly, equality was included only in so far as it helped to safeguard the national interest, rather than a normative principle (Hoskyns, 1996; MacRae, 2010; Garcia, 2021). There is one additional detail to this foundational story about the EU as a gender equality actor. The economic sector that spurred the discussion was textiles. It was the French government that, having just adopted equal pay legislation at the national level, was concerned about unfair competition from Italy in textiles. This example brings together many of the issues discussed previously about market concentration and the subordination of social justice to economic interests.

The lack of institutional engagement with gender in the field of trade is reflected in the fact that it remains a largely under-researched field of policy within the gender scholarship. The first action plan seeking to expand women's participation and representation in international trade was published by the European Commission in 2017. The institutional approach is closely aligned with the 'SheTrades' initiative, thus focusing on individual advancement, economic empowerment and programme funding. This is quite removed from integrating a gender perspective into the actual development of trade policy and the negotiation of new trade agreements that have been called for by feminist political economists (Hannah et al, 2020; 2022a; Gammage, 2022). For the scholars engaged in researching this policy domain, it thus falls short of the calls for transformative change away from growth-driven economic policy that ignores socioeconomic hierarchies. Such an approach 'would move away from the focus on women as economic actors in paid employment, to broader considerations of women's unpaid work in households and caring, and unequal access to resources and power in society' (Garcia, 2021: 285).

Economic rationalities and comparative advantage logics continue to be drivers for foreign trade policy. What this means is that gender and equality provisions are included in trade agreements to address concerns about the competitive advantage derived from inequitable practices associated with lower-paid female labour (Hannah et al, 2020). In this context, it is important to assess whether gender is included in trade agreements in a piecemeal way or co-opted as a tool for the pursuit of established interests either at the national or transnational level. Two countries, Canada and Sweden, with an established track record of gender mainstreaming in trade provide useful case studies for this analysis. Canada has been actively advocating for the inclusion of gender-sensitive analysis and impact assessments since the 2010s. Questions have been asked about the motivations for this advocacy and whether the gender equality discourse is being used to legitimize global hierarchies inherent within trade policy (Hannah et al, 2022b). Similarly, we have already seen how Swedish feminist foreign policy was in part an ambition for a more inclusive foreign policy and in part a branding exercise to assert the position of Sweden as an international actor. Undoubtedly, Sweden's leadership in this space contributed to shaping policy at the World Trade Organization and in the EU. The EU's free trade agreement with Chile was the first to include a gender chapter thanks to efforts of the Swedish Commissioner Cecilia Malmström (Morgan, 2017). Interestingly, what seems to be missing from this discussion is the role of gender experts working within DG Trade and their role in influencing decision-making processes. Whereas policy domains such as security and defence have been subjected to detailed analysis of both the gendered impact of policy as well as representation and participation in decision-making, EU trade policy has remained largely insulated from critiques advanced by feminist political economists. Such analysis would include an examination of key institutional actors, including the positionality of gender experts within the Commission. Additionally, it should establish the pathways for engagement and participation of civil society organizations. Focus on this final actor is particularly important as it highlights the heterogeneous nature of economic interests and bridges the politics of the internal market with EU external action.

Going back to our previous discussion, the interests of market power Europe are resoundingly more central to the EU's identity, and therefore policy action, in the field of trade. Where it seeks to adopt a gender-sensitive approach, it still lacks intrinsic feminist power within the institutional architecture to ensure its approach to inclusive trade is not merely additive but starts to consider the possibilities of a different economic model and future. Delving into alternative futures has to be part of a feminist power approach to European policy making across all areas, especially trade. Most importantly, this approach brings into dialogue diverse economic, social and political interests to overcome the growth and competitive advantage traps that continue to inform international trade policy. The idea of 'feminist power Europe' (Guerrina et al, 2023a) purports a move towards a public and progressive gender regime. However, the EU's post-crisis gender regime is increasingly embedding neoliberal traits (Guerrina et al, 2023b) that challenge Walby's (2004) assessment that it was moving towards a social democratic model.

Conclusion

A feminist analysis of foreign trade policy requires engagement with issues around institutional actors, practices and processes, as well as the impact of policy decisions and programmes on different groups. The application of feminist foreign policy analysis to the domain of trade opens a space for a discussion of the role of institutional actors, civil society organizations and leadership. This approach also allows us to link three distinct bodies of literature: feminist institutionalism, international feminist political economy and gender regimes. Together they provide us with the necessary tools to understand the way gender intersects with trade beyond the asymmetrical impact of this policy domain on different socioeconomic groups. Gendering trade requires us to unpack gender hierarchies in the institutional architecture.

This analysis takes us back to gender regime theory and its application to the analysis of external affairs. Gender regimes shape states' approaches to regulating social reproduction, violence and participation in the economy. They thus help to codify the norms, structures and practices that merge into the idea of 'the national interest' as defined by international trade policy. The idea of gender regimes has largely been used to examine gender inequality in countries of the Global North, however, its application to the field of trade provides an entry point for understanding how gender regimes are produced. A feminist analysis of trade starts by acknowledging the gendered impact of trade, not just on women's participation in the labour market but also in terms of access to services and social reproduction. It also builds on the wide-reaching critique of descriptive representation and women's economic empowerment as proxies for systemic change. Adding women to a system that is designed to support and advance a narrowly defined set of political and economic interests is unlikely to achieve sustained and substantive change, even though it will improve the material reality of some marginalized and minoritized individuals. Feminist foreign policy analysis of international trade opens a space to highlight institutional and political bias and, in so doing, create bridges between a diverse set of interests. Moving beyond the established rationalities will ultimately require a feminist imagination that re-centres the economics of care at a transnational level to redistribute resources and achieve the ambition of the feminist political project.

13

Aid and Development

Rebecca Tiessen

Introduction

This chapter examines the ongoing challenges of and possibilities for renewed thinking in feminist development policies, highlighting the significance of decolonial feminism for guiding future development policies. Feminist development policies are at a critical juncture: they offer the potential to advance a new vision for international development yet fall short in rhetoric and substance for tackling persistent global challenges. Among the enduring challenges in international development are: the failure to address the needs and priorities of the poorest and most marginalized (including women and gender non-conforming individuals) with limited impacts on tackling inequality and poverty; accountability to donors and donor nations, rather than local communities where aid is meant to have the most impact; and insufficient strategies for addressing emerging and compounding global crises that lead to heightened insecurities for the most marginalized. Climate change, pandemics, food insecurity and the growing number of conflicts around the world are examples of crises we currently face, and our limited capacity to address these crises reduces our capacities for meeting global commitments, such as the Sustainable Development Goals (SDGs). Meanwhile, new aid actors are entering the global arena with their own political relationships and distinct development strategies that further limit our progress in meeting our global commitments for a sustainable, equitable and just world.

This chapter begins with an overview of persistent and emerging challenges in foreign aid policy and international assistance. The second section considers the impact of feminist development policies, drawing on critical feminist analyses of current feminist development policies: Canada's 2017 Feminist International Assistance Policy (FIAP) and Germany's 2023

Feminist Development Policy (FDP), with additional examples of foreign aid priorities from Sweden and Australia. The main themes emerging from the analysis of contemporary feminist development policies include neoliberalism and the instrumentalization of women's labour for other political and economic outcomes; the significance of intersectional feminist priorities and the need for clearer definitions of feminism; and strategies for translating policy to practice including funding allocations, monitoring and evaluation, and the potential for inside activists to enact feminist principles. The challenges outlined in this critical evaluation of feminist development policies highlight their current limitations, opportunities for innovation in practice, and the importance of a decolonial feminist vision for addressing the realities of contemporary development challenges and the complexity of compounding global crises.

Drawing on the decolonial feminist insights of Verschuur and Destremau (2012) in their analysis of gender and development, a decolonial perspective establishes new ways of thinking about solutions to global crises and development challenges by centring the perspectives of those most impacted by them and linking the lived experiences of marginalized people to the global political and economic structures of inequality. A decolonial feminist lens challenges Western representations of the 'Third World woman' as a category of analysis that leads to 'Othering' through a 'Western' lens (Mohanty, 1988); offers greater insight and knowledge emerging from Indigenous scholars and Global South activists to guide feminist policy making through an intersectional lens; and centres the local as the knowledge holders, reflecting diversity of voices and lived experiences as they relate to broader political and economic struggles. This chapter ends with a discussion of the possibilities for feminist policy making for aid and development in line with decolonial feminist theory and practice.

Persistent and emerging challenges of foreign aid and development assistance

Foreign aid is marked by persistent challenges in reaching those who need it most and in achieving the impacts that are intended through international assistance. Among the reasons for the limited impact of international assistance commitments is the ease with which foreign aid funding is easily appropriated and used for other foreign policy and defence purposes. International assistance funding can be allocated broadly through a multisector approach with significant flexibility, making it highly fungible and susceptible to other priorities such as defence spending. The United States, for example, classifies one-third of its foreign aid as military aid with funds that come from the Department of Defense to be used for the American military and the militaries of US allies (Concern Worldwide US, 2021), resulting in the securitization of aid (Brown and Grävingholt, 2016), particularly since 11 September 2001 (Miles, 2013). It comes as little surprise, then, that the top recipients of foreign aid allocations for many donor countries are countries where donors have particular security interests and where war and conflict are ongoing.

The securitization of foreign aid has negative impacts on development programming and limits foreign aid's ability to tackle poverty and inequality, including gender inequality (Brown, 2016). Among Germany's top ten aid recipients, for instance, were conflict-affected countries of the Syrian Arab Republic, Afghanistan, Jordan and Yemen (OECD, 2023). Fragile contexts, therefore, receive high levels of support with a gross of US$5.6 billion in 2021, representing 20.1 per cent of Germany's gross bilateral official development assistance (ODA), with only 'twenty-five per cent of this ODA … in the form of humanitarian assistance, 7 per cent to conflict prevention' (OECD, 2023). Similarly, Canada's gross bilateral aid in 2021 was CAD$5 billion, and 17.3 per cent of gross bilateral ODA went to Canada's top ten recipients, nine of which are fragile contexts including Afghanistan, South Sudan and the Syrian Arab Republic (OECD, 2023). Ukraine joined the list of countries with the ranking of the sixth largest recipient of Canada's international assistance at CAD$159.7 million (GAC, 2023). Similarly, in 2021, Germany provided US$525.8 million of gross bilateral ODA to Ukraine to respond to the impacts of Russia's invasion, an amount that rose from 2021 figures of US$223.7 million (out of a total of 27.7 billion of gross bilateral ODA in 2021) (OECD, 2023). Donors have a high degree of discretion regarding what constitutes international assistance. As a result, aid is easily diverted from its intended purpose of development goals for broader security rationales (Feridun, 2014).

Foreign aid allocations by country are also subject to frequent shifts and re-prioritization depending on the government of the day. Under Stephen Harper's Conservative Party governments, for example, Canadian foreign aid was increasingly instrumentalized and reoriented to other priorities to serve national interests, including 'winning hearts and minds' to stop the Taliban insurgency, rather than poverty-related commitments abroad (Brown, 2016: 18). International assistance, when allocated to gender equality or women's empowerment programmes, is also instrumentalized for defence purposes. Several donor countries used 'liberating women and girls' in Afghanistan as part of their justifications for their military activities in Afghanistan, giving foreign aid dollars to support the military mission, and thereby instrumentalizing aid in support of national security interests (Swiss, 2012). Beyond Afghanistan, funding taken from ODA envelopes was increasingly redirected to conflict-affected countries, leading to the 'instrumentalization of gender' (Swiss, 2012: 137) and the instrumentalization of women's rights (Pacwa, 2019) for security related priorities rather than priorities for human rights or gender equality goals. The introduction of pro-gender and feminist foreign policies, and in particular Canada's FIAP and Germany's FDP offer new opportunities to revisit foreign aid priorities, spending strategies, and to create new commitments to justice and equality through a feminist lens. Yet, as the critical review of feminist development policies highlights, and is examined in the next section, little has changed through the design of so-called feminist development policies.

In addition to these persistent challenges are emerging realities that require new thinking for the delivery of development assistance. Among these emerging realities is the changing nature of global aid flows from emerging bilateral donors. Significant increases in aid from China, United Arab Emirates and Turkey, among other newly expanding aid donors, require new thinking about the changing nature of development assistance and the principles that guide it. China's financing of global development (now the sixth largest donor country overall), considers itself 'categorically different' than that of the Organization for Economic Co-operation and Development (OECD) donors with a bigger emphasis on international investments, such as loans made by Chinese enterprises, rather than foreign aid (Johnson and Zühr, 2021: np). While gender equality is one of the main aims of development assistance provided by traditional and multilateral development agencies, it is not a significant priority for some of the emerging aid donors. For example, gender issues are 'largely ignored in the development projects provided by China and rarely discussed in China's foreign policies' (Zhang and Huang, 2023: np).

Despite the growing number of donors engaged in foreign aid ventures, people in need of humanitarian aid have tripled since 2013, with the biggest demands for aid in just 20 countries where climate shocks and violent conflicts are rampant (Miliband as quoted in Goering, 2023). Compounding crises that contribute to intensified and multi-layered insecurities (food insecurity, health insecurity, physical insecurity, among others), require innovative policies that recognize and address the root causes of these global crises, and the needs and priorities of those most affected by them.

Among the challenges contributing to compounding crises and requiring innovative thinking in international assistance programmes are environmental disasters, increasing debt burdens, high rates of unemployment and declining social development investments (in education and health, for example). In addition, the surging autocracy and patriarchy worldwide are resulting in backlash against women's rights, with women, overall, having fewer rights and opportunities than in previous years. Evidence of regression in attitudes towards gender equality is observed in the increasing rates of gender-based and intimate partner violence, as well as perceptions that men should have priority access to food or jobs during times of scarcity (UN Women, 2022a).

Commitments to gender equality are therefore crucial during this 'tipping point for women's rights and gender equality' (Executive Director of UN Women Sima Bahous, quoted in UN News, 2022). In addition to supporting gender equality, feminist priorities are central to tackling a range of issues and crises that lead to injustices, inequalities and insecurities for all. Feminist foreign policies have included priorities and strategies directly linked to development assistance, such as those of Australia and Sweden. Two stand-alone feminist development policies have been launched including Canada's FIAP introduced in 2017 and Germany's FDP launched in 2023. Following the announcement of these feminist development policies, feminist scholars have examined their language and impacts, noting limitations and opportunities for further advancement of feminist priorities.

Critical analyses of the impact of feminist development policies

The two stand-alone feminist development policies – Canada's FIAP and Germany's FDP – are analysed here drawing on the critical feminist scholarship of their impacts in relation to: instrumentalist and neoliberal feminist language; the need for clear definitions of feminism and opportunities for adopting a feminist intersectional lens; and challenges and possibilities for translating policy into practice.

Instrumentalist and neoliberal feminist language

Critical feminist scholars offer essential insights into the ongoing challenges for achieving feminist priorities in feminist development policies including the neoliberalization (Parisi, 2020) or instrumental use of women to achieve other development outcomes. Examples of instrumentalization include the targeting of women and girls for economic growth or peace, and for other foreign policy priorities related to diplomacy, nation branding and norm diffusion. Overall, these critiques highlight a neoliberal logic and limited vision of a feminist approach to development assistance while advancing a particular set of universalist pro-gender equality norms (Aggestam and True, 2020: 144).

Feminist development policies centre 'women and girls' as the conduits for economic growth (with economic growth being the central goal of feminist development policies, rather than gender equality or rights and justice for all). Parisi (2020) describes this approach as the 'neoliberalization of feminism' (Parisi, 2020: 171) for which 'increasing gender equality can … deliver strong economic growth [and] help cut down on extreme poverty' (Parisi, 2020: 170), rendering women 'as objects of development' (Parisi, 2020: 166), rather than as subjects deserving of justice in their own right.

These examples echo the World Bank's approach to 'Gender Equality as Smart Economics' that also guides donor countries' policy making (Parisi, 2020). Consequently, feminist development policy making, like earlier gender equality strategies, such as gender mainstreaming, continues to promote an integrationist or instrumentalist – rather than transformative – approach (Tiessen, 2019; Peterson and Jordansson, 2021), suggesting that the FIAP is 'more of the same' with its emphasis on targeting or using women for other development outcomes (Tiessen, 2019; Parisi, 2020). The argument of 'more of the same' builds on critical analyses of past gender and development strategies. Policies that are focused on a 'women and girl'-centric approach to international assistance are primarily concerned with improved and enhanced participation – or inclusion – of women and girls in development. Drawing on a liberal feminist approach, the Women in Development strategy begins with the question: 'where are the women'? (Enloe, 2014) but does little to uncover and address the gendered power relations that prevent women's participation or perpetuate diverse forms of discrimination based on gender.

While the language of gender equality is increasingly used in foreign policy documents, the discourse falls back on 'women and children'-centric approaches. Under the guise of pro-gender equality norms, donor countries use this rhetoric, in part, to portray themselves as a good, humane donors, as in the case of Canada (Tiessen and Black, 2019). In Sweden, pro-gender norms, gender mainstreaming and feminist foreign policy align with its 'long-held self-images as "good" and/or "women-friendly" and the state's ability to articulate pro-gender priorities in policy rhetoric' (Aggestam and True, 2020: 57). Germany also has a long history of promoting gender equality and women's rights, featured as central to Germany's development policy objectives 'and a consistent design principle and quality feature of German development cooperation' (GIZ, 2021). Feminist international assistance policies can therefore be highly strategic narratives through which states adopt international priorities and gender equality norms as a tool for advancing their own soft power priorities internationally (Zhukova et al, 2022), and as examples of 'value signalling' in order to project national values abroad (Tiessen and Black, 2019). Governments, such as Canada, Sweden and Germany have long used rhetoric around gender equality as part of their image creation and international branding, particularly in international assistance and development programming (Tiessen, 2016). In such cases, women and girls (as development priorities) become the instruments of the donor country's branding exercise to promote itself as a good and caring nation, with gender equality language used as strategic foreign policy rhetoric.

Tackling the challenges of instrumentalized aid under the guise of gender equality priorities requires donors to focus on the power inequalities and structural power relations, which are rooted in patriarchy, racism, sexism, ableism and classism as central to new thinking in feminist development policies. Some examples of these new commitments can be found in Germany's FDP language, which highlights how 'systems of power perpetuate violent and unequal power structures ... and a colonial mindset which continue to have effects today' (Federal Ministry for Economic Cooperation and Development, 2023: 10). Germany's FDP notes the need for a 'gender-transformative' approach that also strives to 'achieve the long-term elimination of gender-specific power hierarchies' by focusing on the causes of inequality, masculinity and patriarchal power relations (Federal Ministry for Economic Cooperation and Development, 2023: 17). These examples offer an alternative discursive and material framework that moves beyond instrumentalist rhetoric with powerful language linking policies to transformative feminist approaches by emphasizing power relations and structural inequalities.

Definitions of feminism and opportunities for adopting a feminist intersectional lens

A clear and articulated definition of feminism within feminist development policies sets the tone for its priorities and commitments. Defining feminism is vital for situating the policy priorities within the debates considered earlier pertaining to instrumentalist or transformative approaches to development assistance. Liberal feminism also tends to instrumentalize women, treating them as tools (or instruments) for other development outcomes or as an 'untapped resource' for economic growth or conduit to peace (Nacyte, 2018). The liberal feminist orientation remains prevalent in many feminist foreign policies, including those of Sweden, Canada, France and Mexico (Zhukova et al, 2022), but it is an insufficient lens for tackling systemic inequalities, such as patriarchy. By contrast, a transformative feminist approach puts power relations and systems of inequality at the centre of development programming. With its emphasis on addressing the underlying causes of gender inequality, a transformative approach challenges masculinities, cultural norms and socially sanctioned power relations that contribute to inequality, marginalization and injustice. Specific examples of transformative feminist programmes include addressing discriminatory laws and practices, uncovering colonial continuities and challenging toxic masculinities. Transformative feminist approaches include activities to engage men and boys through sensitization workshops to foster changes in social relations, attitudes and behaviours, and to ensure women have better access and control of resources or addressing discriminatory practices through education campaigns. While feminist approaches share a common concern for equality of opportunity for all individuals, there are important distinctions to be made across different feminist lenses, thus requiring a clear definition of feminism.

Canada's FIAP does not define feminism and this conceptual vagueness means the FIAP lacks 'a clear policy directive, implementation plan or accountability structure' (Parisi, 2020: 169). Discursive ambiguity in the use of the term feminism may even be a deliberate strategy to reach a broader base (Eyben, 2010; Brown and Swiss, 2018) and to reduce pushback on feminist language. Germany's feminist orientation focuses on the 3Rs: Rights, Resources and Representation: an approach that draws from Sweden's 2014 feminist foreign policy, whereby the focus is on 'women and girls and to strengthen their universal entitlements to rights, representation and resources' (Government of Sweden, 2018a: 9; as quoted in Bergman Rosamond, 2020). The emphasis on entitlements and the centring of a rights-based approach whereby gender equality and women's rights have value in their own right is a significant distinction in language, reinforcing that women and girls are not mere tools to achieve other objectives or outcomes (Thompson et al, 2021).

A rights-based approach to gender equality lends itself, to some degree, to a transformative feminist approach. Gender equality and women's rights are valued in their own right, an approach that seeks to 'advance gender equality for its own sake, as well as in service to other foreign policy priorities' (Thompson et al, 2021: 2). In defining feminism, Germany's FDP begins by recognizing that there are many feminisms. The government of Germany 'recognises that a single concept of feminist does not exist', drawing attention to feminisms that originated in Black feminism and socialist feminist movements, beyond the 'white, Eurocentric perspective' (Thompson et al, 2021: 5). While Germany's FDP considers diverse feminisms it fails to name the feminist approach that guides the official policy, with significant implications for how this policy will translate into practice. Furthermore, Germany's FDP does not explore a decolonial feminist approach which would centre feminist strategies around challenging structural inequalities that arise from racism and patriarchy.

To be more fully inclusive and intersectional, a feminist policy must consider diverse experiences of marginalization, oppression and inequality, drawing on the valuable insights of intersectional feminist scholars. For example, race, age, income, marital status, sexual orientation, ethnicity, religion and many other factors are central to a feminist analysis of inequality and injustice. Yet, women appear in feminist foreign policies as an essentialized group with little attention to the different experiences of inequality, injustice and marginalization within this broad category. The inclusive approach taken in feminist development policies focuses on the improved and enhanced participation of women and girls in existing development programmes, and reinforces neoliberal, Women in Development approaches. For example, Canada's FIAP fails to address the gendered power relations and their impacts on women, within this broad category of women, and on other marginalized groups. Essentializing women and simplifying experiences of inequality and marginalization under the broad umbrella of women is an insufficient strategy for inclusive development programming. Furthermore, the FIAP employs a binary lens of men and women (Nacyte, 2018), leaving out LGBTQIA+ individuals and gender-variant persons who face multiple forms of discrimination, harassment and transphobia (Mason, 2019; Aylward and Brown, 2020; Husband and Tiessen, 2020). Similar challenges were documented in critical analyses of Sweden's feminist foreign policy, whereby foreign policy singled out women and girls (Bergman Rosamond, 2020), creating gaps in our ability to address the gender-specific hardships, violence, and relationships that men and boys and people of diverse genders experience (Bergman Rosamond, 2020).

Germany's 2023 FDP employs a more inclusive and intersectional language by focusing on power-oriented and intersectional realities. For example, Germany acknowledges that gender equality has not been achieved anywhere in the world and links this challenge to patriarchal power structures. Very systematically, Germany's FDP refers to 'women and marginalised persons' (as knowledge-bearers, agents of change, and as those who experience the most extreme forms of inequality, violence and injustice), with an entire page dedicated to intersectionality. Germany's FDP provides greater attention to LGBTQIA+ or sexual orientation and gender inclusion throughout the policy and most specifically in relation to human rights under threat for LGBTQIA+ persons, highlighting the need for 'equal rights and legal equality'. Germany's FDP therefore highlights the possibilities for improvement in language with increased attention to intersectionality and inclusion in feminist policy making.

The discursive analyses of policy documents examined in this section offer valuable contributions to knowledge about the language and priorities of donors. Previous examples and knowledge about the evaluation of policy can be found in the nearly three decades of gender mainstreaming strategies arising from the Beijing Conference on Women in 1995 (True and Parisi, 2012). Several key findings emerge from evaluations of gender mainstreaming policies, including vague – or 'hollow' – language (Daly, 2005: 433) that results in gender mainstreaming priorities being 'everywhere but nowhere' (Tiessen, 2007); and the challenges of translating gender mainstreaming policies into concrete practices (Eveline and Bacchi, 2010; Lombardo et al, 2009; Bacchi, 2017). When gender mainstreaming is limited to checklists of activities (such as appointing gender focal point staff who have little or no influence on the direction of policies and programmes within the organization) (Tiessen, 2007), it loses its political power and transformative orientation, thereby 'diminish[ing] and depoliticiz[ing] gender equality goals' (True and Parisi, 2012: 40). The challenges of translating feminist policy into practice must therefore take into account acts of resistance by institutional actors; the conflation of terms like gender with women (thereby failing to address power relations); the challenges of monitoring for changes in gender relations; and the instrumentalization of gender mainstreaming for other goals and priorities (True and Parisi, 2012). These important lessons from nearly 30 years of gender mainstreaming research and policy analysis offer a useful lens to consider the potential weaknesses or challenges to the implementation of feminist development policies.

Strategies and possibilities for translating policy into practice

Beyond discursive analyses, critical feminist scholars have also considered the challenges of – and potential opportunities for – translating feminist foreign policy into practice, as they relate to: funding commitments; monitoring and auditing strategies; and the role of agents of change or inside activists who support feminist policy and practice.

Funding commitments

Ultimately, the 'true test of a feminist commitment to international assistance is in the delivery of programming' and concrete actions that align with the branding (Tiessen and Black, 2019: 44). To ensure policies translate into practice, feminist development policies need a clear and strong message about financial commitments. Evidence of increased financial commitments to support gender equality programming can be found in pro-gender and feminist foreign policies, including increased funding to support local women's organizations who may be best placed to support feminist programme interventions (Thompson et al, 2021).

To provide context for the significance of funding allocations in feminist development policies, consider average commitments to gender equality priorities among the members of the OECD Development Assistance Committee (DAC), which include commitments of less than half (45 per cent) of overall bilateral official development assistance funds allocated to activities that have gender equality as a principle or significant objective (OECD, 2023). OECD-DAC members with the highest percentage of ODA dedicated to gender equality were also more likely to have developed – or to be in the process of developing – feminist foreign policies or feminist international assistance policies (Sowa, 2023).

Canada's commitments to increased funding in support of gender equality outlined in the FIAP promise a total of 15 per cent of its bilateral international development assistance spending, with earmarked funding for gender equality and the empowerment of women and girls. Canada claims to offer a significant increase in investments for gender equality in its feminist international assistance commitments. Another 80 per cent of bilateral development assistance projects are earmarked for the improved and increased integration of gender equality and the empowerment of women and girls. In total, Canada FIAP promises to commit 95 per cent of its bilateral international development assistance investments to activities that either target or integrate gender equality and the empowerment of women and girls. These percentages are much higher than the OECD-DAC average, summarized earlier. The financial investments are described as the linchpin for establishing Canada as an important feminist donor and a leader in the promotion of the empowerment of women and girls globally (Government of Canada, 2017). Since the launch of the FIAP, Canada has made several commitments to new funding initiatives in support of gender equality, including the launch of the Equality Fund in 2019 which includes a feminist fund of CAD$300 million (to support locally based women's rights organizations fighting for gender equality) as part of the Canadian ODA package. In November 2020, Canada announced CAD$150 million to further support local women's organizations through the Women's Voice and Leadership Program which supports 32 projects across 30 countries and regions (Thompson et al, 2021; Government of Canada, 2023a).

Germany's FDP commits to increasing the proportion of new project funding for the promotion of gender equality to a total of 93 per cent by 2025, an amount that is also significantly higher than the average OECD-DAC commitment. Despite these substantial commitments to ensuring more than 90 per cent of funding to target or integrate gender equality, the terms 'targeted' and 'integrated' remain ambiguous, requiring more careful attention to the specific strategies and priorities needed to ensure gender equality priorities are central to the development programmes. To fully document the extent to which gender equality is indeed a targeted or integrated priority requires innovative data collection and auditing tools that move beyond simple measures that track the number of women who participate in some element of a development project.

Poor measurement tools: monitoring and auditing strategies

To address weak monitoring and evaluation strategies in foreign aid policies, feminist monitoring, evaluation and learning toolkits have been developed. They aim to capture more comprehensive information about feminist and gender equality outcomes, and to better track the translation of policy into practice. Feminist measurements ensure that gender equality outcomes are measured across a range of objectives (social, political, economic, health, among others); that an intersectional lens is used to consider programme impacts on diverse genders and across different groups of women and other groups; and that the programme beneficiaries are able to provide input on empowerment and gender equality outcomes in relation to their local contexts (Government of Canada, 2023b). Feminist measurements offer detailed and analytical information that is not possible when using standard results-based management frameworks since results-based management tools tend to link programme goals explicitly to the priorities of donors (such as economic growth) and not to the locally identified needs and priorities of the communities (Novovic, 2023), and rely heavily on simple data collection such as the number of women and men who attend training or programme activities.

Feminist auditing and measurement approaches demand changes to how programme outcomes are evaluated with new approaches that move to longer-term outcome mapping, and that address the problematic donor control and ownership of project priorities. Building on the lessons learned from gender mainstreaming audits, it is crucial to document locally understood definitions of feminism, and the priorities and processes for achieving gender equality and social inclusion that reflect the 'meanings of gender equality in different global contexts' (True and Parisi, 2012: 40). A feminist approach to auditing focuses on how well policies are linked to programmes, projects, services and funding, combined with strategies to assess organizational performance by identifying 'critical gender gaps and challenges and making recommendations of how they can be addressed through improvements and innovations' (EIGE, 2019: np). In addition, a feminist auditing tool must also keep track of ongoing challenges, resistances and regression in gender equality work. Feminist development policies do not currently require explicit feminist monitoring, evaluation and learning tools for enacting their policies. Thus, the principles of feminist practice of ensuring locally engaged and locally owned project evaluation are not fully considered within feminist or pro-gender foreign policy documents.

Feminist criteria that could be more fully explored in monitoring, evaluation and learning, and in auditing activities, include commitments to working more collaboratively with greater flexibility to support equal partnerships while also recognizing and acknowledging power resulting from the political act of evaluation; supporting agency-focused strategies to ensure evaluation activities are useful and owned by partners; accepting that change is not always linear and regressive practices need to be taken into account in the work we do; understanding that change is needed at different levels from the individual to the systemic; and supporting community-focused and collaborative learning with partners as part of a broader ecosystem (Wyatt et al, 2021).

The role of agents of change and inside activists

A further set of considerations for analysing the translation of pro-gender and/or feminist foreign aid policy into practice is the challenges of the sustained engagement, role and impact of inside activists. While feminist foreign policies have grown in numbers over the past decade to at least 13 official policy documents (at the time of writing), the longevity of these documents is increasingly in question. Shifts in government leadership, particularly to conservative or authoritarian governments, means that feminist foreign policies may not have a particularly long 'shelf life'. Sustained commitments by the government of Sweden to gender equality priorities remain in place despite the rescinding of the feminist framing of its foreign policy, offering some hope for ongoing commitments to feminist-informed practice. Other governments, such as Australia, have had a long-standing commitment to gender equality programming as part of their international assistance portfolio and, in the absence of a feminist development policy, can still play a strategic role in advancing feminist practice and gender equality outcomes. Of central importance to these sustained feminist commitments is the role of inside activists who continue to champion feminist priorities in foreign aid programmes. Inside activists who have been engaged in gender mainstreaming activities are vital to creating changes and building collaborative networks among other feminist activists (True, 2003) as 'astute feminist bureaucrats' (Sandler et al, 2012). The work of feminist inside activists can promote institutional change through their political agency within the bureaucracy and play a vital role in translating feminist policy into practice (Tiessen and Okoli, 2023), particularly when acting in solidarity with locally based women's rights and gender equality organizations.

The discursive challenges and opportunities of feminist development policies and their translation into practice have been summarized in this section. One of the limitations or weaknesses of feminist development policies is their lack of attention to feminist decolonial priorities. In the next section, decolonial feminism is considered as a lens for critically analysing and reformulating feminist development policies to address contemporary challenges and global crises more fully.

The possibilities of decolonial feminism

Acknowledging aid as rooted in neo-colonial systems (Alexander, 2022) whereby Western donors maintain power in their relationships of development assistance with recipient countries, is a useful starting point for introducing a decolonial feminist approach. The impact of such skewed relationships is that aid programming accountability remains upward to donors, linking to one of the persistent challenges in development assistance noted at the start of this chapter. Increased efforts to shift accountability for aid spending to the intended beneficiaries of development assistance is crucial for a feminist decolonial development strategy. Furthermore, to fully embrace a decolonial feminist approach to foreign policy requires a renewed commitment to feminist ethics and practice, as discussed in the chapters on practice (Chapter 7) and power (Chapter 3) of this volume. In so doing, we need to move from 'business as usual' in foreign policy making to a new vision that embraces a decolonial feminist lens in international assistance. Decolonial feminism enacts the critique of 'racialized, colonial, and capitalist heterosexualist gender oppression as a lived transformation of the social' (Lugones, 2010: 745), and moves beyond critical discourse analyses. Core themes to consider when employing a decolonial feminist lens include: the Western representation of the 'Other', or 'Third World woman' (Mohanty, 1988) and the universalizing approach to gender equality through a 'Western' lens; greater insight and knowledge emerging from diverse and intersectional perspectives including Indigenous scholars and activists to guide feminist policy making; and centring local knowledge and lived experiences of the most marginalized in relation to their political and economic struggles. To guide policy making with these decolonial feminist insights in mind, we start with the understanding that 'decolonization is not a metaphor' (Tuck and Yang, 2012) but is instead the enactment of justice and reparations that begins with local ownership of the change processes.

Local ownership in international assistance, as a primary goal of a decolonial approach, requires increased commitments to putting development and humanitarian aid in the hands of local organizations (Gender and Development Network, 2021). As Aksli (2017) argues, feminist development policies may be deemed irrelevant in partner countries if they centre a Western conception of gender equality and women's rights and fail to support strong local development programming. Localization begins with the recognition of power imbalances in donor relations and a commitment to shifting away from Global North (donor) full control of development programming. In this new iteration of aid spending, aid is treated as reparations rather than charity (Lugones, 2010). When aid strategies are designed with reparations and redistribution of wealth at the centre, the focus of development shifts from the rhetoric of failure in the Global South to achieve development indicators, to one that recognizes the structural inequalities perpetuated by powerful corporations and donor nations through unjust trade relations. At the heart of a localization process is allocating more power, resources and control to local organizations. Development policies would benefit, therefore, from a stronger partnership orientation to ensure that development practices are more favourable to locally based communities (Alexander, 2022). Commitments to valuing local and contextual knowledge require consideration in feminist foreign policy making in feminist monitoring, evaluation and learning. Specific strategies that can be employed include working more closely with locally based experts and supporting local ownership of data that is collected through these processes (Wyatt et al, 2021; Government of Canada, 2023b).

Building on the insights of Zilla (2023), a decolonial feminist lens can also build on the notion of transformative feminism by ensuring the policy connects with feminist and anti-racist struggles, linking priorities of development with other commitments to peace and equitable trade relations. The growing calls for decolonization of aid and development involve a demand for power and control over how development is defined (German Development Institute, 2014) and by whom. Decolonial feminists therefore question whether current feminist development policies are tools to 'maintain global hierarchies, due to their colonial underpinnings and universalisms' (Chavez, 2022) or opportunities to transform power relations in favour of justice and equality.

Conclusion

Increasing global inequalities and the rise of compounding crises around the world demand new strategies and priorities in international assistance and aid programming. Persistent aid challenges continue to limit the effectiveness of development programming, including the fungibility of foreign aid funds when used for purposes of security and defence or the instrumentalization of aid for security or other foreign policy priorities that support donor needs and priorities rather than the intended audiences of development assistance. Feminist development policies are examined in this chapter to consider the possibilities and ongoing limitations of two stand-alone feminist development policies. Critical feminist scholars highlight important limitations in feminist development policies including instrumentalist and neoliberal feminist language, which treats women as tools for other policy or development priorities; the need for clear definitions of feminism and for expanding our understanding of gender equality through a feminist intersectional lens; and the strategies used for translating policy into practice. Despite the limitations of feminist development policies addressed in this chapter, several opportunities and possibilities emerge, including advancements in feminist monitoring, evaluation and learning tools, and the work of feminist inside activists who may employ solidaristic strategies to support increased local ownership and control of development programmes.

This chapter began by acknowledging the range of global crises (climate change, pandemics, economic insecurity and rising debt, to name a few) and the disproportionate impact of these crises on the most marginalized. Feminist development policies have the potential to mitigate some of these crises if the needs and priorities of the poorest and most marginalized, and the structural inequalities that perpetuate unequal power relations, are addressed. Decolonial feminism offers an ethics-oriented lens for further critical analyses of policy rhetoric, and for the design of strategies that expose colonial continuities, support local ownership of development programmes, and connect local knowledges and lived realities to political and economic struggles at the global level.

14

Peacemaking

Farkhondeh Akbari

Introduction

Foreign policy is a male-dominated field. Traditionally, foreign policy has centred around the security and national interests of states, largely neglecting women's needs and perspectives in responding to peace and conflict situations (Bell, 2019: 418). The burgeoning scholarship on Women, Peace and Security (WPS) has documented how women are disproportionately affected by war, violence, displacement and poverty, but usually excluded from decision-making processes and peace negotiations (United Nations Security Council, 2003; Davies and True, 2019; Newby and O'Malley, 2021). Yet foreign policy on peacemaking has been slow to adopt a pro-gender approach that recognizes the different roles and experiences of women and men in conflict and post-conflict contexts, and that supports the participation and empowerment of women at all levels of diplomacy. There has been a growing call for reinvigoration of foreign policy to meaningfully implement existing international instruments, such as WPS, and prioritize gender equality in peacemaking efforts. In this chapter, I argue that by prioritizing the voices and experiences of women and other marginalized groups, foreign policy can be transformed into a powerful tool for promoting gender equality and empowering peacemaking efforts around the world.

Pro-gender approaches to peacemaking are essential for achieving sustainable and inclusive peace, but they face many challenges and limitations in foreign policy. Gender approaches refer to the ways of incorporating gender perspectives and promoting gender equality in all aspects of peacebuilding, from conflict prevention and resolution to post-conflict reconstruction and reconciliation. Peacemaking is the process of negotiating and implementing agreements to end or prevent armed conflicts, involving official and unofficial actors at different levels. Foreign policy is the set of goals and actions that a state pursues in its relations with other states and international actors, often influenced by domestic and global factors. Despite the adoption of the WPS agenda by the United Nations Security Council, which recognizes the importance of women's participation and protection in conflict resolution and peacebuilding and the growing pro-gender norms in foreign policies, there is still a gap between rhetoric and reality in many peacemaking contexts.

There is a gap in foreign policy about promoting gender meaningfully in peace processes. Karen Smith (2020: 131) argues that foreign policy analysis (FPA) has generally left out the sex of the decision-maker and the gendered nature of the decision-making process. FPA has largely ignored the influence of women and the effects of gender norms on decision-making. Including a gender perspective in FPA frameworks can lead to a more comprehensive and nuanced understanding of foreign policy making (Aggestam and True, 2020). This can result in greater women's participation, gender mainstreaming and adopting feminist strategies in foreign policies.

This chapter presents a three-pronged framework on gender in peacemaking, which analyses the extent to which gender and feminist perspectives are integrated within foreign policies on peacemaking. The first category examines the mere presence of women in peacemaking. The second category explores the integration of women's wider political interests in peacemaking, particularly through gender-inclusive provisions in peace agreements. The third category critically assesses the extent to which feminist principles of gender equality, empowerment and access to resources are present in the foreign policy of peacemaking, as well as the limitations of the presence and influence of women. The chapter also discusses some recent innovations, such as women mediator networks and civil society mechanisms for women's participation in peace processes, which foreign policy actors have adopted to enhance peacemaking. The chapter aims to shed light on how gender and feminist perspectives have shaped foreign policy on peacemaking. It suggests that gender-inclusive foreign policy towards peacemaking needs to be advanced through feminist principles.

Framework on gender and peacemaking in foreign policy

The framework, which consists of three categories, seeks to analyse the presence, effectiveness and advancement of the role of women in peacemaking. The first category examines the symbolic presence of women and the role of women's bodies in peacemaking. It includes analysing the representation of women in peace processes and the impact of this representation on the adoption of substantive pro-gender policies in peace agreements. The second category explores the influence of women in peacemaking, with a particular focus on gender-inclusive provisions in peace agreements. This includes examining the extent to which women are involved in decision-making processes and the impact of their contributions. Finally, the third category critically assesses the extent to which the foreign policy of peacemaking is informed by feminist principles such as gender equality and empowerment. This includes analysing the limitations of the presence and influence of women in peacemaking.

Presence in peacemaking

In elite peace processes, women are often absent, or their presence is merely symbolic. Peacemaking typically occurs against the backdrop of violent conflict. Conflicting actors are brought to negotiate over conflicting issues and common interests (Bull, 2002: 168; Berridge, 2005: 30). Men, as the traditional power-holders, tend to make up almost all conflicting actors where the diplomacy of peacemaking seeks to engage them either through international, regional or national initiatives. To engage the conflicting actors to negotiate, by default, women who are not directly involved in the conflict are left out in the peacemaking initiative. Data shows that women and girls are affected disproportionately during the war, especially when facing gender-based violence. Research has also confirmed that women's insecurity and lack of socioeconomic rights increase the risk of conflict (Caprioli, 2005; Hudson et al, 2009). Hence, with the emerging norms of gender inclusion in peace processes, peace becomes more durable and less prone to relapse into war (True and Wiener, 2019). With this knowledge of the importance of women in conflict resolution, there have been minor achievements in involving them in the peace process.

In the last two decades there has been formal recognition of the need for women's contribution to peacemaking. The United Nations (UN) Security Council Resolution 1325 (2000) and the WPS agenda have been the milestone international framework to recognize and advocate for the inclusion of women and gender perspectives in all aspects of conflict prevention, resolution and peacebuilding. While acknowledging that women and girls have a vital role to play in preventing conflict, building peace and ensuring security, many countries still lack adequate policies and strategies to implement it effectively as a political objective rather than supplementary to another traditional security objective. According to data from 1992 to 2019, women represented only 13 per cent of negotiators, 6 per cent of mediators and 6 per cent of signatories in major peace processes worldwide (Council for Foreign Relations, nd). These numbers show the marginal and symbolic role of women in peacemaking efforts. As seen during the failed Afghanistan peace process in 2018–2020, only four women were included among the 42 delegates of the Afghan Republic and Taliban groups respectively (Qazi,

2020). In Syria, women made up less than 10 per cent of the participants in the UN-led talks in 2017.

Israeli women have been historically excluded from official negotiations in resolving the complex conflict in the Middle East (Aharoni, 2020). Moreover, the introduction of gender quotas to advance women's political representation in peace or in post-conflict processes is a notable gain but remains problematic and constraining. Gender inclusion in post-conflict as a top-down approach has the consequences of being co-opted and instrumentalized to serve the interests of male political actors and reinforcing patriarchal practices, as seen in the cases of Kenya (Berry et al, 2021) and Nepal (Hewitt, 2017). Inclusion of women does not always advance women's needs and priorities but can instead entrench inequality and patriarchy. One reason for this is the lack of integration of the WPS agenda into foreign policies, which are often dominated by traditional security concerns and designed and implemented accordingly. As a result, foreign policies neglect the gender dimensions of conflict and peace, excluding women's voices and participation from decision-making processes that have an impact on all levels of society. For example, in 2023 only 21 per cent of ambassadors from 193 countries were women (Anwar Gargash Diplomatic Academy (AGDA), 2023).

A foreign policy that does not incorporate the WPS agenda, moreover, can undermine the efforts of other actors, such as civil society organizations, humanitarian agencies and peacekeeping missions, who are working to advance gender equality and women's empowerment on the ground. Oftentimes, in the politics of peacemaking, international frameworks such as WPS tend to be used scarcely and women are either absent or remain symbolic.

Influence in peacemaking

To examine the influence of women in peacemaking, it is important to see beyond the number of women participating in formal negotiations to consider the influence that women make in all peacemaking efforts to shape more gender-equal policies and social outcomes. In their comprehensive research report, Paffenholz et al (2016: 22) argue that the influence women have in peacemaking is more important than merely counting the number of women. Krause et al (2018) measured the meaningful participation of women in peace processes by looking at different types of women political actors, such as female government representatives, female members of armed groups, female delegates from civil society and female signatories on the agreements, and found a 'robust relationship between women signatories and durability of peace' (Krause et al, 2018: 987). Moreover, women's influence is also captured through their informal participation in peacemaking, such as other tracks of diplomacy through civil society networks, protests, media and social media to raise civil society voices and shape the peace narrative as well as highlight women's voices and agendas that are often neglected in formal peace processes. True and Riveros-Morales (2019) found that 32 per cent of peace agreements reached globally included provisions with references to women and/or girls in large part due to the participation of women's formal and informal participation in peace processes.

Women have been actively involved in various informal peacemaking but their roles have been mostly unrecognized and barely acknowledged. For instance, in Syria, women political leaders united across political divides and formed the Syrian Women's Political Movement. They advocated for a democratic and pluralistic Syria that respects human rights and gender equality and contributed to peacemaking by issuing the 'Syrian Women Charter for Peace' (Krause and Enole, 2015). In Libya, UN Women trained women mediators from different regions and backgrounds to facilitate dialogue and reconciliation among local communities and support the national peace process (Parry, 2022). In Iraq, women's organizations fought against women's under-representation in leadership positions and pushed for a quota of 25 per cent of women in parliament and government (Chilmeran, 2022). In Colombia, women's groups led successful campaigns to encourage progress in peace talks between the government and the Revolutionary Armed Forces of Colombia (FARC) rebels and secured a gender perspective in the final peace agreement signed in 2016 (Phelan and True, 2022). In the Philippines, women played a prominent role in the peace negotiations between the government and the Moro Islamic Liberation Front, resulting in a comprehensive peace agreement in 2014 that included provisions on women's rights, transitional justice and development (Duque-Salazar et al, 2022).

Yet the implementation of peace agreements is a complex process, often challenged and delayed with almost half of all agreements failing to be implemented (Bell, 2006). Gender-related provisions in peace agreements are often vague, inconsistent or poorly implemented, resulting in limited impact on the lives and rights of women and gender-diverse people in post-conflict settings (Bell and McNicholl, 2019). For example, in the 2016 peace agreement between the Colombian government and the FARC rebels, which was widely praised for its pro-gender approach, only 5 per cent of the gender-related commitments have been fully implemented so far, while 68 per cent have not started or have made minimal progress (Phelan and True, 2022; Álvarez et al, 2023).

States that have adopted pro-gender norms in their foreign policy, such as Australia, Canada, South Africa, Sweden and Norway, are focused on developmental policies and bottom-up peacebuilding initiatives, rather than integrating pro-gender norms consistently in all areas of foreign policy. However, states with explicit pro-gender equality foreign policies set an international precedent. We would expect them to uphold these principles in all circumstances rather than compromise on these gender equality commitments in difficult and complex situations. However, a foreign policy dilemma may emerge, which places peacemaking at odds with gender equality norms. For example, Norway has a visible pro-gender foreign policy and a focus on peacemaking. Norway's gender equality policies grew out of a strong social and political civil society engagement from grassroots activism combined with state-led implementation of gender equality laws and policies. Skjelsbæk and Tryggestad (2020: 181) argue that gender equality norms and concerns are understood and promoted by Norwegian peace facilitators who balance their pro-gender experiences, values and norms within peacemaking engagements. As one of the facilitators in the Colombian peace process, Norway was able to promote gender equality, while the conflicting parties, the government of Colombia and FARC, adjusted to gender equality norms.

Women were absent at the beginning of the negotiations between the Colombian government and FARC in 2012 to resolve the conflict. Colombian women created movements to raise their voices and pressed the government for their inclusion in the process. As a result, a Gender Subcommittee was created as the first of its kind in the world, to address and streamline gender approaches in the process (Daşlı et al, 2018). Generally, in the Colombian process, there was a strong pro-gender push from the bottom up and this helped facilitators, like Norway who value pro-gender norms, to enrich and enhance the norms by supporting women's spaces and actors in the process. However, the tension arises when conflicting parties are not gender-inclusive or responsible for the push for gender inclusion, which obviously creates difficulty for the facilitator or mediator to find a balance to support peacemaking and gender inclusion. A balance is required to an extent that there should be no fundamental compromise to neglect gender inclusion for the sake of peace. Norway's stance towards the Taliban in Afghanistan during the US–Taliban peace talks and post-2021 is a critical example to understand the tension of peacemaking and integrating pro-gender norms. For example, after the Taliban's forceful takeover in August 2021 and the re-institutionalization of a 'gender-apartheid' regime that discriminates every aspect of women's public and private life, Norway hosted the Taliban's first official trip to Oslo while there were no Afghan women as part of the official delegation (Norwegian Ministry of Foreign Affairs, 2022). In this case, Norway compromised on its stated gender equality norms in its engagement with the Taliban to promote diplomatic engagement. Yet this approach of appeasement of the Taliban has not brought peace or any change to the regime's repressive gender policies. Here, the lack of embeddedness of gender norms in foreign policy even in one of the most progressive states on gender equality is readily apparent. When conflicting parties agree to the inclusion of gender equality norms they may become part of the peacemaking agenda, as in the case of Colombia, but when conflicting parties dispute these norms, they are absent and may be undermined by foreign policies pursuing peacemaking.

Hence, there is an urgent need to identify and address the gaps and barriers that hinder the meaningful integration of gender approaches in peacemaking, as well as promotion of the full and effective participation of women and gender-diverse groups in all stages and levels of peace processes. Foreign policies require accountability mechanisms to address policy failures that affect the lives and security of women and girls.

Feminist principles in peacemaking

As efforts to increase women's participation and influence through the adoption of gender equality provisions in peace processes show, gender in the foreign policy of peacemaking has been limited to mere presence and some influence. While the achievements towards pro-gender norms are applaudable, a feminist approach to peacemaking is vital to achieve the full potential of the contribution that women can make in realizing peace. A feminist approach enshrines feminist principles in the foreign policy towards peacemaking, moving beyond women's presence and influence. Feminist principles entail gender equality and women's rights as core principles that take the political interests of women into account in foreign policy (True, 2016: 225). Therefore, a feminist principled approach to peacemaking ensures that gender perspective is codified and mainstreamed across all aspects and levels of peacemaking policies.

Feminist representation

To understand the feminist approach, it is important to reflect on the types of representation in the diplomacy of peacemaking and where feminist representation can occur. Diplomacy functions through representatives of stakeholders, conflicting actors and the constituents of the conflicted society to negotiate and come to an agreement on the future of the state and the distribution of power and resources. Representation has complexities and dynamics in politics and even more in peacemaking. Hanna Pitkin (1967) identified four different types of representation in politics: formalistic, descriptive, symbolic and substantive. Each type highlights a distinctive feature of representation. Formalistic representation is a clear normative authority of a yes or a no to represent. Descriptive representation is about the resemblance, balance or correspondence between the representative and the represented. Symbolic representation captures the 'technique' the representative uses to stand for the represented, with no influence but mere presence. Symbolic representation is prone to propaganda and often undermines the meaningfulness of representation. Substantive representation is an investigation of the substance and activities of the representative (Pitkin, 1967). The examination would reveal whether the representative is acting on behalf of and in the interest of the represented or a substitute for the represented.

Although attention has been paid to the amount of women's representation in the peace processes and their influence, feminist representation goes beyond examining the numbers and influence of women's participation but adopts a lens that mainstreams women's issues and women's views in all aspects of peacemaking. Feminist representation is the observable and the non-observable – to be present, to influence and integrate women's views in all areas of peacemaking, not only regarding women's issues. As Pitkin defined in her concept of representation, the observable and the un-observable is 'the making present of something which is nevertheless not literally present' (1967: 143). The paradox that Pitkin captures is that representation requires both to be present and not present. Representatives should be responsive to their constituents as well as be able to act independently according to the best interest of the constituents being represented. The autonomy of the represented as well as the representative is to be preserved to fulfil what genuine representation requires. In peacemaking, while it is assumed that a greater number of women ensures women's issues are addressed in the negotiations, it is timely to also identify whether the representation of women in peacemaking is feminist representation by asking 'Do women act for women?' (Childs and Krook, 2009: 125). Women representatives do not always represent women's issues. Women, like all categories or groups of people, are diverse and have different interests (Weldon, 2011). Women's shared interests may be their gender identity as women, but shared identity cannot be the only strong claim about the importance of women's representation. Instead, as Weldon argues, overlapping global and local social structures define 'women' as a social collective. Women across diverse contexts organize to alter this complex configuration, forging relations of solidarity and shared identities. However, this solidarity is not reducible to shared interests. Therefore, women representatives in peace processes who are affiliated with political parties and conflicting actors prioritize party interests over women's issues. This is most observable in the first category and elite process. Therefore, feminist representation is a form of representation that is beyond the body and influence of women, but suggests that the views, needs, diverse interests and insights of women are necessary to adopt for peacemaking. This is a meaningful approach to pro-gender peacemaking that is durable and sustainable.

Revitalizing feminist peacemaking

The emergence of feminist foreign policy is an important initiative for transforming foreign policies on peace and security. Feminist foreign policy also seeks to challenge the dominant and masculinized practices of foreign policy that often ignore or side-line women's experiences and contributions (Aggestam et al, 2019; Wright, 2019). One of the first foreign policies that explicitly included gender as a dimension of peacemaking was Sweden's feminist foreign policy, announced in 2014 by Foreign Minister Margot Wallström. Other countries with feminist foreign policies are Canada, France, Mexico, Germany, Luxembourg, Spain and Chile (UN Women, nd).

The important characteristic of feminist representation is to mainstream the perspectives and insights of women in all aspects of conflict resolution and peacemaking. Therefore, feminist representation goes beyond Hanna Pitkin's list of representations as well as the representations seen in peacemaking, such as influence and presence. Foreign policies can advance feminist representation by embedding the insights and perspectives of women and their interest in all layers of policy for peacemaking. Feminist representation takes a holistic approach that takes into account women's presence and women's diverse insights and interests in designing, operationalizing and implementing peacemaking. Feminist foreign policies have supported the presence and influence of women in peacemaking in new initiatives, such as the women mediation networks (WMNs) but have not been able to go beyond the limits of presence and influence representation to feminist representation. The full effects of WMNs are yet to be assessed considering their short history. However, WMNs may have the potential to advance feminist representation in peacemaking.

Women mediator networks

WMNs have been established and supported by several states and regional organizations to enhance the role and involvement of women in peacemaking processes. These networks include the Nordic Women Mediators, the Mediterranean Women Mediators Network, the Women Mediators across the Commonwealth, the Arab Women Mediators Network, the ASEAN Women's Peace Registry, and the Network of African Women in Conflict Prevention and Mediation. While the networks are rooted in the WPS agenda, their increase has been aligned with the UN Secretary-General Antonio Guterres' pledge to increase the involvement of senior women envoys and mediators (United Nations, 2017). The WMNs come from different geographical and cultural contexts and are created with a specific foreign policy agenda (except FemWise-Africa), funded by foreign ministries. Women mediators have been involved in community-level peacebuilding;

however, WMNs aim to create pools of senior women experts in high-level peace initiatives.

WMNs share the following common objectives across all the initiatives: first, to secure space and increase the visibility of women mediators in high-level peacemaking. Second, to enhance the professional capacity of women mediators through peer-to-peer learning and sharing existing expertise. Third, to build a network and connection between local and global initiatives, centring the visibility of women's mediating role in peacemaking. Fourth, WMNs contribute to strengthening the global peace and security agenda through sustainable peace agreements. WMNs' goal is not limited to increasing the representation of a few women in high-level international processes. Instead, they aim to amplify the voices of all women in mediation, from grassroots peacebuilding organizations that focus on women's participation up to appointing UN Special Envoys. These objectives align with the broader normative framework of WPS and take a comprehensive approach to mediation and women's roles in it, enabling a multi-level approach to both mediation and leadership.

While the WMNs are an innovative approach to addressing the barriers women face in peacemaking, the initiatives have their limitations. There are conceptual limitations as well as structural ones. The conceptual limitation is that WMNs are solely based on mediation activity, which is effective and operational only after the consent of the conflicting parties for a given peace process. Consent is a core norm of mediation, while 'gender' has not been accepted as a core norm of mediation (Federer, 2016). If conflicting parties choose to exclude women, mediators and facilitators have a very limited role only from outside the main process to push for the inclusion of WMNs to play a role.

Second, the structural limitation of the networks is their reliability on national action plans of foreign ministries, their limited resources and limited funding (Fellin and Turner, 2021). National action plan commitments change from one period and often government to another, as does the funding and political support for the WMNs. This limits WMNs from strategically planning mid- to long-term goals. Even further, the WMNs' reliance on foreign ministries ties them to the political objectives of the government in power and its political priorities. Therefore, independent mechanisms for funding WMNs are crucial for their effectiveness. Even if there is women's presence, and women's influence, if the foreign policy lacks a feminist approach, it can unravel the funding and support for WMNs. Therefore, WMNs, considering their limitations and scope, do not fulfil a feminist representation. Feminist representation in peacemaking needs to have a presence, influence and substantive contribution in all aspects of peacemaking and not only mediation. As a new initiative, WMNs can evolve and build the potential to become a feminist representative in peacemaking by addressing the current scope and funding limitations and broadening it to include all activities and tracks of peacemaking diplomacy.

The growing trend of pro-gender norms in foreign policies to create and invest in regional and international WMNs is remarkable, however, they are constrained in their impact, approaches and are tied to political will, government structures and funding. As such, the ability of WMNs to transform the historical discrimination and barriers that women face in the patriarchy of peacemaking is limited. The foreign policies of peacemaking are yet to prioritize gender as an integrative agenda. Therefore, there is a need to revitalize the policy of peacemaking by adopting a feminist approach in peacemaking that is cohesive and holistic to women's empowerment and agency in peace.

Civil society mechanisms

In recent challenging conflicts, such as Syria and Afghanistan, states and the UN have initiated civil society mechanisms to support the inclusion of women marginalized by conflicting parties in formal peace processes. For example, in Syria, women have been leading efforts to promote dialogue, reconciliation and humanitarian assistance across different tracks of peace processes, but they have been largely excluded from formal negotiations and decision-making (Tabbara and Rubin, 2018). Women's inclusion is promoted and enabled up to a certain level, and not in key decision-making and bargaining that can shape the outcome of the peace process. In the Geneva II Conference on Syria, no women were present on behalf of the Syrian government, nor the Syrian opposition actors and neither on behalf of the UN (Moore and Talarico, 2015). Similarly, in the US–Taliban 'peace' deal signed on 29 February 2020, not a single woman was present in the 13 rounds of negotiations and the agreement did not reference a single word on women and women's rights. These examples show that despite the existence of innovative approaches and mechanisms to break women's barriers to participate in peacemaking, they are excluded from formal and top-level negotiations and settings.

The civil society mechanisms are useful but not powerful enough to break through the patriarchal and traditional barriers (Akbari and True, 2024). They are barely an aid and assistance. For example, the UN Women's Peace and Humanitarian Fund launched a finance mechanism called Rapid Response Window (RRW) on Women's Participation in Peace Processes and the Implementation of Peace Agreements (WPHF, 2021). The RRW aims to address the technical and logistical barriers that women and local civil society organizations often face to participate meaningfully in peace processes at all levels, such as travel, childcare, translation, advocacy and capacity-building support. The RRW supported three pilot initiatives led by women's civil society organizations on two continents. In Afghanistan before the Taliban takeover of Afghanistan, RPW supported raising awareness of the essential roles of women in formal conflict resolution processes and facilitating the direct participation of diverse women's civil society organizations in a track two peace process. In Mali, RRW supports local consultations to strengthen advocacy initiatives for women's participation in the implementation of the Agreement for Peace and Reconciliation. This tool aimed to deliver flexible funding to civil society organizations so that women can take their rightful place at the peace table. While such initiatives are essential for practical reasons, there is a need for a feminist approach to include women in all layers and mainstream their perspectives and agendas as central to peacemaking.

Currently, because of the failed peace process in Afghanistan and complete exclusion of women, states, such as the US and European Union countries, have initiated civil society mechanisms to support Afghan women. The US Department initiated the US Afghan Consultative Mechanism (USACM) that brings together Afghan women's coalitions, civil society leaders, journalists, academics and religious scholars from both inside and outside Afghanistan to inform the US on gender issues related to Afghanistan. The European Union initiated the Afghan Women Leaders Forum in 2022 for Afghan women after the Taliban takeover to ensure women's 'active and meaningful participation' in the dialogue about current developments and the future of Afghanistan. These initiatives are helpful but restricted in their influence and impact. Although the forums suggest representing diverse Afghan women inside and outside the country, a close look at the participants shows the elite Afghan women who have been evacuated since August 2021. There is no international mechanism in place to amplify the voice of Afghan women from inside the country nor is there safe mechanism to secure their travels outside the country to attend these forums. Furthermore, the influence of these forums in bringing a positive change to the plight of women is limited at best. Furthermore, the representation of women in these platforms and initiatives is often unclear on what basis women representatives are selected and how these women act for women.

The civil society mechanisms are helpful with logistical issues that support women in participating in peacemaking activities and forums where they are allowed. However, the mechanisms have so far failed to break through the main barrier to women's participation in top-level negotiation that is the core of peacemaking, as shown both in the cases of Syria and Afghanistan. The civil society mechanisms are also lacking the characteristics of feminist representation. Therefore, foreign policies need to advance the peacemaking initiative through feminist principles, and it has to be through a holistic approach to include women and mainstream women in all layers of policy making.

Conclusion

Despite the existing knowledge and evidence on the critical role of women in peacemaking as a crucial prerequisite for achieving lasting and inclusive peace, women face many barriers to contributing to their full potential in peacemaking. The WPS agenda, which aims to address the historical gap in women's participation and needs in peacemaking, has not been able to transform foreign policies of peacemaking with integrative gender approaches. The chapter has suggested a three-pronged framework to gender in peacemaking to analyse how gender and feminist norms have influenced foreign policy on peacemaking. First, it highlights how women are represented symbolically in peacemaking – through their physical presence. Second, it shows how women have contributed to peacemaking beyond presence through their political influence. Third, it evaluates how foreign policies on peacemaking have followed feminist principles and approaches, such as feminist representation, and ways to revitalize peacemaking as a breakthrough. Fourth, it underlines the limits and potential to adopt feminist principles in recent initiatives by foreign policy actors to improve peacemaking, such as networks of women mediators and civil society mechanisms for women's involvement in peace processes. By way of conclusion, this chapter argues that gender-inclusive foreign policy towards peacemaking needs to be advanced through feminist principles. Only through feminist principles, taking a holistic approach and diverse representation of women seriously, a breakthrough is possible to reach sustainable peace. Peacemaking is not only to include women, but have women's views, interests and perspectives codified in the peace process.

15

Global Environmental Challenges

Carol Cohn and Claire Duncanson

Introduction

Any discussion of 'gender perspectives on X' or 'feminist approaches to Y' *must* acknowledge and respond to the extreme precarity of the historical moment in which we live; to fail to do so is suicidal, and ecocidal. According to the Intergovernmental Panel on Climate Change (IPCC, 2022), we have only until 2025 to end the rise of greenhouse gas emissions, and only until 2030 to halve them, if we are to have a chance of avoiding the most catastrophic effects of climate disruption. Even in 2023, we've already seen climate breakdown feedback loops intensifying faster than climate scientists had modelled or predicted (for example, the collapse of Atlantic currents, see Readfearn, 2023; Spratt, 2023; Zhong, 2023). At the same time, ecosystem decline proceeds at a staggering pace – a million species are now threatened with extinction, due not only to the climate crisis, but to the ways humans have also destroyed natural habitats, polluted air, land and water, and overexploited nature's animal and plant life. Sir Robert Watson, Chair of the Intergovernmental Science-Policy Platform on Biodiversity and Ecosystem Services (IPBES), warns that '[t]he health of ecosystems on which we and all other species depend is deteriorating more rapidly than ever. We are eroding the very foundations of our economies, livelihoods, food security, health and quality of life worldwide' (IPBES, 2019).

For this careening towards catastrophe to continue unabated, all that needs to happen is for all of us – including feminists – to just go on doing what we have done before, doing the work we have always done, in the ways that we have always done it. It is wildly irresponsible to let that happen.

Foreign policy, as it is conceptualized and practised, is a prime example of the 'doing-things-as-we-have-always-done-them' that has now become disastrously inadequate to and inappropriate for our tenuous historical present and our even more tenuous future. It is a policy realm whose centre, around which all else spins, is national self-interest. Even though states' foreign policies may commit to a vision of a better, fairer, more peaceful world, their principal aim is always to advance their national security and prosperity through military strength and economic growth. While it might be argued that this made sense in a time when a nation's fortunes were not so clearly tied to and dependent upon the global ecosphere, that was, of course, only true because the healthily functioning ecosphere could (still, then) be assumed. Now, to continue to assume it while blithely continuing to pursue national power is so extremely short-sighted, so blindered, as to defy reason. And yet, it occurs.

Despite the climate-related rhetorical commitments and policy agenda items brought forth annually in response to Conference of Parties (COPs) to the United Nations Framework Convention on Climate Change (UNFCCC) meetings, or commitments to promulgate human rights or women's rights norms, the defining goal of foreign policy remains the same – to ensure the state's security and economic might through regulated competition and alliances with other equally self-interested states. We remain in an international competition to win, or to come away with our share – but our share of what? A ruined planet, rife with despoiled environments and human suffering?

Familiar metaphors – fiddling while Rome burns, rearranging deck chairs on the *Titanic* – articulate both the danger and the utter absurdity: all we need to do is to go on doing what we did before, while ignoring the imminent disaster so quickly upon us. But the metaphors have only a limited fit. Aside from the obvious point – the iceberg is now melting – the *Titanic* itself did not create the iceberg. But the foreign policies of Global North states *did* create and continue to create the disaster we are facing, through their massive militaries and extractive practices in pursuit of political and economic dominance (see, for example, Patel and Moore, 2018; Ghosh, 2021). And, while the *Titanic* apparently could not do anything about the iceberg, we still have the time to do something about our own looming disaster. But that would require a transformation in what we understand the goals and the subjects of foreign policy to be. This is where feminist approaches can, and must, play a critical role.

Thus, what could and should it mean to bring feminist thinking to bear on the urgent need to transform foreign-policy-as-usual in this historical moment of cascading, intensifying eco-crises? And which kinds of feminist approaches have the greatest potential to break through the trap of 'doing-things-as-we-have-always-done-them', or of what might be thought of as 'doing-things-as-we-have-always-done-them-plus-women'? Which feminist approaches can most powerfully respond to the extreme precarity of the historical moment in which we live?

Feminisms, foreign policy and global environmental challenges

Feminist analysis, with its distinctive epistemological and methodological commitments, could radically transform what it means to do foreign policy, in ways that would enable us to respond adequately to the ecological crises we face. For more than a political commitment to gender equality or to the transformation of intersecting inequalities (the goals most commonly associated with feminism in the policy world today), feminist analysis brings powerful epistemological perspectives that enable us to denaturalize the core concepts and narratives that undergird the institutions that hold and structure power in society. In other words, feminist analysis enables us to see what is taken-for-granted, and to 'make it strange'. And it can open our thinking about the bounds of whose experience counts as generating knowledge, what is a worthy idea, and what kinds of analyses it will be generative and meaningful to apply.

A feminist analysis that starts with the ideas and experiences of the most marginalized, including, for example, women, rural communities and peasant populations in the Global South and Indigenous people, draws our attention to the fact that the climate and ecological crises we face are the product of over five centuries of colonialism. Colonialism can be understood as a foreign policy practice based on the extraction and exploitation of the planet's natural resources and its people, in the service of profit-making for the few (Plumwood, 1993; Salleh, 1997; Leach, 2016; Seager, 2019; IPCC, 2022). This extractive model has always been violent, as states and corporations have fought for lands and resources, wielding armed forces to protect their access and secure their position in a global competition (Quijano, 2000; Maathai, 2003; Grove, 2019). That dynamic continues to this day, unabated, in the activities of extractive industries, agro-industrial corporations and powerful states whose practices control the ecological fate of a vast proportion of the world's land, as well as the quality of its air and water and the amount of greenhouse gases that are emitted into the atmosphere (International Resource Panel, 2019; Sultana, 2022).

The kind of feminist approaches that we most need can – and must – help us problematize the assumptions underlying that extractive model, our current economic system, and, indeed, our entire way of structuring humans' relations with each other and the planet. The assumption that the appropriate relationship between 'man' and nature is one of extraction, where the planet's resources are there for man to use and use up as he sees fit, is not universal; rather, it is a particular understanding, based in modern, Western, Christian, White man's theology and philosophy (Merchant, 1980; Plumwood, 1993; Salleh, 1997). The domination, extraction and depletion of nature is assumed to be the natural way of things, and man's God-given purpose on earth, a marker of masculine prowess. Likewise, the idea that the peoples of the world exist in existential competition is assumed to be natural and inevitable, as if it were the only or obvious implication of a world of different cultures and geographical boundaries. For state leaders to outdo others in that competition for power and resources is seen as success, no matter the costs to people or nature; to lose the competition is to be discredited as too weak, soft and compromising – not manly enough – for real leadership (Cohn, 2019).

Feminist analysis reveals the gendered ideas that underpin these destructive assumptions. And, by problematizing what seems natural, it enables us to ask questions that are otherwise unaskable: Should relationships between peoples, nations and states be organized around competition, often violent, or might the values of interdependence guide our foreign policies? Should economic life be organized around using things up (humans, nature's resources) for short-term gain, or might feminist values such as care, nurturance, preservative love, respect for and reciprocity with nature, the flourishing of humans and ecosystems become the basis on which economic life might be reorganized? (Cohn and Duncanson, 2020).

A feminist analytical approach could lead to that sort of fundamental re-examination of foreign policy. It could help state leaders embark on a radically new approach, one commensurate with the ecological crises we face.

The analyses of feminist political ecologists, ecofeminists and decolonial/anti-colonial feminists have shown that forestalling ecological catastrophe will require a reconceptualization of the way we humans relate to nature, with a concomitant reorientation of economic systems towards the goal of human and planetary flourishing (Maathai, 2003; Leach, 2016; Bauhardt and Harcourt, 2018; Parasram and Tilley, 2018; Di Chiro, 2019; Ojeda et al, 2022). What this means for foreign policy is that it needs to be thoroughly re-oriented; states and people across the world need to collaborate, rather than compete, in rethinking and rebuilding economies and communities based on the ideals of regeneration and reciprocity with nature. Instead of prioritizing a narrowly conceived national interest (that is, economic growth, strong borders and military might), states need to work together to tackle ecological crises at their root, by re-orienting economic and social life to focus on delivering human and planetary wellbeing. In other words, this is a vision of collaboration that goes far beyond current practices, such as the negotiation of treaties on environmental protection, as important as such initiatives might be. Rather, it involves a far more thorough-going collaboration to share wealth and resources and to live in harmonious relations with each other and the ecosystems on which we depend.

Feminists provide many blueprints for this radically new approach to organizing social and economic life (AWID, 2020; Muchhala, 2021; UN Women, 2021a; Yahaya, 2021; Naidu, 2022). Although typically these blueprints are not specifically framed as new agendas for foreign policy per se, they hold a wealth of ideas that would be key components of a transformed foreign policy capable of addressing the global environmental challenges we face. These include but are not limited to:

- Generation of the resources needed for a just transition, by: making polluters pay; ending fossil fuel subsidies; cancelling debt; and reforming the global economic and financial architecture.
- Provision of generous climate finance, in the form of reparations and grants, not loans.
- Joint, transnational tackling of corporate power, revising or terminating any economic activities or agreements incompatible or detrimental to human rights and/or the environment.
- International cooperation to realize the goal of limiting the exploitation of nature to 'indispensable extraction' (Gudynas, 2021).
- Negotiation and implementation of agreements on greenhouse gas emissions reductions, way beyond current promises.

These policies require fleshing out, of course, and the elaboration of each would be a book in itself. Not only is each policy complex, but each would require taking on powerful vested interests. And there is also the need for calibrating how each would apply across the continuum from states and companies historically most responsible for carbon emissions and environmental pollution, to increasingly polluting middle-income countries, to essentially non-polluting, very poor, small-island states. Nonetheless, the list conveys the sorts of policies foreign ministries need to be getting together to enact. If this is what feminist analysis can and must inspire vis-à-vis foreign policy, how does it compare to where we are now?

Global North policies towards global environmental challenges: the lack of a feminist transformative vision

When we bring this feminist analytical approach to examining current foreign policies and their response to global environmental challenges, what do we see? In Global North states, mostly, it is 'doing-foreign policy-as-we-have-always-done', with a concern about ecological challenges simply tacked on. We see foreign policies that fail to seriously examine the root causes of our ecological crises and to reckon with the implications. What we don't see is the radical overhaul of foreign policy's goals and methods that is required.

Our analysis starts with Global North states because, as the states that have driven the climate and biodiversity crises, they are the ones with the lion's share of the responsibility to act, which we would hope to see reflected in their foreign policies. Also, as relatively large economic and polluting powers, what they do with their foreign policy has the potential to make a tremendous difference in terms of mitigating and adapting to climate change and biodiversity collapse. We then go on to consider the foreign policies of a sample of Global South states, given they are often affected first and worst, in order to see if there are differences in how they incorporate feminist insights, if at all, into their responses to global ecological crises.

To assess the ways states' foreign policies treat ecological crises, we examined: government websites; relevant foreign policy documents including security, trade and international development strategies, environment strategies, government statements surrounding key diplomatic events (such as the COPs); and, where they existed, feminist foreign policies. In each case, we restricted our analysis to the places where foreign policies make *explicit, direct* mention of climate and other environmental issues. That is, it can well be argued that virtually all aspects of foreign policy (security, development assistance, trade, and so on) have important impacts on the environment (as, indeed, do many aspects of 'domestic' policy). But our aim was not to examine the indirect environmental impacts of the full range of foreign policy; instead, it was to analyse when and how foreign policies explicitly recognize and address global environmental challenges.

In looking at Global North states, we examined the foreign policies of four that have (or have had) explicitly feminist approaches (Sweden, Canada, France and Scotland) and two that do not (United States and United Kingdom). We found that these Global North states are now increasingly focusing on global environmental challenges; all six we looked at named fighting the climate crisis as one of their key priorities, and they also often mentioned other environmental challenges such as biodiversity collapse or plastic pollution. So, we are not suggesting that states fail to realize that the climate crisis and biodiversity collapse are serious challenges. But we are arguing that when states address global environmental challenges in their foreign policies, they do so in ways that do not deviate from the privileging of national self-interest, and that fail to fully apprehend the transformations these challenges necessitate. The key foreign policy documents and websites of each of the states we examined have very little to say about the root causes of the climate crisis and biodiversity collapse. There is little sign they have grasped the consequent requirement to replace competition with collaboration or to transform how they understand humanity's relationship to nature or the imperative to replace extractivism with regenerative, circular economies.

This is the case even for those states that might be seen as having embraced some feminist ideas in their policies addressing global environmental challenges. To the extent that their policies show signs of having been impacted by awareness of feminist perspectives, it is largely as add-ons – 'doing-what-we-have-always-done' but in a somewhat more inclusive way – rather than drawing on feminist insights to rethink foreign policy from the ground up. And 'feminist foreign policies', which one might imagine could be a source for or location of a more thorough-going integration of feminist insights, also fall short in this regard, as we discuss in the next section. Here, though, we focus on our overall claim that foreign policies address global environmental challenges in ways that do very little to trouble business as usual.

There are a few occasional glimmers, though, some evidence of Global North governments reckoning with the causes of the ecological crises we face and seeking to address them in a more transformative way, at least on paper. The Scottish Government (2022b), for example, has committed to decolonizing its International Development Strategy, recognizing the role of colonialism in shaping global inequalities, insecurities and ecological devastation, and the importance of shifting power and wealth to communities in the Global South as part of any just way of responding. It has also framed its pioneering commitment to finance 'Loss and Damage' from climate change as an act of solidarity out of moral responsibility for Scotland's role in driving ecological breakdown (Scottish Government, 2022a). And it has championed the concept of a Wellbeing Economy (Scottish Government, 2023a). Sweden's Strategy for Global Development Cooperation on Sustainable Economic Development 2022–2026 calls for 'economic development that is socially, economically and environmentally sustainable, and promotes the transition to a resource-efficient and toxin-free circular economy within planetary boundaries', acknowledging that global economic growth has 'not, over time, been environmentally sustainable and climate-resilient; rather, it has come at the expense of human health, depleted natural resources, increased pollution and biodiversity loss' (Sweden Ministry for Foreign Affairs, 2022: 3).

There are thus some occasional nods to the toxicity of the dominant economic model and to the need for a radical rethink of the way states operate. But still, the predominant theme remains business as usual. Analysis of foreign policy documents and websites overall makes evident that the first and foremost goal of every state remains its security and its narrowly defined prosperity, and feminist interventions have done little to change that. Indeed, even when states' foreign policies are setting out their ambitions to tackle global environmental challenges, as distinct from their foreign goals overall, they are often careful to explicitly frame their approach as one that is compatible with business as usual, the expansion of (extractive) economic growth as traditionally conceived, and the single-minded pursuit of national interest. In facing global ecological crises as in foreign policy generally, it seems that states must aim to be the best and beat the rest.

In Sweden, for example, the government's global development strategy may call for a new economic model, but government foreign policy speeches portray action on climate as compatible with a competitive national-interest framing: 'We need to make full use of the synergies between climate financing, trade and innovation. The Government will therefore cooperate closely with the business sector to promote exports and foreign trade, investments and Swedish competitiveness' (Billström, 2023).

Similarly, in the UK's Strategic Framework on Climate Action (UK Government, 2023a), '[a]ction on climate and nature is not just about avoiding threats. The transition to a net zero and climate resilient world is a huge opportunity', to be found in 'jobs, growth and export opportunities'. Claiming that transforming to renewable energy technologies is 'expected to result in the largest flow of capital ever seen', the UK can 'reap the benefits' by being at 'the forefront of this transition'. The framing of tackling the climate crisis as a race, where it makes sense to beat other countries, is perhaps particularly dominant in states such as the UK with right-wing, free-market-championing governments, but it exists across all the states we analysed.

The US State Department positions the aim of climate and environment diplomacy as 'to realize economic growth, energy security, and a healthy planet', and addressing the climate crisis is framed as 'a U.S. interest' (U.S. Department of State, nd). Of course, this is in part a strategy to win over citizens who are sceptical about the climate crisis and other global environmental challenges, and resistant to the idea that the US government should be spending any time and resources on it; but it also speaks to the seeming inability that governments have to acknowledging that the prioritization of economic growth and the very idea of national interests is what has got us into the dire situation we are in.

Global North policies towards global environmental challenges: feminism's limited appearance

There is little evidence, then, of Global North foreign policies changing in ways demanded by a feminist analysis of global environmental challenges, their causes and solutions. That is not to say, however, that they are untouched by any kind of feminism. Global North countries' foreign policies, when addressing global environmental challenges, often mention gender, women and sometimes feminism – whether they have adopted an explicitly feminist approach to foreign policy or not. The question, though, is whether the kind of feminism that they are gesturing towards (or sometimes incorporating) has the power to disrupt and transform 'foreign-policy-as-we-have-always-done-it', or whether it serves more to legitimate a slightly more inclusive business-as-usual?

In the Global North countries we examined, the overall emphasis was on how women and gender equality fit within the context of foreign policy responses to global environmental challenges, rather than on how feminist analysis might transform the fundaments of that policy itself. The foreign policies tended to draw on and emphasize two main arguments:

1. Climate change and other environmental crises have devastating and disproportionate impacts on women, in part because of women's culturally ascribed activities, including provisioning for their families.
2. Gendered experiences also give women special knowledge that makes them prime sources of solutions.

As a result, they tend to propose two types of policies:

1. Policies that focus on addressing and ameliorating those negative impacts, through actions such as channelling international development funding to climate adaptation programmes that include a focus on gender equality.
2. Policies to ensure women are supported and empowered to participate in (a) decision-making about climate change or environmental issues, and (b) the management of natural resources.

In what follows, we not only detail how these arguments and policies appear in the Global North foreign policies we examined; we also discuss some of the limitations inherent in this kind of feminist approach.

Impacts

When Global North foreign policies, including feminist foreign policies, mention gender in relation to global environmental challenges, the dominant emphasis tends to be on 'impacts', with analysis and argument stressing the ways in which the impact of climate change or biodiversity collapse is both gender-specific and disproportionately burdensome for women and girls.[1] In these policies, the climate crisis' disproportionate adverse impacts on women are understood to both stem from and exacerbate gender inequality. That is, gender inequality, in the form of women's lack of access to political, economic and material resources, leaves them among the most vulnerable to climate effects, and also among the least able to adapt; and this is seen to be particularly acute because of women's roles in food and water security, agriculture and forestry. In turn, climate effects are seen to

---

[1] This is also the finding of studies that have analysed how gender is included in key environmental policies, such as states' Nationally Determined Contributions and National Communications to the UNFCCC, which all UN Member States that are signatories to the Paris Agreement are obliged to produce. See, for example, WEDO (2020) and UNFCCC (2022).

deepen that gender inequality, with climate frequently appearing in foreign policies nestled within lists of 'challenges' – such as war, humanitarian crises, shrinking democratic space, greater pressure on land use, competition for natural resources, poverty and migration – that increase discrimination, marginalization and vulnerability of women and girls.

Sweden's 2018 *Handbook on Feminist Foreign Policy*, for example, states: '[Climate effects] hit the world's 1.3bn poor people the hardest, and because women have limited access to political, economic and material resources, this has a negative effect on their vulnerability to – and ability to adapt to – climate impact' (Government of Sweden, 2018a: 84). The Canadian Feminist International Assistance Policy (Government of Canada, 2017b: 43–45) echoes the theme, with several pages devoted to ways in which women and girls are particularly at risk. France's International Strategy for Gender Equality (Directorate General for Global Affairs, 2018: 18) similarly notes that '[c]limate variations affect women in a specific way, especially in the Global South, because they contribute significantly to the food security, agriculture, forestry, healthcare and energy sectors'. At COP 26 in Glasgow, the First Minister of Scotland stated:

> One of the great injustices of the climate crisis is that the people and countries who are worst affected are those who have contributed least to its causes. That includes women and girls, with girls more likely to be taken out of school, and women less able to find alternative forms of work as a result of climate impacts. (Scottish Government, 2021)

Even countries that do not have explicit feminist foreign policies tend to mention gender, and when they do, it is in this same way, to highlight gendered impacts. The US government, for example, has used 'Gender Day' at the annual COPs to acknowledge the disproportionate impacts of the climate crisis on women and girls and to announce a range of strategies, initiatives and programmes to address them (Office of the Spokesperson, U.S. Department of State, 2022). The UK government, in its International Women and Girls Strategy (2023b: 9), lists climate change and biodiversity as 'global threats that put women and girls at particular risk'. Its Strategy for International Development reiterates (UK Government, 2023c: 17) the idea of gendered impacts: 'By 2030 climate change and biodiversity loss will have pushed millions into extreme poverty. Women, children and those living in conflict-affected states are most affected.'

Inclusion

In all the foreign policies we examined, the focus on disproportionate impacts on women is matched by a second theme: that women, often because of the knowledge they have developed through their roles in agricultural work and in the use and management of forest and water resources, are an important source of solutions and thus should be included in environmental policy decision-making, and empowered to manage natural resources in their localities. In the countries with feminist foreign policies, spotlighting women's agency, voice and knowledge, and emphasizing the importance of empowering women and girls, is perhaps particularly prominent, in line with feminism's long-standing commitment to the empowerment of women. Thus Sweden's feminist foreign policy states:

> Women are often responsible for the majority of agricultural work and for their families' food security. Women also often play a key role in the use and administration of forest resources and water. Women are thereby important agents for change who can contribute to important perspectives and solutions for dealing with climate change. (Government of Sweden, 2018a: 84)

In Canada's Feminist International Assistance Policy (Government of Canada, 2017a: 39), we see the same ambition to support women because of their key role in sustainable practices: 'We will support local woman-led agricultural businesses, including local women's cooperatives and associations, which are best placed to support food security and economic sustainability at the local level', and emphasis on the importance of women's participation in the design and implementation of climate adaptation or mitigation initiatives, in environmental decision-making and in the renewable energy sector. France's International Strategy on Gender Equality (Directorate-General for Global Affairs, 2018: 18) is similar: 'Greater gender equality and women's empowerment are key elements in curbing climate change.' The Scottish Government has likewise put the inclusion and empowerment of women front and centre in its international climate justice work, funding the Women's Environment and Development Organization (WEDO) to facilitate the attendance of women from the Global South at climate conferences; supporting Indigenous women leaders' climate solutions; and funding a climate focus within its long-standing work with women peacebuilders (Scottish Government, 2023b).

Again, even in the countries without a feminist foreign policy, we see attention to the inclusion and empowerment of women in policies towards global environmental challenges. The US claims to dedicate increasing millions of dollars each year to gender-responsive climate action, which focuses on the inclusion and empowerment of women and girls through initiatives such as 'scaling women's access to green jobs'. The Secretary's Office of Global Women's Issues aims to build a global network of girls working to lead climate solutions in their communities and advocate for climate policies and action both locally and internationally (Office of the Spokesperson, U.S. Department of State, 2022). The UK promises to '[i]ntegrate gender and social inclusion objectives into our climate finance, programmes and strategies, enabling women and girls to be drivers of locally led adaptation and supporting their leadership in a just transition to a green, inclusive economy' (UK Foreign, Commonwealth and Development Office, 2023: 25).

The issues of the disproportionate impacts of ecological crises on women and other marginalized groups, and the importance of including and empowering women, are unquestionably significant. The gendered impacts are real and devastating (UN Women, 2014; 2021); and the level of women's inclusion in climate decision-making is still woefully low (Flavell, 2023; WEDO, nd).

But, as many feminists have pointed out, there are risks attached to any strategy that limits feminist goals to ameliorating disproportionate impacts on women and increasing women's participation in finding solutions. First, it can essentialize women, stereotyping their roles in relation to the family, the community and the environment, failing to recognize the diversity of women, and the intersecting structures of power that shape their opportunities. Second, the positioning of women as 'chief victims and caretakers' (Resurrección, 2013) risks either disempowering women or adding protection of the environment to their already heavy unpaid care and work burdens (Arora-Jonsson, 2011; Buckingham and Le Masson, 2017; Kronsell, 2019).

A third concern about this 'impacts and inclusion' focus lies in the kinds of policy 'solutions' which are repeatedly seen in response. A central characteristic of all of these foreign policies, when they consider gender and environmental challenges, is that they assume that 'if we consult more widely, we can make things better'. They assume that if it is possible to get someone who has experienced the gendered impacts of climate change to participate in climate decision-making or in management of natural resources, then that will address the harms. But we fear this overestimates the difference that marginalized people, even when empowered to speak, can make to transnational political and economic dynamics. And that it leaves the fundamental problem untouched: that the imperative to extract, use and use up natural resources to maximize profits is what is driving insecurity, inequality and planetary collapse. If this fundamental problem is not engaged with, no amount of inclusion is going to make a difference.

In short, we think the focus on impacts and inclusion ends up functioning as a distraction from the kind of feminist approach required to address the crises the world now faces: that is, feminist analysis' potential to radically challenge business-as-usual; to rethink how we organize international relations and how we conceive the goals of our economy; and to re-envision how we understand the relationship between humanity and the rest of nature. These are the contributions of feminist analysis that are absolutely crucial.

Global South states' policies towards global environmental challenges

Is there any evidence that states from the Global South are adopting a more transformative approach to foreign policy, one that would respond to environmental crises by privileging collaboration over competition, and redistribution of wealth and power over the narrow pursuit of national interest? One that prioritizes the transformation of the global economic and financial system over the reinforcement of borders? One that acknowledges the need to replace economies based on extraction of nature to create wealth for the few with ones focused on regeneration to support human and planetary flourishing?

Small island states, the countries most under existential threat from climate disruption, have for decades championed cooperative and justice-based efforts to address the climate crisis (Fresnillo and Crotti, 2022). As far back as 1991, the Alliance of Small Island States started calling for a mechanism to compensate countries affected by sea level rise, and these calls for 'Loss and Damage' payments have risen to a crescendo at recent COPs. In 2023, the Commission of Small Island States on Climate Change and International Law asked the International Court of Justice to clarify the rights and obligations of states under international law with regard to the adverse effects of climate change. They lodged a similar request at the International Tribunal for the Law of the Sea, in an attempt to put more pressure on Global North states to reduce their emissions and provide the requisite climate finance (Client Earth Communications, 2023). Barbados has spearheaded conversations about transformative new mechanisms for just climate finance, such as the Bridgetown Initiative, championed by Prime Minister Mia Mottley.

Some states in the Global South could be said to be making the links between a more collaborative and just response to ecological crises and a feminist approach. For example, Colombia and Chile, both of which have adopted feminist foreign policies that prioritize climate justice, have been trying to utilize the Inter-American Court of Human Rights to clarify the grounds and scope of human rights and women's rights violations caused by the climate crisis; they intend this legal strategy to be a way of putting pressure on the most polluting states to assume their fair share of the costs of responding (Orúe, 2023).

However, the states with more power and wealth are not listening. The Alliance of Small Island States' calls for loss and damage finance at key decision-making fora, such as COPs, are repeatedly blocked, ignored, watered down and/or inadequately implemented. And Global South calls for new mechanisms for climate finance, such as the Bridgetown Initiative, are watered down as soon as they come into contact with more powerful members of the international community.

Notably, in the eyes of some feminists, even the initial guises of these initiatives are not far enough removed from business-as-usual (Feminist Action Nexus, 2023). The Bridgetown Initiative proposes the creation of new instruments and reform of existing institutions to generate climate finance, including: increasing liquidity (via Special Drawing Rights); increasing lending through the multilateral development banks; and other structural shifts in macroeconomic governance. While it is one of the few initiatives that grasps the scale of the finance required and sets it in a context of the need for systemic changes, it does little to challenge the global financial architecture. With its emphasis on generating that finance through loans instead of grants, and through using public funds to leverage private finance, Bridgetown distracts from the hard-won principles associated with feminist and global justice approaches, including that of states' 'common but differentiated responsibilities', and that the polluters should pay. As Mae Buenaventura of the Asian People's Movement on Debt and Development has forcefully argued (Eurodad, 2023), it thus risks further entrenching a debt-based model for climate and development finance, in which the Global South pays the price to mitigate and adapt to climate crises they did not create, and profits continue to flow to investors in the Global North, the very antithesis of a feminist approach.

Conclusion

We are careening towards planetary catastrophe; this has to be the context in which we consider how feminism could improve any aspect of foreign policy. We cannot keep on 'doing-things-as-we-have-always-done-them'. That means not only that how we do foreign policy has to change, but also that the kinds of feminist approaches that have been brought into foreign policy – and arguably all areas of public policy – must change as well.

When 'feminist' is taken to mean a gender equality/women's rights perspective, it allows and lends itself to focusing on impacts: how women are negatively and disproportionately impacted; and how to try to assure that policy responses to the impacts will ameliorate, rather than deepen, gender inequality. Hence, the foreign policy recommendations regarding global environmental challenges focus on initiatives such as 'gender equality strategies' in climate agreements, adaptation plans and finance mechanisms – which themselves are already conceived in and shaped by mainstream policy institutions, free of feminist influence. And women's inclusion in decision-making is then seen as the default mechanism to achieve those strategies.

In other words, this kind of feminist approach is typically brought in as a way of making things better for (some) women, but within the context of continuing the same overall policies, embodying the same methods, goals and underpinning worldview; a slightly more inclusive business-as-usual. Thus, what this understanding of 'feminist' does not lend itself to is addressing climate and eco-crises in their own right, to addressing the root causes of the crises themselves. This approach is not enough. It is not a commensurate response to the precarity of this historical moment. It will not prevent ecological catastrophe.

As feminists, we must ask ourselves, to what extent have we been complicit in the production of business-as-usual? How many of our indicators of success been focused on measuring and evaluating the inclusion of women and other marginalized groups, counting the mentions of gender in policies, and calculating the amount spent on projects that aim at gender equality? How many indicators, by contrast, have related to the policies a feminist analysis demands, such as climate reparations delivered; global tax treaties agreed and implemented; debts cancelled; corporations held to account and broken up; excessive consumption tackled; initiatives taken to transition from linear to circular economies?

Of course, the pull to focus on inclusion and empowerment is entirely understandable: we see all around us a world where many states don't even mention women or gender equality in their environment-focused foreign policy documents, and that those that do focus more on climate change's impacts on women than on the importance of empowering women as a source of solutions (see ICRW, 2023: 44). But we have to ask: will participation in climate conferences such as COP or in national climate change strategies be enough? Will supporting women-led solutions – which usually translates into funding for projects to include them in natural resource management at the grassroots level – be enough? How much can either do to alter the underlying dynamics driving the ecological crises we face?

The frustrating thing is that feminism offers so much more. Feminist analysis provides tremendous resources to get to the root causes of global challenges and thus to generate genuine solutions. It could transform the fundamentals of what foreign policy is understood to be about, and how it is enacted. That is really what we should be using it for. Foreign policy needs to be geared towards collective action: states working together and helping each other to address ecological breakdown at its roots, to reconceptualize the relationship between people and planet, and to facilitate the restructuring of our economies accordingly.

In our analysis of the foreign policies towards global environmental challenges, we see very little evidence of state leaders employing feminist analysis to develop foreign policies that are more genuinely realistic – that is, more reflective of, responsive to and effective in doing something about the most urgent global existential challenges we face. Instead, they nearly all adopt a more limited feminism restricted to ameliorating the gendered impacts of ecological crises and encouraging the participation of women in generating (mostly local) responses.

To reiterate, addressing impacts and increasing inclusion have their own value. But at the end of the day, they represent a policy of 'add gender and stir'. Adding gender to the way things are done now could potentially put a halt to the obscene exclusion of women from control over decisions about how local environments are used and managed, and perhaps about some wider-scale environmental issues as well. It could in the short term improve the lives of some women, promote gender equality and lead to some better decision-making. But it does not address the fact that we are facing an existential threat to humans and other species, which we are careening towards at breakneck speed. Foreign policy, as it has historically been conceived and implemented, is not fit for purpose for addressing that threat. The addition of a gender equality perspective to conventional foreign policy has its virtues, but it is also beside the point. Unless we use feminist analysis to rethink the meaning and purpose of foreign policy itself, we are wasting our time. We may end up with more deckchairs on the *Titanic* that women are allowed to sit in, in more prime locations, with a more comfortable fit, but we will not have moved beyond participating in their rearrangement.

16

The Advancement of Feminist Foreign Policy Analysis

Karin Aggestam and Jacqui True

Introduction

This book has examined the rise of pro- and anti-gender equality norms and feminist principles within and across foreign policy. Studying the foreign policies of selected countries and diverse foreign policies including trade, defence, peacemaking and the environment, we have sought to advance knowledge of how and why diverse gender and feminist approaches and strategies are put into practice. The overarching objective of this book has been to foreground a new subfield of research, feminist foreign policy analysis, which is situated in the intersection of feminist International Relations (IR) and foreign policy analysis. Building on recent efforts to integrate foreign policy analysis in the study of IR and calls for new types of integrative explanations to address the disruptions and new challenges in foreign policy, we argue that the time is now ripe for theoretical innovation in foreign policy analysis. As part of that endeavour, we have advanced a theoretically informed comparative framework for gendering foreign policy, seeking new empirical knowledge to explain why states adopt new and varying foreign policy norms and practices, including avowedly 'feminist' ones (Aggestam and True, 2020; 2021; 2023). Harnessing the insights of feminist international theory as well as IR scholarship on leadership and norm entrepreneurship, transnational networks, foreign policy orientation and state identity, and different conceptions and projections of power is vital for understanding continuity and change in foreign policy in an increasingly contested and turbulent global political order. To further develop the subfield of feminist foreign policy analysis we also need more systematic cross-national studies that examine different foreign policies and conduct comparative institutional analyses of pro- and anti-gender equality foreign policies. With the same feminist foreign policy analysis framework, we can also examine and track progress, contestation and backlash against pro-gender norms in foreign policy.

Juliet Kaarbo and Cameron Thies (2024: 11) recognize that there is little work that connects foreign policy analysis to learning from developments in feminist theory, practice theory, postcolonialism, ethics and so on. Yet, as we have argued elsewhere, synergies are to be found particularly between foreign policy analysis and feminist theory (Aggestam and True, 2020). Feminism is a key theoretical tradition to which foreign policy analysis can connect (Kaarbo and Thies, 2024: 11) and foreign policy analysis can benefit from feminism's interrogation of gendered leadership, ethics and IR feminist empirical exploration of networks and non-state actors in foreign policy. Both subfields reject the separation of domestic and international politics. Foreign policy is domestic policy embedded in transnational issues, such as immigration, climate change and cybersecurity transgressing the inside–outside boundaries of the state. Moreover, both address a wide variety of actors (non-state actors, such as transnational networks and non-Western, post-colonial states, not just 'great powers') and new policy areas beyond security (for example, disinformation and social media, trade and the environment). They also embrace multi-level and multi-factorial analysis drawing on ideational and interdisciplinary analysis. Finally, foreign policy analysis and feminism examine the subjective (gendered) perceptions of leaders and (gendered) institutional performances set within a variety of dynamics and how they influence foreign policy making (Aggestam and True, 2020; 2021). For instance, only through feminist foreign policy analysis can we understand current efforts by the US Biden administration to elevate gender equality as fundamental to democracy and US foreign policy, the rapid reversals and removal of feminist and gender language from foreign policy strategy most recently in Sweden, and contemporary campaigns by Russia asserting that entrance into the North Atlantic Treaty Organization requires the acceptance of Western gender relations and that the international response to the country's invasion of Ukraine is akin to 'cancel culture' (see Kratochvíl and O'Sullivan, 2023).

Results from feminist foreign policy analysis

This book deliberately promotes new avenues for research as part of the consolidation of feminist foreign policy analysis as a subfield. We have focused on theoretical examinations of core concepts central to feminist foreign policy analysis. The investigation has also centred on pro-gender equality and/or feminist norms and practices within diverse foreign policies across countries and areas of foreign policy. In what follows we assess the latest state-of-the-art in research and suggest new avenues to theoretically and empirically advance the field of study of feminist foreign policy analysis.

Explaining the rise of pro- and anti-gender foreign policy

The growing presence of authoritarian, repressive regimes has increased the relevance and the contestation of feminist and pro-gender equality foreign policies. We have argued that analysing variation in the presence, adoption or practice of pro-gender norms in foreign policy will enhance analytical precision in the emerging field of feminist foreign policy analysis (Aggestam and True, 2020: 13–14). Various explanations might be advanced to understand the international variation in foreign policy pro- and anti-gender norms across countries and foreign policies. We can explain why states adopt gendered norms and practices by assessing the foreign policy beliefs of men and women leaders (for example, Bjarnegård and Melander, 2017); the role of advocacy networks pushing pro- and anti-gender norms within and across states (for example, Ayoub, 2015); state compliance with liberal international rules in trade and security; the relative material capabilities versus soft power focus of a state (Bergman Rosamund, 2020; Aggestam and True, 2020); the militaristic or humanitarian orientation of a state as judged by rising or declining military and aid expenditures and reception by other states (for example, Barnes and O'Brien, 2018; Engberg-Pedersen, 2018).

Klaus Brummer and Karen E. Smith argue that there are a range of factors propelling states to adopt various pro-gender and/or feminist foreign policies: International recognition and aid versus political legitimacy and engagement on the domestic political front (Chapter 8, this volume). Building on foreign policy analysis scholarship, they explain that a permissive strategic environment, national role conception compatible with pro-gender norms as well as the presence of an executive-level policy leader driving foreign policy change are key. But a key question is how seemingly similar conditions might give rise to markedly different outcomes concerning pro- and anti-gender foreign policy leadership. Feminist foreign policy analysis can help us to understand illiberal as well as liberal states and why they use strategies of gender-washing versus gender-bashing and norm spoiling (see Thomson, Chapter 4).

Networks matter

Pro-gender norms may spark resistance and contestation contributing to changed dynamics and divisions in global politics. The rise of pro-gender and feminist foreign policy, for instance, has been accompanied by the emergence of new types of transnational feminist networks more focused on the state than previously. These networks also often take a critical stance on state foreign policy action, seeking to break down hegemonies, whether masculine or liberal hegemonies, and to promote transformative foreign policy outcomes (Aggestam and True, 2023: 206–207). Innovative ideas about foreign policy may be developed in the network and diffused from there, rather than just adopted by peer demonstration among states emulating one another. As Daniela Philipson García and Victoria Scheyer argue, states rely on civil society networks not only because of their knowledge but also for legitimacy (Chapter 5, this volume). The state cannot achieve their goals without civil society. As they state, '[f]eminist networks and civil society are the gatekeepers of feminist knowledge, values and practices that produce feminist-informed foreign policy and governance'. Networks hold governments accountable for their foreign policy commitments to realize greater rights and security for women and transform gendered inequalities. Yet, while states have conservatively balanced their feminist or pro-gender foreign policies with often combative defence policies, transnational feminist networks have been more sceptical. Ethical tensions and disagreements, however, pervade feminist networks regarding military intervention and self-defence, gender identity and transgender activism.

How gendered analysis advances foreign policy analysis

Feminist foreign policy analysis identifies new issues that transcend the so-called domestic and foreign policy divide and present challenges to existing governance structures. Gendered disinformation in the realm of foreign policy is one example of this, featured in the volume. Elsa Hedling argues that disinformation challenges the status of gender norms in liberal state foreign policies by exposing the vulnerabilities of domestic polarization over gender equality (Chapter 10, this volume). For instance, we could imagine the Chinese state, not only misogynist domestic opponents, engaging in online technology-facilitated abuse that explicitly targets women politicians in liberal states. That is, gender-based threats are becoming deliberate threats to democracy at the same time. As Hedling states, 'gendered disinformation adds to the list of how gender norms and their policy outcomes become situated in the interests of and interactions between states in the international system'. Across political contexts, there are differences in how foreign policy discourses intersect or clash with gender norms and how anti-gender, anti-women and anti-feminist discourses shape foreign policy. What we broadly observe, however, is that these discourses are increasingly inextricable. Moreover, current foreign policies that seek to 'combat online security threats often sideline gender perspectives' and tend to privilege 'the aggressor (foreign interference) and defence of the state over responses to (gendered) vulnerabilities' (Hedling, Chapter 10). Feminist foreign policy analysis is crucially needed here to inform and guide statecraft in a polarized world wherein values, as well as norms regarding gender equality, are part of foreign policy contestation.

The centrality of strategic leadership action

The turn to 'practice' in IR and the analysis of foreign policy is a significant trend in recent scholarship, but one that hardly considers feminist theories and gendered analysis of power dynamics in everyday interactions including by foreign policy actors as discussed by Ekatherina Zhukova (Chapter 7, this volume; see also Chessé and Sondarjee, 2024). Here the leadership and novel foreign policy practices purported by feminist leaders are salient. Former US Secretaries of State, Madeleine Albright and Hillary Clinton, initiated novel practices of foreign policy as feminist leaders. Albright developed a women's empowerment policy platform with other foreign policy leaders. Clinton flipped the script on foreign state visits, requesting 'take me to your (ordinary) women' rather than 'take me to your leader'. Hence, to successfully promote gender equality and human rights, foreign policy leadership must be both strategic and political. Gender-neutral policies only reinforce patriarchal structures and norms. One Afghan woman activist recently made this point unabashedly, referring to visits by female foreign diplomats to her country, in which they observed a kind of dress code, which is an everyday foreign policy practice: 'When the representatives of the powerful countries and the international organizations are dressed according to the principles of the Taliban and drink coffee and laugh with the Taliban officials, then we can't expect the Taliban to change' (Sadat, 2022).

Moreover, feminist foreign policy analysis emphasizes the capacity to act and to understand the gendered dynamics to promote gender equality and improve local women's security and rights. As Farkhondeh Akbari asks in her chapter on peacemaking, does the foreign policy promotion of women in peace processes amount to feminist representation where 'women act for women' (quoted from Childs and Krook, 2009: 125) (Chapter 14, this volume)? She argues that foreign policy can advance feminist representation by embedding the heterogeneous and intersectional perspectives and needs of women in all layers of peacemaking, its design and implementation. Incipient networks of women mediators working across the tracks of peace processes could achieve this goal (Turner, 2020). Strategic leadership action is vital in many foreign policies. As Guerrina emphasizes in her chapter on foreign trade policy, mainstreaming gender in trade depends on political leadership that establishes gender equality as a core objective of trade policy (Chapter 12, this volume).

Looking further afield to historical and non-Western contexts, as Khushi Singh Rathore does, reveals decolonial feminist practices of import for contemporary foreign policy (Chapter 9, this volume). Indian women diplomats Vijaya Lakshmi Pandit and Lakshmi Menon are foregrounded as key foreign policy thinkers promoting Asian unity and international solidarity in the early years following India's independence. It is important to recognize past struggles including decolonial struggles where feminist and pro-gender equality ideas were significant, and their relevance to contemporary foreign policy challenges. The methods of decolonial feminist historiography being used to excavate women's international thought in non-Western and well as Western contexts have the potential to be a vital resource for the consolidation of the field of feminist foreign policy analysis taking into account power and intersectionality (see also Owens et al, 2022).

The crucial nexus of gendered power relations and intersectionality

Feminist foreign policy analysis pays attention to individual and structural gendered power relations in the systems of power that underpin inequality and injustice at a global scale. As highlighted in this book, explicitly naming a feminist approach to achieving goals, such as gender equality, peace and sustainable development, is a significant move in foreign policy. While feminist approaches to foreign policy recognize gender inequality is underpinned by unequal power relationships based on gender, they also go beyond gender analysis. Intersectional power analysis, as discussed by Columba Archilleos-Sarll, highlights patriarchy, colonialism and exploitative capitalism as systems of power produced and reproduced by the state and through foreign policy (Chapter 3, this volume). Feminist scholars and advocates argue that foreign policy actors need to engage meaningfully with intersectional power analysis and local understandings of feminism to ensure they are not imposing Western or minority world understanding of feminism on partner or aid recipient countries. An emancipatory, feminist concept of power embraces agency as well as resistance and is captured by 'the feminist theory of power ... as energy and competence rather than dominance' (Chapter 3, this volume). This feminist concept is helpful for the analysis of foreign policy and the range of different foreign policy actors deploying power, including non-state actors, small and middle-power states, corporations and multilateral organizations. Connections between feminist principles and Indigenous values can also be made via the framework of transforming systems of power, as highlighted in Fiona Robinson's chapter on ethics (Chapter 2). Some states, for example, have promoted an Indigenous foreign policy that shares commitments to addressing power inequalities with feminist or pro-gender equality foreign policies. Fiona Robinson illustrates these synergies with the example of Aotearoa New Zealand, a state that has adopted an Indigenous rather than a feminist branding of foreign policy that centres marginalized people and relational perspectives in its approach to engaging with other states and peoples (Chapter 2, this volume).

Resistance intertwined with sustainability

Throughout the book, questions are raised about the sustainability of foreign policies given the volatility and increasing conflict in international politics. Current global politics, marked by tension and polarization, are not conducive to normative agendas or to rethinking foreign policy beyond the traditional tools of statecraft. Crucial to the sustainability of pro-gender and feminist foreign policy is the supporting institutional infrastructure in ministries of foreign affairs, which is highlighted by Katarzyna Jezierska and Ann Towns in Chapter 6. New institutions, such as thematic ambassadors for gender equality and gender equality branches or focal areas within the foreign affairs bureaucracy have aimed to embed pro-gender and feminist norms in foreign policy. Yet as Jezierska and Towns recognize, diplomacy is a gendered foreign policy institution that is slow to change, making it relatively easy to enact reversals of controversial policy innovations. They trace its evolution from the active marginalization of women in diplomacy to concerted inclusion efforts today. Yet across historical and contemporary periods they argue that pushback against institutional innovation is a constant pattern. This is why we should not be surprised at the reactions to current feminist institution-building in foreign policy, such as the swift removal of the feminist brand in Sweden where feminist foreign policy originated (Wright and Bergman Rosamond, 2024).

Despite resistance and backlash, pro-gender and feminist foreign policies provide a framework of practical strategies to advance and defend rights across all areas. Moreover, as Rebecca Tiessen argues, such foreign policies can avoid a neo-colonial approach by taking guidance from local feminist movements (Chapter 13, this volume). As several scholars in this volume, including Tiessen, emphasize, feminist principles require states to go beyond a focus on mere inclusion to understanding and ultimately seeking to transform the underlying structures of power, which perpetuate inequality and marginalization. They also demand we challenge the instrumental approach to aid recipient countries and the professionalization or 'NGOization' of feminism (Alvarez, 2009) that marginalizes grassroots women and women's organizations through growth-based foreign development and trade policies (see also Chapter 12 and Chapter 15). We further discuss this issue of whose voices are heard and silenced in foreign policy, including pro-gender and feminist foreign policy versions as we consider feminist approaches to navigating geopolitics in the next part.

Feminist foreign policy analysis responding to a turbulent global world

The advancement of feminist and pro-gender foreign policy reflects both a gradual power shift in gender relations as women's economic and political participation increases worldwide and in geopolitical power with the reality that soft power tools projecting a country's values and normative commitments are a major mechanism of foreign policy. Contestation of pro-gender and feminist norms through antagonistic discourses and non-implementation of international human rights and gender equality commitments, however, is a prevalent widespread pattern in today's global politics (Aggestam and True, 2020: 17). The rise of illiberal authoritarian regimes and state violence has heightened the attacks against the rights of women, gender, ethnic and religious minorities. Nowhere has this been more evident than in Afghanistan – where the chaotic withdrawal of the US and Western powers after a 20-year liberal state-building intervention following a 'global war on terror' has abandoned women and girls to edicts of the Taliban, a violent extremist, ideological group. The regression of women's rights in that country is unprecedented in world history and sets a precedent, further endangering marginalized groups. Whereas in the past, states have deployed instrumental arguments about economic growth and national security to promote gender equality and women's rights in their foreign policies, soft power persuasion may be less compelling in an increasingly belligerent global environment. Patriarchal structures are deeply entrenched in states and global politics and resistance to change may be readily activated (Akbari and True, 2024). Indeed, as Hedling in Chapter 10 argues, 'the trend in proclaiming "feminist foreign policies" instrumentalizes confrontation over gender norms through global positionings and externalization of feminist state identities'. How then do pro-gender equality and/or feminist foreign policy leaders and states navigate geopolitics?

Responding to contemporary geopolitics demands a more politically astute approach to diplomacy and foreign policy encompassing strategic feminist leadership, institutions and global alliances. It must go beyond the perception of nation branding to be salient in foreign policy actions. Effective pro-gender or feminist foreign policy needs to have positions on defence and security as well as diplomacy and justice. In this book, we have sought to analyse a range of foreign policies, including those often left out of existing pro-gender and feminist foreign policy agendas, such as foreign defence, defence and climate policies. Heightened defence spending and militarization, triggered in part by Russia's invasion of Ukraine but also by the resurgence of great power competition with China's rising influence have largely not been the focus of pro-gender or feminist foreign policies, as Annika Bergman Rosamond and Katharine A.M. Wright argue in Chapter 11. Yet, they seem to run contrary to feminist approaches to conflict resolution in foreign policy and suggest the potential for the securitization of feminist and pro-gender foreign policies in the current climate of conflict. With heightened geopolitical insecurity, navigating the complexities of defending state borders from a feminist perspective must balance support for defensive capacities to protect people's human rights with preventative capacities involving diplomatic tools and strategy. Fundamentally, feminist approaches to foreign policy must contrast with hyper-masculine and strongman approaches that are destabilizing norms of democracy, human rights and peace.

To successfully navigate geopolitical tensions, feminist and pro-gender foreign policy requires clear messaging and a values-based strategy. States must live up to their own espoused values and norms in domestic as well as in foreign policy. They should adopt concrete, unambiguous language and communication strategies to uphold the rights of marginalized groups and to avoid legitimizing regimes in violation of these international norms. Foreign policy actors must prioritize relationships with the 'most affected' in situations of regional and global crisis and insecurity. Former US Secretary of State Hillary Clinton paved the way in her bilateral state visits by requesting to be taken to meet grassroots women's initiatives related to US foreign policy goals. Other high-level officials must maintain this stance. From a pro-gender and feminist foreign policy perspective, geopolitical insecurity calls for development assistance on a par with the defence budget to support civil society, especially feminist civil society, and their efforts to build peace, maintain livelihoods and expand the spaces for cooperation.

Alliances across foreign policy areas have been building on the incipient pro-gender and feminist foreign movement calling for a 'feminist post-COVID-19 recovery' and 'feminist peace' (Aggestam and True, 2023). States can further build on this narrative and network, harnessing actors at all levels in a new foreign policy alliance, which could be influential in existing multilateral forums. For example, in September 2023, 20 countries convened as an FFP+ group at the UN General Assembly's 78th session to advocate for a gender equality and peace agenda through a feminist foreign policy framework. Such alliances are enabled and supported by transnational knowledge, governance and advocacy networks that we have examined in this book. In states where the governments have not adopted an explicit pro-gender or feminist foreign policy, for instance, civil society actors have launched coalitions to advance strategies and options for advancing transformative foreign policies (International Women's Research Centre and Feminist Foreign Policy Collaborative, 2019). Feminist and pro-gender foreign policy goals cannot be achieved without these networks or without efforts to build a feminist civil society by centring and resourcing the knowledge, expertise and lived experience of those most affected by conflict and geopolitical competition and yet most under-represented in debates (Hendl et al, 2023; O'Sullivan and Krulišová, 2023).

The relevance of feminist foreign policy analysis

Feminist foreign policy analysis has great potential to generate new critical knowledge and policy-relevant insights about how to tackle the many challenges in contemporary global politics. Gender intersects with various national and global security threats including terrorism, organized crime and cybersecurity. Understanding the gender dimensions of these threats is essential for developing effective prevention and responsive foreign policy practices. Feminist foreign policy analysis highlights and uncovers how gendered power structures and traditional notions of masculinity inform state behaviour, foreign policy and international relations. It brings attention to the experiences and perspectives of groups most marginalized in contemporary geopolitical discourses, thereby offering a more comprehensive understanding of the complexities of global politics. By challenging the patriarchal norms and structures that underpin contemporary global politics feminist foreign policy analysis reveals how patriarchy operates at the domestic, international and transnational levels and how gendered hierarchies influence state practices and diplomacy. At the same time, gender intersects with other identities, such as race, class, sexuality and nationality, which explains how different forms of oppression and privilege interact to shape contemporary geopolitics. Next, we identify three avenues particularly ripe for feminist foreign policy analysis.

First, there is a 'credibility gap' in feminist and pro-gender foreign policies since they are hardly talked about or operationalized in the context of myriad foreign policy crises. For instance, studies could examine the salience of feminist foreign policy options and strategies in political and humanitarian crises, such as, for example, in situations like Afghanistan, Ukraine, Israel and Palestine (Chehab, 2023; Hendl et al, 2023; Akbari and True, 2024). Gender shapes both the causes and consequences of conflict and insecurity. Patriarchal norms also perpetuate cycles of violence and exacerbate conflict dynamics. Women often experience conflict differently than men and are often disproportionately affected by gender-based violence, displacement and economic insecurity during times of war, which increase vulnerabilities to exploitation. Thus, feminist foreign policy analysis of policy-making processes sheds insights into how gender norms shape priorities and agenda-setting processes in foreign policy, which has significant implications for global politics, security and development. Recognizing and addressing these gender-specific impacts are essential for developing effective conflict prevention practices and building sustainable peace. Moreover, gender analysis is increasingly recognized as a critical component in addressing environmental challenges, such as climate change and environmental degradation. Again, women are often disproportionately affected by environmental changes and natural disasters, yet they are also key agents of change in sustainable resource management and resilience-building efforts as Cohn and Duncanson highlight in Chapter 15.

Second, the critical question of how pro-gender and feminist foreign policy leaders and states are tackling pushback in the multilateral system expressed in confrontation, bandwagoning, cautious diplomacy or other plausible strategies needs to be thoroughly examined. Furthermore, feminist foreign policy analysis could assess the emerging and varied toolboxes of feminist foreign policy and suggest a broader set of practices to counter the backlash against human rights globally. It could identify new sources of 'feminist power' to envision what is possible. For instance, with a feminist institutionalist approach empirical studies could identify new foreign policy actors, such as civil society coalitions and special ambassador offices[1] focused on gender equality as a key instrument for the development and practice of feminist and pro-gender foreign policy and its connection with other like-minded countries and encouraging champions across state institutions.

Third, there is a need to move beyond descriptive visible representation and focus more on 'feminist representation' in foreign policy. Overall, feminist representation seeks to challenge gender norms and transform institutions and gendered structures to create more inclusive, equitable and just institutions. This can be analysed and assessed more systematically in various foreign policies, ranging from diplomacy and defence to the practice of foreign policy leadership, encompassing critical analyses of positions of power, leadership roles and feminist norms, perspectives, agency and priorities in foreign policy. Many foreign policies give lip service to gender equality and human rights, but do not integrate or implement them across all areas of foreign policy. Using 'feminist criteria' to evaluate policies, as Rebecca Tiessen does vis-à-vis international development policy in Chapter 13, can be an approach in other areas of foreign policy as well. 'Following the money' is a vital feminist method and, as such, tracking where countries spend their defence and development aid dollars matters for assessing the implementation of pro-gender and feminist foreign policies (see Davies and True, 2022). Financing must back up and support key allies and groups that can safeguard women's human rights as well as build local constituencies for gender equality, peace and democracy by distributing resources to them. There is also an opportunity to monitor feminist approaches to climate diplomacy and an equitable approach to energy transitions which means ensuring inclusive representation in decision-making and adaptation

---

[1] For example, the following countries have adopted these special ambassador offices for gender equality: Sweden, United States, Seychelles, United Kingdom, Iceland, Spain, Netherlands, Norway, Australia, Finland, Canada and Luxembourg (see https://www.cfr.org/blog/ambassadors-gender-equality-who-they-are-what-they-do-and-why-they-matter).

outcomes; both involving diverse women and civil society delegates and their knowledge and experience of climate change at multilateral fora is a minimum standard. Pro-gender equality foreign policies should support solutions-focused local partnerships that showcase how just and equitable energy transitions, shifting from a fossil-fuel-based economy to a low-carbon and renewable energy system, can be achieved while upholding women's human rights and advancing social and environmental justice.

Conclusion

Feminist foreign policy analysis highlights the exclusion of women and other political minorities from the substance and conduct of foreign policy making. As such, the new emerging field studies foreign policy efforts instigated by key activist states, beginning with Sweden, to counter discriminatory and patriarchal structures around the globe. It also studies the 'anti-gender' and 'feminist' foreign policies that fuel hyper-masculinity, and may reinforce marginalization and gender-based violence, and suppress diverse gender identities to restore traditional male domination in the social and global order.

From a feminist perspective, foreign policy leadership and actions are needed to defend gender equality, peace and democracy against hyper-masculine, aggressive and extremist state and non-state actors. The new subfield of feminist foreign policy analysis will produce meaningful and actionable knowledge on how to understand and respond to current global politics through foreign policy that takes seriously their implications for women's rights and security. It promotes decolonial feminist analysis of foreign policy and across foreign policies. While the meanings of feminism and gender equality vary across contexts and groups, transformative politics and foreign policy are urgently needed to promote a more just and peaceful world.

References

Acharya, A. (2004) How ideas spread: whose norms matter? Norm localization and institutional change in Asian regionalism, *International Organization*, 58(2): 239–275.

Achilleos-Sarll, C. (2018) Reconceptualising foreign policy as gendered, sexualised and racialised: towards a postcolonial feminist foreign policy (analysis), *Journal of International Women's Studies*, 19(1): 34–49.

Achilleos-Sarll, C., Thomson, J., Färber, K., Cohn, C. and Kirby, P. (2023) The past, present, and future(s) of feminist foreign policy, *International Studies Review*, 25(1): viac068. https://doi.org/10.1093/isr/viac068

Ackerly, B. and True, J. (2008) Reflexivity in practice: power and ethics in feminist research on International Relations, *International Studies Review*, 10(4): 693–707.

Ackerly, B. and True, J. (2020) *Doing Feminist Research in Political and Social Science*, 2nd edn, London: Bloomsbury Publishing.

Action contre la Faim (2019) Open letter to the president, *Action contre la Faim*. https://www.actioncontrelafaim.org/en/press/civil-societys-concerns-regarding-ngo-participation-in-the-g7/

Aggestam, K. (2018) WPS, peace negotiations, and peace agreements, in S.E. Davies and J. True (eds) *The Oxford Handbook of Women, Peace, and Security*, Oxford University Press: Oxford.

Aggestam, K. and Bergman Rosamond, A. (2016) Swedish feminist foreign policy in the making: ethics, politics, and gender, *Ethics and International Affairs*, 30(3): 323–334.

Aggestam, K. and Towns, A. (2018) *Gendering Diplomacy and International Negotiation*, Cham: Palgrave Macmillan.

Aggestam, K. and Bergman Rosamond, A. (2019) Re-politicising the gender-security nexus: Sweden's feminist foreign policy, *European Review of International Studies*, 5(3): 30–48.

Aggestam, K. and Towns, A.E. (2019) The gender turn in diplomacy: a new research agenda, *International Feminist Journal of Politics*, 21(1): 9–28.

Aggestam, K. and True, J. (2020) Gendering foreign policy: a comparative framework for analysis, *Foreign Policy Analysis*, 16(2): 143–162.

REFERENCES

Aggestam, K. and Bergman Rosamond, A. (2021) Peace and feminist foreign policy, in *The Palgrave Encyclopaedia of Peace and Conflict Studies*, Cham: Springer, pp 1–8.

Aggestam, K. and True, J. (2021) Political leadership and gendered multilevel games in foreign policy, *International Affairs*, 97(2): 385–404.

Aggestam, K. and True, J. (2023) The rise of feminist governance in foreign policy, in M. Sawer, L.A. Banaszak, J. True and J. Kantola (eds) *Handbook of Feminist Governance*, Cheltenham: Edward Elgar, pp 203–215.

Aggestam, K. and True, J. (2024) Foreign policy analysis and feminism, in J. Kaarbo and C.G. Thies (eds) *The Oxford Handbook of Foreign Policy Analysis*, Oxford: Oxford University Press.

Aggestam, K., Bergman Rosamond, A. and Kronsell, A. (2019) Theorising feminist foreign policy, *International Relations*, 33(1): 23–39.

Agius, C. and Edenborg, E. (2019) Gendered bordering practices in Swedish and Russian foreign and security policy, *Political Geography*, 71: 56–66.

Agius, C., Rosamond, A.B. and Kinnvall, C. (2020) Populism, ontological insecurity and gendered nationalism: masculinity, climate denial and Covid-19, *Politics, Religion & Ideology*, 21(4): 432–450.

Agostino, K. (1998) The making of warriors: men, identity and military culture, *Journal of Interdisciplinary Gender Studies*, 3(2): 58–75.

Aharoni, S.B. (2020) No entry: how Israeli women were barred from peacemaking, *Palestine-Israel Journal of Politics, Economics and Culture*, 25(3–4): 70–75.

Akbari, F. and True, J. (2022) One year on from the Taliban takeover of Afghanistan: re-instituting gender apartheid, *Australian Journal of International Affairs*, 76(6): 624–633.

Akbari, F. and True, J. (2024) Bargaining with patriarchy in peacemaking: the failure of the Women, Peace and Security in Afghanistan, *Global Studies Quarterly*, 4(1). https://doi.org/10.1093/isagsq/ksae004

Aksli, M. (2017) Canada's feminist international assistance risks not being relevant to its development partners and not enjoying strong local ownership, *Policy Options*, 17 October.

Alexander, J. (2022) Aid policy trends to watch in 2022, *The New Humanitarian*. https://www.thenewhumanitarian.org/analysis/2022/1/3/aid-policy-trends-to-watch-in-2022

Allen, A. (2022) Feminist perspectives on power, in E.N. Zalta and U. Nodelman (eds) *The Stanford Encyclopaedia of Philosophy*, Stanford, CA, https://plato.stanford.edu/entries/feminist-power/

Allen, G. (2019) The rise of the ambassadress: English ambassadorial wives and early modern diplomatic culture, *The Historical Journal*, 62(3): 617–638.

Allison, G.T. and Zelikow, P. (1999) *Essence of Decision: Explaining the Cuban Missile Crisis*, 2nd edn, New York: Longman.

Álvarez, J., Fajardo Farfán, J.S., Gómez Vásquez, M., Balen Giancola, M., Forero Linares, B., Gutiérrez Pulido, E., et al (2023) Time is running out to implement the gender approach: progress, challenges, and opportunities six years after the Colombian final peace accord's signing, *Peace Accords Matrix/Kroc Institute for International Peace Studies/Keough School of Global Affairs*. https://doi.org/10.7274/0z708w35r0b

Alvarez, S. (2000) Translating the global effects of transnational organizing on local feminist discourses and practices in Latin America, *Meridians: Feminism, Race, Transnationalism*, 1(1): 29–67.

Alvarez, S. (2009) Beyond NGO-ization? Reflections from Latin America, *Development*, 52: 175–184.

Amigot, P. and Pujal, M. (2009) On power, freedom, and gender: a fruitful tension between Foucault and feminism, *Theory & Psychology*, 19(5): 646–669.

Ankit, R. (2016) Between vanity and sensitiveness: Indo–British relations during Vijayalakshmi Pandit's High-Commissionership (1954–61), *Contemporary British History*, 30(1): 20–39.

Ansorg, N., Haastrup, T. and Wright, K.A.M. (2021) Foreign policy and diplomacy: Feminist interventions, *Routledge Handbook of Feminist Peace Research*, Routledge, 202–211.

Anwar Gargash Diplomatic Academy (AGDA) (2023) *Women in Diplomacy Index,* https://www.agda.ac.ae/docs/default-source/2023/women-diplomacy.pdf?sfvrsn=6189673b_3#:~:text=Results%20of%20the%202023%20Women,are%20women%20(Figure%201).

Aran, A. and Brummer, K. (2024) Feminist foreign policy in Israel and Germany? The Women, Peace and Security agenda, development policy, and female representation, *European Journal of International Security*, 1–20, https:// doi:10.1017/eis.2024.6

Arora-Jonsson, S. (2011) Virtue and vulnerability: discourses on women, gender and climate change, *Global Environmental Change*, 21(2): 744–751.

Atkinson, J. (2002) *Trauma Trails, Recreating Song Lines: The Transgenerational Effects of Trauma in Indigenous Australia*, North Melbourne: Spinifex Press.

AWID (2020) *Bailout Manifesto: From a Feminist Bailout to a Global Feminist Economic Recovery*, AWID. https://www.awid.org/publications/bailout-manifesto-feminist-bailout-global-feminist-economic-recovery

Aylward, E. and Brown, S. (2020) Sexual orientation and gender identity in Canada's 'feminist' international assistance, *International Journal*, 75(3): 367–382.

Ayoub, P.M. (2015) Contested norms in new-adopter states: international determinants of LGBT rights legislation, *European Journal of International Relations*, 21(2): 293–322.

Bacchi, C. (1999) Women, *Policy and Politics: The Construction of Policy Problems*, New York: Sage, pp 1–256.

REFERENCES

Bacchi, C. (2017) Policies as gendering practices: re-viewing categorical distinctions, *Journal of Women, Politics & Policy*, 38(1): 20–41.

Barnes, T.D. and O'Brien, D. (2018) Defending the realm, *American Journal of Political Science*, 62(2): 355–368.

Barnett, M. and Duvall, R. (2005) Power in international politics, *International Organization*, 59(1): 39–75.

Barr, H. (2023) Israel's unlawful blockade of Gaza sparks women's rights crisis – lack of treatment, medicine pose risk to women and girls, *Human Rights Watch*, 24 October, https://www.hrw.org/news/2023/10/24/israels-unlawful-blockade-gaza-sparks-womens-rights-crisis

Barr, J. (2007) *Peace Came in the Form of a Woman: Indians and Spaniards in the Texas Borderlands*, Chapel Hill: University of North Carolina Press.

Bashevkin, S. (2014) Numerical and policy representation on the international stage: women foreign policy leaders in Western industrialised systems, *International Political Science Review*, 35(4): 409–429.

Bashevkin, S. (2018) *Women as Foreign Policy Leaders: National Security and Gender Politics in Superpower America*, Oxford: Oxford University Press.

Batliwala, S. (1993) *Empowerment of Women in South Asia: Concepts and Practices*.

Bauhardt, C. and Harcourt, W. (eds) (2018) *Feminist Political Ecology and the Economics of Care: In Search of Economic Alternatives*, London: Routledge.

Bedford, K. (2008) Governing intimacy at the World Bank, in S. Rai and G. Waylen (eds) *Global Governance: Feminist Perspectives*, London: Palgrave, pp 84–106.

Bell, C. (2006) Peace agreements: their nature and legal status, *The American Journal of International Law*, 100(2): 373–412.

Bell, C. (2019) Women, peace negotiations, and peace agreements: opportunities and challenges, in F. Ní Aoláin, N. Cahn, D.F. Haynes and N. Valji (eds) *The Oxford Handbook of Gender and Conflict*, Oxford: Oxford University Press, pp 417–429.

Bell, C. and McNicholl, K. (2019) Principled pragmatism and the 'Inclusion Project': implementing a gender perspective in peace agreements, *Feminist @Law*, 9(1): 1–51.

Bellamy, A. and McLoughlin, S. (2018) *Rethinking Humanitarian Intervention- Rethinking World Politics*, London: Bloomsbury Publishing.

Beltrán, W.M. and Creely, S. (2018) Pentecostals, gender ideology and the peace plebiscite: Colombia 2016, *Religions*, 9(12): 418, https://doi.org/10.3390/rel9120418.

Benford, R.D. and Snow, D.A. (2000) Framing processes and social movements: an overview and assessment, *Annual Review of Sociology*, 26: 611–639.

Benkler, Y., Faris, R. and Roberts, H. (2018) *Network Propaganda: Manipulation, Disinformation, and Radicalization in American Politics*, Oxford: Oxford University Press.

Bennett, L.W. and Livingston, S. (2018) The disinformation order: disruptive communication and the decline of democratic institutions, *European Journal of Communication*, 33(2): 122–139.

Bennett, L.W. and Livingston, S. (2020) *The Disinformation Age*, Cambridge: Cambridge University Press.

Bergman, A. (2007) Co-constitution of domestic and international welfare obligations: the case of Sweden's social democratically inspired internationalism, *Cooperation and Conflict*, 42(1): 73–99.

Bergman Rosamond, A. (2015) Swedish internationalism and development aid, in J. Pierre (ed) *The Oxford Handbook of Swedish Politics*, Oxford: Oxford University Press, pp 462–478.

Bergman Rosamond, A. (2020) Swedish feminist foreign policy and 'gender cosmopolitanism', *Foreign Policy Analysis*, 16(2): 217–235.

Bergman Rosamond, A. (2022) Glöm nu inte feminismen! NATO, *Sydsvenskan*, 6–7.

Bergman Rosamond, A. (2024) The abandonment of Sweden's feminist foreign policy: militarism and gendered nationalism, in H. Partis-Jennings and C. Eroukhmanoff (eds) *Feminist Policymaking in Turbulent Times: Critical Perspectives*, Oxford: Routledge.

Bergman Rosamond, A. and Kronsell, A. (2018) Cosmopolitan militaries and dialogical peacekeeping: Danish and Swedish women soldiers in Afghanistan, *International Feminist Journal of Politics*, 20(2): 172–187.

Bergman Rosamond, A. and Wibben, A. (2021) Feministiska institutioner? Utrikespolitik och nationellt försvar, in E. Edenborg et al (eds) *Feministiska perspektiv på global politik*, Lund: Universitetslitteratur, pp 83–94.

Bergman Rosamond, A. and Kronsell, A. (2022) Cosmopolitanism and individual ethical reflection: the embodied experiences of Swedish veterans, *Critical Military Studies*, 8(2): 159–178.

Bergman Rosamond, A. and Wright, K.A.M. (2023) Digital celebrity diplomacy in the UN Security Council elections: Canada, Ireland and Kenya, *The Hague Journal of Diplomacy*, 19(1): 17–48.

Bergqvist, C. (2015) The welfare state and gender equality, in J. Pierre (ed) *The Oxford Handbook of Swedish Politics*, Oxford: Oxford University Press, pp 55–68.

Berik, G. (2011) Gender aspects of trade, in M. Jansen, R. Peters and J.M. Salazar Xirinachs (eds) *Trade and Employment: From Myths to Facts*. http://www.ilo.org/wcmsp5/groups/public/---ed_emp/documents/genericdocument/wcms_166465.pdf

Berridge, G. (2005) *Diplomacy: Theory and Practice*, Basingstoke: Palgrave Macmillan.

Berry, M.E., Bouka, Y. and Kamuru, M.M. (2021) Implementing inclusion: gender quotas, inequality, and backlash in Kenya, *Politics & Gender*, 17(4): 640–664.

REFERENCES

Bhagavan, M. (2012) *The Peacemakers: India and the Quest for One World*, Noida: HarperCollins.

Bias, L. (2023) Authoritarian othering back and feminist subversion: rethinking transnational feminism in Russia and Serbia, *Social Politics* [Preprint].

Bigo, D. and Walker, R.B.J. (2007) Political sociology and the problem of the international, *Millennium*, 35(3): 725–739.

Bilgin, P. and Ling, L.H.M. (2017) *Asia in International Relations: Unlearning Imperial Power Relations*, London: Routledge.

Billström, T. (2023) Statement of government policy in the parliamentary debate on foreign affairs Wednesday 15 February 2023, *Government of Sweden*. https://www.government.se/speeches/2023/02/statement-of-foreign-policy-2023/

Bjarnegård, E. and Zetterberg, P. (nd) Genderwashing or genderbashing? Reconciling the different faces of modern autocrats, The Loop, *https://theloop.ecpr.eu/genderwashing-or-genderbashing-reconciling-the-different-faces-of-modern-autocrats/* (Accessed 20 July 2024).

Bjarnegård, E. and Melander, E. (2017) Pacific men: how the feminist gap explains hostility, *The Pacific Review*, 30(4): 478–493.

Bjarnegård, E. and Zetterberg, P. (2022) How autocrats weaponize women's rights, *Journal of Democracy*, 33(2): 60–75.

Blackwell, J. (2021) Foreign policy's 'indigenous moment' is here, *The Interpreter*, 12 February.

Blok, A. (2008) Contesting global norms: politics of identity in Japanese pro-whaling countermobilization, *Global Environmental Politics*, 8(2): 39–66.

Bloomfield, A. (2016) Norm antipreneurs and theorising resistance to normative change, *Review of International Studies*, 42: 310–333.

BMZ (Bundesministerium für Wirtschaftliche Zusammenarbeit und Entwicklung) (2023) *Feministische Entwicklungspolitik. Für gerechte und starke Gesellschaften weltweit*, Bonn: BMZ.

Bodur Ün, M. (2019) Contesting global gender equality norms: the case of Turkey, *Review of International Studies*, 45: 828–847.

Bodur Ün, M. (2023) Contestation of the global norm against violence against women in Turkey, *Turkish Studies*, 25(4): 1–22.

Bouka, Y. (2021) Make foreign policies as if Black and Brown lives mattered, in M. Mackenzie and N. Wegner (eds) *Feminist Solutions for Ending War*, London: Pluto Press, pp 121–137.

Bourgault, S. (2022) Jacques Rancière and care ethics: four lessons in (feminist) emancipation, *Philosophies*, 7(3): 62.

Bourgault, S., FitzGerald, M. and Robinson, F. (2024) *Decentering Epistemologies and Challenging Privilege: Critical Care Ethics Perspectives*, New Brunswick: Rutgers University Press.

Bouza García, L. and Oleart, A. (2023) Regulating disinformation and big tech in the EU: a research agenda on the institutional strategies, public spheres and analytical challenges, *JCMS: Journal of Common Market Studies,* https://doi.org/10.1111/jcms.13548

Bradshaw, S. and Henle, A. (2021) The gender dimensions of foreign influence operations, *International Journal of Communication,* 15: 23, https://ijoc.org/index.php/ijoc/article/view/16332

Bremberg, N. (2016) Making sense of the EU's response to the Arab uprisings: foreign policy practice at times of crisis, *European Security,* 25(4): 423–441.

Bro, A. and Turkington, R. (2020) Ambassadors for gender equality: who they are, what they do, and why they matter, *Council on Foreign Relations Blog.* https://www.cfr.org/blog/ambassadors-gender-equality-who-they-are-what-they-do-and-why-they-matter

Brown, S. (2016) The instrumentalization of foreign aid under the Harper government, *Studies in Political Economy,* 97(1): 18–36.

Brown, S. and Grävingholt, J. (2016) Security, development and the securitization of foreign aid, in S. Brown and J. Grävingholt (eds) *The Securitization of Foreign Aid,* London: Palgrave Macmillan, pp 1–17.

Brown, S. and Swiss, L. (2018) Canada's feminist international assistance policy: game changer or feminist fig leaf?, in K.A.H. Graham and A.M. Maslove (eds) *How Ottawa Spends 2017–2018,* Ottawa: Carleton University School of Public Policy and Administration, pp 117–131. https://carleton.ca/hos/wp-content/uploads/How-Ottawa-Spends-2017-2018-Ottawa-@150.pdf

Brummer, K. and Kießling, F. (eds) (2019) *Zivilmacht Bundesrepublik? Bundesdeutsche außenpolitische Rollen vor und nach 1989 aus politik- und geschichtswissenschaftlichen Perspektive,* Baden-Baden: Nomos.

Brysk, A. and Mehta, A. (2014) Do rights at home boost rights abroad? Sexual equality and humanitarian foreign policy, *Journal of Peace Research,* 51(1): 97–110.

Buckingham, S. and Le Masson, V. (2017) *Understanding Climate Change through Gender Relations,* London: Taylor & Francis.

Bueger, C. (2014) Pathways to practice: praxiography and international politics, *European Political Science Review,* 6(3): 383–406.

Bueger, C. and Gadinger, F. (2015) The play of international practice, *International Studies Quarterly,* 59(3): 449–460.

Bull, H. (2002) *The Anarchical Society: A Study of Order in World Politics,* Basingstoke: Palgrave.

Bush, S.S. and Zetterberg, P. (2021) Gender quotas and international reputation, *American Journal of Political Science,* 65(2): 326–341.

Cadesky, J. (2020) Built on shaky ground: reflections on Canada's Feminist International Assistance Policy, *International Journal,* 75: 298–312.

REFERENCES

Caiani, M. (2023) Framing and social movements, *Discourse Studies*, 25(2): 195–209.

Calkin, S. (2015) Feminism, interrupted? Gender and development in the era of 'smart economics', *Progress in Development Studies*, 15: 295–307.

Caprioli, M. (2005) Primed for violence: the tole of gender inequality in predicting internal conflict, *International Studies Quarterly*, 49(2): 161–178.

Carty, L. and Mohanty, C.T. (2015) Mapping transnational feminist engagements, in R. Baksh and W. Harcourt (eds) *The Oxford Handbook of Transnational Feminist Movements*, 1st edn, Oxford: Oxford University Press. doi: 10.1093/oxfordhb/9780199943494.001.0001, pp 116–130.

Cassidy, J.A. (2017) Conclusion: progress and policies towards a gender-even playing field, in J.A. Cassidy (ed) *Gender and Diplomacy*, London: Routledge.

Chacko, P. (2011) The internationalist nationalist: pursuing an ethical modernity with Jawaharlal Nehru, in R. Shilliam (ed) *International Relations and Non-Western Thought: Imperialism, Colonialism and Investigations of Global Modernity*, 1st edn, New York: Routledge. https://doi.org/10.4324/9780203842126

Chadha Behera, N. (2007) Re-imagining IR in India, *International Relations of the Asia-Pacific*, 7(3): 341–368.

Chandler, D. (2003) Rhetoric without responsibility: the attraction of 'ethical' foreign policy, *The British Journal of Politics and International Relations*, 5(3): 295–316.

Chapnick, A. (2019) The origins of Canada's feminist foreign policy, *International Journal*, 74(2): 191–205.

Chappell, L. (2016) *The Politics of Gender Justice at the International Criminal Court: Legacies and Legitimacy*, New York: Oxford University Press.

Chappell, L. and Guerrina, R. (2020). Understanding the gender regime in the European External Action Service, *Cooperation and Conflict*, 55(2): 261–280.

Chavez, M.P.R. (2022) Feminist foreign policy: coloniality in new clothes?, *Feminist Perspectives*, King's College London, 11 August. https://www.kcl.ac.uk/feminist-foreign-policy-coloniality-in-new-clothes

Chehab, S.J. (2023) Feminist foreign policy and the war in Ukraine: hollow framework or allying Fofrce?, *Journal of International Women's Studies*, 25(6). https://vc.bridgew.edu/jiws/vol25/iss6/4

Chenoweth, E. and Marks, Z. (2022) Revenge of the patriarchs: why autocrats fear women, *Foreign Affairs*, 101(2): 103–116.

Chessé, A. and Sondarjee, M. (2024) A feminist critique of international practices, *International Studies Quarterly*, 68(2): sqae009, https://doi.org/10.1093/isq/sqae009

Childs, S. and Krook, M.L. (2009) Analysing women's substantive representation: from critical mass to critical actors, *Government and Opposition*, 44(2): 125–145.

Chilmeran, Y. (2022) Women, peace and security across scales: exclusions and opportunities in Iraq's WPS engagements, *International Affairs*, 98(2): 747–765.

Clayton, S.D. and Crosby, F.J. (1992) *Justice, Gender, and Affirmative Action*, Ann Arbor: University of Michigan Press.

Client Earth Communications (2023) *How Small Island States Are Leading the Legal Charge against Climate Change*. https://www.clientearth.org/latest/latest-updates/news/how-small-island-states-are-leading-the-legal-charge-against-climate-change/

Cloward, K. (2016) *When Norms Collide: Local Responses to Activism against Female Genital Mutilation and Early Marriage*, Oxford: Oxford University Press.

Cohn, C. (1987) Sex and death in the rational world of defense intellectuals, *Signs: Journal of Women in Culture and Society*, 12(4): 687–718.

Cohn, C. (2019) Gender and national security: thinking complexly and creatively about security, *Ploughshares Fund*, 3 April. https://ploughshares.org/issues-analysis/article/gender-and-national-security

Cohn, C. and Duncanson, C. (2020) Women, peace and security in a changing climate, *International Feminist Journal of Politics*, 22(5): 742–762.

Cohn, C., Kinsella, H. and Gibbings, S. (2004) Women, Peace and Security Resolution 1325, *International Feminist Journal of Politics*, 6(1): 130–140.

Collins, P.H. (1986) Learning from the outsider within: the sociological significance of black feminist thought, *Social Problems*, 33(6): 14–S32.

Collins, P.H. (2003) Toward an Afrocentric feminist epistemology, in E. Lincoln and N.K. Denzin (eds) *Turning Points in Qualitative Research: Tying Knots in a Handkerchief*, New York: Rowman & Littlefield.

Concern Worldwide US (2021) Foreign aid, explained: 5 things you should know, *Concern Worldwide US*, 10 February. https://concernusa.org/news/foreign-aid-explained/

Concord (2017) How Feminist is Sweden's Foreign Policy, available at https://concord.se/wp-content/uploads/2018/05/eng-summary-how-feminist-swedens-foreign-policy-2017.pdf

Connell, R.W. (1987) *Gender and Power: Society, the Person and Sexual Politics*, Stanford: Stanford University Press.

Conway, J.M. (2017) Troubling transnational feminism(s): theorising activist praxis, *Feminist Theory*, 18(2): 205–227.

Cornwall, A. (2018) Beyond 'empowerment lite': women's empowerment, neoliberal development and global justice, *Cadernos Pagu*, 52, :e185202, https://www.scielo.br/j/cpa/a/9zJqwjXHP4KbgfsLRCY7WpC/?format=pdf&lang=en

Cornwall, A. and Rivas, A.M. (2015) From 'gender equality' and 'women's empowerment' to global justice: reclaiming a transformative agenda for gender and development, *Third World Quarterly*, 36(2): 396–415.

Council of the European Union (2023) *Council Conclusions on EU Digital Diplomacy: Council Conclusions Approved by the Council at its Meeting on 26 June 2023*. https://data.consilium.europa.eu/doc/document/ST-11088-2023-INIT/en/pdf

Council of Foreign Relations (nd) *Women's Participation in Peace Processes*. https://www.cfr.org/womens-participation-in-peace-processes/

Crenshaw, K.W. (1989) Demarginalizing the intersection of race and sex: a black feminist critique of antidiscrimination doctrine, feminist theory and antiracist doctrine, *University of Chicago Legal Forum*, 1(8): 139–167.

Cueva, B., Rosa, A., Griffin, P. and Shepherd, L.J. (2023) Logics of empowerment in the women, peace and security agenda, *Journal of International Relations and Development*, 26(3): 453–480.

Cupać, J. and Ebetürk, I. (2021) Backlash advocacy and NGO polarization over women's rights in the United Nations, *International Affairs*, 97(4): 1183–1201.

Daly, M. (2005) Gender mainstreaming in theory and practice, *Social Politics: International Studies in Gender, State and Society*, 12(3): 433–450.

Damro, C. (2012) Market power Europe, *Journal of European Public Policy*, 15(5): 682–699.

Daşlı, G., Alıcı, N. and Poch Figueras, J. (2018) Peace and gender: the Colombian peace process, *Research Center for Peace, Democracy and Alternative Politics*. https://www.researchgate.net/publication/323433901_Peace_and_Gender_The_Colombian_Peace_Process

Datzer, V. and Lonardo, L. (2022) Genesis and evolution of EU anti disinformation policy: entrepreneurship and political opportunism in the regulation of digital technology, *Journal of European Integration*, 45(3): 1–16.

David, M. and Guerrina, R. (2013) Gender and European external relations: dominant discourses and unintended consequences of gender mainstreaming, *Women's Studies International Forum*, 39: 53–62.

David, M., Guerrina, R. and Wright, K. (2023) Nakedly normative, *Journal of Common Market Studies*. https://onlinelibrary.wiley.com/doi/full/10.1111/jcms.13496

Davies, S.E. and True, J. (2017) Norm entrepreneurship in foreign policy: William Hague and the prevention of sexual violence in conflict, *Foreign Policy Analysis*, 13(3): 701–721.

Davies, S.E. and True, J. (2019) Women, peace, and security: a transformative agenda?, in S.E. Davies and J. True (eds) *The Oxford Handbook of Women, Peace and Security*, New York: Oxford University Press, pp 1–16.

Davies, S.E. and True, J. (2022) Follow the money: assessing norm implementation through financing for gender-inclusive peace, *Review of International Studies*, 48(4): 668–688.

De Almagro, M.M. (2018) Lost boomerangs, the rebound effect and transnational advocacy networks: a discursive approach to norm diffusion, *Review of International Studies*, 44: 672–693.

Dean, R.D. (2001) *Imperial Brotherhood: Gender and the Making of Cold War Foreign Policy*, Amherst: University of Massachusetts Press.

Delap, L. (2021) *Feminisms: A Global History*, London: Pelican Books.

Delgado, M. (2020) Mexico's feminist foreign policy, *Transatlantic Policy Quarterly*, 19(1): 35–39.

Demel, J.A. (2020) Female 'diplomats' in Europe from 1815 to the present, *Encyclopédie d'histoire numérique de l'Europe*. https://ehne.fr/en/node/12323

Deslandes, A. (2020) Checking in on Mexico's feminist foreign policy, *Foreign Policy*, 30 December. https://foreignpolicy.com/2020/12/30/mexico-feminist-foreign-policy-one-year-in/

Deveaux, M. (1994) Feminism and empowerment: a critical reading of Foucault, *Feminist Studies*, 20(2): 223–247.

Di Chiro, G. (2019) Care not growth: imagining a subsistence economy for all, *The British Journal of Politics and International Relations*, 21(2): 303–311.

Di Meco, L. and Brechenmacher, S. (2020) Tackling online abuse and disinformation targeting women in politics, *Carnegie Endowment for International Peace*, 30 November, https://carnegieendowment.org/research/2020/11/tackling-online-abuse-and-disinformation-targeting-women-in-politics?lang=en

Di Meco, L. and Wilfore, K. (2021) *Gendered Disinformation is a National Security Problem*, Washington, DC: Brookings Institute, https://www.brookings.edu/articles/gendered-disinformation-is-a-national-security-problem/

Directorate-General for Global Affairs (2018) *France's International Strategy on Gender Equality (2018–2022)*. https://www.diplomatie.gouv.fr/en/french-foreign-policy/human-rights/women-s-rights/france-s-international-strategy-for-genderequality-2018-2022/

Dombroski, K., Healy, S. and McKinnon, K. (2018) Care-full community economies, in *Feminist Political Ecology and the Economics of Care*, New York: Routledge, pp 99–115.

Donno, D., Fox, S. and Kaasik, J. (2022) International incentives for women's rights in dictatorships, *Comparative Political Studies*, 55: 451–492.

Doty, R. (1996) *Imperial Encounters: The Politics of Representation in North-South Relations*, Minnesota: University of Minnesota Press.

Doucet, A., Jewell, E. and Watts, V. (2024) Indigenous and feminist ecological reflections on feminist care ethics: encounters of care, absence, punctures, and offerings, in S. Bourgault, M. FitzGerald and F. Robinson (eds) *Decentering Epistemologies and Challenging Privilege: Critical Care Ethics Perspectives*, New Brunswick: Rutgers University Press, https://philpapers.org/rec/DOUIAF

REFERENCES

Drumond, P. and Rebelo, T. (2023) Norm spoiling, gender washing and the pushback against women's rights in Brazilian foreign policy, *Globalizations*, 21(3): 1–19, DOI:10.1080/14747731.2023.2202106

Dukalskis, A. (2023) A fox in the henhouse: China, normative change, and the United Nations Human Rights Council, *Journal of Human Rights*, 22(3): 334–350.

Duncanson, C. (2013) *Forces for Good? Military Masculinities and Peacebuilding in Afghanistan and Iraq*, Basingstoke: Palgrave.

Duncanson, C. (2019) Beyond liberal vs liberating: women's economic empowerment in the United Nations' Women, Peace and Security agenda, *International Feminist Journal of Politics*, 21(1): 111–130.

Duque-Salazar, D., Forsberg, E. and Olsson, L. (2022) Implementing gender provisions: a study of the Comprehensive Agreement on the Bangsamoro in the Philippines, *International Negotiation*, 26(1): 1–23.

Duriesmith, D. (2018) Manly states and feminist foreign policy: revisiting the liberal state as an agent of change, in S. Parashar, J.A. Tickner and J. True (eds) *Revisiting Gendered States: Feminist Imaginings of the State in International Relations*, Oxford: Oxford University Press, pp 51–68.

Edenborg, E. (2022a) Putin's anti-gay war on Ukraine, *Boston Review*, 14 March. https://bostonreview.net/articles/putins-anti-gay-war-on-ukraine/

Edenborg, E. (2022b) Disinformation and gendered boundarymaking: Nordic media audiences making sense of 'Swedish decline', *Cooperation and Conflict*, 57(4): 496–515.

Edkins, J. (1999) *Poststructuralism & International Relations: Bringing the Political Back in*, Boulder: Lynne Rienner Publishers.

EIGE (2019) *Gender Mainstreaming: Gender Audit*. https://eige.europa.eu/publications/gender-mainstreaming-gender-audit

Eisenstein, H. (1996) *Inside Agitators: Australian Femocrats and the State*, Philadelphia: Temple University Press.

Elias, J. and Rai, S.M. (2019) Feminist everyday political economy: space, time, and violence, *Review of International Studies*, 45(2): 201–220.

Elias, J. and Roberts, A. (2016) Feminist political economy of the everyday: from bananas to bingos, *Globalizations*, 13(6): 787–800.

Elshtain, J.B. (1987) *Women and War*, Chicago: University of Chicago Press.

Engberg-Pedersen, L. (2018) Do norms travel, *Progress in Development Studies*, 18(3): 153–171.

Enloe, C. (2000) *Manoeuvres: The International Politics of Militarizing Women's Lives*, Berkeley: University of California Press.

Enloe, C. (2004) *The Curious Feminist*, Berkeley: University of California Press.

Enloe, C. (2010) *Nimo's War, Emma's War: Making Feminist Sense of the Iraqi War*, Berkeley: University of California Press.

Enloe, C. (2013) *Seriously!: Investigating Crashes and Crises as if Women Mattered*, Berkeley: University of California Press.

Enloe, C. (2013) Interview – Cynthia Enloe. https://www.e-ir/2013/03/13/interview-cynthia-enloe/

Enloe, C. (2014) *Bananas, Beaches and Bases: Making Feminist Sense of International Politics*, Berkeley: University of California Press.

Enloe, C. (2017) *The Big Push: Exposing and Challenging the Persistence of Patriarchy*, Berkeley: University of California Press.

Enloe, C. (2023) *Twelve Feminist Lessons of War*, Berkeley: University of California Press.

Esposito, E. (2023) Online gendered and sexualised disinformation against women in politics, in S.M. Maci, M. Demata, M. McGlashan and P. Seargenat (eds) *The Routledge Handbook of Discourse and Disinformation*, Routledge, pp 292–305.

Etchart, L. (2015) Demilitarizing the global: women's peace movements and transnational networks, *Review of International Studies*, 44(4): 672–693.

EU DisinfoLab and #ShePersisted (2022) *Gender-Based Disinformation 101: Theory, Examples, and Need for Regulation*. https://www.disinfo.eu/wp-content/uploads/2022/10/20221012_TechnicalDocumentGBD-1.pdf

Eurodad (2023) *Reform or Regress? From the World Bank's Evolution Roadmap to the Bridgetown Agenda* [webinar], 6 April. https://www.eurodad.org/reform_or_regress_from_the_world_bank_s_evolution_roadmap_to_the_bridgetown_agenda#:~:text=This%20panel%20will%20explore%20to,close%20the%20climate%20finance%20gap

European Commission (2018) *EU Code of Practice on Disinformation*. https://digital-strategy.ec.europa.eu/en/library/2018-code-practice-disinformation

European Commission (2020) *Evaluation of the EU's External Action Support to Gender Equality and Women's and Girls' Empowerment (2010–2018): Final Report, Volume I – Main Report*.

European External Action Service (2023) *FIMI Targeting LGBTIQ+ People: Well-Informed Analysis to Protect Human Rights and Diversity*, https://neighbourhood-enlargement.ec.europa.eu/system/files/2020-11/gewe_eval_-_final_report_-_main_report_-_november_2020.pdf

European Parliament (2018) *Gender Equality and Trade*. https://www.europarl.europa.eu/RegData/etudes/ATAG/2019/633163/EPRS_ATA(2019)633163_EN.pdf

European Parliament and the Council of the European Union (2022) *Regulation (EU) 2022/2065 of the European Parliament and of the Council of 19 October 2022 on a Single Market for Digital Services and Amending Directive 2000/31/EC (Digital Services Act)*. https://eur-lex.europa.eu/legal-content/EN/TXT/?uri=CELEX%3A32022R2065&qid=1666857835014

Eveline, J. and Bacchi, C. (2010) What are we mainstreaming when we mainstream gender?, in C. Bacchi and J. Eveline (eds) *Mainstreaming Politics: Gendering Practices and Feminist Theory*, Adelaide: University of Adelaide Press, pp 87–109.

Eyben, R. (2010) Subversively accommodating: feminist bureaucrats and gender mainstreaming, *IDS Bulletin*, 41(2): 54–61.

Faas, T. and Klingelhöfer, T. (2022) German politics at the traffic light: new beginnings in the election of 2021, *West European Politics*, 45(7): 1506–1521.

Fahrmeir, A. (2017) Historiography of foreign policy analysis, *Oxford Research Encyclopedia of Politics*, https://doi.org/10.1093/acrefore/9780190228637.013.370.

Farkas, J. and Neumayer, C. (2020) Mimicking news: how the credibility of an established tabloid is used when disseminating racism, *Nordicom Review*, 41(1): 1–17.

FAZ (Frankfurter Allgemeine Zeitung) (2022) Der feministische Dreiklang, *FAZ*, 12 September, p 5.

Federal Foreign Office (2021) *The German Federal Government's Action Plan for the Women, Peace and Security Agenda 2021 to 2024*. http://1325naps.peacewomen.org/wp-content/uploads/2021/04/aktionsplan-1325-2021-2024-en-data.pdf

Federal Foreign Office (2022a) Rede von Außenministerin Annalena Baerbock bei der Konferenz 'Shaping Feminist Foreign Policy', 12 September. https://www.auswaertiges-amt.de/de/newsroom/feministische-aussenpolitik/2551358

Federal Foreign Office (2022b) Rede von Außenministerin Annalena Baerbock beim Feminist Foreign Policy Summit, 13 April. https://www.auswaertiges-amt.de/de/newsroom/baerbock-cffp/2522322

Federal Foreign Office (2023a) Rede von Außenministerin Annalena Baerbock zur Vorstellung der Leitlinien zur Feministischen Außenpoliti, 1 March. https://www.auswaertiges-amt.de/de/newsroom/baerbock-leitlinien-ffp/2585138

Federal Foreign Office (2023b) *Shaping Feminist Foreign Policy*, Berlin. https://www.auswaertiges-amt.de/blob/2585076/4d2d295dad8fb1c41c6271d2c1a41d75/ffp-leitlinien-data.pdf

Federal Ministry for Economic Cooperation and Development (2023) *Feminist Development Policy: For Just and Strong Societies Worldwide*, https://www.bmz.de/resource/blob/153806/bmz-strategy-feminist-development-policy.pdf

Federal Republic of Germany (2023) *Feminist Development Policy*, German Governments Federation for Economic Cooperation and Development. https://www.bmz.de/en/issues/feminist-development-policy

Federer, J. P. (2016) *On Gender: The Role of Norms in International Peace Mediation*, Swisspeace Essential, 1. Bern.

Fellegi, Z., Kočí, K. and Benešová, K. (2023) Work and family balance in top diplomacy: the case of the Czech Republic, *Politics & Gender*, 19(1): 220–246.

Fellin, I. and Turner, C. (2021) Women's mediator networks: reflections on an emerging global trend, in C. Turner and T. Svensson (eds) *Rethinking Peace Mediation: Challenges of Contemporary Peacemaking Practice*, Bristol: Policy Press, pp 285–300.

Feminist Action Nexus (2023) Unpacking the Bridgetown Initiative: a systemic feminist analysis & critique, *Women's Empowerment & Development Organization*. https://wedo.org/wp-content/uploads/2023/06/ActionNexus_BridgetownBrief_EN_June2023.pdf

Feminist Foreign Policy Plus Group (2023) Political declaration on feminist approaches to foreign policy, *Government of The Netherlands*, 20 September. https://www.government.nl/documents/diplomatic-statements/2023/09/20/political-declaration-on-feminist-approaches-to-foreign-policy

Feminist Foreign Policy Working Group (2021) *Be Bold, Be Brave: Recommendations for Canada's Feminist Foreign Policy*. https://interpares.ca/sites/default/files/resources/ffp_be_brave_be_bold_en.pdf

The Feminist Initiative Group (2022) *'The Right to Resist': A Feminist Manifesto*. https://commons.com.ua/en/right-resist-feminist-manifesto/

Feridun, M. (2014) 'Foreign aid fungibility and military spending: the case of North Cyprus', *Defence and Peace Economics*, 25(5): 499–508.

Fetzer, J.H. (2004) Information: does it have to be true?, *Minds and Machines*, 14: 223–229.

Finnemore, M. (1996) Norms, culture, and world politics: insights from sociology's institutionalism, *International Organization*, 50(2): 325–347.

Finnemore, M. and Sikkink, K. (1998) International norm dynamics and political change, *International Organization*, 52: 887–917.

Finnemore, M. and Sikkink. K. (2001) Taking stock: the constructivist research program in international relations and comparative politics, *Annual Review of Political Science*, 4(1): 391–416.

FitzGerald, M. (2022) *Care and the Pluriverse: Rethinking Global Ethics*, Bristol: Bristol University Press.

FitzGerald, M. (2023) Rethinking the political in the pluriverse: the ethico-political significance of care, *Journal of International Political Theory*, 19(3): 252–268, https://doi.org/10.1177/17550882231178884

Flavell, J. (2023) Lessons from the women and gender constituency: interrogating civil society strategies for organising in the UNFCCC, *International Journal of Politics, Culture, and Society*, 36(3): 385–403.

Flowers, P.R. (2022) Gender representation in Japan's national and international diplomacy, *The Hague Journal of Diplomacy*, 17(3): 488–517.

Fodor, E. (2022) *The Gender Regime of Anti-Liberal Hungary*, Cham: Palgrave Pivot.

Foreign & Commonwealth Office (2021) *Diversity and Equality Report 2019 to 2020*. https://www.gov.uk/government/publications/fco-diversity-and-equality-report-2020/foreign-commonwealth-office-diversity-and-equality-report-2019-to-2020

Foreign, Commonwealth & Development Office (2022) *Gender Pay Gap Report 2022*. https://www.gov.uk/government/publications/fcdo-gender-pay-gap-report-2022/fcdo-gender-pay-gap-report-2022

Foster, D.M. (2008) 'Comfort to our adversaries'? Partisan ideology, domestic vulnerability, and strategic targeting, *Foreign Policy Analysis*, 4(4): 419–436.

Foucault, M. (1977) *Discipline and Punish: The Birth of the Prison*, trans A. Sheridan, New York: Vintage.

Franceschet, S. and Piscopo, J. (2013) Equality, democracy, and the broadening and deepening of gender quotas, *Politics & Gender*, 9(3): 310–316.

Freelon, D. and Wells, C. (2020) Disinformation as political communication, *Political Communication*, 37(2): 145–156.

Fresnillo, I. and Crotti, I. (2022) Riders on the storm – how debt and climate change are threatening the future of small island developing states, *Eurodad*, 11 October. https://www.eurodad.org/debt_in_sids

Friedland, L.A., Hove, T. and Rojas, H. (2006) The networked public sphere, *Javnost-the Public*, 13(4): 5–26.

Frost, M. (1999) Putting the world to rights: Britain's ethical foreign policy, *Cambridge Review of International Affairs*, 12(2): 80–89.

Fry, C. (2013) Perceptions of influence: the Catholic diplomacy of Queen Anna and her ladies, 1601–1604', in N. Akkerman and B. Houben (eds) *The Politics of Female Households: Ladies-in-Waiting across Early Modern Europe*, Leiden: Brill, pp 265–285.

Fukuyama, F. (1998) Women and the evolution of world politics, *Foreign Affairs*, 77(5): 24–40.

GAC (Global Affairs Canada) (2023) *Report to Parliament on the Government of Canada's International Assistance 2021–2022*. https://www.international.gc.ca/transparency-transparence/international-assistance-report-rapport-aide-internationale/2021-2022.aspx?lang=eng

Gammage, C. (2022) Empowering women in trade: how gender responsive are the EU's trade agreements?, in E. Fahey and I. Mancini (eds) *Understanding the EU as a Good Global Actor*, Cheltenham: Edward Elgar, pp 158–174.

Ganguly, S. and Pardesi, M. (2015) Foreign policy analysis in India, in K. Brummer and V. Hudson (eds) *Foreign Policy Analysis Outside North America*, Boulder: Lynne Rienner, pp 57–76.

García, D.P. (2022) Mexico aims to lead the way, *The World Today*, February and March.

Garcia, M. (2021) Trade policy, in G. Abels, A. Krizsán, H. MacRae and A. van der Vlueten (eds) *The Routledge Handbook on Gender and EU Politics*, London: Routledge, pp 278–289.

Garcia, M. and Masselot, A. (2015) The value of equality in the EU-Asian trade policy, *Asia Europe Journal*, 13(3): 241–252.

Gaweda, B. (2021) Europeanization, democratization, and backsliding: trajectories and framings of gender equality institutions in Poland, *Social Politics*, 28: 629–655.

Gender and Development Network (2021) Decolonising aid, *Briefings*, June. https://static1.squarespace.com/static/536c4ee8e4b0b60bc6ca7c74/t/60ef2c1f33c2d110098feca5/1626287136282/Decolonising+Aid-+Briefing+.pdf

The Gender Security Project (2023) *Luxembourg*. https://www.gendersecurityproject.com/post/luxembourg-s-feminist-foreign-policy

Georgetown University (2002) *U.S.-Afghan Women's Council*. https://usawc.georgetown.edu/

German Development Institute (2014) 'Beyond aid' and the future of development cooperation, *Briefing Paper*, German Development Institute. https://www.idos-research.de/uploads/media/BP_6.2014_.pdf

Getachew, A., Bell, D., Enloe, C. and Thakur, V. (2022) Theorizing the history of women's international thinking at the 'end of international theory', *International Theory*, 14(3): 394–418.

Ghosh, A. (2021) *The Nutmeg's Curse*, Chicago: University of Chicago Press.

Gilby, L., Koivusalo, M. and Atkins, S. (2021) Global health without sexual and reproductive health and rights? Analysis of United Nations documents and country statements, 2014–2019, *BMJ Global Health*, 6: e004659.

Gilligan, C. (1993) *In a Different Voice: Psychological Theory and Women's Development*, 2nd edn, Cambridge, MA: Harvard University Press.

GIWPS (Georgetown Institute for Women, Peace and Security) and PRIO (Peace Research Institute Oslo) (2021) *Women, Peace, and Security Index 2021/22 Summary: Tracking Sustainable Peace through Inclusion, Justice, and Security for Women*, Washington, DC: GIWPS and PRIO.

GIZ (The Germany Agency for International Development) (2021) *Promoting Gender Equality and Women's Rights*. https://www.giz.de/en/worldwide/65544.html

Glenn, E.N. (2015) Settler colonialism as structure: a framework for comparative studies of US race and gender formation, *Sociology of Race and Ethnicity*, 1(1): 52–72.

Global Affairs Canada (2017) Feminist International Assistance Policy, www.international.gc.ca

Gobierno de México (2020) Mexico adopts feminist foreign policy, Press Release 15, 9 January. https://www.gob.mx/sre/prensa/mexico-adopts-feminist-foreign-policy?idiom=en

REFERENCES

Gobierno de México (2023a) Martha Delgado resigns as Undersecretary for Multilateral Affairs and Human Rights, Press Release 191, 2 May. https://www.gob.mx/sre/prensa/martha-delgado-resigns-as-undersecretary-for-multilateral-affairs-and-human-rights

Gobierno de Mexico (2023b) The Government of Mexico will conduct a responsible, humane and feminist foreign policy: Alicia Bárcena, 7 July. https://www.gob.mx/sre/articulos/the-government-of-mexico-will-conduct-a-responsible-humane-and-feminist-foreign-policy-alicia-barcena-339369

Goering, L. (2023) Analysis: as world's poor face 'compounding crises', what could curb risks?, *Reuters*, 19 May. https://www.reuters.com/article/climate-change-humanitarian-crisis-idUSL8N37A0FD

Goetz, A.M. (2020) The new competition in multilateral norm-setting: transnational feminists & the illiberal backlash, *Daedalus*, 149: 160–179.

Golovchenko, Y. (2022) Fighting propaganda with censorship: a study of the Ukrainian ban on Russian social media, *The Journal of Politics*, 84(2): 639–654.

Government of Canada (2017a) *Feminist International Assistance Policy*, https://www.international.gc.ca/world-monde/assets/pdfs/iap2-eng.pdf?_ga=2.163114300.1047690429.1651252240-2075300383.1651252240

Government of Canada (2017b) *Canada's Feminist International Assistance Policy*, Government of Canada, 7 June. https://www.international.gc.ca/world-monde/issues_development-enjeux_developpement/priorities-priorites/policy-politique.aspx?lang=eng

Government of Canada (2018) Speech by the Honourable Chrystia Freeland, Minister of Foreign Affairs, to the Standing Committee on Foreign Affairs and International Development, February 8, 2018, https://www.canada.ca/en/global-affairs/news/2018/02/speech_by_the_honourablechrystiafreelandministerofforeignaffairs.html

Government of Canada (2023a) Canada announces expansion and renewal of Women's Voice and Leadership program, *Global Affairs Canada*, 27 April. https://www.canada.ca/en/global-affairs/news/2023/04/canada-announces-expansion-and-renewal-of-womens-voice-and-leadership-program.html

Government of Canada (2023b) Gender equality and empowerment measurement tool. https://www.international.gc.ca/world-monde/funding-financement/introduction_gender_emt-outil_renforcement_epf.aspx?lang=eng

Government of Chile (2023) *Feminist Foreign Policy*. https://politicaexteriorfeminista.minrel.gob.cl/home

Government of the Netherlands (2023) *Political Declaration on Feminist Approches to Foreign Policy*. https://www.government.nl/documents/diplomatic-statements/2023/09/20/political-declaration-on-feminist-approches-to-foreign-policy

Government of New Zealand (2021) *Inaugural Foreign Policy Speech to Diplomatic Corps*. https://www.beehive.govt.nz/speech/inaugural-foreign-policy-speech-diplomatic-corps

Government of Spain (2021) *Política Exterior Feminista: Impulsando la Iqualdad en la Axxión Exterior Española*. https://www.exteriores.gob.es/es/PoliticaExterior/Paginas/ PoliticaExteriorFeminista.aspx

Government of Sweden (2015) *Statement of Foreign Policy 2015*, 11 February. https://www.government.se/speeches/2015/02/statement-of-foreign-policy-2015/

Government of Sweden (2017) *Sweden's Feminist Foreign Policy: Examples from Three Years of Implementation*.

Government of Sweden (2018a) *Handbook: Sweden's Feminist Foreign Policy*. https://www.swedenabroad.se/globalassets/ambassader/zimbabwe-harare/documents/handbook_swedens-feminist-foreign-policy.pdf

Government of Sweden (2018b) *The Government's Statement of Foreign Policy 2018*, 14 February. https://www.government.se/speeches/2018/02/the-governments-statement-of-foreign-policy-2018/

Government of Sweden (2020) *The Government's Statement of Foreign Policy 2020*, 12 February. https://www.government.se/speeches/2020/02/2020-statement-of-foreign-policy/

Green, C., Kozielska, M. and Smith, K.E. (2023) Is feminist foreign policy driving progress for women's representation in diplomacy?, *London School of Economics and Political Science*, Strategic Update.

Greenberg, J. (2023) *At War with Women Military Humanitarianism and Imperial Feminism in an Era of Permanent War*, New York: Cornell University Press.

Grove, J.V. (2019) *Savage Ecology: War and Geopolitics at the End of the World*, Durham, NC: Duke University Press.

Gudynas, E. (2021) *Extractivisms: Politics, Economy and Ecology*, Black Point: Fernwood.

Guerrina, R. and Slootmaeckers, K. (2023) *The Sound of Silence: EDI in the European Studies Canon*, UACES. https://www.uaces.org/edi-report

Guerrina, R. Chappell, L. and Wright, K.A.M (2018) Transforming CSDP? feminist triangles and gender regimes, *Journal of Common Market Studies*, 56(5): 1036–1052.

Guerrina, R., Haastrup, T. and Wright, K.A.M. (2023a) Contesting feminist power Europe: is feminist foreign policy possible for the EU?, *European Security*, 32(3): 485–507.

Guerrina, R., MacRae, H. and Masselot, A. (2023b) Between a rock and a hard place: the EU's gender regime in crisis, *Women's Studies International Forum*, 99: 102722.

Haastrup, T. (2020) Gendering South Africa's foreign policy: toward a feminist approach?, *Foreign Policy Analysis*, 16(2): 199–216.

Haastrup, T. (2023) Building gender norms into regional governance and the limits of institutionalising feminism, in M. Sawer, L.A. Banaszak, J. True and J. Kantola (eds) *Handbook of Feminist Governance*, Cheltenham: Edward Elgar, pp 371–384.

Haastrup, T. and Hagen, J.J. (2020) Global racial hierarchies and the limits of localization via national action plans, in S. Baus, P. Kirby and L.J. Shepherd (eds) *New Directions in Women, Peace and Security*, Bristol: Bristol University Press, pp 133–152.

Hameleers, M. (2023) Disinformation as a context-bound phenomenon: toward a conceptual clarification integrating actors, intentions and techniques of creation and dissemination, *Communication Theory*, 33(1): 1–10.

Hamilton, K. and Langhorne, R. (2011) *The Practice of Diplomacy: Its Evolution, Theory and Administration*, London: Routledge.

Hamington, M. (2020) Care ethics and improvisation: can performance care?, in A.S. Fisher and J. Thompson (eds) *Performing Care: New Perspectives on Socially Engaged Performance*, Manchester: Manchester University Press.

Hannah, E., Roberts, A. and Trommer, S. (2020) Towards a feminist global trade politics, *Globalizations*, 18(1): 70–85.

Hannah, E., Roberts, A. and Trommer, S. (2022a) Gender in global trade: transforming or reproducing trade orthodoxies?, *Review of International Political Economy*, 29(4): 1368–1393.

Hannah, E., Roberts, A. and Trommer, S. (2022b) Canada's 'feminist' trade policy?, in D. Carment, L. Macdonald and J. Paltiel (eds) *Canada and Great Power Competition*, Cham: Springer International Publishing, pp 71–96.

Hannah, E., Roberts, A. and Trommer, S. (2023) Feminist interventions in trade governance, in M. Sawer, L.A. Banaszak, J. True and J, Kantola (eds) *Handbook of Feminist Governance*, Cheltenham: Edward Elgar, pp 250–261.

Hansel, M., Khan, R. and Levaillant, M. (2017) *Theorizing Indian Foreign Policy*, Abingdon: Routledge.

Hansen, L. (2006) *Security as Practice: Discourse Analysis and the Bosnian War*, London: Routledge.

Haraldsson, A. and Wängnerud, L. (2019) The effect of media sexism on women's political ambition: evidence from a worldwide study, *Feminist Media Studies*, 19(4): 525–541.

Haraway, D. (1988) Situated knowledges: the science question in feminism and the privilege of partial perspective, *Feminist Studies*, 14: 575–599.

Harcourt, W., Ling, L.H.M., Zalewski, M. and Swiss International Relations Collective (2015) Assessing, engaging, and enacting worlds, *International Feminist Journal of Politics*, 17(1): 158–172.

Harding, A. (2020) The loyalty oath keeping Rwandans abroad in check, *BBC News*. https://www.bbc.com/news/world-africa-54801979

Harnisch, S. (2011) Role theory: operationalization of key concepts, in S. Harnisch, C. Frank and H.W. Maull (eds) *Role Theory in International Relations: Approaches and Analyses*, London and New York: Routledge, pp 7–15.

Hartsock, N. (1983) *Money, Sex, and Power: Toward a Feminist Historical Materialism*, Boston: Northeastern University Press.

Hedling, E. (2021) Transforming practices of diplomacy: the European External Action Service and digital disinformation, *International Affairs*, 97(3): 841–859.

Hedling, E. (2023) Emotional labour in digital diplomacy: perceptions and challenges for European diplomats, *Emotions and Society*, 1(aop): 1–19.

Hekman, S.J. (1995) *Moral Voices, Moral Selves*, Cambridge: Polity Press.

Hendl, T., Burlyuk, O., O'Sullivan, M. and Arystanbek, A. (2023) (En)countering epistemic imperialism: a critique of 'Westsplaining' and coloniality in dominant debates on Russia's invasion of Ukraine, *Contemporary Security Policy*, 45(2): 171–209.

Henry, M. (2021) On the necessity of critical race feminism for women, peace and security, *Critical Studies on Security*, 9(1): 22–26.

Hernes, H.M. (1987) *Welfare State and Woman Power: Essays in State Feminism*, Oslo: Norwegian University Press.

Hewitt, S. (2017) Money, power and muscles: women in Nepalese politics, *Australian Outlook*, 12 May. https://www.internationalaffairs.org.au/australianoutlook/local-elections-womens-participation-nepal/

Hickman, K. (2002) *Daughters of Britannia: The Lives and Times of Diplomatic Wives*, New York: HarperCollins.

Hill, C. (2016) *Foreign Policy in the Twenty-First Century*, 2nd edn, London: Palgrave.

Hocking, B. (2016) Diplomacy and foreign policy, in C.M. Constantinous, P. Kerr and P. Sharp (eds) *The SAGE Handbook of Diplomacy*, Los Angeles: SAGE, pp 67–78.

Holsti, K.J. (1970) National role conceptions in the study of foreign policy, *International Studies Quarterly*, 14(3): 233–309.

hooks, b. (2015) *Feminist Theory: From Margin to Center*, New York: Routledge.

Hoskyns, C. (1996) *Integrating Gender: Women, Law and Politics in the European Union*, London: Verso.

Hozic, A.A. and True, J. (eds) (2016) *Scandalous Economics: Gender and the Politics of Financial Crises*, Oxford: Oxford University Press.

Htun, M. and Weldon, S.L. (2018) *The Logics of Gender Justice: State Action on Women's Rights around the World*, Cambridge: Cambridge University Press.

Hudson, H. (2005) Doing security as though humans matter: a feminist perspective on gender and the politics of human security, *Security Dialogue*, 36(2): 155–174.

Hudson, V.M. and Leidl, P. (2015) *The Hillary Doctrine: Sex and American Foreign Policy*, New York: Columbia University Press.

Hudson, V., Caprioli, M., Ballif-Spanvill, B., McDermott, R. and Emmett, C.R. (2008) The heart of the matter: the security of women and the security of states, *International Security*, 33(3): 7–45.

Hughes, M.M., Krook, M.L. and Paxton, P. (2015) Transnational women's activism and the global diffusion of gender quotas, *International Studies Quarterly*, 59(2): 357–372.

Humprecht, E., Esser, F., van Aelst, P. and Staender, A. (2023) The sharing of disinformation in cross-national comparison: analyzing patterns of resilience, *Information, Communication & Society*, 26(7): 1342–1362.

Husband, T. and Tiessen, R. (2020) Beyond the binary: sexual orientation and gender identity in Canadian foreign policy, in M. Tremblay and J. Everitt (eds) *The Palgrave Handbook of Gender, Sexuality and Canadian Politics*, London: Palgrave Macmillan, pp 581–611.

Hutchings, K. (2013) A place of greater safety: securing judgement in international ethics, in A. Russell Beattie and K. Schick (eds) *The Vulnerable Subject: Beyond Rationalism in International Relations*, London: Palgrave.

Hutchings, K. (2018) *Global Ethics: An Introduction*, 2nd edn, Cambridge: Polity Press.

Hutchings, K. (2019) From just war theory to ethico-political pacifism, *Critical Studies on Security*, 7(3): 191–198.

Ibarra, P. (2023) *Moving from Theory to Practice: Countering Gendered Political Disinformation*. https://www.oecd-forum.org/posts/moving-from-theory-to-practice-countering-gendered-political-disinformation

ICRW (2023) *Feminist Foreign Policy Index: A Qualitative Evaluation of Feminist Commitments*, International Centre for Research on Women. https://www.icrw.org/publications/feminist-foreign-policy-index-a-qualitative-evaluation-of-feminist-commitments/

The Independent (2021) 'We cannot have long term peace while American troops are here' says celebrated Afghan activist Malalai Joya, *The Independent*, 6 August.

Independent Commission for Aid Impact (2020) *The UN's Preventing Sexual Violence in Conflict Inititiative*, icai.independent.gov.uk

Internacional Feminista (2023) Open letter to ICRW regarding the feminist foreign policy index, *Internacional Feminista*, March. https://docs.google.com/document/d/14fh98BCXKP16ZehtBDoQTh357g6eW7We2ckRKNebCNk/edit

International Centre for Research on Women (2022) Feminist Foreign Policy: A Framework. New York, https://www.icrw.org/publications/feminist-foreign-policy-a-framework/

International Women's Research Centre and Feminist Foreign Policy Collaborative (2019) *Defining Feminist Foreign Policy, A Global Partner Network for Feminist Foreign Policy*, https://www.ffpcollaborative.org/defining-ffp

International Peace Institute (2018) Margot Wallström: 'without women, how can we achieve sustainable peace?', 27 September. https://www.ipinst.org/2018/09/women-and-international-peace-way-forward#7

International Resource Panel (2019) *Global Resources Outlook 2019: Natural Resources for the Future We Want*, Nairobi: UN Environment Programme. https://www.resourcepanel.org/reports/global-resources-outlook

International Trade Centre (nd) *Inclusive Trade: SheTrades Initiative.* https://intracen.org/our-work/projects/inclusive-trade-shetrades-initiative

IPBES (2019) UN report: nature's dangerous decline 'unprecedented'; species extinction rates 'accelerating', *UN Sustainable Development Goals*, 6 May. https://www.un.org/sustainabledevelopment/blog/2019/05/nature-decline-unprecedented-report/

IPCC (2022) *Climate Change 2022: Impacts, Adaptation and Vulnerability. Summary for Policymakers. Working Group II Contribution to the Sixth Assessment Report of the Intergovernmental Panel on Climate Change*, International Panel on Climate Change (IPCC). https://www.ipcc.ch/report/ar6/wg2/downloads/report/IPCC_AR6_WGII_FinalDraft_FullReport.pdf

Irish Defence Forces (2020) *Defence Forces Third Action Plan for the Implementation of UNSCR 1325 and Related Resolutions 2020–2024*, Dublin, Ireland.

Iyigun, M. (2014) Lessons from the Ottoman harem on culture, religion and war, *Economic Development and Cultural Change*, 61(4): 693–730.

IWDA (International Women's Development Agency) (2021) *From Seeds to Roots: Trajectories Towards Feminist Foreign Policy.* https://iwda.org.au/resource/from-seeds-to-roots-trajectories-towards-feminist-foreign-policy/

James, C. and Sluga, G. (2016) Introduction: the long international history of women and diplomacy, in G. Sluga and C. James (eds) *Women, Diplomacy and International Politics Since 1500*, London: Routledge, pp 1–12.

Jayakumar, K. (2023) How have states with feminist foreign policies responded to the Palestine question?, *The Gender Security Project*. https://www.gendersecurityproject.com/post/how-have-states-with-feminist-foreign-policies-reacted-to-the-palestine-question#:~:text=Israel%20allowed%20aid%20to%20pass,foreign%20policy%20at%20work%20here

Jensen, M. (2018) Russian trolls and fake news: information or identity logics?, *Journal of International Affairs*, 71(1.5): 115–124.

Jezierska, K. and Towns, A. (2018) Taming feminism? The place of gender equality in the 'Progressive Sweden' brand, *Place Branding and Public Diplomacy*, 14: 55–63.

Johnson, S. (2021) Women deserve better: a discussion on COVID-19 and the gendered organization in the new economy, *Gender, Work, & Organization*, 29(2): 639–649.

Johnson, Z. and Zühr, R. (2021) A new era?, *Donor Tracker*, SEEK Development. https://donortracker.org/publications/new-era-trends-chinas-financing-international-development-cooperation

Kaarbo, J. and Thies, C.G. (2024) Repositioning foreign policy analysis in international relations, in J. Kaarbo and C.G. Thies (eds) *The Oxford Handbook of Foreign Policy Analysis*, Oxford: Oxford University Press.

Kabeer, N. (1994) *Reversed Realities: Gender Hierarchies in Development Thought*, London: Verso, pp 1–12.

Kaczynski, J. (2019) 'Party leader calls LGBT rights an imported threat to Poland', AP, https://apnews.com/general-news-6cb144f6838e409c828cb32a19834a2a

Kamaara, E.K., Vasko, E.T. and Viau, J.E. (2012) Listening and speaking as two sides of the same coin: negotiating dualisms in intercultural feminist collaboration, *Journal of Feminist Studies in Religion*, 28(2): 49–67.

Kannan, A.V. (2018) *The Third World Women's Alliance: History, Geopolitics, and Form*, PhD dissertation, Syracuse University.

Kantola, J. and Dahl, H.M. (2005) Gender and the state: from differences between to differences within, *International Feminist Journal of Politics*, 7(1): 49–70.

Keck, M. and Sikkink, K. (1998) *Activists Beyond Borders: Advocacy Networks in International Politics*, New York: Cornell University Press.

Kenny, M. and Mackay, F. (2009) Already doin' it for ourselves? Skeptical notes on feminism and institutionalism, *Politics & Gender*, 5(2): 271–280.

Keohane, N.O. (2020) Women, power and leadership, *Daedulus*, 149(1): 236–250.

Kinsella, D. (2005) No rest for the democratic peace, *American Political Science Review*, 99(3): 453–457.

Kirby, P. (2015) Ending sexual violence in conflict: the Preventing Sexual Violence Initiative and its critics, *International Affairs*, 91: 457–472.

Kirste, K. and Maull, H.W. (1996) Zivilmacht und Rollentheorie, *Zeitschrift für Internationale Beziehungen*, 3(2): 283–312.

Korinek, J., Moïsé, E. and Tange, J. (2021) Trade and gender: a framework of analysis, *OECD Trade Policy Papers*, No. 246, Paris: OECD Publishing.

Korolczuk, E. (2020a) Counteracting challenges to gender equality in the era of anti-gender campaigns: competing gender knowledges and affective solidarity, *Social Politics*, 27: 694–717.

Korolczuk, E. and Graff, A. (2018) Gender as 'ebola from Brussels': the anticolonial frame and the rise of illiberal populism, *Signs: Journal of Women in Culture and Society*, 43: 797–821.

Kratochvíl, P. and O'Sullivan, M. (2023) A war like no other: Russia's invasion of Ukraine as a war on gender order, *European Security*, 32(3): 347–366.

Krause, J. and Enloe, C. (2015) A wealth of expertise and lived experience: conversations between international women peace activists at the Women Lead to Peace Summit preceding the Geneva II Peace Talks on Syria, January 2014, *International Feminist Journal of Politics*, 17(2): 328–338.

Krause, J. Krause, W. and Bränfors, P. (2018) Women's participation in peace negotiations and the durability of peace, *International Interactions*, 44(6): 985–1016.

Krinsky, J. and Crossley, N. (2014) Social movements and social networks: introduction, *Social Movement Studies*, 13(1): 1–21.

Kronsell, A. (2012) *Gender, Sex and the Postnational Defence: Militarism and Peacekeeping*, Oxford: Oxford University Press.

Kronsell, A. (2019) WPS and climate change, in S.E. Davies and J. True (eds) *The Oxford Handbook of Women, Peace and Security*, New York: Oxford University Press, pp 729–738.

Krook, M.L. and Mackay, F. (2011) Introduction: gender, politics, and institutions, in M.L. Krook and F. Mackay (eds) *Gender, Politics and Institutions: Towards a Feminist Institutionalism*, Basingstoke: Palgrave Macmillan, pp 1–20.

Krook, M.L. and True, J. (2012) Rethinking the life cycles of international norms: the United Nations and the global promotion of gender equality, *European Journal of International Relations*, 18(1): 103–127.

Kuhar, R. and Paternotte, D. (2017) *Anti-Gender Campaigns in Europe: Mobilizing against Equality*, New York: Rowman & Littlefield.

Kühnel, F. (2022) The ambassador is dead – long live the ambassadress: gender, rank and proxy representation in early modern diplomacy, *The International History Review*, 44(5): 1004–1020.

La Cour, C. (2020) Theorising digital disinformation in international relations, *International Politics*, 57(4): 704–723.

Lanoszka, A. (2019) Disinformation in international politics, *European Journal of International Security*, 4(2): 227–248.

Larking, E. (2019) Challenging gendered economic and social inequalities: an analysis of the role of trade and financial liberalisation in deepening inequalities, and of the capacity of economic and social rights to redress them, in S. Harris Rimmer and K. Ogg (eds) *Research Handbook on Feminist Engagement with International Law*, Cheltenham: Edward Elgar.

Lawler, P. (2013) The 'good state' debate in international relations, *International Politics*, 50: 18–37.

Lawrinson, B. (2023) The limits of state-led norm entrepreneurship: the United Kingdom and the Preventing Sexual Violence in Conflict Initiative (PSVI), *British Journal of Politics & International Relations*, 25: 260–276.

Lazarus, J. and Steigerwalt, A. (2018) *Gendered Vulnerability: How Women Work Harder to Stay in Office*, Ann Arbor, MI: University of Michigan Press.

Leach, M. (ed) (2016) *Gender Equality and Sustainable Development*, London and New York: Routledge.

Lee-Koo, K. (2020) Pro-gender foreign policy by stealth: navigating global and domestic politics in Australian foreign policy making, *Foreign Policy Analysis*, 16(2): 236–249.

Leguey-Feilleux, J.-R. (2009) *The Dynamics of Diplomacy*, Boulder: Lynne Rienner Publishers.

Lequesne, C., Castillo, G., Holm. M., Bin Abdullah, W.J., Leira, H., Tiwary, K. and Wong, R. (2022) Ethnic diversity in the recruitment of diplomats: why ministries of foreign affairs take the issue seriously, in C. Lequesne (ed) *Ministries of Foreign Affairs in the World: Actors of State Diplomacy*, The Hague, Netherlands: Nijhoff, Brill, pp 1–23.

Levaillant, M. (2017) The contribution of neo-institutionalism to the analysis of India's diplomacy in the making, in M. Hansel, R. Khan and M. Levaillant (eds) *Theorizing Indian Foreign Policy*, New York: Routledge.

Lima, R.d.C. and de Oliveira, A.J.S.N. (2018) Continuity and change in the Ministry of Foreign Affairs: a profile of the diplomatic corps and career patterns, *Revista de Administração Pública*, 52: 797–821.

Linde, A. (2017) Speech by Minister for EU Affairs and Trade Ann Linde at the WTO Ministerial Conference, 12 December 2017, Government Offices of Sweden.

Lindio-McGovern, L. (2019) Neoliberal globalization and transnational women's movements in the early twenty-first century, in B. Berberoglu (ed) *The Palgrave Handbook of Social Movements, Revolution, and Social Transformation*, Cham: Springer International Publishing, pp 353–372.

Ling, L.H.M. (2017) The missing other: a review of Linklater's violence and civilization in the western states-system, *Review of International Studies*, 43(4): 621–636.

Lombardo, E., Meier. P. and Verloo, M. (eds) (2009) *The Discursive Politics of Gender Equality Stretching, Bending and Policy-Making*, London: Routledge.

Lugones, M. (2010) Towards a decolonial feminism, *Hypathia*, 25(4): 742–759.

Lyytikainen, M., Yadav, P., Confortini, C.C., Wibben, A.T.R. and Jauhola, M. (2021) Unruly wives in the household of peace research: toward feminist genealogies for peace research, *Cooperation & Conflict*, 56(1): 3–25.

Maathai, W. (2003) *The Green Belt Movement: Sharing the Approach and the Experience*, New York: Lantern Books.

Mackay, F. (2014) Nested newness, institutional innovation, and the gendered limits of change, *Politics & Gender*, 10(4): 549–571.

Mackay, F., Kenny, M. and Chappell, L. (2010) New institutionalism through a gender lens: towards a feminist institutionalism?, *International Political Science Review*, 31(5): 573–588.

MacRae, H. (2010) The EU as a gender equal polity: myths and realities, *Journal of Common Market Studies*, 48(1): 155–174.

Mallavarapu, S. (2015) Theorizing India's foreign relations, in D.M. Malone, C.R. Mohan and S. Raghavan (eds) *The Oxford Handbook of Indian Foreign Policy*, Oxford: Oxford University Press, pp 35–48.

Mansregh, N. (1947) Asian Relations Conference, *International Affairs*, 23(3): 295–306.

March, J.G. and Olsen, J.P. (1996) Institutional perspectives on political institutions, *Governance (Oxford)*, 9(3): 247–264.

Markland, A. (2020) *NGOs, Knowledge Production and Global Humanist Advocacy: The Limits of Expertise*, New York: Routledge.

Martens, B., Aguiar Wicht, L., Gomez-Herrera, M.E., Muller-Langer, F. (2018) *The Digital Transformation of News Media and the Rise of Disinformation and Fake News*, Brussels: European Commission, https://joint-research-centre.ec.europa.eu/reports-and-technical-documentation/digital-transfo rmation-news-media-and-rise-disinformation-and-fake-news_en#authors

Martin, L.J. (1982) Disinformation: an instrumentality in the propaganda arsenal, *Political Communication*, 2(1): 47–64.

Martín de Almagro, M. (2018) Producing participants: gender, race, class, and women, peace and security, *Global Society*, 32(4): 395–414.

Martins Yassine, A. (2022) The rise of women's organizations of diplomats (WODs): insights from the Group of Brazilian female diplomats, Paper presented at the 3rd International GenDip Conference, University of Gothenburg.

Marwick, A.E., Losh, E., Schlüter, M., Markham, A. and Phipps, E.B. (2022) Feminist approaches to disinformation studies, *AoIR Selected Papers of Internet Research*, https://doi.org/10.5210/spir.v2022i0.12961.

Mason, C. (2019) Buzzwords and fuzzwords: flattening intersectionality in Canadian aid, *Canadian Foreign Policy Journal*, 25(2): 203–219.

Mathers, J. (2020) Women, war and austerity: IFIs and the construction of gendered economic insecurities in Ukraine, *Review of International Political Economy*, 27(6): 1235–1256.

Mathers, J. and Kvit, A. (2023) Ukraine war: attitudes to women in the military are changing as thousands serve on front lines, *The Conversation*.

Matthews, J.V. (1997) *Women's Struggle for Equality: The First Phase, 1828–1828*, Rowman & Littlefield.

Maull, H.W. (1990) Germany and Japan: the new civilian powers, *Foreign Affairs*, 69(5): 91–106.

McBride, K. and Wibben, A.T.R. (2012) The gendering of counterinsurgency in Afghanistan, *Humanity*, 3(2): 199–215.

McCarthy, H. (2014) *Women of the World: The Rise of the Female Diplomat*, London: Bloomsbury.

McClintock, A. (2016) No longer in a future heaven: gender, race and nationalism, *Space, Gender, Knowledge: Feminist Readings*, Routledge, pp 409–424.

McEwen, H. (2023) The (geo)politics of gender and sexuality diversity in a multipolar world: reading African anti-Genderisms beyond the transatlantic, *Politique africaine (Paris, France: 1981)*, 168: 95–113.

McInnis, K.J., Jensen, B. and Wharton, J. (2022) Why dictators are afraid of girls: rethinking gender and international security, *War on the Rocks Blog*, 7 November. https://warontherocks.com/2022/11/why-dictators-are-afraid-of-girls-rethinking-gender-and-national-security/

Meger, S. (2016) *Rape, Loot, Pillage: The Political Economy of Sexual Violence in Armed Conflict*, New York: Oxford University Press.

Mejias, U.A. and Vokuev, N.E. (2017) Disinformation and the media: the case of Russia and Ukraine, *Media, Culture & Society*, 39(7): 1027–1042.

Mendez, K. (2021) *At the Intersection of Race, Gender, and Class: Honoring the Revolutionary Feminist Legacy of the Third World Women's Alliance*, Black Women Radicals. https://www.blackwomenradicals.com/blog-feed/at-the-intersections-of-race-gender-and-class-honoring-the-revolutionary-feminist-legacy-of-the-third-world-womens-alliance

Menon, L. (nd) 'Our foreign policy', File no. 62, Lakshmi Menon Papers, Nehru Memorial Museum and Library, New Delhi, India.

Menon, L. (1955) 'India's foreign and economic policies', File no. 32, Lakshmi Menon Papers, Nehru Memorial Museum and Library, New Delhi, India.

Menon, L. (1962) 'Speech delivered at the University of Syracuse, New York', File no. 20, Lakshmi Menon Papers, Nehru Memorial Museum and Library, New Delhi, India.

Merchant, C. (1980) *The Death of Nature: Women, Ecology, and the Scientific Revolution*, HarperOne.

Miles, W. (2013) Deploying development to counter terrorism: post-9/11 transformation of U.S. foreign aid to Africa, *African Studies Review*, 55(3): 27–60.

Ministère de l'Europe et des Affaires Étrangères (2019) *Female Diplomats in France: From 1930 to Tomorrow*. https://www.diplomatie.gouv.fr/en/french-foreign-policy/human-rights/women-s-rights/events-6401/article/exhibition-female-diplomats-in-france-from-1930-to-tomorrow

Ministry of Defence (2019) *JSP 1325 Human Security in Military Operations*, https://www.gov.uk/government/publications/human-security-in-military-operations-jsp-1325

Ministry of Defence (2021) *JSP 985 Human Security in Defence*, https://www.gov.uk/government/publications/human-security-in-defence-jsp-985

Ministry of Foreign Affairs of the Republic of Belarus (2015) *Group of Friends of the Family Launched at the UN*, Press release, 4 February. https://mfa.gov.by/en/press/news_mfa/f8ff663d7481c615.html

Minow, M. (1990) *Making all the Difference: Inclusion, Exclusion, and American Law*, Ithaca: Cornell University Press.

Mintrom, M. and Luetjens, J. (2018) Policy entrepreneurs and foreign policy decision making, in C.G. Thies (ed) *The Oxford Encyclopedia of Foreign Policy Analysis*, Oxford: Oxford University Press, vol 2, pp 394–411.

Mintrom, M. and Luetjens, J. (2019) International policy entrepreneurship, in D. Stone and K. Moloney (eds) *The Oxford Handbook of Global Policy and Transnational Administration*, Oxford: Oxford University Press, pp 111–128.

Moghadam, V. (2005) *Globalizing Women*, Baltimore: Johns Hopkins University Press.

Moghadam, V. (2015) Transnational feminist activism and movement building, in R. Baksh-Soodeen and W. Harcourt (eds) *The Oxford Handbook of Transnational Feminist Movements*, New York: Oxford University Press, pp 53–81.

Mohanty, C.T. (1984) Under western eyes: feminist scholarship and colonial discourses, *Boundary 2*, 12(3): 333–358, doi: doi.org/10.2307/302821

Mohanty, C.T. (1988) Under western eyes: feminist scholarship and colonial discourses, *Feminist Review*, 30: 61–88.

Mohanty, C.T. (2003) 'Under western eyes' revisited: feminist solidarity through anticapitalist struggles, *Signs: Journal of Women in Culture and Society*, 28(2): 499–535.

Moore, C. and Talarico, T. (2015) Inclusion to exclusion: women in Syria, *Emory International Law Review*, 30(2): 213–260.

Morgan, S. (2017) EU wants gender chapter included in Chile trade deal update, Euractive, https://www.euractiv.com/section/economy-jobs/news/eu-wants-gender-chapter-included-in-chile-trade-deal-update/

Morgan, S. (2018) Fake news, disinformation, manipulation and online tactics to undermine democracy, *Journal of Cyber Policy*, 3(1): 39–43.

Mori, J. (2015) How women make diplomacy: the British Embassy in Paris, 1815–1841, *Journal of Women's History*, 27(4): 137–159.

Moss, K. (2017) Russia as the saviour of European civilization: gender and the geopolitics of traditional values, in R. Kuhar and D. Paternotte (eds) *Anti-Gender Campaigns in Europe: Mobilizing against Equality*, London: Rowman & Littlefield, pp 195–214.

Muchhala, B. (2021) *A Feminist and Decolonial Global Green New Deal: Principles, Paradigms and Systemic Transformations*, Action Nexus for Generation Equality. https://wedo.org/wp-content/uploads/2021/06/FemEconClimate-ActionNexus_Brief_FemGND-1.pdf?blm_aid=26261

Müller, H. and Risse-Kappen, T. (1993) From the outside in and from the inside out: international relations, domestic politics, and foreign policy, in D. Skidmore and V.M. Hudson (eds) *The Limits of State Autonomy*, Boulder: Westview Press, pp 25–48.

Müller, P. and Gazsi, D. (2023) Populist capture of foreign policy institutions: the Orbán government and the de-Europeanization of Hungarian foreign policy, *Journal of Common Market Studies*, 61(2): 397–415.

Nacyte, L. (2018) Canada's feminist international assistance policy: security for whom?, *Engenderings*, London: London School of Economics. https://blogs.lse.ac.uk/gender/2018/01/22/canadas-feminist-international-assistance-policy-security-for-whom/

Nadelmann, E.A. (1990) Global prohibition regimes: the evolution of norms in international society, *International Organization*, 44(4): 479–526.

Naidu, K. (2022) The world is waking up!, in *Reimagining a Feminist, Social Contract for People & Planet*, Christian Aid. https://www.christianaid.org.uk/news/policy/world-waking

Nair, D. (2020) Sociability in international politics: golf and ASEAN's Cold War diplomacy, *International Political Sociology*, 14(2): 196–214.

Nair, J. (1994) On the question of agency in Indian feminist historiography, *Gender & History*, 6: 82–100.

Narayan, U. (1995) Colonialism and its others: considerations on rights and care discourses, *Hypatia*, 10(2): 133–140.

Narlikar, A. (2022) German feminist foreign policy: an inside-outside perspective, *Observer Research Foundation*, 12 September. https://www.orfonline.org/expert-speak/german-feminist-foreign-policy/

Nash, P. (2020) American women at the UN: from breakthrough to dumping ground?, *History News Network*, 19 April. https://historynewsnetwork.org/article/175049

NATO (2022) *NATO 2022 Strategic Concept*, 29 June. https://www.nato.int/strategic-concept/

Nee, R.C. and De Maio, M. (2019) A 'presidential look'? An analysis of gender framing in 2016 persuasive memes of Hillary Clinton, *Journal of Broadcasting & Electronic Media*, 63(2): 304–321.

Neumann, I.B. (2012) *At Home with the Diplomats: Inside a European Foreign Ministry*, Ithaca: Cornell University Press.

Neumann, I.B. (2020) *Diplomatic Tenses: A Social Evolutionary Perspective on Diplomacy*, Manchester: Manchester University Press.

Newby, V. and O'Malley, A. (2021) Introduction: WPS 20 years on where are the women now?', *Global Studies Quarterly*, 1(3): 1–13.

Nguyễn, S., Kuo, R., Reddi, M., Li, L. and Moran, R.E. (2022) Studying mis-and disinformation in Asian diasporic communities: the need for critical transnational research beyond Anglocentrism, *Harvard Kennedy School Misinformation Review*, 3(2), https://misinforeview.hks.harvard.edu/wp-content/uploads/2022/03/nguyen-_diasporic_communities_research_beyond_anglocentrism_20220324.pdf

Niklasson, B. (2020) The gendered networking of diplomats, *The Hague Journal of Diplomacy*, 15(1–2): 13–42.

Niklasson, B. and Robertson, F. (2018) The Swedish MFA: ready to live up to expectations?, in K. Aggestam and A.E. Towns (eds) *Gendering Diplomacy and International Negotiation*, Cham: Palgrave Macmillan, pp 65–85.

Niklasson, B. and Towns, A.E. (2022) Introduction: approaching gender and ministries of foreign affairs, *The Hague Journal of Diplomacy*, 17(3): 339–369.

Niklasson, B. and Towns, A.E. (2023) Diplomatic gender patterns and symbolic status signaling: introducing the GenDip dataset on gender and diplomatic representation', *International Studies Quarterly*, 67(4): sqad089.

Nisancioglu, K. (2020) Racial sovereignty, *European Journal of International Relations*, 26(S1): 39–63.

Nordberg, J. (2015) Who's afraid of a feminist foreign policy?, *The New Yorker*, 15 April. https://www.newyorker.com/news/news-desk/swedens-feminist-foreign-minister

Norwegian Agency for Development Cooperation (2015) *Unit 10: The Role of the Gender Focal Point*.

Norwegian Ministry of Foreign Affairs (2022) *Norway Invites Taliban to Oslo for Meetings*. https://www.regjeringen.no/en/aktuelt/talks_oslo/id2897938/

Novovic, G. (2023) Dispelling fairy tales: the Auditor General's misinterpretation of Canada's Feminist International Assistance Policy, *The McLeod Group*, Guest Blog, 11 April. https://www.mcleodgroup.ca/2023/04/dispelling-fairy-tales-the-auditor-generals-misinterpretation-of-canadas-feminist-international-assistance-policy/

Nye, J.S. (1990) Soft power, *Foreign Policy*, 80, 153–171.

Nye, J.S. (2011) Power and foreign policy, *Journal of Political Power*, 4(1): 9–24.

Odysseos, L. (2017) Prolegomena to any future decolonial ethics: coloniality, poetics and 'being human as praxis', *Millennium: Journal of International Studies*, 45(3): 447–472.

OECD (Organization for Economic Cooperation and Development) (2023) Development co-operation profiles: Canada. https://www.oecd-ilibrary.org/sites/aa7e3298-en/index.html?itemId=/content/component/0079f636-en&_csp_=2e70060d368b5fc38b205b10ce2ddda6&itemIGO=oecd&itemContentType=chapter

Off, G. (2023) Gender equality salience, backlash and radical right voting in the gender-equal context of Sweden, *West European Politics*, 46(3): 451–476.

Office of the Spokesperson, U.S. Department of State (2022) *At COP27, Our Climate Future Is Female: A Progress Report on Implementing U.S. Efforts to Advance Women and Girls' Climate Action*, 14 November. https://www.state.gov/at-cop27-our-climate-future-is-female-a-progress-report-on-implementing-u-s-efforts-to-advance-women-and-girls-climate-action/

Ojeda, D., Nirmal, P., Rocheleau, D. and Emel, J. (2022) Feminist ecologies, *Annual Review of Environment and Resources*, 47(1): 149–171.

Okin, S.M. (1989) *Justice, Gender and the Family*, New York: Basic Books.

openDemocracy (2023) Right to resist: how war changed Ukraine's feminist movement. https://www.opendemocracy.net/en/odr/war-with-russia-changed-ukraine-feminist-movement/

Oppermann, K., Brummer, K. and van Willigen, N. (2017) Coalition governance and foreign policy decision-making, *European Political Science*, 16(4): 489–501.

Orbán, V. (2022) Speech by Prime Minister Viktor Orbán at the opening of CPAC Texas, 3 August. https://abouthungary.hu/speeches-and-remarks/speech-by-prime-minister-viktor-orban-at-the-opening-of-cpac-texas

Orbán, V. (2023) Prime Minister Viktor Orban's 'State of the Nation' address, 18 February. https://abouthungary.hu/speeches-and-remarks/prime-minister-viktor-orbans-state-of-the-nation-address-63f319616e193

Orchard, X., Saldaña, M., Pavez, I., et al (2023) 'Does she know how to read?' An intersectional perspective to explore Twitter users' portrayal of women Mapuche leaders, *Information, Communication & Society*, 26(13): 2554–2574.

Örden, H. (2022) Securitizing cyberspace: protecting political judgment, *Journal of International Political Theory*, 18(3): 375–392.

Orúe, J.D.R. (2023) The Inter-American Court of Human Rights and the climate emergency, 8 March. https://cil.nus.edu.sg/blogs/the-inter-american-court-of-human-rights-and-the-climate-emergency/

OSAGI (2001) *UN System-wide Gender Focal Point Study*, Executive summary. http://www.un.org/womenwatch/osagi/gmfpstudy.htm

O'Sullivan, M. and Krulišová, K. (2023) Women, Peace and Security in central Europe: in between the western agenda and Russian imperialism, *International Affairs*, 99(2): 625–643.

Owens, P., Rietzler, K. Hutchings, K. and Dunstan, S.C. (eds) (2022) *Women's International Thought: Towards a New Canon*, Cambridge: Cambridge University Press.

Oxfam Canada (2022) Canada commits to bold and unprecedented global investments to support a caring economy and advance women's rights, *Oxfam Canada*, 30 June. https://www.oxfam.ca/news/canada-commits-to-bold-and-unprecedented-global-investments-to-support-a-caring-economy-and-advance-womens-rights/

Pacwa, J. (2019) *War on Terror as a 'Fight for the Rights and Dignity of Women': A Discourse Analysis of the U.S. 'Liberation' Campaign for Afghan Women*, Thesis. https://digitalcommons.pepperdine.edu/etd/1101

Paffenholz, T., Ross, N., Dixon, S., Schluchter, A. and True, J. (2016) *Making Women Count – Not Just Counting Women: Assessing Women's Inclusion and Influence on Peace Negotiations*, Geneva: Inclusive Peace and Transition Initiative (The Graduate Institute of International and Development Studies) and UN Women.

Pandit, V.L. (nd) S/W by her, File no 14, VLP Papers, IInd Instalment, NMML.

Papagioti, F. (2023) *Feminist Foreign Policy Index: A Qualitative Evaluation of Feminist Commitments*, Washington, DC: International Center for Research on Women.

Parashar, S., Tickner, J.A. and True, J. (2018) Introduction: feminist imaginings of twenty-first-century gendered states, in S. Parashar, A. Tickner and J. True (eds) *Revisiting Gendered States: Feminist Imaginings of the State in International Relations*, New York: Oxford University Press, USA, pp 1–15.

Parasram, A. and Tilley, L. (2018) Global environmental harm, internal frontiers and indigenous protective ontologies, in O. U. Rutazibwa and R. Shilliam (eds) *Routledge Handbook of Postcolonial Politics*, Routledge, pp 302–317.

Paris Peace Forum (2022) Global partner network for FFP, *Paris Peace Forum*. https://parispeaceforum.org/en/projects/global-partner-network-for-ffp/#:~:text=The%20Global%20Partner%20Network%20for,feminist%20foreign%20policies%20(FFPs)

Parisi, L. (2020) Canada's new feminist international assistance policy: business as usual?, *Foreign Policy Analysis*, 16(2): 163–180.

Park-Kang, S. (2011) Utmost listening: feminist IR as a foreign language, *Millennium*, 39(3): 861–877.

Parkes, A. (2021) From burden to benefit: reframing the conversation on care, *Oxfam Canada*, 6 April. https://www.oxfam.ca/story/from-burden-to-benefit-reframing-the-conversation-on-care/

Parry, J. (2022) *Women's Participation in Local Mediation: Lessons from Iraq, Libya, Syria and Yemen*, UN Women, https://arabstates.unwomen.org/en/digital-library/publications/2022/06/womens-participation-in-local-mediation-lessons-from-iraq-libya-syria-and-yemen

Patel, R. and Moore, J.W. (2018) *A History of the World in Seven Cheap Things: A Guide to Capitalism, Nature, and the Future of the Planet*, Chicago: University of Chicago Press.

Peez, A. (2022) Contributions and blind spots of constructivist norms research in international relations, 1980–2018: a systematic evidence and gap analysis, *International Studies Review*, 24(1): viab055.

Peirce, L.P. (1993) *The Imperial Harem: Women and Sovereignty in the Ottoman Empire*, Oxford: Oxford University Press.

Peterson, H. and Jordansson, B. (2021) Gender mainstreaming in Swedish academia: translating policy into practice, *Journal of Gender Studies*, 31, DOI: https://doi.org/10.1080/09589236.2021.2004539

Peterson, V.S. (ed) (1992) *Gendered States: Feminist (Re)Visions of International Relations Theory*, Bolder: Lynne Rienner Publishers.

Pettersen, T. (2021) Feminist care ethics, in T. Väyrynen, S. Parashar, É. Féron and C.C. Confortini (eds) *Routledge Handbook of Feminist Peace Research*, 1st edn, London: Routledge. doi: 10.4324/9780429024160

Phelan, A. and True, J. (2022) Navigating gender in elite bargains: women's movements and the quest for inclusive peace in Colombia, *Review of International Studies*, 48(1): 171–194.

Philipson García, D. (2022) Mexico's feminist foreign policy: in name only, *VENRO*, 19 August. http://blog.venro.org/mexicos-feminist-foreign-policy-in-name-only/

Philipson García, D. and Velasco, A. (2022) Feminist foreign policy: a bridge between the global and the local, *Yale Journal of International Affairs*, 29 April. https://www.yalejournal.org/publications/feminist-foreign-policy-a-bridge-between-the-global-and-local

Phillips, S. and Martsenyuk, T. (2023) Women's agency and resistance in Russia's war on Ukraine: from victim of the war to prominent force, *Women's Studies International Forum*, 98, https://theconversation.com/ukraine-war-attitudes-to-women-in-the-military-are-changing-as-thousands-serve-on-front-lines-198195

Pitkin, H.F. (1967) *The Concept of Representation*, Los Angeles: University of California Press.

Plumwood, V. (1993) *Feminism and the Mastery of Nature*, New York: Routledge. https://www.crcpress.com/Feminism-and-the-Mastery-of-Nature/Plumwood/p/book/9780415068109

Porobić, N. (2022) *Holding Onto Nonviolence and Feminism in the Midst of War*. https://www.wilpf.org/holding-onto-nonviolence-and-feminism-in-the-midst-of-war/

Pouliot, V. (2008) The logic of practicality: a theory of practice of security communities, *International Organization*, 62(2): 257–288.

Pratt, N. (2013) Reconceptualizing gender, reinscribing racial–sexual boundaries in international security: the case of UN Security Council Resolution 1325 on 'Women, Peace and Security', *International Studies Quarterly*, 57(4): 772–778.

Pratt, S.F. (2020) From norms to normative configurations: a pragmatist and relational approach to theorizing normativity in IR, *International Theory*, 12: 59–82.

Prügl, E. (2016) How to wield feminist power, in M. Bustelo, L. Ferguson and M. Forest (eds) *The Politics of Feminist Knowledge Transfer: Gender Training and Gender Expertise*, Basingstoke: Palgrave Macmillan, pp 25–42.

Qazi, S. (2020) Who are the Afghan women negotiating peace with the Taliban, *Al Jazeera*, 7 October. https://www.aljazeera.com/features/2020/10/7/who-are-the-afghan-women-negotiating-peace-with-taliban

Quijano, A. (2000) Coloniality of power and Eurocentrism in Latin America, *International Sociology*, 15(2): 215–232.

Rajagopalan, S. (2009) Women in the Indian Foreign Service, *Hindustan Times Blog 'Wordly Wise'/PSW Weblog*. https://keepingcount.wordpress.com/2009/04/17/women-in-the-indian-foreign-service/

Rankin, J. (2021) EU parliament condemns Hungary's anti-LGBT law, *The Guardian*, 9 July. https://www.theguardian.com/world/2021/jul/08/eu-parliament-condemns-hungary-anti-lgbt-law

Raza, A. (2020) *Revolutionary Pasts: Communist Internationalism in Colonial India*, Cambridge: Cambridge University Press.

Razack, S. (2005) Geopolitics, culture clash, and gender after September 11, *Social Justice*, 32(4[102]): 11–31.

Readfearn, G. (2023) Antarctica warming much faster than models predicted in 'deeply concerning' sign for sea levels, *The Guardian*, 2 September.

Reddi, M., Kuo, R. and Kreiss, D. (2023) Identity propaganda: racial narratives and disinformation, *New Media & Society*, 25(8): 2201–2218.

Rengger, N. (2002) On the just war tradition in the twenty-first century, *International Affairs*, 78(2): 353–363.

Resurrección, B.P. (2013) Persistent women and environment linkages in climate change and sustainable development agendas, *Women's Studies International Forum*, 40(September): 33–43.

Reyntjens, F. (2011) Constructing the truth, dealing with dissent, domesticating the world: Governance in post-genocide Rwanda, *African Affairs*, 110(438): 1–34.

Riordan, S. (2019) *Cyberdiplomacy: Managing Security and Governance Online*, Hoboken, NJ: John Wiley & Sons.

Ripsman, N.M., Taliaferro, J.W. and Lobell, S.E. (2016) *Neoclassical Realist Theory of International Politics*, New York: Oxford University Press.

Roberts, A. (2016) *Gendered States of Punishment and Welfare: Feminist Political Economy, Primitive Accumulation and the Law*, New York: Routledge.

Robinson, F. (2009) Feminist ethics in world politics, in P. Hayden (ed) *The Ashgate Research Companion to Ethics and International Relations*, London: Ashgate, pp 79–96.

Robinson, F. (2011) Stop talking and listen: discourse ethics and feminist care ethics in International Political Theory, *Millennium*, 39(3): 845–860.

Robinson, F. (2020) Resisting hierarchies through relationality in the ethics of care, *International Journal of Care and Caring*, 4(1): 11–23.

Robinson, F. (2021a) Feminist foreign policy as ethical foreign policy? A care ethics perspective, *Journal of International Political Theory*, 17(1): 20–37.

Robinson, F. (2021b) Considering care in Canada's feminist foreign policy, *The McLeod Group*, Guest Blog, 10 February.

Rosén Sundström, M. and Elgström, O. (2020) Praise or critique? Sweden's feminist foreign policy in the eyes of its fellow EU members, *European Politics and Society*, 21(4): 418–433.

Ruddick, S. (1995) *Maternal Thinking: Towards a Politics of Peace*, London: The Women's Press.

Rupert, J. (2015) Sweden's foreign minister explains feminist foreign policy. Margot Wallström and colleagues face 'the giggling factor', *United States Institute for Peace*, 9 February. https://www.usip.org/publications/2015/02/swedens-foreign-minister-explains-feminist-foreign-policy

Sadat, M. (2022) Public floggings, women banned from parks: this is the Taliban 2.0, *The Toronto Star*, 22 November. https://www.thestar.com/news/world/2022/11/25/public-floggings-women-banned-from-parks-this-is-the-taliban-20.html

Sailer, G. (2021) Vatican: more and more women ambassadors to the Holy See, *Vatican News*. https://www.vaticannews.va/en/vatican-city/news/2021-07/vatican-diplomatic-corps-women-ambassadors-accredited-holy-see.html

Salleh, A. (1997) *Ecofeminism as Politics: Nature, Marx, and the Postmodern*, London and New York: Zed Books.

Sanders, R. (2018) Norm spoiling: undermining the international women's rights agenda, *International Affairs*, 94: 271–291.

Sanders, R. and Jenkins, L.D. (2022) Control, alt, delete: patriarchal populist attacks on international women's rights, *Global Constitutionalism*, 11: 401–429.

Sandler, J., Rao, A. and Eyben, R. (2012) Strategies of feminist bureaucrats: United Nations experiences, *Institute of Development Studies. IDS Working Paper*, 397: 1–35.

Sawer, M. and Grey, S. (2009) *Women's Movements: in Abeyance or Flourishing in New Ways*, New York: Routledge.

Schild, V. (2014) Institutional feminist networks and their 'poor': localizing transnational interventions, *Latin American Policy*, 5(2): 279–291.

Schimmelfennig, F. (2001) The community trap: liberal norms, rhetorical action, and the eastern enlargement of the European Union, *International Organization*, 55(1): 47–80.

Schmitt, O. (2018) When are strategic narratives effective? The shaping of political discourse through the interaction between political myths and strategic narratives, *Contemporary Security Policy*, 39(4): 487–511.

Schneiker, A. (2021) Norm sabotage: conceptual reflection on a phenomenon that challenges well-established norms, *International Studies Perspectives*, 22: 106–123.

Scott, J. (1986) Gender: a useful category of historical analysis, *The American Historical Review*, 91(5): 1053–1075.

Scott, S.V. and Bloomfield, A. (2017) Norm entrepreneurs and antipreneurs: chalk and cheese, or two faces of the same coin?, in A. Bloomfield and S.V. Scott (eds) *Norm Antipreneurs and the Politics of Resistance to Global Normative Change*, London and New York: Routledge, pp 231–250.

Scottish Government (2021) Gender equality and climate change, *International Leaders Sign Joint Statement at COP26* (blog), 11 February. https://www.gov.scot/news/gender-equality-and-climate-change/

Scottish Government (2022a) *COP27 – Loss and Damage Panel: First Minister's Speech – 8 November 2022*. http://www.gov.scot/publications/cop27-loss-damage-panel-first-ministers-speech-8-november-2022/

Scottish Government (2022b) *Scotland's Feminist Approach to Foreign Policy: Background Note*. http://www.gov.scot/publications/background-note-scotlands-feminist-approach-foreign-policy/

Scottish Government (2023a) *Equality, Opportunity, Community: Our Programme for Government 2023 to 2024*, The Scottish Government. http://www.gov.scot/publications/programme-government-2023-24/

Scottish Government (2023b) *Taking a Feminist Approach to International Relations*, The Scottish Government. https://www.gov.scot/binaries/content/documents/govscot/publications/strategy-plan/2023/11/taking-feminist-approach-international-relations/documents/taking-feminist-approach-international-relations/taking-feminist-approach-international-relations/govscot%3Adocument/taking-feminist-approach-international-relations.pdf

Scrinzi, F. and Blee, K. (2023) *The Racialization of Sexism: Men, Women and Gender in the Populist Radical Right*, 1st edn, New York: Routledge.

Seager, J. (2019) *Earth Follies: Feminism, Politics and the Environment*, New York: Routledge.

Sen, G. and Grown, C. (1987) *Development Crises and Alternative Visions: Third World Women's Perspectives*, New York: Monthly Review Press.

Sessa, M.G. (2020) Misogyny and misinformation: an analysis of gendered disinformation tactics during the COVID-19 pandemic, *Disinfo.eu*, https://www.disinfo.eu/publications/misogyny-and-misinformation:-an-analysis-of-gendered-disinformation-tactics-during-the-covid-19-pandemic/.

She Decides (nd) *Our Focus*, https://www.shedecides.com/our-focus/

Shepherd, L.J. (2008) *Gender, Violence and Security: Discourse as Practice*, London: Zed Books.

Shepherd, L.J. (2011) Sex, security, and superhero(in)es: from 1325 to 1820 and beyond, *International Feminist Journal of Politics*, 13: 504–521.

Shire, K. and Walby, S. (2020) Introduction: advances in theorising varieties of gender regimes, *Social Politics*, 27(3): 409–413.

Sil, R. and Katzenstein, P.J. (2010) Analytic eclecticism in the study of world politics: reconfiguring problems and mechanisms across research traditions, *Perspectives on Politics*, 8(2): 411–431.

Sjoberg, L. (2006) *Gender, Justice, and Wars in Iraq: A Feminist Reformulation of Just War Theory*, New York: Lexington Books.

Sjoberg, L. (2008) Why just war needs feminism now more than ever, *International Politics*, 45(1): 1–18.

Sjoberg, L. (2011) Gender, the state, and war redux: feminist international relations across the 'levels of analysis', *International Relations*, 25(1): 108–134.

Sjoberg, L. (2013) *Gendering Global Conflict: Towards a Feminist Theory of War*, New York: Columbia University Press.

Sjoberg, L. (2016) Witnessing the protection racket: rethinking justice in/of wars through gendered lenses, *International Politics*, 53(3): 361–384.

Skjelsbæk, I. and Tryggestad, T.L. (2020) Pro-gender norms in Norwegian peace engagement: balancing experiences, values, and interests, *Foreign Policy Analysis*, 16(2): 181–198.

Slootmaeckers, K., Touquet, H. and Vermeersch, P. (2016) *The EU Enlargement and Gay Politics: The Impact of Eastern Enlargement on Rights, Activism and Prejudice*, London: Springer Nature ebook.

Smith, K.E. (2017) Group politics in the debates on gender equality and sexual orientation discrimination, *The Hague Journal of Diplomacy*, 12(2): 138–157.

Smith, K.E. (2019) Missing in analysis: women in foreign policy-making, *Foreign Policy Analysis*, 16(1): 130–141.

Smith, N.R. and Holster, B. (2023) New Zealand's 'Maori foreign policy' and China: a case of instrumental relationality?, *International Affairs*, 99(4): 1575–1593.

Schneiker, A. (2021) Norm sabotage: conceptual reflection on a phenomenon that challenges well-established norms, *International Studies Perspectives*, 22: 106–123.

Sowa, T. (2023) In my view: are feminist foreign policies translating into real action?, *OECD: Development Cooperation Report 2023: Debating the Aid System*. https://read.oecd-ilibrary.org/development/development-co-operation-report-2023_337d6469-en#page1

Spector, A.J. (2019) Decade of turbulence: social movements and rebellion in the 1960s, in B. Berberoglu (ed) *The Palgrave Handbook of Social Movements, Revolution, and Social Transformation*, Cham: Springer International Publishing. doi: 10.1007/978-3-319-92354-3

Spratt, D. (2023) Faster than forecast, climate impacts trigger tipping points in the earth system, *Bulletin of the Atomic Scientists* (blog), 19 April. https://thebulletin.org/2023/04/faster-than-forecast-climate-impacts-trigger-tipping-points-in-the-earth-system/

Squires, J. (2005) Is mainstreaming transformative? Theorising mainstreaming in the context of diversity and deliberation, *Social Politics: International Studies in Gender, State & Society*, 12(3): 366–388.

Srivastava, S. (2021) Algorithmic governance and the international politics of Big Tech, *Perspectives on Politics*, 21(3): 989–1000, doi:10.1017/S1537592721003145

Standfield, C. (2022) Who gets to be a virtuoso? Diplomatic competence through an intersectional lens, *The Hague Journal of Diplomacy*, 17(3): 371–401.

St. Denis, V. (2017) Feminism is for everybody: Aboriginal women, feminism and diversity, in J. Green (ed) *Making Space for Indigenous Feminism*, Winnipeg: Fernwood Publishing, pp 33–52.

Stensöta, H., Wängnerud, L. and Svensson, R. (2015) Gender and corruption: the mediating power of institutional logics, *Governance*, 28(4): 475–496.

Stephenson, E. (2024) *The Face of the Nation: Gendered Institutions in Australian International Affairs*, Oxford: Oxford University Press.

Stephenson, E. and Blackwell, J. (2022) Towards a feminist First Nations foreign policy, *Broad Agenda*, University of Canberra. https://www.broadagenda.com.au/2022/towards-a-feminist-first-nations-foreign-policy/

Stern, M. and Stavrianakis, A. (2018) Militarism and security: dialogue, possibilities and limits, *Security Dialogue*, 59(1–2): 3–18.

Stetson, D. M., and Mazur, A. (eds) (1995) *Comparative State Feminism*, Thousand Oaks, CA: Sage.

Stirling, A. (2015) Emancipating transformations, in Scoones, I., Leach, M. and Newell, P. (eds) *The Politics of Green Transformation*, New York: Routledge, pp 54–67, https://library.oapen.org/bitstream/handle/20.500.12657/52753/1/9781317601128.pdf

Strange, S. (1988) *States and Markets*, London: Bloomsbury Publishing.

Sultana, F. (2022) The unbearable heaviness of climate coloniality, *Political Geography*, 99: 102638.

Sundström, M.R. and Elgström, O. (2020) Praise or critique? Sweden's feminist foreign policy in the eyes of its fellow EU members, *European Politics and Society*, 21(4): 418–433.

Suzor, N., Dragiewicz, M., Harris, B., Gillett, R., Burgess, J. and Van Geelen, T. (2019) Human rights by design: the responsibilities of social media platforms to address gender-based violence online, *Policy & Internet*, 11(1): 84–103.

Swamy, A., Knack, S., Lee, Y. and Azfar, O. (2001) Gender and corruption, *Journal of Development Economics*, 64(1): 25–55.

Swedish Ministry for Foreign Affairs (2016) *Swedish Foreign Action Plan for Feminist Foreign Policy 2015–2018 Including Focus Areas for 2016*, Government Offices of Sweden.

Sweden Ministry for Foreign Affairs (2022) *Strategy for Sweden's Global Development Cooperation on Sustainable Economic Development 2022–2026*. https://www.government.se/contentassets/38225ad1ff5c425f9c212ff5d cfeec6c/strategy-sustainable-economic-development-2022-2026.pdf

Swiss, L. (2012) Gender, security, and instrumentalism: Canada's foreign aid in support of national interest?, in S. Brown (ed) *Struggling for Effectiveness: CIDA and Canadian Foreign Aid*, Montreal and Kingston: McGill-Queen's University Press, pp 135–159.

Sylvester, C. (1994) Empathetic cooperation: a feminist method for IR, *Millennium*, 23(2): 315–334.

Sylvester, C. (2013) *War as Experience: Contributions from International Relations and Feminist Analysis*, London: Routledge.

Tabbara, H. and Rubin, G. (2018) *Women on the Frontlines of Conflict Resolution and Negotiation: Community Voices from Syria, Iraq and Yemen*, UN Women. https://arabstates.unwomen.org/sites/default/files/Field%20Office%20A rab%20States/Attachments/2018/Women%20on%20the%20frontlines-WEB-REV.PDF

Tarrow, S.G. (2011) *Power in Movement: Social Movements and Contentious Politics*, revised and updated 3rd edn, Cambridge and New York: Cambridge University Press.

Thakur, V. (2013) India's diplomatic entrepreneurism: revisiting India's role in the Korean crisis, 1950–52, *China Report*, 49(3): 273–298.

Thakur, V. (2019) An Asian drama: the Asian relations conference, 1947, *The International History Review*, 41(3): 673–695.

Thompson, F. (2023) Why feminist foreign policy doesn't have all the answers to the humanitarian crisis in Israel-Palestine, *LSE Blog*, 31 October. https:// blogs.lse.ac.uk/internationaldevelopment/2023/10/31/why-feminist-fore ign-policy-doesnt-have-all-the-answers/

Thompson, L. and Clement, R. (2019) Is the future of foreign policy feminist?, *Journal of Diplomacy and International Relations*, 20(2): 76–94.

Thompson, L., Ahmed, S., and Khokar, T. (2021) *Defining Feminist Foreign Policy: An Update*, International Center for Research on Women. https:// www.icrw.org/wp-content/uploads/2022/01/FFP-2021Update_v4.pdf

Thomson, J. (2020) What's feminist about feminist foreign policy? Sweden's and Canada's foreign policy agendas, *International Studies Perspectives*, 21: 424–437.

Thomson, J. (2022a) Gender norms, global hierarchies, and the evolution of feminist foreign policy, *European Journal of Politics and Gender*, 5(2): 173–190.

Thomson, J. and Whiting, S. (2022) Women, Peace and Security national action plans in anti-gender governments: the cases of Brazil and Poland, *European Journal of International Security*, 7(4): 531–550.

Tickner, J.A. (1992) *Gender in International Relations: Feminist Perspectives on Achieving Global Security*, New York: Columbia University Press.

Tickner, J.A. (1995) Hans Morgenthau's principles of political realism: a feminist reformulation (1988), *International Theory: Critical Investigations*, London: Palgrave Macmillan, pp 53–71.

Tickner, J.A. (2001) *Gendering World Politics: Issues and Approaches in the Post-Cold War Era*, New York: Columbia University Press.

Tickner, J.A. (2004) Feminist responses to international security studies, *Peace Review*, 16(1): 43–48.

Tickner, J. A. and True, J. (2018) A century of international relations feminism: from World War I women's peace pragmatism to the women, peace and security agenda, *International Studies Quarterly*, 62(2): 221–233.

Tiessen, R. (2007) *Everywhere/Nowhere: Gender Mainstreaming in Development Institutions*, West Hartford: Kumarian Press.

Tiessen, R. (2016) Gender equality and the two CIDAs, in S. Brown, M. den Heyer and D. Black (eds) *Rethinking Canadian Aid*, Ottawa: University of Ottawa Press, pp 195–211.

Tiessen, R. (2019) What's new about Canada's feminist international assistance policy and why 'more of the same' matters, *SPP Research Papers*, The School of Public Policy, University of Calgary, 12(44) December.

Tiessen, R. and Black, D. (2019) Canada's feminist international assistance policy: to whom is Canada back?, in R. Nimijean and D. Carment (eds) *Canada, Nation Branding and Domestic Politics*, New York: Routledge, pp 39–46.

Tiessen, R. and Okoli, N. (2023) Towards a transformative vision for gender and Canadian international policy: the role and impact of 'feminist inside activists', *International Journal: Canada's Journal of Global Policy Analysis*, Online first. DOI: https://doi.org/10.1177/00207020231163490

Tomz, M. and Weeks, J.L. (2020) Public opinion and foreign electoral intervention, *American Political Science Review*, 114(3): 856–873.

Towns, A. (2009) The status of women as a standard of 'civilization', *European Journal of International Relations*, 15: 681–706.

Towns, A. (2010) *Women and States: Norms and Hierarchies in International Society*, Cambridge: Cambridge University Press.

Towns, A. (2019) Global patterns and debates in the granting of women's suffrage, in S. Francheschet, M.L. Krook and N. Tan (eds) *The Palgrave Handbook of Women's Political Rights*, London: Palgrave Macmillan.

Towns, A. (2020) 'Diplomacy is a feminine art': feminised figurations of the diplomat, *Review of International Studies*, 46(5): 573–593.

Towns, A. (2022) WAW, no women? Foucault's reverse discourse and gendered subjects in diplomatic networks, *Global Society*, 36(3): 347–367.

Towns, A., Karlsson, E. and Eyre, J. (2014) The equality conundrum: gender and nation in the ideology of the Sweden Democrats, *Party Politics*, 20(2): 237–247.

Towns, A., Bjarnegård, E. and Jezierska, K. (2023) *More Than a Label, Less Than a Revolution: Sweden's Feminist Foreign Policy*, The Expert Group for Aid Studies (EBA) Report 2023:02.

Towns, A., Jezierska, K. and Bjarnegård, E. (2024) Can a feminist foreign policy be undone? Reflections from Sweden, *International Affairs*, 100(3): 1263–1273.

Tripp, A.M. (2015) *Women and Power in Post-Conflict Africa*, Cambridge: Cambridge University Press.

Tripp, A.M. (2019) *Seeking Legitimacy: Why Arab Autocracies Adopt Women's Rights*, Cambridge: Cambridge University Press.

Tronto, J.C. (1993) *Moral Boundaries: A Political Argument for an Ethic of Care*, New York: Routledge.

True, J. (2003) Mainstreaming gender in global public policy, *International Feminist Journal of Politics*, 5(3): 368–396.

True, J. (2009) Trading-off gender equality for global Europe: the European Union and free trade agreements, *European Foreign Affairs Review*, 14(4): 723–742.

True, J. (2010) Gender mainstreaming in international institutions, in L.J. Shepherd (ed) *Gender Matters in Global Politics*, New York: Routledge.

True, J. (2012) *The Political Economy of Violence Against Women*, New York and Oxford: Oxford University Press.

True, J. (2016) Explaining the global diffusion of the Women, Peace and Security agenda, *International Political Science Review*, 37(3): 307–323.

True, J. (2017) Gender and foreign policy, in M. Beeson and S. Hameiri (eds) *Navigating the New International Disorder: Australia in World Affairs 2011–2015*, Oxford: Oxford University Press, pp 224–242.

True, J. (2018) Feminism, in R. Devetak and J. True (eds) *Theories of International Relations*, London: Bloomsbury, pp 141–163.

True, J. (2019) Gender research and the study of institutional transfer and norm diffusion, in M. Sawer and K. Baker (eds) *Gender Innovation in Political Science: New Norms, New Knowledge*, London: Palgrave.

True, J. (2024) Of norms and networks: theorising the vital link between norm contestation and network globalisation, in P. Orchard and A. Wiener (eds) *Contesting the World: Norm Research in Theory and Practice*, Cambridge: Cambridge University Press, pp 199–218.

True, J. and Mintrom, M. (2001) Transnational networks and policy diffusion: the case of gender mainstreaming, *International Studies Quarterly*, 45(1): 27–57.

True, J. and Parisi, L. (2012) Gender mainstreaming strategies in international governance, in G. Caglar, E. Prugl and S. Zwingel (eds) *Feminist Strategies in International Governance*, New York: Routledge, pp 37–56.

True, J and Prügl. E. (2014) Equality means business? Governing gender through transnational public-private partnerships, *Review of International Political Economy*, 21(6): 1137–1169.

True, J. and Morales-Riveros, Y. (2019) Toward inclusive peace: analysing gender-sensitive peace agreements 2000–2016, *International Political Science Review*, 40(1): 1–18.

True, J. and Wiener, A. (2019) Everyone wants (a) peace: the dynamics of rhetoric and practice on 'Women, Peace and Security', *International Affairs*, 95(3): 553–574.

True, J. and Davies, S.E. (2020) Gender, governance and security, in C. De Jonge and M.E. Brown (eds) *The Gender and Security Agenda: Strategies for the 21st Century*, New York: Routledge.

Truong, T.-D., Wieringa, S. and Chhachhi, A. (2006) *Engendering Human Security: Feminist Perspectives*, New Delhi: Woman Unlimited.

Tryggestad, T.L. (2009) Trick or treat? The UN and implementation of Security Council Resolution 1325 on Women, Peace, and Security, *Global Governance*, 15(4): 539–557.

Tsymbalyuk, D. and Zamuruieva, I. (2022) Why we as feminists must lobby for air defence for Ukraine, *Open Democracy*. https://www.opendemocracy.net/en/odr/ukraine-russia-war-feminists-we-must-lobby-for-air-defence/

Tsymbalyuk, D., Zamuruieva, I., Iakovlenko, K., Khvyl, A. and Kostyshyna, I. (2022) We talked to fellow feminists from Ukraine about military aid, here's what they told us, *Blok*. https://blokmagazine.com/we-talked-to-fellow-feminists-from-ukraine-about-military-aid-heres-what-they-told-us/

Tuck, E. and Yang, K.W. (2012) Decolonization is not a metaphor, *Decolonization: Indigeneity, Education and Society*, 1(1): 1–40.

Tuck, E. and McKenzie, M. (2014) *Place in Research: Theory, Methodology, and Methods*, New York: Routledge.

Tuhiwai Smith, L. (2021) *Decolonizing Methodologies: Research and Indigenous Politics*, 3rd edn, London: Zed Books.

Turner, C. (2020) 'Soft ways of doing hard things': women mediators and the question of gender in mediation, *Peacebuilding*, 8(4): 383–401.

UK Foreign, Commonwealth and Development Office (2023) *International Women and Girls Strategy 2023–2030*, UK Government. https://www.gov.uk/government/publications/international-women-and-girls-strategy-2023-to-2030

UK Government (2023a) *2030 Strategic Framework for International Climate and Nature Action*, Department for Energy Security and Net Zero, Department for Environment, Food & Rural Affairs, and Foreign, Commonwealth & Development Office. https://www.gov.uk/government/publications/2030-strategic-framework-for-international-climate-and-nature-action

REFERENCES

UK Government (2023b) *International Women and Girls Strategy 2023 to 2030*, The Foreign, Commonwealth & Development Office. https://www.gov.uk/government/publications/international-women-and-girls-strategy-2023-to-2030

UK Government (2023c) *UK Government's Strategy for International Development*. https://www.gov.uk/government/publications/uk-governments-strategy-for-international-development

Uličná, I. (2023) Shifting the gender quota debate from underrepresentation of women to overrepresentation of men within diplomacy, *Policy Paper for Think Visegrad*. https://www.sfpa.sk/wp-content/uploads/2021/08/ulicna-intempl-final-kopie-kopie.pdf

Ün, M.B. (2019) Contesting global gender equality norms: the case of Turkey, *Review of International Studies*, 45(5): 828–847.

UNFCCC (2022) *Implementation of Gender-Responsive Climate Policies, Plans, Strategies and Action as Reported by Parties in Regular Reports and Communications under the UNFCCC*, United Nations. https://unfccc.int/documents/613847.

United Nations (2017) *System-wide Strategy on Gender Parity*, https://www.un.org/gender/sites/ www.un.org.gender/files/gender_parity_strategy_october_2017.pdf

United Nations (2023a) *Launch of the Updated Ukraine National Action Plan for Women, Peace and Security (CSWG & Side Event)*. https://webtv.un.org/en/asset/k1t/k1t551ac2p

United Nations (2023b) *Report of the Special Rapporteur on the Promotion and Protection of the Right to Freedom of Opinion and Expression, Irene Khan*. https://documents-dds-ny.un.org/doc/UNDOC/GEN/N23/233/65/PDF/N2323365.pdf?OpenElement

United Nations Security Council (2003) Women suffer disproportionately during and after war, Security Council told during day-long debate on women, peace and security. https://press.un.org/en/2003/sc7908.doc.htm

UN News (2022) Without investment, gender equality will take nearly 300 years: UN report, *United Nations*. https://news.un.org/en/story/2022/09/1126171

UN Secretary-General (2022) *Annual Report on Women, Peace and Security to the UN Security Council*, October.

UN Women (2014) *World Survey on the Role of Women in Development 2014: Gender Equality and Sustainable Development*, UN Women. https://www.unwomen.org/en/digital-library/publications/2014/10/world-survey-2014

UN Women (2015) *Preventing Conflict, Transforming Justice, Securing the Peace*, New York: UN.

UN Women (2021a) *Beyond COVID-19: A Feminist Plan for Sustainability and Social Justice*, UN Women. https://www.unwomen.org/en/digital-libr ary/publications/2021/09/beyond-covid-19-a-feminist-plan-for-sustain ability-and-social-justice

UN Women (2021b) *Increasing Women's Participation in Mediation Processes.* https://www.unwomen.org/sites/default/files/Headquarters/Attachme nts/Sections/Library/Publications/2021/Increasing-womens-participat ion-in-mediation-processes-en.pdf

UN (United Nations) Women (2022a) *UN Women Reveals Concerning Regression in Attitudes Towards Gender Roles During Pandemic in New Study*, UN Women. https://www.unwomen.org/en/news-stories/press-release/ 2022/06/un-women-reveals-concerning-regression-in-attitudes-towards-gender-roles-during-pandemic-in-new-study

UN Women (2022b) *Feminist Foreign Policies: An Introduction.* https://www. unwomen.org/en/digital-library/publications/2022/09/brief-feminist-foreign-policies

U.S. Department of State (nd) Climate and environment, *Policy Issues.* https://www.state.gov/policy-issues/climate-and-environment/

U.S. Department of State (2023a) *Gendered Disinformation: Tactics, Themes, and Trends by Foreign Malign Actors.* https://www.state.gov/gendered-dis information-tactics-themes-and-trends-by-foreign-malign-actors/

U.S. Department of State (2023b) *Summary of the UK-U.S. Roundtable on Countering Gendered Disinformation at the 67th United Nations Commission on the Status of Women.* https://www.state.gov/summary-of-the-uk-u-s-rou ndtable-on-countering-gendered-disinformation-at-the-67th-united-nati ons-commission-on-the-status-of-women/

Van Sant, K., Fredheim, R. and Bergmanis-Korats, G. (2021) *Abuse of Power: Coordinated Online Harassment of Finnish Government Ministers*, Riga: NATO Strategic Communications Centre of Excellence. https:// stratcomcoe. org/pdfjs

Vastapuu, L. and Lyytikäinen, M. (2022) *Gender Equality in Finnish Foreign Affairs from 2019 to 2022*, Independent study commissioned by the Ministry for Foreign Affairs of Finland. https://um.fi/documents/35732/0/Gen der+equality+in+foreign+affairs_Vastapuu_Lyytikainen.pdf/4aef250d-4d89-41cd-d390-6059951d4aa9?t=1668426670061

Velasco, A. and Philipson García, D. (2023) Feminist foreign policy: accountability matters, *Internacionale Feminista*, blog post, 6 March. https:// www.internacionalfeminista.com/blog/feminist-foreign-policy-account ability-matters

Velasco, M., Enrique, A. et al (2022) Sustainable development, occupation, and cities. The case of Oaxaca, Mexico, *Secuencia,* 114.

Verschuur, C. and Destremau, B. (2012) Decolonial feminisms, gender, and development: history and narratives of southern feminisms and women's movements, *Revue Tiers Monde*, 209(1): 7–18.

von der Leyen, U. (2023) Speech by President von der Leyen on EU-China relations to the Mercator Institute for Chinese Studies and the European Policy Centre, 30 March. https://ec.europa.eu/commission/presscorner/detail/en/speech_23_2063

Wagle, R., Pillay, S. and Wright, W. (2020) *Feminist Institutionalism and Gendered Bureaucracies: Forestry Governance in Nepal*, Singapore: Springer Singapore.

Walby, S. (2004) The European Union and gender equality: emergent varieties of gender regime, *Social Politics: International Studies in Gender, State & Society*, 11(1): 4–29.

Walby, S. (2015) *Crisis*, London: Wiley.

Walby, S. (2020) Varieties of gender regimes, *Social Politics*, 27(3): 414–431.

Walby, S. (2023) Authoritarianism, violence and varieties of gender regimes: violence as an institutional domain, *Women's Studies International Forum*, 98(May–June): 102677.

Watson, M. (2016) Historicising Ricardo's comparative advantage theory, challenging the normative foundations of liberal international political economy, *New Political Economy*, 22(3): 257–272.

Waylen, G. (2014) Informal institutions, institutional change, and gender equality, *Political Research Quarterly*, 67(1): 212–223.

WEDO (nd) *Gender Climate Tracker*. https://genderclimatetracker.org/

WEDO (2020) *Spotlight on Gender in NDCs: An Analysis of Parties' Instruments, Plans and Actions Supporting Integration of Gender Equality Principles and Practices*, Women's Environment and Development Organization. https://wedo.org/spotlight-on-gender-in-ndcs/

Weisbrode, K. (2017) Diplomacy in foreign policy, in *Oxford Research Encyclopedia of Politics*, Oxford: Oxford University Press.

Weldon, L. (2011) Perspectives against interests: sketch of a feminist political theory of 'women', *Politics & Gender*, 7(3): 441–446.

Weldon, L. and Htun, M. (2012) Feminist mobilisation and progressive policy change: why governments take action to combat violence against women, *Gender & Development*, 21: 231–247.

Wellons, T. (2019) Affirmative action is still an effective and necessary tool, *Contexts*, 18(1): 80.

Wells, C. and Friedland, L.A. (2023) Recognition crisis: coming to terms with identity, attention and political communication in the twenty-first century, *Political Communication*, 40(1): 1–19.

Weston-Scheuber, K. (2012) Gender and the prohibition of hate speech, *QUT Law & Justice Journal*, 12(2): 132–150.

Whyte, K.P. and Cuomo, C.J. (2017) Ethics of caring in environmental ethics: indigenous and feminist philosophies, in S.M. Gardiner and A. Thompson (eds) *The Oxford Handbook of Environmental Ethics*, Oxford: Oxford University Press, pp 253–266.

Wiener, A. (2004) Contested compliance: interventions on the normative structure of world politics, *European Journal of International Relations*, 10: 189–234.

Wiener, A. (2023) Norm(ative) change in international relations, in H. Krieger and A. Liese (eds) *Tracing Value Change in the International Legal Order*, Oxford: Oxford University Press. https://doi.org/10.1093/oso/9780192855831.003.0002

Wijermars, M. and Makhortykh, M. (2022) Sociotechnical imaginaries of algorithmic governance in EU policy on online disinformation and FinTech, *New Media & Society*, 24(4): 942–963.

Wilcox, L. (2015) *Bodies of Violence: Theorizing Embodied Subjects in International Relations*, Oxford: Oxford University Press.

Wilcox, L. (2017) Practising gender, queering theory, *Review of International Studies*, 43(5): 789–808.

Wilfore, K. (2022) Security, misogyny, and disinformation undermining women's leadership, in G. Haciyakupoglu and Y. Wong (eds) *Gender and Security in Digital Space*, London: Routledge, pp 124–142.

WILPF (1915) *WILPF Resolutions: The Hague Congress 1915*. https://wilpf.org/wp-content/uploads/2012/08/WILPF_triennial_congress_1915.pdf

WILPF (2023) *X* post, 31 October. https://x.com/WILPF/status/1719041642475233703?s=20

Winston, C. (2018) Norm structure, diffusion, and evolution: a conceptual approach, *European Journal of International Relations*, 24(3): 638–661.

Woodward, A. (2015) Travels, triangles and transformations: implications for new agendas in gender equality policy, *TVGN*, 18(1): 5–18.

World Bank (nd) *World Bank Open Data Bank*. https://data.worldbank.org/indicator/SG.GEN.PARL.ZS

World Economic Forum (2021) *135 Years in the Estimated Journey Time to Gender Equality*, https://www.weforum.org/agenda/2021/04/136-years-is-the-estimated-journey-time-to-gender-equality/

WPHF (Women's Peace and Humanitarian Fund) (2021) *Women's Peace and Humanitarian Fund*. https://wphfund.org/quotes/

Wright, H. (2019) 'Masculinities perspectives': advancing a radical Women, Peace and Security agenda?, *International Feminist Journal of Politics*, 22(5): 652–674.

Wright, K.A.M. (2022a) Gendered silences in western responses to the Russia-Ukraine war, *Place Branding and Public Diplomacy*, 19: 237–240.

Wright, K.A.M. (2022b) Where is Women, Peace and Security? NATO's response to the Russia–Ukraine war, *European Journal of Politics and Gender*. 1–3.

Wright, K.A.M. (2022c) WPS and defence, *CSSF Women, Peace and Security Helpdesk*. https://wpshelpdesk.org/wp-content/uploads/2022/11/Helpdesk-report-WPS-and-Defence_FINAL_uploaded.pdf

Wright, K.A.M. (2024) Towards a feminist defence policy: challenges for feminist foreign policy?, in H. Partis-Jennings and C. Eroukhmanoff (eds) *Feminist Policy-Making*, New York: Routledge.

Wright, K. and Bergman Rosamond, A. (2024) Sweden, NATO and gendered silences on feminist foreign policy, *International Affairs*, 100(2): 589–607.

Wyatt, A., Podems, D., Durieux, M. and Evans, K. (2021) Feminist approaches to monitoring, evaluation and learning: overview of current practices, *Equality Fund*. https://equalityfund.ca/wp-content/uploads/2021/09/Feminist-MEL-Research-Overview-Paper-FINAL-1.pdf

Yahaya, D. (2021) A feminist agenda for people and planet: principles and recommendations for a global feminist economic justice agenda, *Action Nexus for Generation Equality*. https://wedo.org/wp-content/uploads/2021/06/Blueprint_A-Feminist-Agenda-for-People-and-Planet.pdf?blm_aid=26261

Yildirim, T.M., Kocapınar, G. and Ecevit, Y.A. (2021) Status incongruity and backlash against female legislators: how legislative speechmaking benefits men, but harms women, *Political Research Quarterly*, 74(1): 35–45.

Young, I.M. (1990) *Throwing Like a Girl and Other Essays in Feminist Philosophy and Social Theory*, Bloomington: Indiana University Press.

Young, I.M. (1992) Five faces of oppression, in T. Wartenberg (ed) *Rethinking Power*, Albany: State University of New York Press, pp 174–195.

Zhang, C. and Huang, Z. (2023) Foreign aid, norm diffusion, and local support for gender equality: comparing evidence from the World Bank and China's aid projects in Africa, *Studies in Comparative International Development*. https://doi.org/10.1007/s12116-023-09381-4

Zhong, R. (2023) Warming could push the Atlantic past a 'tipping point' this century, *International New York Times*, 25 July.

Zhukova, E. (2023) Postcolonial logic and silences in strategic narratives: Sweden's feminist foreign policy in conflict-affected states, *Global Society*, 37(1): 1–22.

Zhukova, E., Rosén Sundström, M. and Elgström, O. (2022) Feminist foreign policies (FFPs) as strategic narratives: norm translation in Sweden, Canada, France, and Mexico, *Review of International Studies*, 48(1): 195–216.

Zilla, C. (2023) Feminist foreign and development policy in ministerial documents and debates, *Feminist Policy Reorientation, SWP*. https://www.swp-berlin.org/10.18449/2023C22/

Zwingel, S. (2005) From intergovernmental negotiations to (sub)national change: a transnational perspective on the impact of CEDAW, *International Feminist Journal of Politics*, 7: 400–424.

Zwingel, S. (2013) Translating international women's rights norms: CEDAW in context, in G. Caglar, E, Prügl and S. Zwingel (eds) *Feminist Strategies in International Governance*, New York: Routledge, pp 111–126.

Zwingel, S. (2015) *Translating International Women's Rights*, London: Palgrave Macmillan.

Zwingel, S. (2016) *Translating International Women's Rights: The CEDAW Convention in Context*, London: Palgrave Macmillan.

Zwingel, S. (2017) Women's rights norms as content-in-motion and incomplete practice, *Third World Thematics: A TWQ Journal*, 2: 675–690.

Index

References to footnotes show both the page number and the note number (29n1).

A

abortion as a human right, legal 58–59
accountability mechanisms to address policy failures in peacemaking 205
activists, role of inside 195
actors, non-state and state 70–71
affirmative action and active recruitment efforts by ministries of foreign affairs 81–82
Afghan feminists
  call for withdrawal of troops from Afghanistan by 159n2
  criticism of dress code adhered to by female foreign diplomats in Afghanistan 232
Afghan Republic, inclusion of women among delegates from in Afghanistan peace process (2018–2020) 201
Afghan women
  civil society mechanisms to support 210
  rights and livelihoods of 158–159
Afghan Women Leaders Forum 210
Afghanistan
  abandonment of women and girls to edicts of Taliban 235
  as recipient of aid from Canada 185
  as recipient of aid from Germany 185
  conflict in 209
  empowerment of girls and women in 44–45
  failed peace process (2018–2020) 201, 210
  justification of military engagements in 44, 185
  peacemaking in 15, 210
  rapid response window (RPW) support in raising awareness of women's essential roles in formal conflict resolution 210
  resurgence of the Taliban in 158
  Taliban takeover of 210
  use of Female Engagement Teams in 159
  withdrawal of NATO forces from 155, 158–159, 235

African Americans, increase in number of in diplomacy 81
African anti-colonial movements 65
African MFAs 83
African Women's Development and Communication Network (FEMNET) 71
African Women's Movement, President Kagame's 2016 winning of Gender Champion Award from 60
Afro-Brazilians, offering of scholarships to 81
agency 34, 45
agenda 4, 47, 82, 157, 179
agents of change 42–43, 51, 77
  and inside activists, role of 194–195
Agreement for Peace and Reconciliation in Mali 210
aid and development 15, 183–198
Albright, Madeleine 232, 236
Alliance of Small Island States 224
alliances across foreign policy areas 236
alternative institutional spaces 85
ambassadresses 78–79
Ambassadors for Gender Equality 86–87
Ambassadors for Women 75–76, 78
American military and allies 184–185
Amnesty International 71
Anishinaabe worldviews 23
anti-abortion Geneva Consensus Declaration (2020) 58
anti-gender governments and leadership 108–109, 113, 116–117
anti-liberal actors 57
antipreneurs and antipreneurship 57, 113
Aotearoa New Zealand foreign policy 28–30, 233
Arab Women Mediators Network 207
Asia, demands for freedom and dignity in 130
Asian People's Movement on Debt and Development 225

289

Asian Relations Conference (ARC) (1947) 129, 130–134
Asian solidarity, roadmap for 133–134
Asian unity, Pandit's roadmap for 129–130, 233
Association of Southeast Asian Nations (ASEAN) Women's Peace Registry 207
Association of Southeast Asian Nations (ASEAN) states 84
Australia
 adoption of pro-gender norms in foreign policy by 203
 agency of political leaders in 8, 9
 appointment of ambassadors/envoys 86
 commitment to gender equality programming 195
 feminist foreign policy 187
 foreign aid priorities 184
 transnational feminist networks (TFNs) in 67
Australian Defence Force 157
Australian Feminist Foreign Policy Coalition 70, 71
autocracies 59–60

B

backlash
 against feminist and pro-gender norms in foreign policy 49, 57–61
 from families and communities 25
Baerbock, Annalena 116, 118, 147
Barbados, spearheading of conversations about new mechanisms for just climate finance by 224
Bárcena, Alicia 116
barriers, patriarchal and traditional 209–210
Beijing Conference on Women (1995) 191
Beijing Platform for Action 65
biases, institutionalization of 178
Billström, Tobias 55
binary gender 36, 43
Bishop, Julie 8, 9
Black feminists 22
Black people 22
Black women
 political organizing of 22–23
 quilting of 22
Black women's abolitionist activists 65
Boer War, violence against women and children during 64
Brazilian Itamaraty 81
Bridgetown Initiative 224–225
Britain, early women's suffrage movement in 64
Brundtland, Gro-Harlem 8
Buenaventura, Mae 225
bundled norms 51, 54, 59 *see also* democracy; human rights
burden of care 24–25, 44

bureaucrats, proliferation of feminist foreign policy 72–73
Burundi, implementation of WPS agenda in 63

C

Canada
 achievement of the requisite levels of equality, peace and security by 45
 adoption of pro-gender norms in foreign policy by 203
 agency of political leaders in 8
 appointment of ambassadors/envoys by 86
 commitments to increased funding 192–193
 Conservative Party government 185
 as donor country 188
 Equality Fund 193
 feminist foreign policy in 9, 16, 18, 19, 24–26, 47, 183, 189, 207
 Feminist International Assistance Policy (FIAP) 186, 187, 190–193, 222
 foreign policy shifts in 17
 gender mainstreaming in 180
 holding of the G7 presidency in 2018 and 2019 by 98
 human rights violations in 27
 increased number of female ambassadors 88
 nation rebranding in 10
 Official Development Assistance (ODA) Package 193
 putting of empowerment into discourse 41–43
 state actor in Global Partners Network (GPN) 70
 top ten aid recipients 185
 Women's Voice and Leadership Program 193
Canadian Feminist International Assistance Policy 221
Canadian International Development Agency 41
cancel culture 229
care ethics and the care economy 21–22, 24–26, 70
Caribbean
 diplomats-only networks 84
 transnational feminist networks (TFNs) in 67
Chile
 European Union's free trade agreement with 180
 feminist foreign policy in 46, 87, 207, 224
 state actor in Global Partners Network 70
China
 increases in aid from 186
 possible online technology-facilitated abuse targeting women politicians in liberal states 231

INDEX

rising influence of 235
tensions with United States 110
choice, rhetoric of 22–23
civil society 175
  development and implementation of key policy objectives 172
civil society mechanisms 209–210
climate and biodiversity crises 216–217
climate change crisis 220, 224
climate finance, provision of 216
Clinton, Hillary 53, 53n1, 138, 232, 236
coalition building 10–11, 12
Coalition for Feminist Foreign Policy in the United States 70, 71
Cold War 133, 169
collaborative engagement through different spaces 94, 97–101
collective recognition of social reproductive labour 25
Colombia
  arms deal signed with Sweden 56
  campaigns led by women's groups to encourage progress in peace talks 203
  feminist foreign policy in 46, 224
  negotiations between the Colombian government and FARC (2012) 203, 204
  peacemaking agenda in 205
colonialism 30, 214
colonization on racial and gender hierarchies, effects of 29
Colombia, adoption of pro-gender norms in peace agreements 10
Commission of Small Island States on Climate Change and International Law 224
Commission on the Status of Women (1946) 65
commodities, high-value 169
Communism 130
compatibility of feminist foreign policy goals with states' key national role conceptions 117
Conference of Parties (COPs) 203, 224
conflicts
  between and among values and interests 29
  within community of practice 99
constructivism
  versus feminist international relations theory 6–7
  viewpoint 14
content-in-motion 49
contested compliance 51
Convention on the Elimination of All Forms of Discrimination Against Women 49
Cooperative for Assistance and Relief Everywhere (CARE) 71
corporate power, joint, transnational tackling of 216
Costa Rica, reinvestment of whole defence budget in health services 154n1

Council of the European Union 148
credibility gap, handling of 237–238
cultural exchange 133
cultural extractivism 30
Czechoslovakian ministry of foreign affairs 82

D

Declaration of Commitment to End Sexual Violence in Conflict 54
decolonial feminism, possibilities of 195–197
decolonial solidarity 130–131
defence/military 15, 154–166
  in pro-gender and feminist foreign policy, absence of 155–157
Delgado, Martha 116, 118
delivery of development assistance 186
demands for aid 186
democracy 10, 59, 60, 75, 113, 119, 130
democratic control 64–65
democratic representation 133
Denmark, appointment of ambassadors/envoys 86
development, market-based logic of 45
development assistance 24
developmental objectives 44
dialogue, inclusive 93–94, 98–99, 100–101, 105
diffusion and contestation on gender and feminism in foreign policy 3–4
digital disinformation, rise of 139–141
Digital Services Act (2023) 148
diplomacy
  advancement of women in formal 80
  and feminist foreign policies 87–88
  and foreign policy 75–76, 78, 80, 81
  gender segregation and division of labour in 79–80
  as a gendered practice 76
  and heterosexual marriage 79
  new institutional features that advance women in 80–88
diplomatic exchange of information and views 133
diplomatic infrastructure 74–89
diplomatic wives 79 *see also* ambassadresses
discriminatory racist and misogynist agendas 3
disengagement 6
diverse experiences of marginalization, oppression and inequality 190–191
diversity and diversification 7, 22, 81, 104, 105
Dlamini-Zuma, Nkozasana 8, 9
domestic political context 114–115
domination 36

E

Ebrard, Marcelo 116
ecological crises 215, 217

291

economic development and policy 45
economic development initiatives 37
economic empowerment 46–47
economic growth
  and poverty reduction 39
  women and children as conduits for 187–188
economic logic 37, 38
economic rationalities and comparative advantage logics 180–181
economic rights and empowerment 40
elite, educated middle and upper-class 99
embodied listening through all stages of foreign policy 101–104
empathy, care and dialogue 163–164
empowerment 2, 33–34, 36–37, 41–42
  -as-efficiency 45
  lite, superheroines and structural transformation 43–47
  putting of in discourse 37–43
empowerment narratives 43–44
epistemology and ontology 29–30
equality and women's rights, regression in 3
ethical in feminist foreign policy 19–20
ethical questions, avoidance of 164
ethics 14, 16–31
Euro-Western cultures 29
Europe, market power 179, 181
European ambassadors 78
European colonial powers 78
European Commission 180
  Directorate General (DG) for Trade 181
  positionality of gender experts within 181
European diplomatic systems 78
European ministries of foreign affairs 83
European Parliament 148, 158
European Union 39, 51, 59, 84, 119, 149, 169
  Action Plan on Women, Peace and Security 178
  Ambassador for Gender and Diversity 86
  claims to link social and economic agenda 179
  Code of Practice on Disinformation (2018) 148
  Common Security and Defence Policy 158
  countering of disinformation 148
  criticism of conservative changes in Hungary 113
  external action 181
  free trade agreement 180
  initiation of civil society mechanisms to support Afghan women 210
  trade policy 178, 181
event organization 98
exclusive gender binary, reinforcement of 25
expertise, thematic and technical 66–67
extractive model 214–215

F

familial relations, straining of 25
female ambassador postings, increase in 87–88
female suffrage 50–51
femicides 26
feminism
  definitions of 189–192
  just war and pacifism 161–165
  NGOization of feminism 234
  silencing of 161
feminism's limited appearance 219–224
feminisms, foreign policy and global environmental challenges 214–216
feminist critiques of global trade structures 169–171
feminist decolonial historiography 120–136
feminist development policies, critical analyses of the impact of 187–195
feminist ethics 20–24
feminist foreign goals 118
feminist foreign policies 14, 27–28, 56, 87–88
feminist foreign policy
  absence of defence/military in 155–157
  advancement of 228–239
  in Australia 187 see also Australian Feminist Foreign Policy Coalition
  in Canada see feminist foreign policy in under Canada
  in Chile see feminist foreign policy in under Chile
  in Colombia see feminist foreign policy in under Colombia
  ethical in 19–20
  in France see feminist foreign policy in under France
  future of 237–239
  in Germany see feminist foreign policy in under Germany
  goals 117, 118
  in Libya see feminist foreign policy in under Libya
  in Luxembourg see feminist foreign policy in under Luxembourg
  in Mexico see feminist foreign policy in under Mexico
  new avenues for research into 7–13
  in New Zealand see feminist foreign policy in under New Zealand
  in Norway see feminist foreign policy in under Norway
  non-adoption of by Finland 108
  and power 34–36
  proliferation of bureaucrats in 72–73
  responding to a turbulent global world 234–236
  results from 229–234
  saviour narrative of 17

INDEX

in Spain *see* Feminist Foreign Policy *under* Spain
in Sweden *see* feminist foreign policy in *under* Sweden
in the United Nations *see* Feminist Foreign Policy + Group *under* United Nations
in the US *see* Coalition for Feminist Foreign Policy in the United States
see also feminist foreign policy analysis; feminist foreign policy networks; Feminist Foreign Policy Plus states; Global Partners Network for Feminist Foreign Policy; *Handbook on Feminist Foreign Policy*; International Centre for Research on Women's Feminist Foreign Policy's framework; and feminist foreign policy *under* ministries of foreign affairs; Shaping Feminist Foreign Policy
feminist foreign policy analysis (FFPA) 1, 2, 3, 4, 5, 8, 14–15, 16–17, 21, 95–96, 112–113
  advancement of 228–239
  future of 237–239
  new avenues for research into 7–13
  responding to a turbulent global world 234–236
  results from 229–234
feminist foreign policy networks 70–71
  see also transnational feminist networks
Feminist Foreign Policy Plus (FFP+) states 70, 71, 165
feminist Indigenous scholars 23
feminist-informed foreign policy, incorporation of defence into 158
feminist institutionalism 75, 76–78, 82, 86–87
feminist international assistance 25–26
Feminist International Assistance Policy (FIAP) 19, 24–25, 41, 42–43, 44–46, 183, 186, 188
feminist International Relations (IR) theory 1–2, 3, 5, 6–7, 8, 11, 12, 21, 23, 32, 90–92, 144, 155–156, 168, 228
feminist intersectional lens, opportunities for adopting a 189–192
feminist language and policies 24, 67–69
feminist leadership styles 8–9
feminist neoliberalism 42
feminist peacemaking, revitalizing of 207
feminist power 179
  Europe 181
feminist principles in peacemaking 205–210
feminist representation in foreign policies 205–206, 238–239
feminist understandings of just war, pacifism and self-defence 156–157
feminist values and practices 27, 69–70
feminist vanguards and reactionaries 108–109
FemSolution 163

FemWise-Africa 207
Finland, non-adoption of feminist foreign policy by 108
Finnish Ambassador for Gender Equality 86
First-Nations foreign policy 18
First World War 64
foreign aid allocations by country 185–186
foreign aid and development assistance, persistent and emerging challenges of 184–187
foreign policy
  and gendered vulnerabilities 143–149
  introspection and gendered resilience in 149–153
  practising of inclusive dialogue through 94–104
foreign policy analysis (FPA) 1–3, 5–7, 32, 74, 75, 200
  how gendered analysis advances 231–232
  power in 11
  see also feminist foreign policy analysis
foreign policy change 2–3
foreign policy engagements, feminist-informed 157–161
formal diplomatic institutional features 77–78
framework on gender and peacemaking in foreign policy 200–201
framing of collective understandings of injustices and inequalities 62
France
  adoption of equal pay legislation at national level 180
  clampdowns on pro-Palestinian protests in 160
  co-organization of Generation Equality Forum by 98
  declaration of feminist diplomacy 87
  feminist foreign policy in 207
  holding of the G7 presidency by 98, 99
  increased number of female ambassadors 88
  International Strategy for Gender Equality (2018–2022) 46, 221, 222
  state actor in Global Partners Network (GPN) 70
  support for Ukraine war efforts 159
free trade agreements (FTAs) 176
Freedom House 60
Freeland, Chrystia 16
funding commitments 192–193

G

games, gendered multilevel 11–12
Garcia, Daniela Philipson 27
gay-friendliness 50–51
Gaza, responses to the war in 160–161
gender
  concept of within international discourse and practice 7
  and democracy 10

293

in European Union trade policy 178–181
feminisms and foreign policy 1–15
feminist branding and foreign policy
 orientation 9–11
and feminist epistemic community 99
and feminist strategies in foreign policy 2
and foreign policy leadership 109–117
inclusion of in key environmental
 policies 220n1
role of in adversarial geopolitics 144–145
in trade 173–174, 180
as useful category of historical
 analysis 126–127
gender articulation 9
gender-based violence (GBV) 26
gender bashing 51, 59
gender biases 96
gender blindness in foreign policy analysis
 (FPA) 5
gender categories 43–44
gender chapters 174–175
gender cosmopolitanism 10
gender equality 2, 3, 4, 12, 14, 39, 41, 42,
 49–50, 51, 53–54, 55–57, 59, 60–61, 65,
 66, 82, 85, 97, 114, 187, 190, 219–220
Gender Equality Ambassadors 97
gender focal points 85–86
 in Ministries of Foreign Affairs and
 embassies 14
gender ideology 59
gender inequality
 defining problem of 33, 37–38, 39
 resources and 34–35
 and violence 27–28
gender-justice 43, 48
gender mainstreaming 40–41, 69, 191–192
'gender-neutral' categories, challenging
 of 126
gender norms *see* gender and foreign policy
 under norms
gender quotas
 mandatory 81–82
 used to advance women's political
 representation 202
gender regimes theory 172–173, 182
gender relations 11–12
 transformation of 34
gender representation, rising stakes
 of 146–148
gender subordination 33
gender washing 51, 60–61
gendered analyses 5
gendered diplomatic infrastructure 14, 77
gendered disinformation 15, 137–153
 as a security concern 141–143
gendered dynamics in foreign policy 7–9, 32
gendered effects of war, conflict and
 militarism on women's lives and political
 communities 156

gendered entanglements between domestic
 gender regimes and foreign trade
 policy 171–173
gendered experiences leading to knowledge
 development 220
gendered norms, adoption of 11, 60, 68
gendered power relations 34–35
 commitment to challenging 17
 and intersectionality 233
gendered states 35
gendered structures in foreign policy and
 global politics 11–13
gendered violence of settler-colonialism 45
gendering of Indian foreign policy
 narratives 125–135
gendering of international trade policy 171, 181
gendering trade and the global political
 economy 169–171
General Smuts 129
Generation Equality Forum 2021 96, 97
Geneva Conventions 39
Geneva II Conference on Syria 209
geopolitical themes and interests 3, 149,
 235–236
Germany
 civilian power role conception 113
 Federal Minister for Economic Cooperation
 and Development 116
 Federal Office 158
 Feminist Development Policy (FDP)
 183–184, 186, 187, 189, 190, 191, 193
 feminist foreign policy in 110, 115–116,
 190, 207
 Green party 116, 147, 158
 history of promotion of gender equality and
 women's rights 188
 Merkel governments (2005–2021)
 115–116, 118
 Ministry of Defence 158
 policy towards Ukraine 159–160
 Social Democrats 116
 state actor in Global Partners Network
 (GPN) 70
 support for Israel's right to self-defence 160
 transnational feminist networks in 67
 top ten aid recipients 185
 WPS national action plan (2021–2024) 158
Global Affairs Canada 24
global class inequality 99
Global Day of Action for Access to Safe and
 Legal Abortion 67
global environmental challenges 13, 15,
 212–227
global feminist political economy challenges 177
Global Gag rule 58
global investment in the care economy 24–25
Global North
 foreign policies 213
 foreign policy actors from 101

framing of development and human rights shortcomings 27
gender inequality in 182
governmental addressing of ecological crises in transformative way in 218
history of feminist networks relevant to foreign policy 65
Mexico's model for states in 27, 28
policies towards global environmental challenges 216–224
pressure placed on states to reduce emissions 224
profits flowing to investors in 225
use of National Action Plans (NAPs) by 95
women's peace and anti-war networks in 64
Global Partners Network (GPN) for Feminist Foreign Policy 70, 71, 93
global production chains, exploitation of women by 170
Global South
activists 184
contribution to international peacekeeping operations 158
empowerment of women and girls in 36, 44
feminist scholars 72
foreign policy actors from 101
framing of development and human rights shortcomings 27
funding of WEDO to facilitate attendance of women from at climate conferences 222
importance of shifting power and wealth to communities in 218
masculinities in 25
networks in 63
positioning of Mexico as leader in 111
representation of 101
rhetoric of failure in 196
states linking collaborative, just response to ecological crises and feminist approach 224–225
states' policies towards global environmental challenges 14, 224–225
use of National Action Plans by 95
women and girls from the 45
women's history of resistance in 65
women's rights networks in 65
writing in women from 47
see also Mexico
Global Summit to End Sexual Violence in Conflict (London, 2014) 54
globetrotting sneaker 169, 170
governance feminism 47
government representatives, meetings of 133
greenhouse gas emissions reductions, negotiation and implementation of agreements on 216
Guterres, Antonio 207

H

The Hague, first international women's congress convened in 64
Hague, Lord William 54
Handbook on Feminist Foreign Policy 38, 39n1, 55, 68, 95, 176–177, 221
hard power versus soft power 34
Harper, Stephen 185
Harris, Kamala 147
hierarchies in Mexico, challenging 26–28
Hillary doctrine 52, 53–54, 61
history, recollecting, rewriting and reconceptualizing 124–127
human rights 2, 4, 16, 19, 27–28, 39–40, 60, 66, 68, 112–113, 224, 236, 238–239
human security approach 19–20
Hungary
appeal to Christian, pro-family values 113
Orbán as key policy entrepreneur and leader of fight against international liberal order 111, 113, 117, 119
outright rejection of feminist foreign policy goals by 118
teaching of gender studies banned in 59

I

illiberal states 57–58
impacts, emphasis on in Global North foreign policies 220–221
inclusion, emphasis on in Global North foreign policies 221–224
impacts and inclusion focus 223–224
inclusion and exclusion, institutionalizing patterns of 27
Independent Commission for Aid Impact (ICAI) 54
India
independence of 233
international relations and foreign policy analysis, women in 14–15, 121–125, 127–128
reservations in place in the foreign service 81
women envoys in 123
women's movements in 65
Indian foreign policy (IFP) and international relations 14–15, 122, 123–128
Menon's vision for 134–135
Indian women diplomats *see* Menon, Lakshmi; Pandit, Vijaya Lakshmi
indigeneity and feminism in New Zealand's foreign policy 28–30
Indigenous ethico-ontologies and onto-epistemologies 23, 28–29
Indigenous ethics and epistemologies 23
Indigenous Māori inhabitants and British settlers 28
Indigenous networks, women's history of resistance in 65
Indigenous people, violence endured by 23
Indigenous rights 66

Indigenous scholars 23, 184
Indigenous thought 23
Indigenous ways of being and knowing 23
individual experience 163–164
individual-in-relation 22
individual uniqueness 22
influence in peacemaking 202–205
information, collection and dissemination of 133
institutional analyses 77
institutional structures, inclusion of gender equality norms and programmes in established 175–176
institutional turf battles 149
institutionalized masculinized diplomacy, history of 78–80
Inter-American Court of Human Rights 224
interdependence and coexistence 134–135
interests, formulation of national economic 172
Intergovernmental Panel on Climate Change 212
Intergovernmental Science-Policy Platform on Biodiversity and Ecosystem Services (IPBES) 212
Internacional Feminista 18, 26–27
international assistance funding for paid and unpaid care work 24
international assistance programmes, challenges requiring innovative thinking in 186
International Center for Research on Women 26
International Center for Research on Women's Feminist Foreign Policy's (2022) framework 176
international cooperation to limit exploitation of nature 216
International Council of Women 64, 65
International Court of Justice 224
International Gender Equality Strategy 67
international leadership, opportunities for 109–111, 117
international non-governmental organizations (INGOs) and donors 99
international polarization 111
International Practice Theory (IPT) 90, 91, 101
international relations (IR) 21, 23, 32, 50, 52, 57, 102, 144, 168
Non-Western 120, 121
see also feminist International Relations theory; international relations and foreign policy analysis, women in under India
International Trade Centre 'SheTrades Initiative' 175
International Tribunal for the Law of the Sea 224
International Women Deliver conference 60
International Women's Conferences (1975, 1980, 1985, 1995) 65

internationalism and foreign policy 134
intersectionality 44, 103–104
introspection and reflexivity 150–151
Iraq, quota of women in parliament and government 202
Ireland, Defence Action Plan (2020) 157
Israel
  conflict in Gaza 160
  Hamas attacks on Israeli civilians 160
Israeli women, exclusion from official Middle East negotiations 202
Italy, unfair competition in textiles 180

J

Jolie, Angelina 54
Jordan, as recipient of aid from Germany 185
jus ad bellum 160
jus in bello 160
jus post bellum 160

K

Kaczynski, Jaroslaw 59
Kagame, President Paul 60
Kenya, gender inclusion in post-conflict in 202
knowledge
  contextual 103
  production and transnational feminist networks 66–70, 72
  reflective conscious and unreflective background 92
  and truth 29–30

L

language
  development of gender-inclusive 68
  of gender equality and mainstreaming 188–189, 191–192
  inclusive and intersectional 191
  instrumentalist and neoliberal feminist 187–189
  use of around transformation 42, 68–69
  use of empowerment 45, 48
Latin America
  gender ideology 146
  ministries of foreign affairs in 83
  transnational feminist networks in 67
  see also Mexico
leadership 14, 106–119
  strategic 232–233
LGBT movement 59
LGBTQIA+
  community 146–147
  individuals 141, 191
  language 68–69
  `rights 58, 59, 65, 66, 108, 138, 145
  workers in the UK Foreign & Commonwealth Office 80
liberal approach 44
liberal democracy 59, 119

liberal feminist concerns 41
liberal gendered rights 49
liberal order, erosion of rule-based 13
liberalism
Liberia, implementation of WPS agenda in 63
Libya
  failure to adopt a WIPS National Action Plan, despite feminist foreign policy 4
  feminist foreign policy in 46
  peacemaking in 15
  training of women mediators by UN Women 202
Linde, Ann 110
listener and learner 30
listening 30
  inclusive 93
local context 102
local ownership in international assistance 196–197
Löfven, Stefan 115
logics, challenging of 47 see different logics of empowerment, e.g. economic logic
Loncon, Elisa 147
Luxembourg
  feminist foreign policy in 158, 207
  state actor in GPN 70
  support for Ukraine war efforts 159

M

Mahuta, Nanaia 16, 28
mainstreaming of women's issues and views in peacemaking 206, 207
male ethical agenda within the just war tradition 161
Mali, RRW support of women's participation in implementation of Agreement for Peace and Reconciliation 210
Malmström, Cecilia 180
Māori
  principles 16
  values 28
  way 29n1
marginalized, centring of ideas and experiences of 45
measurement tools, poor 193–194
Mediterranean Women Mediators Network 207
Meloni, Giorgia 116
MENA region, religion and culture in 95
Menon, Lakshmi 121, 128–129, 134–135, 233
Mexico
  co-organization of Generation Equality Forum by 98
  feminist foreign policy in 18, 26, 46, 111, 118, 189, 207
  foreign policy shifts in 17
  international feminist ambitions 113
  key policy entrepreneurs 116
  militarization of public security 26

neutral response to war in Gaza 160
restriction of feminist foreign policy to a single department by 118
state actor in GPN 70
Middle East
  empowerment of girls and women in 44
  implementation of UN Resolution 1325 in 95
  ministries of foreign affairs in 83
  official negotiations to resolve conflict in 202
  organization of gay pride parade in capital city in 102–103
military
military
  and defence 15
  operationalization and integration of the WPS agenda in the 157
ministries of foreign affairs (MFAs) 75
  affirmative action in recruitment of diplomats 81
  career advancement of women in 81
  and feminist foreign policy 87
  formal hierarchy of 77
  institutional changes undergone by 80–81
  institutional gender patterns in 79–80
  reliance on diplomatic wives 79
  women's networks developed within 83
ministry of foreign affairs gender focal points 76, 85–86
mobilization around key values and identities 110
Moderaterna 55
moral duties to protect rights and interests of others 17
moral language 27
moral theories 20–21 see also ethics
moral thinking 26
moral universalism, problem of 20
moral value of attentiveness to the needs of others 25
morality 92–93
Moro Islamic Liberation Front 203
Mottley, Mia 224
Muslim women 103

N

Naidu, Sarojini 130
nation branding 9–10
national
  interest 9, 217
  role conceptions, compatibility with 111–113
National Action Plans (NAPs) 95
national committee, formation of 133
Native American polities 78
Native polities 78
nego-feminism 94, 96
Nehru, Jawaharlal 129, 131, 134

297

neoliberal approach 41
neoliberal capitalism 40
neoliberal economic policy 45
neoliberal feminism 42
neoliberal logic of empowerment 42
neoliberal market logic 22–23
neoliberal narratives 42
neoliberal and social democratic public gender regimes, distinction between 172
neoliberal terms 45
neoliberalization of feminism 24, 72
Nepal, gender inclusion in post-conflict in 202
Netherlands
  appointment of ambassadors/envoys 86
  She Decides campaign 58
  state actor in GPN 70
  support for Israel's right to self-defence 160
  support for Ukraine war efforts 159
Network of African Women in Conflict Prevention and Mediation 207
networks 62–73, 230–231
  of female diplomats 83–85
New Zealand
  female suffrage in 50
  feminist foreign policy in 18
  foreign policy shifts in 17
  Indigenous foreign policy 16, 28
  Indigenous rights 28
  Indigenous values 28
NGO Working Group on Women, Peace and Security 66, 68
non-alignment 135
non-Western anti-imperial solidarity 132
non-Western foreign policy imaginations 122
non-Western histories of international relations 125
Nordic countries
  appointment of ambassadors/envoys 86
  diplomats-only networks 84
  suffrage in 50
  see also Norway; Sweden
Nordic Women Mediators 207
norm antipreneurs 107
norm entrepreneurs 9, 38 *see also* Canada; Sweden
norm life cycle model 50–51
norm localization 51
norm saboteurs 57
norm spoiling 57–58
norm translation 51
normative configuration 50, 52, 57
normative foreign policy, pursuit of 110
normative rules, creation of 92
normative values and principles 4
normativity 22, 25–26
norms 49–61
  clashing 144–146
  diffusion of 7

gender and foreign policy 5, 7, 12, 50–52, 67, 93, 145–146
post-introduction stage of new 12–13
North Africa, empowerment of girls and women in 44
North Atlantic Treaty Organization (NATO) 56, 229
  membership 159
  recognition of Ukraine's entitlement to self-defence 163
  Resolute Support Mission 159
  Special Representative on Women Peace and Security 86
  Sweden's seeking to join 157
  withdrawal of forces from Afghanistan 155, 158–159
North/South divide 71, 72
Norway
  adoption of pro-gender norms in foreign policy by 203, 204
  agency of political leaders in 8
  feminist foreign policy in 9–10, 26, 108
  non-adoption of feminist foreign policy by 108
  playing of femininity 84
  stance towards Taliban in Afghanistan 204

O

Obrador, López 116
obstacles to inclusive dialogue 98–99
OECD Development Assistance Committee (DAC) 192, 193
official development assistance (ODA) 185
oppression, exclusions and forms of 21, 27
Orbán, Viktor 59, 113, 117, 119
Organization for Economic Co-operation and Development (OECD) 186
Organization for Security and Co-operation in Europe 84
organization of social and economic life 215–216
Oslo, Taliban's first official trip to 204
Oxfam Canada 24–26

P

Pacific Feminist Forum (Fiji, 2023) 67
pacifism
  differentiation between absolute and contingent 164–165
  not synonymous with feminist foreign policy 159
  versus self-defence 72
Palestinian women and girls as victims in Gaza conflict 160
Pandit, Vijaya Lakshmi 121, 128–134, 135, 232–233
participation
  in decision-making institutions 40
  deterring of women from political and civic 147–148

INDEX

of women in decision-making processes 68
of women in trade 175
particularism 20
partner-oriented listening 94
party ideology 118
patriarchal structural and hierarchical principles 5, 8, 13, 27
peace agreements, implementation of 203
peacemaking 10, 15, 199–211
personal
  and international 35
  and political 20–21
Philippines
  role played by women in peace negotiations 203
  women's movements in 65
PiS (Law Justice) political party 59
pluriverse 30
Poland, presentation of gender in 59
polarization of and global politics 3
policies and rhetoric, lack of coherence between 26
policies ensuring that women's participation is supported and empowered 220
policies focused on addressing and ameliorating negative environmental impacts 220
policy, link between domestic and international 172
policy documents 94–95
policy entrepreneurs 114–119
policy making, transformative approaches to 176
political leadership 8–9
political logic 37, 42–43
politics of forgetting 27
polity and effectiveness of scrutiny and accountability processes 172
post-Cold War efforts to develop ethical foreign policy 16–17, 19
post-Soviet region, feminist networks in 72
post-Western international order 58
power and power dynamics 6, 11, 14, 16, 23, 24, 27, 30, 32–48, 103–104, 179
power-over 34, 35
practice 90–105
  and feminist theory 91–94
presence in peacemaking 201–202
President Macron 87, 99
Preventing Sexual Violence Initiative 10–11
Priority Area I, Peace and Security 26
pro- and anti-gender foreign policy, rise of 230
pro-gender equality norms in foreign policy 9, 52–57
pro-gender norms in foreign policy, upholding of 203–204
productive network of power 35
professionalization of feminist non-governmental organizations 72–73

public state responses 149
pushback in the multilateral system, tackling 238

R

racial and gender justice 24
racial stereotypes, reinscription of 25
Rapid Response Window (RRW) on Women's Participation in Peace Processes and the Implementation of Peace Agreements 209–210
Reaching Critical Will 67
Reactionaries 117
realpolitik 17, 79
recognition of misogynistic disinformation campaigns 151–152
reflexivity 21
reform, structural and system 29
relational ethics of accountability to people and place 23
relational feminist values 24
relationality and power 20–24, 28–29, 30, 31, 35–36
reproductive justice 22–23
reproductive rights 58–59
resilience, fostering of 150–151
resistance
  to foreign policies 36
  to structures of power 36
  and sustainability 234
resource, power as 34–35, 47
resources
  of gender focal points 85–86
  generation of needed for a just transition 216
  meaning attached to different 34–35
  opportunities and power 40
  redistribution of 35
  unequal distribution of 34–35
restrictive international environment 110
revisionist foreign policy trends 2
Revolutionary Armed Forces of Colombia (FARC) 203, 204
rights-based approach to gender equality 190
risks attached to limited strategy 223
routines and innovation 92
Russia
  advancement of traditional values doctrine 145
  assertion by that entrance into NATO requires acceptance of Western gender relations 229
  invasion of Ukraine 72, 110, 157, 149, 158, 159–160, 162–164, 185, 229, 235
Rwanda
  championing of women's rights and empowerment 60
  designated Not Free by Freedom House 60
  intimidation of political opponents in 60

S

safeguarding representation of women in public and political life 146
same-sex marriage 50–51
Saudi Arabia, Sweden's selling of arms to 56
saviour narrative of feminist foreign policy 17
Scholz, Olaf 115–116
Schulze, Svenja 116
Scottish Government
  championing of the concept of a Wellbeing Economy 218
  commitment to decolonizing its International Development Strategy 218
  funding of WEDO 222
  perception of climate crisis voiced at COP 26 (Glasgow) 221
second wave of norms scholarship 51, 52
securitization of foreign aid 185
Security Council Resolutions on 'Women, Peace and Security 45
security logic 37, 42–43
security objectives 44
Self and Other 94, 184
self-interest and sharing, state 28
self-reflection 105
settler colonial care and contexts 23, 45
sexual violence in conflict initiative, preventing 54–55
sexual violence in conflict (London, 2022), international summit on 55
sexual violence in war in Gaza 160
sexuality 72
Seychelles, appointment of ambassadors/envoys 86
Shaping Feminist Foreign Policy (Berlin, 2022) 67
She Decides campaign 58
SheTrades initiative 176, 180
siloed projects 100
Slovenia, support for Ukraine war efforts 159
smart economics 39
  gender equality as 188
social hierarchies, entrenchment of in decision-making processes around trade 177–178
social logic 37, 38, 41
socioeconomic inequalities 170
soft political issue 53
soft power 11, 41
  arguments, tools and practices, use of in foreign policies 3, 13
solidarity-building in feminist spaces 69, 72
South Africa
  adoption of pro-gender norms in foreign policy by 203
  agency of political leaders in 8, 9
  Pandit's victory over General Smuts on floor of UNGA 129
South Asia, disinformation along lines of division on gender, religion and caste 146
South Sudan as recipient of aid from Canada 185
Spain
  appointment of ambassadors/envoys 86
  Feminist Foreign Policy (2021–2026) 46, 207
  incorporation of gender training in its military operations 158
  state actor in GPN 70
  support for Ukraine war efforts 159
Special Drawing Rights 225
speech versus silence 30
Sri Lanka, women's movements in 65
state feminism 9–10
state-of-the-art on gender, feminism and foreign policy analysis 5–7
state responses 148–149
state security and economic growth 53
Statement to Parliament on Sweden's Foreign Policy position (2019) 55–56
states and state policy 6
Stockholm's Forum on Gender Equality 2018 96, 98, 115
strategic leadership action, centrality of 232–233
strategies
  monitoring and auditing 193–194
  and possibilities for translating policy into practice 192
Strategy for Global Development Cooperation on Sustainable Economic Development (2022–2026) 2188
structural privileges, effect of on wellbeing 103
structural transformations 44
sub-Saharan Africa, women's rights activists and gender rights defenders 146
superheroines, women as 45
Sustainable Development Goals (SDGs) 168–169, 175, 183
  Goal 5 (gender equality) 65, 173–174, 175
  Goal 8 (decent work and economic growth) 175
  Goal 17 (partnership for goals) 175
Sweden
  achievement of the requisite levels of equality, peace and security by 45
  action on climate as compatible with competitive national-interest framing 218–219
  adoption of pro-gender norms in foreign policy by 203
  agency of political leaders in 8, 9
  ambassadorial team 86
  approach of to international trade 176–177
  arms trade 177
  coalition Social Democratic and Green Party government 19

INDEX

commitment to gender equality priorities 195
Conservative-led government's dropping of feminist framing of foreign policy 157–158
failure to link domestic and international action 55
feminist foreign policy in 9–10, 16, 17–18, 19, 26, 33, 41–42, 45, 47, 52–53, 55–57, 61, 68, 73, 87, 108, 110, 115, 118, 119, 176–177, 180, 187, 188, 189, 190, 222
focus on trade as part of its feminist foreign policy commitments 176–177
foreign aid priorities 184
gender mainstreaming in 180
government foreign policy speeches 218–219
human rights violations in 27
increased defence commitment 157–158
increased number of female ambassadors 88
MFA 87
National Action Plan 19
Network formed in 83
non-adoption of feminist foreign policy by 108
playing of femininity 84
promotion of values in foreign policy 177
putting of empowerment into discourse 38–41
removal of feminist and gender language from foreign policy strategy in 229
restriction of migration policy 55
rights, representation and resources (3Rs) in 19, 38–39
use of Female Engagement Teams in Afghanistan by 159
WPS agenda as consistent pillar of defence policy of 157–158
Swedish Democrats 55–56
Swedish Foreign Service and Ministry 68
Swedish International Development Agency (SIDA) 100
Syria
conflict in 209
peacemaking in 15, 210
percentage of women participants in UN-led talks (2017) 202
uniting of women political leaders across political divides 202
Syrian Arab Republic, as recipient of aid from Canada and Germany 185
as recipient of aid from Germany 185
Syrian Women Charter for Peace 202
Syrian Women's Political Movement 202
systemic factors and state action 109
Szijjártó, Péter 117

T

Taliban
expectations of change 232

groups, inclusion of women among delegates from in Afghanistan peace process (2018–2020) 201
insurgency 159, 185
Norway's stance towards 204
peace talks with US 204, 209
takeover of Afghanistan 210, 235
targeting of women in positions of power and visibility 146–147
technocratic governance and foreign policy omissions 173–178
techno-solutionism 149
TEDWomen Conference 53n1
third space 91, 91n1, 98
Third World, women's movements in 65
Third World woman 184, 196
Third World Women 69
Third World Women's Alliance (TWWA) 65
3Rs (rights, representation and resources) 38–40, 68, 116, 190 *see also* feminist representation in foreign policies; human rights; resources
toxicity of the dominant economic model 218
trade 15, 167–182
Trade for All strategy 178
traditional international relations 23
transcontinental non-Western anti-imperial solidarity 132
transnational activism 63
transnational feminist networks (TFNs) 62–73, 230–231
role of 6–7, 12–13, 14
treaties, inclusion of gender equality norms in founding 179–180
Treaties of Rome (1957), Article 119 179
Treaty of Amsterdam (1998) 178
Treaty of Lisbon (2009) 178
Treaty of Waitangi 28
Trudeau, Justin 8, 10, 24, 41
Trump, Donald 111
Turkey, increases in aid from 186

U

Ukraine
feminist networks in 72
as recipient of aid from Canada and Germany 185
Russian invasion of 110, 149, 157, 158, 159–160, 162–164, 185, 229, 235
updating of National Action Plan on WPS 160
ungendering, task of 25
United Arab Emirates
increases in aid from 186
as recipient of aid from Canada 185
United Kingdom
appointment of ambassadors/envoys 86

attention paid to pressing moral problems by 19
Department for International Development 80n2
Foreign & Commonwealth Office 80n2
Foreign, Commonwealth and Development Office 86
International Women and Girls Strategy 221
Joint Service Publication 985 (2021) 157
Preventing Sexual Violence in Conflict Initiative (PSVI) 10–11, 52–53, 54–55, 56, 61
promises to integrate gender and social inclusion objectives 223
Special Envoy for Gender Equality 86
Strategic Framework on Climate Action 219
Strategy for International Development 221
United Nations 53, 54, 59, 65, 84, 107, 133, 134
  agencies 67
  Charter 134
  'dumping ground' for US female diplomats 80
  Feminist Foreign Policy + Group 56
  Framework Convention on Climate Change (UNFCCC) 213
  gender justice within work of 19
  General Assembly (UNGA) 71, 128, 129, 133
  initiation of civil society mechanisms to support inclusion of marginalized women 209
  organizations 98
  resolutions 19
  Secretary General 207
  Special Envoys 208
  Women 157, 165, 202
  Women's Participation in Peace Processes and the Implementation of Peace Agreements 209
  World Conferences on Women 37
  see also Women, Peace, Security
United Nations (UN) Secretary-General on Sexual Violence in Conflict, Special Representative of the 115
United Nations (UN) Security Council 10, 67, 157
  Resolution 1325 on WPS 4, 7, 19, 39, 44–46, 49, 68, 95, 201
United States (US)
  Afghan Consultative Mechanism (USACM) 210
  Aid (USAID) mission internships 81
  appointment of Ambassador-at-Large for Global Women's Issues 86
  Biden administration 229
  contribution to gender-responsive climate action 222
  Department of Defense 184–185

female secretaries of state and endorsement of pro-gender norms 8
Obama administration 53
initiation of civil society mechanisms to support Afghan women 210
Secretaries of State 8, 232 see also Albright, Madeleine; Clinton, Hillary
Secretary's Office of Global Women's Issues 222–223
–Taliban peace talks 204, 209
tensions with China 110
Trump and Bush presidencies 58
use of Gender Day at annual COPs to acknowledge aspects of climate change 221
withdrawal of forces from Afghanistan 158–159, 235
United States foreign policy 229
  as 'dumping ground' for US female diplomats 80
US Conservative Political Action Conference (Dallas, Texas, August 2022) 111
US Department of State 81, 219
  Ambassador-at-Large for Global Women's Issues 86
  Women's Action Organization 83
useable history 122–123

V

vanguards 117
Velasco, Ana 27
Vietnam, women's movements in 65
violence
  against Indigenous people 23–24, 45
  against women and girls 26–27, 45, 54
  pursuit of the national interest and 172
vision, lack of a feminist transformative 216–219
voice 30

W

Wallström, Margot 8, 9, 16, 19, 39n1, 55–56, 110, 115, 118, 207
war, lived experience of those subjected to war 163–164
Watson, Sir Robert 212
WE-Care programme 24–25
weaponized information capacities 148
Western
  boundary-making 143
  camp 108
  -centrism 125
  commitment to progressive values 144
  conception of rational individual 22
  conflict of ideologies and ambitions 134
  countries, agreement of 132
  democratic leaders 14
  donors 195
  feminist defence of pacifism 155
  feminists and feminist ethico-ontology 23, 72, 163

gender relations 229
geographies 122
governments, use of language of ethics by 19
imperialist intentions 131
implementation of Resolution 1325 95
imports 160
international relations 124, 127–128
interventionism 161
liberal feminism 31
moral high ground of states 28
multilateral peacekeeping operations 158
norms of feminism 25
notions 29, 59, 122, 135–136
perspectives 102, 184
polarization 141
power workings 134, 235
representations of the Other and 'Third World woman' 184, 196
states 17, 27, 59
subject 45
theology and philosophy 214
theorizations of care 23
values 107, 146, 162
world 50
Western modernity 30
hierarchical boundaries of 27, 30
White Paper on Canada's feminist foreign policy 24
White, Western theorizations of care 23
women
  impact of globalization and trade liberalization on social, political and economic rights of 170–171
  relocation of 127–135
  roles of in informal peacemaking mostly unrecognized and barely acknowledged 203
  and state security 53–54
  Ukrainian 160, 162–164
women ambassador networks 84–85
women ambassadors in Asian, African and American capitals 84
Women Ambassadors' Network in the Vatican 84
Women Ambassadors of Warsaw (WAW) 83, 84–85
women entrepreneurs, change in terms of policy and support for 175
Women in Development 41, 188, 190

women mediator networks (WMNs) 207–209
Women Mediators across the Commonwealth 207
Women, Peace, Security (WPS)
  agenda 1, 10, 12, 19, 45, 53, 54–55, 65, 67, 68, 150, 156, 157–158, 161, 164, 200, 201, 202, 207, 211
  appointment of ambassadors for 86
  coalition of friends of 10
  community of practice 7
  foreign policy 7
  National Action Plan 4, 160
  principles 165
  protection and prevention pillars 68
  research exploring close relationship between feminist foreign policies and agenda of 156
  scholarship 199
women pioneers in foreign policy 128–129
Women's Action Organization, US Department of State 83
Women's Environment and Development Organization (WEDO) 67, 71, 222
women's inclusion in climate decision-making, low level of 223
women's contribution to peacemaking, formal recognition of the need for 201–202
women's economic empowerment 175
women's economic equality, advancement of 24
Women's Global Network for Reproductive Rights (WGNRR) 67
Women's International League for Peace and Freedom (WILPF) 64–65, 67, 68
women's rights 108
women's ways of knowing 22
work–family balance in diplomacy 82
World Bank 188
World Health Organization 67
World Trade Alliance (WTA) 176
World Trade Organization 180
  Declaration 174
worlds 30

Y

Yemen
  as recipient of aid from Germany 185
  period of conflict in 56